STRATEGIC MARKETING
FOR
NONPROFIT ORGANIZATIONS

D1317480

STRATEGIC MARKETING
FOR
NONPROFIT ORGANIZATIONS
Cases and Readings

THIRD EDITION

PHILIP KOTLER
Northwestern University

O.C. FERRELL
Texas A & M University

CHARLES LAMB
Texas Christian University

PRENTICE-HALL, INC., Englewood Cliffs, NJ   07632

Library of Congress Cataloging-in-Publication Data

Strategic marketing for nonprofit organizations.

  Rev. ed. of: Cases and readings for marketing for nonprofit organizations. c1983.
  Includes bibliographies.
    1. Corporations, Nonprofit—Marketing.
  2. Corporations, Nonprofit—Marketing—Case studies.
  3. Marketing—Case studies. I. Kotler, Philip.
  II. Ferrell, O. C. III. Lamb, Charles W.
  IV. Cases and readings for marketing for nonprofit organizations.
  HF5415.C2854 1987   658.8   86-25262
  ISBN   0-13-851312-0

Editorial/production supervision and interior design: Maureen Wilson
Cover design: Lundgren Graphics, Ltd.
Manufacturing buyer: Ed O'Dougherty

© 1987 by Prentice-Hall, Inc.
A Division of Simon & Schuster
Englewood Cliffs, New Jersey 07632

© 1983 by Prentice-Hall, Inc., under the title
Cases and Readings for Marketing for Nonprofit Organizations

All rights reserved. No part of this book may be
reproduced, in any form or by any means,
without permission in writing from the publisher.

Printed in the United States of America

10 9 8 7 6 5 4 3 2 1

ISBN 0-13-851312-0   01

Prentice-Hall International (UK) Limited, *London*
Prentice-Hall of Australia Pty. Limited, *Sydney*
Prentice-Hall Canada Inc., *Toronto*
Prentice-Hall Hispanoamericana, S.A., *Mexico*
Prentice-Hall of India Private Limited, *New Delhi*
Prentice-Hall of Japan, Inc., *Tokyo*
Prentice-Hall of Southeast Asia Pte. Ltd., *Singapore*
Editora Prentice-Hall do Brasil, Ltda., *Rio de Janeiro*

CONTENTS

PART II
STRATEGIC PLANNING AND ORGANIZATION

Readings

PART III
DESIGNING THE MARKETING MIX

Readings

Cases

PART IV
CONTROLLING MARKETING STRATEGIES

Readings

PART V
COMPREHENSIVE CASES

Cases

PREFACE

In our first edition we stated that "marketing is relevant not only to businesses but to every organization that provides (something of value) to clients or the public." Today, business organizations such as colleges, hospitals, museums, arts organizations, charities, politicians, and just about any organization that attempts to provide "something of value" to individuals or groups is involved in developing marketing strategies. Marketing and strategic planning offer new ways to serve the public or client and help the organization to achieve its own goals too.

Many nonprofit organizations have appointed or are in the process of appointing marketing managers. Many of these managers are moving from learning about marketing's usefulness to using marketing concepts in dealing with their publics. This edition moves from the "discovery of marketing" stage to the "strategic marketing" stage in the evolution of the use of marketing in nonprofit organizations. Decision makers in governmental agencies, social cause organizations, and similar organizations can use this book to improve their efficiency and effectiveness in strategic marketing. Also, students of marketing with limited or no experience in nonprofit organizations can utilize this book to learn more about the application of marketing in nonprofit organizations.

Strategic Marketing for Nonprofit Organizations: Cases and Readings represents a joint effort by the editors to provide articles and cases to broaden and apply strategic marketing to nonprofit organizations. Most of the selected articles are new to this edition and describe specific applications of marketing strategies for nonprofit organizations as well as discuss the adaptation of marketing strategy to nonprofit organizations. In addition, most of the cases are new and illustrate specific real-world applications of marketing strategies in nonprofit organizations and most are based on real situations and identify the actual organization.

The articles and cases selected for this book utilize the same organization as the third edition of *Strategic Marketing for Nonprofit Organizations* by Philip Kotler and Alan Andreasen. Both books are divided into four major parts; however, this book has an extra section with comprehensive cases. Part I ("Developing a Customer Orientation") explains the nature of marketing in nonbusiness organizations, consumer behavior, and market segmentation. Part II ("Strategic Planning and Organization") covers strategic planning, marketing research, and fundraising. Part III ("Designing the Marketing Mix") discusses the four major variables in the marketing mix—product, price, distribution, and promotion. Part IV ("Controlling Marketing Strategies") covers marketing audits and control processes in marketing management. The chart on pp. viii-ix will aid you in coordinating the study of the readings and cases in this text with the corresponding chapters in the Kotler-Andreasen text.

Since learning should be an active process, the cases provide an opportunity for students to make decisions or evaluate the marketing activities of nonprofit organizations. Each case should illustrate marketing strategies and encourage discussion about the salient issues. These cases provide an integrative focus for conceptual marketing material

Correlation of contents with: **Kotler-Andreasen, Strategic Marketing for Nonprofit Organizations** / **Kotler-Ferrell-Lamb, Strategic Marketing for Nonprofit Organizations: Cases and Readings**

	Marketing in the Nonprofit Environment	The Marketing Philosophy	Understanding Customer Behavior	Market Segmentation and Customer Targeting	The Strategic Marketing Planning Process	Marketing Research	Market Measurement and Forecasting	Marketing Planning	Organizing for Implementation	Leveraging Limited Resources	Fundraising	Designing and Analyzing Marketing Programs	Developing New Offerings	Managing Offerings Over the Life Cycle	Strategies for Products, Services, and Social Behaviors	Managing Perceived Costs	Managing the Marketing Channel	Formulating Communications Strategies for Influencing Behavior	Managing Advertising and Sales Promotion	Managing Public Relations	Managing Personal Selling	Marketing Evaluation and Control
PART I: DEVELOPING A CUSTOMER ORIENTATION																						
Articles																						
Strategies for Introducing Marketing into Nonprofit Organizations	1	2			2																	
The Marketing of Social Causes: The First 10 Years	1	2			2																	
Mickey Mouse Marketing		1	2	2	2																	
More Mickey Mouse Marketing		1	2		2																	
How to Initiate a Marketing Perspective in a Health Services Organization		1			1				2													
Marketing: One YMCA Attacks the Problems	2	1	1																			
Predictors of Attendance at the Performing Arts			2	1																		
A Market Segmentation Approach to Transit Planning, Modeling, and Management				2	1																	
Communicating Cancer Information: New Messages, New Approaches, and New Potential	2		1	1																		
Cases																						
Family Service, Inc.			2	1	2	1	1															
Lady Indian Basketball				1	2		1			2												2
PART II: STRATEGIC PLANNING AND ORGANIZATION																						
Articles																						
Cost-Conscious Marketing Research						1	1															
Strategic Planning for Higher Education								1		1												
Strategic Planning for Nonprofit Health Care Organization Funding								1		2	1	2										
The Baptists Want You!								1												1		

PART III: DESIGNING THE MARKETING MIX
Articles

PART IV: CONTROLLING MARKETING STRATEGIES
Articles

PART V: COMPREHENSIVE CASES
Cases

1–Primary use.
2–Secondary use.

found in the readings and in *Strategic Marketing for Nonprofit Organizations*. Variety in case length and complexity allows instructors to match cases to the course and level of students.

The articles were selected to be practical and useful in making marketing decisions for nonprofit organizations. The articles focus on how marketing concepts can be applied to specific nonprofit marketing problems. Most marketing texts and articles deal with institutions and practices found in the private-for-profit sector. This makes it difficult for nonprofit organization managers—public administrators, educators, museum directors, hospital administrators, family planners, religious leaders, foundation directors, social activists, urban planners, and others—

to gain a direct and comprehensive idea of marketing that is relevant to their types of organizations. The articles selected provide an introduction to marketing for these administrators.

The editors would like to express their sincere appreciation to all participants in the development of this book. We would like to thank the authors and the case writers who were willing to share their ideas and experiences with us. Their contributions made this project possible and their cooperation in allowing us to publish or reprint their work is appreciated. All contributors' authorship is indicated on each case and article.

Finally, we want to thank our students for their comments and insight on the cases and readings included in this book.

Philip Kotler
O.C. Ferrell
Charles Lamb

STRATEGIC MARKETING
FOR
NONPROFIT ORGANIZATIONS

PART I

DEVELOPING A CUSTOMER ORIENTATION

Most people associate marketing with the business sector of the economy. Marketing practice began and has attained its highest level of development in this sector. Today, many public and private nonprofit organizations recognize that they have publics or clients to work with from a marketing point of view. The private nonprofit sector accounts for more than one-fourth of the American economy. Although there are unique characteristics of the nonprofit sector, application of marketing principles used in the business sector provides an opportunity for improved management of public and private nonprofit organizations.

In Part I we examine how managers in the nonprofit sector can develop a more comprehensive consumer orientation. Marketing's evolving role in nonprofit organizations and the importance of an organization's commitment to customer satisfaction are valuable attributes in determining the success of an organization. A firm grasp of the marketing environment is necessary for a successful application of a customer orientation.

In the first article, "Strategies for Introducing Marketing into Nonprofit Organizations," Philip Kotler points out the marketplace problems associated with the nonprofit arena. This article stresses the importance of a customer/market orientation and outlines a number of steps involved in increasing nonprofit marketing effectiveness. Kotler considers the transferability of traditional marketing principles to a largely reluctant nonprofit sector.

The second article, "The Marketing of Social Causes: The First 10 Years," by Karen F. A. Fox and Philip Kotler, examines the evolution of social marketing and discusses a number of key questions pertaining to this controversial field.

The third and fourth articles, "Mickey Mouse Marketing" and "More Mickey Mouse Marketing" by N. W. (Red) Pope, contend that the financial industry would do well to emulate the marketing effectiveness of Mickey Mouse. Although this article was written for financial managers, we believe that the ingredients of success used by Disney are useful considerations for nonprofit organizations. One of the world's most famous characters has become a respected and envied symbol of the very best there is in target marketing, sales techniques, and customer relations. The leader which sets the standards that others in the theme park industry seek to match is the Disney organization. Many nonprofit organizations could utilize some aspects of the Disney consumer-oriented philosophy.

In the fifth article, "How to Initiate a Marketing Perspective in a Health Services Organization," William R. George and Fran Compton examine a successful internal marketing approach in order to provide a marketing orientation to individuals who, traditionally, have not viewed themselves as being part of the marketing domain. They also stress the importance of the customer-consciousness aspect of an internal marketing strategy.

The sixth article is "Marketing: One YMCA Attacks the Problems" by Jacqueline Janders. This selection examines how a nonprofit organization such as the YMCA can use marketing technology. The Milwaukee YMCA developed and implemented some marketing plans and found the experience very rewarding.

Alan R. Andreasen and Russell Belk in their article "Predictors of Attendance at the Performing Arts" discuss ways of determining who will be the most likely market segments to attend performing arts programs and how to attract their attention.

The eighth article in this section is "A Marketing Segmentation Approach to Transit Planning, Modeling, and Management" by Christopher Lovelock. The author notes that services that are developed, priced, distributed, and promoted to a mass market may fall short of their potential because people's needs and behavior patterns often differ sharply. By segmenting the market into different groups based on such factors as individual characteristics, attitudes, behavior, and location, important insights can often be obtained into market dynamics. This makes it possible to develop services which are closely tailored to the needs of specific segments. This article examines alternative ways of segmenting the market for public transportation services and considers the implications for marketing strategy.

The last article, written by William O. Novelli, "From 'General Audience' to 'Quiet Pessimists': Sharpening the Focus in Cancer Audience Segmentation," examines the process of informing, educating, and motivating public audiences about cancer prevention and control. It delves into the identification of who is at risk in terms of contracting cancer and how marketing is being used to reach and inform these people.

Two cases are included in Part I. "Family Service, Inc." presents the market research findings of an image study performed by a social service agency. After interpreting the findings, the analyst is faced with providing recommendations for improving the agency's marketing program.

"Lady Indian Basketball" also presents survey data that requires interpretation. This case illustrates some of the challenges associated with marketing a sport. Decisions must be made regarding how to better market intercollegiate women's basketball.

Strategies for Introducing Marketing into Nonprofit Organizations

PHILIP KOTLER

Marketing is a topic of growing interest to nonprofit organization managers as their organizations confront new, complex marketplace problems. These institution heads are taking their first, tentative steps toward marketing, often confusing it with its advertising and selling subfunctions. Nonprofit institutions can introduce marketing in a number of ways, such as appointing a marketing committee or task force, hiring an advertising agency or marketing research firm, hiring a marketing consultant, or appointing a marketing director or marketing vice president.

In most societies of the world, economic activity is a function of the actions and interactions of a profit sector and a governmental sector. The American economy, however, contains an important third sector made up of tens of thousands of private, not-for-profit organizations ranging from The Society for the Preservation and Encouragement of Barber Shop Quartet Singing in America to major foundations, colleges, hospitals, museums, charities, social agencies, and churches.

This strong third sector constitutes a *middle way* for meeting social needs, without resorting to the profit motive on the one hand or government bureaucracy on the other. Third sector organizations tend to be socially responsive and service-oriented. They specialize in the delivery of social services that are not adequately provided by either business or government.

While Big Business is healthy and Big Government continues to grow, the third sector, unfortunately, is in trouble. Third sector organizations depend upon the support of private citizens and upon grants from the other two sectors. Many colleges, hospitals, churches, social agencies, performance groups, and museums are increasingly feeling the pinch of rising costs and stable or declining revenues. Consider the following:

- More than 170 private colleges have closed their doors since 1965, unable to get either enough students or funds or both. Tuition at Stanford and Yale is now over $6,000; if college costs continue to climb at the current rate, the parents of a child born today will have to put aside $82,830 to buy that child a bachelor's degree at one of the better private colleges (Pyke, 1977).
- Hospital costs continue to soar, leading to daily room rates of $300 or more in some large hospitals; many hospitals are experiencing underutilization, particularly in the maternity and pediatrics sections. Some experts have predicted the closing of 1,400–1,500 hospitals in the next 10 years.
- The Catholic Church drew as many as 55% of all adult Catholics under 30 years of age

Philip Kotler, "Strategies for Introducing Marketing into Nonprofit Organizations," *Journal of Marketing*, Vol. 43 (January 1979), pp. 37–44.

Reprinted from *Journal of Marketing*, published by the American Marketing Association.

to church in a typical week in 1966. By 1975 the figure had fallen to 39% and further declines in weekly attendance were expected.

- Many performance groups cannot attract large enough audiences. Even those which have seasonal sellouts, such as the Lyric Opera Company of Chicago, face huge operating deficits at the end of the year.
- Many third sector organizations that flourished in earlier years—the YMCA, Salvation Army, Girl Scouts, and Women's Christian Temperance Union—presently are reexamining their mission in an effort to reverse membership declines.

In a word, these third sector organizations have marketplace problems. Their administrators are struggling to keep them alive in the face of rapidly changing societal needs, increasing public and private competition, changing client attitudes, and diminishing financial resources. Board members and supporters are asking administrators tough questions about the organization's mission, opportunities, and strategies. Unfortunately, many administrators are mere "Monday-morning quarterbacks" when it comes to strategic planning. At a time when these organizations face uncertain prospects, the lack of management depth poses a serious threat to survival.

Let us examine a major requirement for such survival: third sector administrators must begin to think like marketers. Ten years ago, Sidney J. Levy and I advanced the thesis that marketing is not just a business function—it is a valid function for nonbusiness organizations as well—and that all organizations have marketing problems and all need to understand marketing (Kotler and Levy, 1969). The article created considerable controversy. Many academic marketers attacked it, saying that marketing made

sense only in profit-oriented enterprises. However other marketing professors found the idea stimulating and, without necessarily agreeing that it was valid, began to study and experiment with it. Initial interest was confined to academia. The issue was of little concern to businessmen, and was largely ignored by administrators of nonprofit institutions.

More articles followed in the 1970s, reporting applications of marketing technology to such areas as college recruiting, fund raising, membership development, population problems, public transportation, health services, religion, and arts organizations.[1] Benson Shapiro's article in the September–October 1973 issue of the *Harvard Business Review* elicited many favorable comments, published in the following issue of *HBR*. The only textbook on the subject, *Marketing for Nonprofit Organizations,* appeared in 1975 and has enjoyed a growing readership (Kotler, 1975). Recently Gaedeke (1977) published a book of readings, Lovelock and Weinberg (1977) a book of cases, Lovelock (1977) a bibliography of over 100 cases, and Nickels (1978) a general marketing textbook giving equal attention to business and nonbusiness marketing. It appears that marketing for nonprofit organizations is an idea whose time has come.

How have administrators of nonprofit organizations responded? Are they interested or aware? Enthusiastic? Do they know how to use marketing? Is it making a difference anywhere? On this tenth anniversary of the idea's launching, we are in a position to supply some answers.

[1] A relevent 43-page bibliography lists over 600 references. See Michael L. Rothschild (1977), *An Incomplete Bibliography of Works Relating to Marketing for Public Sector and Nonprofit Organizations,* Second Edition (Boston, MA: Intercollegiate Case Clearing House 9-577-771).

ENTER MARKETING

Of all the classic business functions, marketing has been the last to arrive on the nonprofit scene. Some years earlier, nonprofit managers began to get interested in accounting systems, financial management, personnel administration, and formal planning. Marketing lagged, except where the nonprofit institution experienced a decline in clients, members, or funds. As long as institutions operated in a sellers' market—as colleges and hospitals did throughout the 1960s—marketing was ignored, but as customers and/or resources grew scarce the word "marketing" was heard with increasing frequency, and organizations suddenly discovered marketing or reasonable facsimiles thereof.

Colleges

Colleges provide a good example of this development. By the mid-1970s, they were reading this grim scenario: (1) the annual number of high school graduates would decline from a peak of 3.2 million in 1977 to 2.8 million in 1982-83; (2) the proportion of high school students electing to go to college might decline; (3) a higher proportion of the college-bound students would elect to attend community colleges instead of four-year colleges; and (4) the absolute and relative future level of tuition would deter college-going in general and hurt private colleges in particular.[2]

What are college administrators doing about this? One group is doing nothing. Either enrollment hasn't slipped, or if it has, the administrators believe the decline is temporary. Many believe it is "unprofessional" to go out and "sell" their colleges.

[2] See *A Role for Marketing in College Admissions* (New York: College Entrance Examination Board, 1976), 54 and elsewhere.

A second group has responded with "marketing," which in too many cases means aggressive promotion unaccompanied by any real improvements in competitive positioning, teaching quality, or student services. For example:

- The admissions office at North Kentucky State University planned to release 103 balloons filled with scholarship offers.
- The admissions staff of one college passed out promotional frisbees to high school students vacationing on the beaches of Fort Lauderdale, Florida, during the annual Easter break.
- St. Joseph's College in Rensselaer, Indiana, achieved a 40% increase in freshmen admissions through advertising in *Seventeen* and on several Chicago and Indianapolis rock radio stations. The admissions office also planned to introduce tuition rebates for students who recruited new students ($100 finders fee), but this was cancelled.
- Bard College developed a same-day admission system for students who walk into their office and qualify.
- Worcester Polytechnic Institute offers negotiable admission in which credit is negotiated for previous study or work experience to shorten the degree period.
- The University of Richmond has spent $13,000 to create a 12-minute film for showings to high school students and other interested publics.
- Drake University advertised on a billboard near Chicago's O'Hare Airport that "Drake is only 40 minutes from Chicago" (if one flies).
- Duke University paid for a supplement in *The New York Times* to tell its story.

Promotional competition has not yet led to premiums given to students for enrollment (free radio, typewriter) or offers of "satisfaction guaranteed or your money back,'' but these may come.

In equating marketing with intensified promotion, there are several dangers. Aggressive promotion tends to produce strong negative reactions among the school's constituencies, especially the faculty, who regard hard selling as offensive. Also, such promotion may turn off as many prospective students and families as it turns on. Aggressive promotion can attract the wrong students to the college—students who drop out when they discover they don't have the qualifications to do the work or that the college is not what it was advertised to be. Finally, this kind of marketing creates the illusion that the college has undertaken sufficient response to declining enrollment—an illusion which slows down the needed work on product improvement, the basis of all good marketing.

Promotion alone doesn't always work. Briarcliff College, a long-established women's college, faced an enrollment drop from 688 in 1969 to 280 in 1973. The college president scrambled to find ways to ''sell'' Briarcliff to prospects, including advertising and more high school visits. He personally went on the road to talk up Briarcliff, managing to raise enrollment to 350. But his effort was too little and too late. Briarcliff's finances continued to deteriorate and the college finally closed its doors in 1977.[3]

A genuine marketing response has been undertaken by a relatively small number of colleges. Their approach is best described as *market-oriented institutional planning*. In this approach, marketing is recognized as much more than mere promotion, and indeed, the issue of promotion cannot be settled in principle until more fundamental issues are resolved. These issues are shown in Exhibit 1. By doing its homework on market, resource, and missions analysis, a college is

[3] See ''Rest in Peace,'' *Newsweek*, April 11, 1977, 96.

in a better position to make decisions that improve student and faculty recruitment and institutional fundraising.

As an example, the University of Houston

EXHIBIT 1: Issues in market-oriented institutional planning facing colleges and universities

MARKET ANALYSIS

1. What important trends are affecting higher education? (Environmental analysis)
2. What is our primary market? (Market definition)
3. What are the major market segments in this market? (Market segmentation)
4. What are the needs of each market segment? (Need assessment)
5. How much awareness, knowledge, interest, and desire is there in each market segment concerning our college? (Market awareness and attitude)
6. How do key publics see us and our competitors? (Image analysis)
7. How do potential students learn about our college and make decisions to apply and enroll? (Consumer behavior)
8. How satisfied are current students? (Consumer satisfaction assessment)

RESOURCE ANALYSIS

1. What are our major strengths and weaknesses in faculty, programs, facilities, etc.? (Strengths/weaknesses analysis)
2. What opportunities are there to expand our financial resources? (Donor opportunity analysis)

MISSION ANALYSIS

1. What business are we in? (Business mission)
2. Who are our customers? (Customer definition)
3. Which needs are we trying to satisfy? (Needs targeting)
4. On which market segments do we want to focus? (Market targeting)
5. Who are our major competitors? (Competitor identification)
6. What competitive benefits do we want to offer to our target market? (Market positioning)

recently completed an intensive institutional audit using several faculty task forces. The final report presented recommendations on the university's mission, strategy, and portfolio. The portfolio section recommended which components of the university's "product mix" (schools and departments) should be built, maintained, phased down, or phased out. The criteria included: (1) the centrality of that academic program to the mission of the university, (2) the program's academic quality, and (3) the program's marketing viability. Thus, a department of women's studies that is marginal to the mission of the school, of low national reputation, and unable to attract an adequate number of students, would be slated for phasing down or out. A few other schools such as New York University, Northwestern University, and Kent State University are taking marketing initiatives to bring strategic planning and marketing into their operating frameworks.

Hospitals

Hospitals are beginning to treat marketing as a "hot" topic. A few years ago, health professionals scorned the idea of marketing, imagining that it would lead to ads such as "This week's special—brain surgery, only $195." Hospital administrators also argued that patients didn't choose hospitals, their doctors did; so marketing, to be effective, would have to be directed to doctors.

Thus, it came as a surprise when a single and tentative session on marketing for hospital administrators, sandwiched between several other sessions during the 1975 convention of the American College of Hospital Administrators, drew about one-third of the 2,000 attendees. Perhaps they were tired of hearing panels on rising hospital costs and money collection problems, but more probably they were beginning to sense an oppor-

tunity, in marketing, to halt their declining occupancy rates.

As did many colleges, some hospitals rushed into marketing with more enthusiasm than understanding, believing it to consist of clever promotional gimmicks. For example:

- Sunrise Hospital in Las Vegas ran a large advertisement featuring the picture of a ship with the caption, "Introducing the Sunrise Cruise, Win a Once-in-a-Lifetime Cruise Simply by Entering Sunrise Hospital on Any Friday or Saturday: Recuperative Mediterranean Cruise for Two."
- St. Luke's Hospital in Phoenix introduced nightly bingo games for all patients (except cardiac cases), producing immense patient interest as well as a net annual profit of $60,000.
- A Philadelphia hospital, in competing for maternity patients, let the public know that the parents of a newborn child would enjoy a steak and champagne candlelight dinner on the eve before the mother and childs' departure from the hospital.
- A number of hospitals, in their competition to attract and retain physicians, have added "ego services," such as saunas, chauffeurs, and even private tennis courts.

Fortunately, some hospitals are now beginning to apply marketing to a broader set of problems. Where should the hospital locate a branch or ambulatory care unit? How can the hospital estimate whether a new service will draw enough patients? What should a hospital do with a maternity wing that is only 20% occupied? How can the hospital attract more consumers to preventive care services, such as annual medical checkups and cancer screening programs? How can a hospital successfully compete in the recruitment of more highly trained specialists who are in short supply? What marketing programs can attract nurses, build community goodwill, attract more contributions?

The marketing naivete of the typical hospital is well-illustrated by a hospital in southern Illinois that decided to establish an Adult Day Care Center as a solution to its underutilized space. It designed a whole floor to serve senior citizens who required personal care and services in an ambulatory setting during the day, but who would return home each evening. The cost was $16 a day and transportation was to be provided by the patient's relatives. About the only research that was done on this concept was to note that a lot of elderly people lived within a three-mile radius. The Center was opened with a capacity to handle thirty patients. Only two signed up!

Not all hospital administrators launch new services without research and testing of market size and interest. An increasing number are now attending marketing seminars to learn more about marketing research and new service development. The Evanston Hospital, Evanston, Illinois, a major 500-bed facility, appointed the world's first hospital vice president of marketing. Recently, MacStravic (1977) published an entire book devoted to hospital marketing, and many articles are now appearing on health care marketing.[4]

Other Institutions

In addition to colleges and hospitals, other institutions are paying more attention to marketing. The YMCA is taking a fresh look at its mission, services, and clients in order to develop new services and markets for the 1980s. Major charities like the Multiple Sclerosis Society, the American Heart Association, and the March of Dimes are investigating marketing ideas that go beyond selling and advertising. Marketing successes have been reported by arts institutions,[5] family planning associations (Roberto, 1975), and energy conservation groups (Henion, 1976). It is likely that within 10 years, much of the third sector will have some understanding and appreciation of the marketing concept.

IMPLEMENTING MARKETING

The interesting thing about marketing is that all organizations do it whether they know it or not. When this dawns on a nonprofit organization, the response is much like Moliere's character in *Le Bourgeois Gentilhomme* who utters: "Good Heavens! For more than forty years I have been speaking prose without knowing it." Colleges, for example, search for prospects (students), develop products (courses), price them (tuition and fees), distribute them (announce time and place), and promote them (college catalogs). Similarly, hospitals, social agencies, cultural groups, and other nonprofit organizations also practice marketing, wittingly or unwittingly; whether they do it well is a separate issue. For institutions which would like to improve their marketing effectiveness, I recommend consideration of the six steps shown in Exhibit 2. The "steps" really represent alternative approaches to the introduction of marketing into a nonprofit institution rather than a rigid sequence of steps.

Marketing Committee

As early as possible, the head of the institution should consider appointing a marketing committee to examine the institution's

---

[4] See, for example, the special issue on marketing of hospitals, *Journal of the American Hospital Association*, June 1, 1977.

[5] See Danny Newman (1977), *Subscribe Now! Building Arts Audiences through Dynamic Subscription Promotion*, (New York: Theatre Communications Group, Inc.). This book deals primarily with the use of promotion as a marketing tool rather than with overall marketing strategy.

EXHIBIT 2: Approaches to introducing marketing in a nonprofit institution

1. Appoint a marketing committee
2. Organize task forces to carry out an institutional audit
3. Hire marketing specialist firms as needed
4. Hire a marketing consultant
5. Hire a director of marketing
6. Hire a vice president of marketing

---

problems and look into the potentialities of marketing. In a college, for example, such a marketing committee might consist of the president, vice presidents of faculty and development, director of admissions, dean of students, and one or two school deans. The committee should also include a marketing professor and/or a marketing practitioner. The marketing committee's objectives are (1) to identify the marketing problems and opportunities facing the institution; (2) to identify the major needs of various administrative units for marketing services; and (3) to explore the institution's possible need for a full-time director of marketing.

Task Forces

The chief administrator should consider appointing task forces to carry out various phases of an institutional audit. The aim is to discover how the institution is seen by key publics, what its main constituencies want that institution to be, which programs are strong and which weak, and so on. The task force's reports should adduce a consensus on institutional goals, positioning, and strategies. Even when task forces fail to find dramatic solutions, the members usually gain a deeper appreciation and understanding of the institution's problems and the need to work together to solve them.

Marketing Specialist Firms

From time to time, the organization should engage the services of marketing specialist firms, such as marketing research firms, advertising agencies, direct mail consultants, and recruitment consultants. A marketing research firm might be hired to survey the needs, perceptions, preferences, and satisfaction of the client market. An advertising agency might be hired to develop a corporate identification program or an advertising campaign. High quality marketing specialist firms bring more than their specific services to the client; they take a total marketing viewpoint and raise important questions for the institution to consider concerning its mission, objectives, strategies, and opportunities.

Marketing Consultant

As a further step, the organization should seek a marketing consultant to carry out a comprehensive *marketing audit* on the problems and opportunities facing that organization. The marketing consultant could be someone affiliated with the institution—such as a marketing professor, or a board member who is a marketing specialist. However, volunteers tend to give less attention than is necessary to the project, and often lack objectivity. It is usually preferable to engage a professional marketing consultant, one who has experience in that nonprofit subsector of the economy. In education, for example, several consulting firms have emerged specializing in college marketing and management. Alternatively, the institution could seek the services of a general consulting firm. In any event, the institution should make an effort to invite at least three proposals from which to select the best consultant. A contract should be written which specifies the objectives, the time frame, the research plan, and the billing. A liaison person within the institution should be assigned to work with the consultant, arrange interviews, read and comment on the emerging reports, and make arrangements for the final presentation and implementation of proposals.

The marketing consultant will interview representative sets of people connected with the institution. In the case of a college, he or she will interview the president, members of the board of trustees, major vice presidents, directors of admissions and public relations, several school deans, several department chairmen, several professors, several students, representative alumni, and outside opinion leaders. The marketing consultant would seek to answer the following questions for each *academic program* studied:

What is happening to student size and quality?

How successful is the program in attracting qualified students?

What are the main competitive programs and their positions in the market?

What are the image and reputation of this program?

What is the mission and what are the objectives of this program over the next five years?

What budget is needed to accomplish these objectives?

What fund raising potentials exist in the program?

What marketing problems face the program and what marketing activities are being pursued?

What useful services could a marketing director contribute to this program?

On the basis of this survey, the marketing consultant will develop and present a set of findings and recommendations regarding the institution's operations, opportunities, and needs in the marketing area. One of the recommendations will specifically deal with whether the institution is ready to effectively utilize a marketing director or vice president of marketing.

Marketing Director

Eventually the organization might become convinced of the need to appoint a director of marketing. This requires the development of a job description which specifies to whom this person reports, the scope of the position, the position concept, the functions, responsibilities, and major liaisons with others in the institution. Exhibit 3 presents a job description in a university context. The job is conceived as a middle management position, one in which the occupant primarily provides marketing services to others in the institution.

A major issue is where this person should be located in the organization and his or her relationships with kindred functions. Specifically, what is the marketing director's relationship to planning, public relations, and fundraising? A good case could be made for locating the marketing director within the planning office and therefore reporting to the vice president of planning. It would not make sense for the marketing director to report to public relations or fundraising because this would overspecialize the use made of marketing. The solution used by a large, eastern hospital consisted of appointing a vice president of institutional relations to whom directors of marketing, public relations, fundraising and planning reported.

Some public relations directors have been uncomfortable about the emergence of marketing directors, out of fear that they may eventually be reporting to the latter. Some public relations directors argue that marketing isn't needed, or that it is being done, or that they can do it. To the extent that marketing is thought to be aggressive promotion, public relations people feel they are best

---

EXHIBIT 3: Job description: Director of marketing for a university

POSITION TITLE: Director of Marketing

REPORTS TO: A vice president designated by the president

SCOPE: University-wide

POSITION CONCEPT: The director of marketing is responsible for providing marketing guidance and services to university officers, school deans, department chairmen, and other agents of the university.

FUNCTIONS: The director of marketing will:

1. Contribute a marketing perspective to the deliberations of the top administration in their planning of the university's future
2. Prepare data that might be needed by any officer of the university on a particular market's size, segments, trends, and behavioral dynamics
3. Conduct studies of the needs, perceptions, preferences, and satisfactions of particular markets
4. Assist in the planning, promotion, and launching of new programs
5. Assist in the development of communication and promotion campaigns and materials
6. Analyze and advise on pricing questions
7. Appraise the workability of new academic proposals from a marketing point of view
8. Advise on new student recruitment
9. Advise on current student satisfaction
10. Advise on university fundraising

RESPONSIBILITIES: The director of marketing will:

1. Contact individual officers and small groups at the university to explain services and to solicit problems
2. Prioritize the various requests for services according to their long run impact, cost saving potential, time requirements, ease of accomplishment, cost, and urgency
3. Select projects of high priority and set accomplishment goals for the year
4. Prepare a budget request to support the anticipated work
5. Prepare an annual report on the main accomplishments of the office

MAJOR LIAISONS: The director of marketing will:

1. Relate most closely with the president's office, admissions office, development office, planning office, and public relations department
2. Relate secondarily with the deans of various schools and chairmen of various departments

---

equipped to carry out this function. To the extent that marketing is seen to consist of market analysis, new services development, marketing strategy, product line evaluation, and so on, public relations personnel are not equipped insofar as their training is basically in the fields of journalism and communications, not economics and business analysis. However, public relations persons can, of course, take courses in marketing and attempt to promote the concept of a combined office of marketing and public relations.

Marketing Vice President

The ultimate solution is the establishment of a vice president of marketing position. This is an upper level management position which gives more scope, authority, and influence to marketing. A vice president of marketing not only coordinates and supplies analytical services but also has a strong voice in the determination of where the institution should be going in terms of its changing opportunities.

The vice president of marketing would be responsible for planning and managing relations with several publics. The person's title may be altered to that of vice president of institutional relations or external affairs to avoid unnecessary semantic opposition. Thus far, only a few nonprofit organizations have gone this route.

The top marketing job should be tailored to the specific institution. Consider the

YMCA, often called "the General Electric of the social service business." The YMCA is in not one, but several "businesses": recreation, education, camps, physical fitness, hotels, and so on. Central headquarters must wrestle with decisions on where to build new facilities, what new programs to introduce, what programs to drop, how to promote membership, and dozens of other matters. Were a vice president of marketing appointed, this person would be responsible for defining better ways to serve various constituencies. Reporting to the vice president would be functional marketing specialists (marketing research, pricing, promotion, and planning), product managers (recreational programs, educational programs, camps), and market managers (teens, young marrieds, senior adults). These people would design programs and offer services to the various YMCA units throughout the country. There is no question that marketing decisions are being made all the time throughout the YMCA system but they are made, unfortunately, without professional marketing expertise.

Let us assume that an institution decides to hire a marketing vice president. This person's contribution will be carefully scrutinized. The new appointee will have to develop a strategy to make marketing visible and useful.

The marketing executive is not likely to be immediately swamped with requests for services, because many administrators initially will not understand marketing. The marketing executive should spend the first few months meeting various groups within the institution to learn about their problems. For example, Evanston Hospital's new marketing vice president arranged separate meetings with senior physicians, residents, interns, senior nurses, and others. At each meeting he described his job position, explained the nature of marketing, indicated the kinds of problems he could solve and services that he could offer, and then opened the meeting to discussion. He sought suggestions of projects that he might conduct. At the end of two months, he found more than enough useful projects. His problem, in fact, was to set priorities for the many projects, and he did so by rating each potential project using the following criteria (on five-point scales): (1) the importance or centrality of the project to the future of the institution; (2) the magnitude of the improved service or cost savings that it might effect; (3) its probable cost; (4) the difficulty of carrying it out; and (5) the length of time it would take to complete. An ideal project was one that was very important, would effect great cost savings, and would cost little to do, could be easily carried out, and could be completed in a short time. It became clear which projects went to the top of the list, and he concentrated his efforts in the first year on these projects.

The marketing executive will be expected to prepare an annual marketing plan listing major projects and a required budget. Much of the budget will go toward buying the services of outside marketing research firms and advertising agencies for needed projects. At each year's end, the executive will prepare a report summarizing levels of accomplishment and savings. Eventually, the nature of this position will become well understood within the organization and easy to assess its contributions toward institutional survival and growth.

CONCLUSION

At the present time, the marketing idea is beginning to attract the interest of administrators in the third sector. This is evidenced by the growing literature on college, hospital, and other third sector marketing, as well as by increased attendance at specialized marketing conferences for nonprofit organizations. Interest is not likely to abate; indeed, it is likely to increase as more administrators come to see their institution's future in marketing terms. For an institution, marketing offers a much richer understanding of what is happening and throws light on new opportunities.

Despite the growing interest in marketing, however, many nonprofit organizations still resist it. Many groups within these organizations see marketing as a threat to their autonomy or power. Eventually, out of necessity, marketing ideas will filter into these organizations. Marketing will initially be viewed as advertising and promotion rather than as a revolutionary new way to view the institution and its purposes. A few institutions will lead the others in developing an advanced understanding of marketing. They will start performing better. Their competitors will be forced to learn their marketing. Within another decade, marketing will be a major and accepted function within the nonprofit sector.

The issue that frightens some observers is not that marketing will be ineffective but that it may be too effective. They see funds and clients flowing to institutions that are willing to spend the largest sums of money on advertising and promotion. They fear that large scale promotional warfare will ruin the smaller institutions that cannot afford marketing, and will create a competitive stalemate among the larger institutions. This fear is based, once again, on the fallacy of viewing marketing as primarily promotional.

The real contribution of marketing thinking is to lead each institution to search for a more meaningful position in the larger market. Instead of all hospitals offering the same services, marketing leads each hospital to shape distinct service mixes to serve specific market segments. Marketing competition, at its best, creates a pattern of varied institutions, each clear as to its mission, market coverage, need specialization, and service portfolio.

Administrators and businessmen who have a stake in the third sector are beginning to recognize the contributions that marketing thinking can make. Marketing will lead to a better understanding of the needs of different client segments; to a more careful shaping and launching of new services; to a pruning of weak services; to more effective methods of delivering services; to more flexible pricing approaches; and to higher levels of client satisfaction. Altogether, marketing offers a great potential to third sector organizations to survive, grow, and strengthen their contributions to the general welfare.

REFERENCES

Gaedeke, R. M. (1977), *Marketing in Private and Public Nonprofit Organizations: Perspectives and Illustrations.* Santa Monica, CA: Goodyear Publishing Co.

Henion, Karl E. (1976), *Ecological Marketing.* Columbus, OH: Grid, Inc.

Kotler, Philip (1975), *Marketing for Nonprofit Organizations.* Englewood Cliffs, NJ: Prentice-Hall, Inc.

———, and Sidney J. Levy (1969), "Broadening the Concept of Marketing," *Journal of Marketing,* 33 (January), 10–15.

Lovelock, Christopher H., ed. (1977), *Nonbusiness Marketing Cases,* 8-378-001. Boston, MA: Intercollegiate Case Clearing House.

———, and Charles B. Weinberg (1977), *Cases in Public and Nonprofit Marketing.* Palo Alto, CA: The Scientific Press.

———, and Charles B. Weinberg (1978), "Public and Non-profit Marketing Comes of Age," in *Review of Marketing 1978,* Gerald Zaltman and T. Bonoma eds. Chicago, IL: American Marketing Association, 413–452.

MacStravic, Robin E. (1977), *Marketing Health*

Care. Germantown, MD: Aspen Systems Corp.

Nickels, William G. (1978), *Marketing Principles.* Englewood Cliffs, NJ: Prentice-Hall, Inc.

Pyke, Donald L. (1977), "The Future of Higher Education: Will Private Institutions Disappear in the U.S.?" *The Futurist,* 374.

Roberto, Eduardo (1975), *Strategic Decision-Making in a Social Program: The Case of Family-Planning Diffusion.* Lexington, MA: Lexington Books.

Shapiro, Benson (1973), "Marketing for Nonprofit Organizations," *Harvard Business Review,* 51 (September–October), 123–132.

The Marketing of Social Causes: The First 10 Years

KAREN F. A. FOX • PHILIP KOTLER

The application of marketing to the promotion of social causes was proposed a decade ago. The authors position social marketing as an approach to social change, describe its evolution, and review social marketing applications and assess their impact.

During the past decade the "territory" of marketing has expanded to include the marketing tasks of nonprofit organizations and the marketing of worthwhile social causes. Kotler (1979) reviewed the accomplishments in the first area, describing how an increasing number of nonprofit organizations—particularly hospitals, colleges, social service agencies, and cultural organizations—are applying marketing concepts and techniques to improve the marketing of their services. Despite earlier controversy, few marketers dispute the relevance of marketing to the management of nonprofit organizations (Nickels, 1974).

The time is now appropriate to evaluate the status of work in the area of social cause marketing—social marketing. Here the applicability of marketing is more hotly contested. Social marketing as a distinct application area for general marketing theory was advanced about a decade ago (Kotler and Zaltman, 1971). Since then, various reform groups and government agencies have applied social marketing to such causes as family planning, energy conservation, im-

Karen F. A. Fox and Philip Kotler, "The Marketing of Social Causes: The First 10 Years," *Journal of Marketing*, Vol. 44 (Fall 1980), pp 24–33.

Reprinted from *Journal of Marketing*, published by the American Marketing Association.

proved nutrition, antismoking, prevention of alcohol and drug abuse, safer driving, and myriad other causes. Yet no review of these efforts and of the issues and problems connected with social marketing has been published. In fact, some recent articles—written by academic marketers rather than practitioners—question the appropriateness and ethics of social marketing just as it is being more widely adopted (e.g., Laczniak, Lusch, and Murphy, 1979). G. D. Wiebe's (1951–52) question of 30 years ago, "Why can't you sell brotherhood like you sell soap?", persists along with the newer question, "Should you be selling brotherhood?" Furthermore, the whole discussion is plagued by confusion about what social marketing is. As the technology of social marketing will shortly mark its first decade, an assessment of its nature, successes, limitation, and future is now warranted.

As background for such an assessment, we undertook an extensive review of the literature in marketing and in public health (where many of the applications of social marketing have been carried out). We interviewed key people in two leading social marketing firms to learn what problems they have tackled and what successes and frustrations they have encountered, and interviewed people in federal government agencies concerned with health and nutrition about their awareness of and experience with social marketing. Our findings are presented in the form of answers to the following questions:

- What is social marketing?
- What situations call for social marketing?
- What has social marketing accomplished?
- What are the major criticisms of social marketing?
- What are the hurdles in successful social marketing?
- What is the future of social marketing?

WHAT IS SOCIAL MARKETING?

Social marketing was originally defined as:

. . . the design, implementation, and control of programs calculated to influence the acceptability of social ideas and involving considerations of product planning, pricing, communications and marketing research (Kotler and Zaltman, 1971, p. 5).

Thus social marketing was conceived to be an application of marketing concepts and techniques to the marketing of various socially beneficial ideas and causes instead of products and services in the commercial sense. Synonymous terms might be "social cause marketing," "social idea marketing," or "public issue marketing."

The term "social marketing" unfortunately has been given different meanings by other writers. For example, Lazer and Kelley (1973) published *Social Marketing: Perspectives and Viewpoints* which includes articles on marketing's social responsibilities and social impacts, as well as the marketing of social ideas, under the term "social marketing." In a recent article entitled "Social Marketing: Its Ethical Dimensions," Laczniak, Lusch, and Murphy (1979) confuse social marketing with nonprofit organization marketing by improperly including the marketing of political candidates and urban police departments as examples of "social marketing." Our position is that social marketing should be distinguished from "societal marketing" on the one hand and "nonprofit organization marketing" on the other.

The Evolution of Social Marketing

One can best understand social marketing by seeing it in relation to the major broad approaches to producing social change—the legal, technological, economic, and informational approaches. Consider how these approaches apply in inducing people to reduce their cigarette consumption. The *legal* approach is to pass laws that make cigarette smoking either illegal, costly, or difficult (e.g., prohibiting smoking in public places). The *technological* approach is to develop an innovation that will help people reduce their smoking or the harm thereof (e.g., an antismoking pill, a harmless cigarette). The *economical* approach is to raise the price or cost of smoking (e.g., higher cigarette taxes, higher insurance rates for smokers). Finally, the *informational* approach is to direct persuasive information at smokers about the risks of smoking and the advantages of not smoking (e.g., "Warning: The Surgeon General Has Determined That Smoking Is Dangerous to Your Health").

The roots of social marketing lie in the informational approach, in the form known as *social advertising*. Many cause groups, struck by the apparent effectiveness of commercial advertising, began to consider its potential for changing public attitudes and behavior. Family planning organizations in India, Sri Lanka, Mexico, and several other countries have sponsored major advertising campaigns attempting to sell people on the idea of having fewer children. Messages on billboards and over radio tell the public that they can have a higher standard of living with fewer children (India) or be happier (Sri Lanka). Nutrition groups have also used advertising extensively to encourage people to adopt better eating habits. The U.S. Department of Energy has plans for a multi-million-dollar advertising campaign to promote energy conservation to the American people.

Properly designed, these campaigns can influence attitudes and behavior. The problem is that all too often these campaigns are the only step taken to motivate new behavior and, by themselves, are usually inadequate. First, the message may be inadequately re-searched. For example, media campaigns to encourage people in developing countries to improve their diets miss the point that many people lack knowledge of which foods are more healthful, they may lack the money to buy these goods, and, in remote areas, they may not find certain foods available. Second, many people screen out the message through selective perception, distortion, and forgetting. Mass communications have much less direct influence on behavior than has been thought, and much of their influence is mediated through the opinion leadership of other people. Third, many people do not know what to do after their exposure to the message. The message "Stop smoking—it might kill you" does not help the smoker know how to handle the urge to smoke or where to go for help.

As these limitations were recognized, social advertising evolved into a broader approach known as *social communication*. Much of current social marketing has moved from a narrow advertising approach to a broad social communication/promotion approach to accomplish its objectives. Social communicators make greater use of personal selling and editorial support in addition to mass advertising. Thus, the family planning campaign in India utilizes a network of agents, including doctors, dentists, and barbers, to "talk up" family planning to people with whom they come in contact. Events such as "Family Planning Day" and family planning fairs, together with buttons, signs, and other media, get across the message.

Only recently has *social marketing* begun to replace social communication as a larger paradigm for effecting social change. Social marketing adds at least four elements that are missing from a pure social communication approach.

One element is sophisticated *marketing research* to learn about the market and the probable effectiveness of alternative marketing approaches. Social advertising amounts to "a shot in the dark" unless it is preceded by careful marketing research. Thus social marketers concerned with smoking would examine the size of the smoking market, the major market segments and the behavioral characteristics of each, and the benefit–cost impact of targeting different segments and designing appropriate campaigns for each.

The second element added by social marketing is *product development*. Faced with the problem of getting people to lower their thermostats in winter, a social advertiser or communicator will see the problem largely as one of exhorting people to lower the thermostat, using patriotic appeals, fuel-cost-saving appeals, or whatever seems appropriate. The social marketer, in addition, will consider existing or potential products that will make it easier for people to adopt the desired behavior, such as devices that automatically lower home heat during the middle of the night or that compute fuel cost savings at various temperature settings. In other words, whenever possible the social marketer does not stick with the existing product and try to sell it—a sales approach—but rather searches for the best product to meet the need—a marketing approach.

The third element added by social marketing is *the use of incentives*. Social communicators concentrate on composing messages dramatizing the benefits or disbenefits of different kinds of behaviors. Social marketers go further and design specific incentives to increase the level of motivation. For example, social marketers have advised public health officials who are running immunization campaigns in remote villages to offer small gifts to people who show up for vaccinations. Some hospitals in South America run "price specials" on certain days whereby people who come in for health checkups

pay less than the normal charge. The sales promotion area is rich with tools that the marketer can use to promote social causes.

The fourth element added by social marketing is *facilitation*. The marketer realizes that people wishing to change their behavior must invest time and effort, and considers ways to make it easier for them to adopt the new behavior. For example, smoking cessation classes must be conveniently located and conducted in a professional manner. Marketers are keenly aware of the need to develop convenient and attractive response channels to complement the communication channels. Thus they are concerned not only with getting people to adopt a new behavior, but also with finding ways to facilitate maintenance of behavior.

Our discussion of how social marketing goes beyond social advertising and social communication can be summarized by saying that social marketing involves all "four Ps," not just one. Social marketing involves coordinating product, price, place, and promotion factors to maximally motivate and facilitate desired forms of behavior. Furthermore, social marketing calls for marketing research and for preparation of a full marketing plan, strategy, and budget to get initial "sales" and to reinforce the new behavior over time.

WHAT SITUATIONS CALL FOR SOCIAL MARKETING?

Social marketing potentially can be applied to a wide variety of social problems. It appears to be particularly appropriate in the following three situations.

When New Information and Practices Need to Be Disseminated

In many situations people need to be informed of an opportunity or practice that will improve their lives. In developing nations, social marketers have had to tackle such challenges as:

- Convincing people to boil their water and keep the water supply covered.
- Encouraging people to build and use latrines.
- Explaining to mothers the advantages of continuing to breastfeed their babies instead of switching them to less nourishing gruel at an early age.
- Encouraging people to buy and use iodized salt to prevent goiter.
- Showing parents a simple way to treat infant diarrhea at home—important because infant diarrhea is a major cause of infant mortality in less developed countries.

In industrialized nations the social marketer often must disseminate new information resulting from scientific research, including significant changes in high blood pressure treatment, in childhood immunization, in cancer detection and treatment, and in recommended diet.

Consider the changing concepts of what constitutes a good diet. In the early 1950s American elementary school children were taught about the seven basic food groups and were told to eat foods from each group daily. The 1969 USDA Yearbook entitled *Food For Us All* indicated that the American population was well fed and reported that "sugar or a sweet in some form is a daily necessity" (Mikesh and Nelson, 1969, p. 232). Yet in 1979, the Surgeon General's Report on health promotion and disease prevention criticized the typical American diet, linking a diet high in fat, sugar, cholesterol, and salt, and low in dietary fiber to heart disease, dental caries, high blood pressure, and colon cancer (U.S. Public Health Service, 1979). These shifts in our knowledge of sound

health practices suggest that we cannot simply relegate new health information to a slot in the elementary school curriculum, trusting that the next generation will be better informed and thus healthier than their parents. New information must be transmitted much more widely and more rapidly along with facilitation, price, and innovation steps to stimulate and reinforce new behavior.

When Countermarketing Is Needed

In various nations of the world, companies are promoting the consumption of products that are undesirable or potentially harmful—for example, cigarettes, alcoholic beverages, and highly refined foods which contribute to lung and heart disease, liver damage, overweight, and other problems. The large promotional budgets behind these products tend to crowd out opposing views, because those who disagree are often too fragmented, too few in number, or have inadequate resources to present the counterposition. Social marketing is now viewed by many public interest groups and government agencies as a way to present the other side of the story and stimulate people to adopt more healthful behavior. Sweden, for example, has taken vigorous steps to countermarket alcohol consumption, including running ad campaigns stigmatizing drunk behavior, restricting the availability of alcoholic beverages, raising the prices of alcoholic beverages, establishing stiff penalties for drunken driving, and increasing anti-alcohol school education programs.

Another current example of countermarketing has come in response to the promotion of infant formula in Third World countries. Borden, Nestlé, and other infant formula manufacturers, faced with declining birth rates in developed countries, began aggressive marketing to mothers in Africa, Latin America, and other less developed regions characterized by poverty, illiteracy, lack of pure water, lack of facilities for sterilizing bottles, and lack of refrigeration for storing mixed formula (Post and Baer, 1978). Social marketing campaigns have been carried out to counter such powerful slogans as "Give your baby love and Lactogen" and to inform mothers of the advantages of breastfeeding.

When Activation Is Needed

Often people know what they should do, but do not act accordingly. For example, nine out of 10 smokers interviewed in a 1975 government survey said they would like to quit, yet 57% expected to be smoking five years later (Fisher, 1977). Likewise, many people "know" they should lose weight, get more exercise, floss their teeth, and do other things, but they do not do them. In part their inertia is related to the myriad alternatives they have and the countervailing media messages to enjoy life and maintain current habits ("Have a Coke and a smile" instead!). Furthermore, the benefits may be obtainable only by sustained effort, and the personal "payoff" over a lifetime may be exceedingly difficult to estimate. As one elderly man reportedly said, "If I had known I was going to live this long, I would have taken better care of my health" (*Forbes*, 1979).

In such situations, the task of social marketing is to move people from intention to action. Marketers have studied the many factors that affect the readiness of people to act, and have developed several approaches to motivate and facilitate action. In the future, various national or local emergencies—such as water shortages, oil shortages, and epidemics—may increase the need for public

agencies to know how to activate people quickly.

WHAT HAS SOCIAL MARKETING ACCOMPLISHED?

Although social marketing is an appealing social change approach in theory, to what extent has it been effective in practice? At this time, we can only review the accomplishments of social marketing on an impressionistic basis. The bona fide applications of social marketing—as distinguished from social advertising or social communication—are too few to provide a full data base. Moreover, because social marketing often has been carried out without experimental controls, it is difficult to know whether behavioral changes were due to social marketing efforts or to other factors.

We consider two major areas of application—family planning and motivating healthier life styles—and a sampling of other interventions which reflect elements of a social marketing approach.

Family Planning

Family planning has been a major focus of social marketing efforts, reflected in a growing literature. Roberto (1975) provides an excellent exposition of social marketing theory applied to the problem of family planning. The Population Information Program at The Johns Hopkins University recently published a detailed review of social marketing applications, including information on features of specific programs and their effectiveness (Population Information Program, 1980). The report defines the basic goal of such programs as providing contraceptives "efficiently, economically, and conveniently to people who will use them" (p. J-395). The majority of campaigns to market family planning are government-sponsored, motivated by the availability of effective birth control products and by the growing awareness that economic and social gains can be wiped out by rapid population growth. Many of these social marketing campaigns have been successful, as the following cases show.

A successful social marketing campaign in Sri Lanka (formerly Ceylon) was based on principles of marketing research, brand packaging, distribution channel analysis, and marketing management and control. Consumer research prior to the campaign indicated widespread approval of the idea of family planning but little knowledge and use of contraception. The government, in cooperation with several agencies, centered its efforts on achieving widespread usage of condoms as a means of birth control. A brand was developed named "Preethi" (meaning happiness), and was sold in a three-pack for four cents (U.S.), one of the lowest costs in the world. Preethi achieved distribution in more than 3,600 pharmacies, tea-houses, grocery and general stores, as well as by direct mail. Literature and order forms for condoms were distributed by agricultural extension workers on their regular visits to farm families. The sale of condoms was supported through a mass media campaign, including newspaper and radio ads, films, and a booklet entitled "How to Have Children by Plan and Not by Chance." Distributors also received large point-of-purchase displays. As a result of this orchestrated marketing approach, Preethi sales grew from 300,000 per month (in mid-1974) to an average of 500,000 per month in 1977. It was estimated that 60,000 unwanted pregnancies were averted by this social marketing project (Population Services International, 1977).

Similar campaigns have been successful in parts of India, Thailand, Bangladesh, and other countries. For example, in Bangladesh this type of campaign resulted in the monthly use of more than 1.5 million condoms and about 100,000 cycles of oral contraceptives, providing full contraceptive protection for approximately 400,000 couples at a yearly cost of about $4 per couple. In Thailand, the Community-Based Family Planning Services marketing program for promoting birth control includes some novel features. The agency stages contests with prizes to the person who inflates the biggest "balloon"— a condom—as a way to break down taboos about contraception. Contraceptives are accepted in rural villages, where villagers often ask local Buddhist monks to bless newly arrived shipments of contraceptives. The agency has recruited 5,000 rural distributors, including rice farmers, shopkeepers, village elders, and others who receive a one-day training course on selling condoms and keeping records, for which they receive a modest commission. The cost of all this effort is $3.50 per recipient per year, less than half of the cost of a similar government program in Thailand not using a marketing approach (Mathews, 1976).

In Mexico, family planners face a tougher challenge because traditional values oppose the idea of family planning, as did past government policy designed to increase the population. Manhood and womanhood have traditionally been measured by the number of children produced. The dominant Catholic culture and widespread ignorance of birth control further hamper family planning efforts. Yet in 1974 the Mexican government established the National Population Council (NPC) to slow the country's galloping rate of population increase. The NPC adopted a classic social marketing approach with the following elements. All promotional materials feature a logo showing a mother, a father, and two children. The family planning messages are carried by posters, booklets, and radio and TV spots. Family planning commercials are broadcast virtually every half hour on the radio. Free contraceptives are available at about 950 hospitals and clinics operated by the Ministry of Health and at 930 clinics run by an affiliate of the International Planned Parenthood Foundation (Wille, 1975).

The effectiveness of social marketing of family planning can be assessed by looking at sales data, distribution systems, changes in knowledge, attitudes, and practices of consumers, cost-effectiveness, and, at the macro level, changes in fertility and birth rates. The Population Information Program reports micro-level measures indicating positive results. Positive results also can be claimed at the macro level. Bogue and Tsui (1979), analyzing the effect of several different variables, found that family planning efforts explain much more of the birth rate reduction since 1968 than does any other factor, including changes in economic and social development which usually have been given most of the credit. According to their data, the recent decline in the world fertility rate has been primarily due to "the worldwide drive by Third World countries to introduce family planning as part of their national social-development services" (pp. 99–100).

Heart Disease Prevention

Coronary disease is a byproduct of "the good life." Though nearly nonexistent in most of the world, it has reached epidemic proportions in Western industrialized countries. Between 1972 and 1975 the Stanford Heart Disease Prevention Program carried out an interdisciplinary intervention to determine ways to reduce risk of coronary disease through long-term changes in health practices—decreasing dietary cholesterol consumption and cigarette use, and increasing exercise levels.

Though fundamentally a sophisticated use of social communication, carried out by public health and communications research specialists, the program embodied many of the elements of a social marketing approach. As in the case of family planning, the goal of long-term behavior change required carefully designed and implemented interventions. To facilitate evaluation, the program was carried out in three similar rural California communities: in one community a mass media campaign alone was used; in a second, a mass media campaign was combined with personal instruction for a sample of high-risk individuals; in the third, neither treatment was used.

The extensive media campaign in the first two communities consisted of radio and TV spots and minidramas; "doctor's columns" and columns on diet in local newspapers; printed items, including an information booklet, a heart health calendar, and a cookbook, mailed to all residents; and billboards and bus posters. Residents in the second community also received personal instruction utilizing modeling and reinforcement to encourage them to quit smoking, lose weight, and get more exercise. In each of the three communities a sample of people was selected and tested at the beginning of the program and followed up annually.

The mass media were used to teach specific behavioral skills whenever possible, rather than simply to exhort people to change. Maccoby and Alexander (1979) cite several other key features of the study which match marketing considerations, including:

- The establishment of specific objectives for each component of the campaign over time.
- Clearly defined audience segments.
- The creation of clear, useful, and salient messages through formative research and pretesting.

- Utilization of creative media scheduling to reach the audience with adequate frequency.
- Stimulation of interpersonal communication to encourage a synergistic effect of multiple channels.
- Promotion of clear and well-paced behavioral changes in messages.
- Use of feedback to evaluate the campaign's progress over time.
- The use of a long-term campaign to avoid threshold effect considerations.

The program demonstrated that long-term changes in habits and significant reduction in risk for heart disease could be assisted through communitywide interventions utilizing the mass media (Meyer and Maccoby, 1978). Both interventions yielded a significant increase in knowledge of risk factors and of desirable practices and a significant reduction in overall risk, with the media-plus-direct-instruction intervention producing the greater changes.

A social marketer might consider ways of extending the effectiveness of the Stanford Heart Program. For example, participants might be given special incentives or reinforcements for conforming to good health habits. Grocery stores might participate by highlighting healthful foods, as is now being done by Giant Food Stores in the Washington, D.C., area. The direct support of local doctors and dentists could be enlisted because they are particularly likely to see high-risk individuals.

Other Applications of Social Marketing

A growing number of health improvement programs reflect or have been consciously developed with a social marketing approach:

1. The Cancer Information Office of the National Institutes of Health has produced and pilot-tested a "Helping Smokers Quit" kit to encourage physicians to use their influence with patients who smoke. The kit includes a brief guide for the doctor, patient education materials, and a followup letter and brochure to be sent to the patient after the office visit.

2. The U.S. Department of Agriculture is supporting a project to use mass media and other channels to improve children's eating habits. The project began with extensive consumer research—interviews with children about their food preferences and eating habits.

3. The American Hospital Association's Center for Health Promotion is working to encourage preventive health measures and healthy "life habits" through programs run by hospitals, businesses, and community organizations. The Center recently conducted a workshop for hospital decision makers on marketing health promotion programs to local industry.

4. When infant immunization levels in Missouri dropped to ominous levels, a marketing plan was designed on the basis of a statewide study of the social–psychological factors affecting the problem (Houston and Markland, 1976). The market was segmented and promotional material was directed to parents and expectant parents, as well as to the staff of the Missouri Division of Health. The campaign spokesman, "Marcus Rabbit, M.D.," was created to link the program to children, but to appeal to adults.

5. Public health specialists are using new channels to provide diagnostic services. A team of homosexual male clinicians from the Denver Metro Health Clinic conducted weekly VD screening in one of Denver's three steam baths catering to homosexuals (Judson, Miller, and Schaffnit, 1977).

6. The National Heart, Lung, and Blood

Institute changed eating habits in a National Institutes of Health employee cafeteria through a "Food for Thought" game. Food information was presented on playing-card-like cards which employees received each time they went through the serving line. Small prizes were awarded to those who acquired sets of cards. An increase in purchases of skim milk and decreases in purchases of bread and desserts and in total calories consumed were measured with the aid of the existing inventory control cash register system which automatically recorded every food item selected (Zifferblatt, Wilbur, and Pinsky, 1980).

Although many of these campaigns are still to be evaluated, especially in terms of benefit/cost criteria and long-term effects, the use of conscious social marketing planning by cause organizations is clearly on the upswing.

WHAT ARE THE MAJOR CRITICISMS OF SOCIAL MARKETING?

Not surprisingly, the increasing application of social marketing has been accompanied by questions about its legitimacy and possible negative impacts. The following four classes of criticism have appeared.

Social Marketing Is Not Real Marketing

Some marketers still feel that marketing is largely a business discipline with little or no application to social causes. They believe that marketing is valid only where there are markets, transactions, and prices. As stated by Laczniak and Michie (1979), marketers should "take enough pride in the scope of traditional marketing."

Every discipline has its orthodox group which is content to ply familiar waters, believing either that their discipline has nothing to offer in the new territory or that, if it does, others will resent the intrusion. However, we believe that scholars and practitioners have a right, indeed, an obligation, to venture out and look freshly at phenomena from their discipline's perspective. Such ventures have produced such new fields as political sociology, economic anthropology, social psychology, and quantitative geography. If the new framework or findings are accepted, then the discipline has made a contribution.

Social Marketing Is Manipulative

Many of the issues in social marketing call for changing people's attitudes and behavior, urging them to give up or cut back on comfortable habits. In contrast, commercial marketing frequently supports and encourages present habits, including those that are potentially harmful. Given that commercial marketing is often accused of being manipulative (primarily in persuading people to buy more things or in convincing them that one brand will satisfy a given need better than another brand), it is not surprising that social marketing is charged with being even more manipulative. For example, Laczniak, Lusch, and Murphy (1979) believe that social marketing is potentially unethical in giving power to a group to influence public opinion on such contested issues as pornography and abortion.

The word "manipulative" is something of a red herring in this discussion. The word "manipulative" usually connotes hidden and unfair ends and/or means used in the influence process. We argue that if a cause is marketed openly with the purpose of influencing someone to change his or her behavior, then the process is not manipulative, any more than is the activity of a lawyer, religious leader, or politician trying to convince others. If the social marketer simply makes the strongest possible case in favor of a cause without distorting the facts, the approach is not manipulative. Social marketing, especially when used in countermarketing, can provide a voice for those with competing points of view.

Social Marketing Is Self-Serving

Some critics might be distressed that some social marketers who are promoting a cause are also making a profit in the process. Consider the following examples.

- Seat belt manufacturers are major supporters of auto safety legislation, partly because they stand to gain.
- Bottled water manufacturers in France have backed efforts to influence French citizens to reduce their alcohol consumption.
- Condom manufacturers have lent support to campaigns against VD because they stand to gain through greater use of condoms.
- Life insurance companies are encouraging people to jog, cut down on fats and sugar, install smoke alarms, and in other ways reduce illness, accidents, and premature deaths, thus cutting insurance claims and raising company profits.

Clearly commercial enterprises will increasingly support social marketing programs as they see financial benefits accruing to their companies while they also promote beneficial social change. This development appears to us to be desirable because it increases the incentive for commercial marketers to consider the best interests of consumers. Too often, social marketing efforts are undertaken by underfinanced cause organizations which run the risk of creating excessive demands on their limited resources

when they achieve a major success, a phenomenon which Houston and Homans (1977) term "the failure of success."

A more troublesome issue is the use of tax money by government agencies to promote politically motivated efforts. For example, a booklet on energy conservation measures was delivered to every home in New England at the start of the 1979–80 heating season, paid for by the Department of Energy and private corporate contributions. Critics pointed to the "coincidence" of the upcoming New Hampshire primaries and President Carter's need to improve his image as an effective leader on conservation. In contrast, most government-sponsored social marketing efforts are likely to be fairly uncontroversial when used to increase the effectiveness of legislatively mandated social programs. Social marketing is already being applied in this way by several federal agencies.

Social Marketing Will Damage the Reputation of Marketing

Some marketers fear that applications of social marketing might arouse negative public sentiment toward marketing. Social marketing might acquire a bad name in two ways. First, it might be attacked for promoting unpopular causes, such as abortion or family planning. Second, it might influence people to accept a new behavior that turns out not to be in their best interest. The public might ultimately turn against social marketing and call for its curbing or regulation. Such attacks might strengthen present criticisms of commercial marketing and result in a setback to both.

There is some irony in this scenario because social marketing should, if anything, add luster rather than disrepute to marketing's image as the public sees marketing used to enhance the quality of their lives.

WHAT ARE THE REAL HURDLES TO SUCCESSFUL SOCIAL MARKETING?

The most devastating blow to social marketing would be to demonstrate that it is ineffective, that it does not change anything. Ineffective marketing is wasteful of resources and may lead people to expect results which cannot be produced. Novelli (1980) notes that managers and planners looking for a panacea or a "quick fix" may rush to embrace social marketing with inflated expectations: "When these quick solutions are not forthcoming, they are disappointed and view marketing as having failed." Some social issues are not likely to be affected by social marketing because the costs, although mainly nonmonetary, are too great and because the level of consumer involvement is either too low to overcome inertia—e.g., antilittering campaigns—or so high that producing behavior change will require great facilitation effort—e.g., antismoking campaigns (Rothschild, 1979).

Social marketing practitioners are the first to admit that social marketing will have a different degree of effectiveness with different social causes, and that most social marketing problems will be more formidable than the typical marketing problems facing commercial marketers. William Novelli, a leading social marketing practitioner, admits, "It's a thousand times harder to do social marketing than to do package goods marketing." He and Paul Bloom recently reviewed the major hurdles faced by social marketers, and their observations are summarized hereafter (Bloom and Novelli, 1979).

First, the market is usually harder to analyze. Social marketers have less good quality secondary data about their consumers. They have more difficulty in obtaining valid and reliable measures of salient consumer attributes, and in sorting out the relative influence of various determinants of consumer behavior. They have more difficulty getting consumer research studies funded, approved, and completed in a timely fashion.

Second, target market choice is more difficult. There is often public pressure to attempt to reach the whole market rather than to zero in on the best target groups. Thus a family planning campaign is restrained from focusing on the families who have the most children because of charges of racial or religious discrimination. When the relevant groups can be targeted, these groups are usually the most negatively predisposed to adopt the desired behavior, and thus success is harder to achieve.

Third, formulating product strategy is more difficult. The antismoking crusader should really invent a safe cigarette but this is not easy to do, and therefore the range of product innovation options is smaller. For many causes the reformer must get people to do something that is unpleasant rather than offering them something that would be even more pleasant than their present behavior.

Fourth, social marketers have fewer opportunities to use pricing and must rely more on other approaches that would increase or decrease the cost to consumers of certain behavior. Thus getting people to stop littering is not accomplished as well through a fine (very difficult to enforce) as by reducing the cost of not littering by providing more refuse containers in parks and on busy thoroughfares.

Fifth, channels of distribution may be harder to utilize and control. For example, a family planning organization may be able to get many retailers to carry condoms but has less control over how they will display them, price them, sell them, and replace them when out of stock.

Sixth, communication strategies may be more difficult to implement. Some groups may oppose the use of certain types of appeals that otherwise would be very effective. The particular cause may require a longer explanation than is available within the confines of a short message. The budget may be too low to permit pretesting the message or to ensure its wide distribution or the evaluation of its impact.

Seventh, cause organizations are often backward in their management and marketing sophistication. Many cause organizations are small, rely mainly on volunteers, and have little familiarity with marketing concepts or planning approaches. They may not be able to handle a large demand for their service, should it arise. The staff may not really be committed to solving the problem, especially if they will lose their jobs when they succeed.

Eighth, the results of social marketing efforts are often difficult to evaluate. For example, should the success of a family planning campaign be measured by total births averted or by births averted in high fertility groups? Or should the measure be the number of people who become aware of family planning, or who begin to show an interest in adopting it? Even after an appropriate measure is determined, the contribution of the marketing program to the final outcome is often difficult to estimate.

The resolution of these problems will depend in part on the accumulation of additional experience in applying and evaluating social marketing, on continuing efforts to integrate and disseminate findings from social marketing programs, and on theoretical and empirical work to improve our understanding of factors that can be used to increase the impact of such programs (Bloom, 1980; Cook and Campbell, 1979; Cook and McAnany, 1979; Fine, 1979; Fox, 1980; Rothschild, 1979).

WHAT IS THE FUTURE OF SOCIAL MARKETING?

The 1980s outlook for social marketing is one of continued growth and application to an ever-widening range of issues. More and more cause organizations and government agencies will turn to social marketing in a search for increased effectiveness. Many will come to social marketing only by passing through the stages of social advertising and social communication first. Large and expensive advertising blitzes may be attempted, rather than integrated social marketing campaigns. The risk is that if such social advertising campaigns fail, critics may charge that marketing does not work when in fact it was not really tried.

Clearly there will be a need for more and better trained social marketers rather than simply social advertisers. The ideal training would have several components. Business marketing training which stresses market analysis, economic analysis, and management theory would be desirable. Because social marketers are involved in trying to change attitudes and behavior rather than simply to meet existing needs, they should study the social science disciplines, particularly sociology, psychology, and anthropology. They should also be trained in communication theory. In addition, social marketers will need to acquire a social problem-solving perspective which will lead them to search for possible technological solutions that may eventually replace present solutions based on self-denial, regulation, or economic incentives.

Social marketers working in multicultural contexts in the United States and in overseas development projects will need particular sensitivity to cultural differences, a knowledge of relevant aspects of the cultures in which they work, and facility in language or in working with persons who have the necessary language competence. It is no wonder that many social marketers now working in overseas projects have been Peace Corps volunteers or have studied or worked overseas for extended periods. Courses in language, history, and anthropology contribute to this preparation.

Though at present many social marketers are outside consultants, a look into the future suggests that organizations may attract or develop their own "in house" social marketers. These people may already be educators, public health specialists, policy analysts, and communications experts, for example. Or organizations may attract business-trained marketers who are able to cross over by gaining an understanding of the specific issues and tasks that confront a specific organization or field, such as health promotion. In effect, social marketers will be dual specialists who can apply marketing to specific social causes.

SUMMARY

What impact is social marketing likely to have on promoting beneficial social change in an effective manner? The evidence from the first decade of social marketing applications is promising. We have described social marketing as the application of marketing thinking and tools to the promotion of social causes, and have traced its evolution through social advertising and social communication. Cases from family planning, heart disease prevention, and other health areas are presented to illustrate the range and impact of social marketing applications, though we acknowledge that many are not fully elaborated examples of social marketing.

A growing number of cause organizations and governmental agencies are turning to social marketing. Groups that once relied on social advertising alone are now moving toward social communication and social marketing. Applications of social marketing have achieved some notable results and provide insights into the challenge confronting social marketers. We foresee that social marketing specialists, combining business marketing skills with additional training in the social sciences, will be working on a wider range of social causes with increasing sophistication. Advances in conceptualizing social marketing problems and in evaluating the impacts of social marketing programs will further enhance their effectiveness.

REFERENCES

Bloom, Paul N. (1980), "Evaluating Social Marketing Programs: Problems and Prospects," *1980 Educators Conference Proceedings.* Chicago: American Marketing Association.

——, and William D. Novelli (1979), "Problems in Applying Conventional Marketing Wisdom to Social Marketing Programs," paper presented at American Marketing Association Workshop, "Exploring and Developing Government Marketing," Yale University.

Bogue, Donald J., and Amy Ong Tsui (1979), "Zero World Population Growth?" *The Public Interest*, 55 (Spring), 99–113.

Cook, Thomas D., and Donald T. Campbell (1979), *Quasi-Experimentation: Design and Analysis Issues for Field Settings.* Chicago: Rand McNally College Publishing.

——, and Emile G. McAnany (1979), "Recent United States Experiences in Evaluation Research with Implications for Latin America," in *Evaluating the Impact of Nutrition and Health Programs*, Robert E. Klein et al., eds. New York: Plenum.

Fine, Seymour H. (1979), "Beyond Money: The Concept of Social Price," working paper, Rutgers University.

Fisher, Lucille (1977), "National Smoking Habits and Attitudes," American Lung Association.

Forbes (1979), 123 (September 17), 25.

Fox, Karen F. A. (1980), "Time as a Component of Price in Social Marketing," *1980 Educators Conference Proceedings*. Chicago: American Marketing Association.

Houston, Franklin S., and Richard E. Homans (1977), "Public Agency Marketing: Pitfalls and Problems," *MSU Business Topics*, 25 (Summer), 36–40.

———, and Robert Markland (1976), "Public Agency Marketing—Improving the Adequacy of Infant Immunization," in *Proceedings*, American Institute for Decision Sciences, 461–63.

Judson, Franklyn N., Kenneth G. Miller, and Thomas R. Schaffnit (1977), "Screening for Gonorrhea and Syphilis in the Gay Baths—Denver, Colorado," *American Journal of Public Health*, 67 (August), 740–42.

Kotler, Philip (1979), "Strategies for Introducing Marketing into Nonprofit Organizations," *Journal of Marketing*, 43 (January), 37–44.

———, and Gerald Zaltman (1971), "Social Marketing: An Approach to Planned Social Change," *Journal of Marketing*, 35 (July), 3–12.

Laczniak, Gene R., Robert F. Lusch, and Patrick E. Murphy (1979), "Social Marketing: Its Ethical Dimensions," *Journal of Marketing*, 43 (Spring), 29–36.

———, and Donald A. Michie (1979), "The Social Disorder of the Broadened Concept of Marketing," *Journal of Marketing Science*, 7 (Summer), 214–31.

Lazer, William, and Eugene J. Kelley (1973), *Social Marketing: Perspectives and Viewpoints*, Homewood, IL: Richard D. Irwin, Inc.

Maccoby, Nathan, and Janet Alexander (1979), "Field Experimentation," in *Research in Social Contexts: Bringing About Change*, R. F. Munoz, L. R. Snowden, and J. G. Kelly, eds. San Francisco: Jossey-Bass.

Mathews, Linda (1976), "What Makes Mechai Run, or How to Curb the Births of a Nation," *Wall Street Journal* (January 15), 1.

Meyer, Anthony J., and Nathan Maccoby (1978), "The Role of Mass Media in Maintaining Health," in *Vestinnan Virtauksia*, Erja Erholn and Leif Aberg, eds. Keruu, Finland: Delfiinikirkat.

Mikesh, Verna A., and Leona S. Nelson (1969), "Sugar, Sweets Play Roles in Food Texture and Flavoring," in *Food for Us All*, 1969 Yearbook of the United States Department of Agriculture, Washington, D.C.: Government Printing Office, 232–36.

Nickels, William G. (1974), "Conceptual Conflicts in Marketing," *Journal of Economics and Business*, 27 (Winter), 140–43.

Novelli, William G. (1980), personal communication, January 3.

Population Information Program (1980), "Social Marketing: Does It Work?" *Population Reports*, Family Planning Programs, Series J, number 21, The Johns Hopkins University.

Population Services International (1977), "Preethi Project Transferred to Sri Lanka FPA," *PSI Newsletter* (November&December), 4.

Post, James E., and Edward Baer (1978), "Demarketing Infant Formula: Consumer Products in the Developing World," *Journal of Contemporary Business*, 7 (4), 17–35.

Roberto, Eduardo (1975), *Strategic Decision-Making in a Social Program: The Case of Family-Planning Diffusion*. Lexington, MA: Lexington Books.

Rothschild, Michael L. (1979), "Marketing Communication in Nonbusiness Situations: or Why It's So Hard to Sell Brotherhood Like Soap," *Journal of Marketing*, 43 (Spring), 11–20.

U.S. Public Health Service (1979), *Healthy People: The Surgeon General's Report on Health Promotion and Disease Prevention*. Washington, D.C.: Government Printing Office.

Wiebe, G. D. (1951–52), "Merchandising Commodities and Citizenship on Television," *Public Opinion Quarterly*, 15 (Winter), 679–91.

Wille, Lois (1975), "Mexico Battles the Baby Boom," *Cicago Daily News* (December 3), 5.

Zifferblatt, Steven M., Curtis S. Wilbur, and Joan L. Pinsky (1980), "Changing Cafeteria Eating Habits: A New Direction for Public Health Care," *Journal of the American Dietetic Association*, 76 (January), 15–20.

Mickey Mouse Marketing

N. W. (RED) POPE

The financial industry would do well to emulate the marketing acumen of Mickey Mouse.

The world's most famous character has become a respected and envied symbol of the very best there is in target marketing, salesmanship and customer relations. The leader which sets the standards that others in the attraction industry seek to match is the Disney Organization.

And in that marketing magic initially concocted by Walter Elias Disney over 50 years ago there are some very valuable lessons for the financial industry. For while the business of entertainment and the business of finance appear as far apart as an X-rated movie and a Disney G release, there is one obvious and necessary common denominator both share.

People.

People inside, and people outside. Customers and employees.

How Disney looks upon people, internally and externally, handles them, communicates with them, rewards them is, in my view, the basic foundation upon which its five decades of success stands. The banking and thrift industry, conversely, has appeared to put more emphasis on results, solutions, growth and problems than on the basic method for achieving results or growth or solving problems with solutions—i.e., people.

People. Inside and outside. Customers and employees.

Sitting as I do everyday in the shadow of Cinderella's Castle (East), and exposed to the Pixie Dust which permeates the atmosphere hereabouts, I have come to observe closely and with reverence the theory and practice of selling satisfaction and serving millions of people on a daily basis successfully. It is what Disney does best. It is one of the things banking needs to improve on most.

If anyone better understood the direct relationship between employees and customers I haven't heard about him or her. If ever there was an organization built on people interfacing with people, it is Disney.

For two articles I will relate to the financial industry some of the personnel policies and customer relations theories of the late Walt

Reprinted with permission from *American Banker*, July 25, 1979.

Disney and his successors in the theme park business, with the obvious hope that our customers will someday be able to say what almost every person who has been to Disneyland or Walt Disney World has said: "It was everything I expected, it was worth every penny, and I was served to my satisfaction by people who were enthusiastic, knowledgeable and pleasant."

The articles will dwell on the internal side—the people on the theme park payroll—and the customers, those who pay. But to Disney the two are so intertwined it may be difficult to separate one from the other. As you follow the piece, always keep your bank's policies, theories, philosophies and methods in mind in relation to how Disney does it. Compare your way with the Disney way.

Put aside the fact the Disney organization has been at the entertainment business for more than 50 years and in the theme park business for almost 20 years.

And don't consider the fact Walt Disney Productions has an ample supply of cash and financial support to do some rather remarkable things now and again. In the early days the exact opposite was true. So the Disney strength of today grew out of some rather lean times of yesterday. My point has more to do with attitude, philosophy, direction and execution than cash or credit.

The beauty of it all is that the "Disney Way" has been in effect since Steamboat Willie changed his name to Mickey Mouse. Success did not prompt Walter Elias Disney to establish specific consumer and staff procedures and approaches. Rather, his innovative usual methods of people management brought about Disney's overall success as an organization.

There's little question about the fact that Disney is in the entertainment business. So it is natural that show business terms are employed. Instead of Personnel, there is Casting. That alone gets the average young man or woman in the right frame of mind when he or she goes in for a job. And that's important at Disney. The frame of mind is the difference between being an employee, or being a Cast Member. Show biz, if you will.

At Disney if your job has you interfacing with the public in any way whatsoever, you're "onstage" when you do your thing. If your work is not public-interfacing, you're "backstage." One is not better than the other. That is emphasized. It takes both to "put on the show," as the Disney people say it, and they mean just that.

No little, insignificant jobs at all. That is emphasized. It takes many people, doing many types of jobs, to put on the show every day. No job is without its importance to the show. The first time a new Disney cast member goes to his or her job there is a feeling of being a part of the overall success.

The most obvious element at Casting is the professionalism. Those who interview and hire and place are pros in the personnel business. They know what they are doing, and how to do it. An interview at Disney is impressive to the thousands of people, most of them young, who apply for jobs. And there are up to 14,000 jobs at Walt Disney World in season. Be aware that first impressions on the potential employee are as important as those on the employer.

What kind of people are interviewing job applicants at your bank? Do they give the proper impression to applicants? Is your personnel function really professional?

The new Cast Member, once hired, is given written instructions as to the steps he/she will go through in preparation-to-work stages. Written information, not verbal. He is told when to report, where to report, what to wear to report, how long he will be in each training phase. He is provided a booklet that tells him, or her, what is expected in appearance, hair style and length, from makeup to jewelry, from clean fingernails to acceptable shoes. Regardless of age or sex or job to be performed, there is conformity to the code. Everything is in writing. No chance for misinformation, misinterpretation. Attention to detail.

Everyone must attend Disney University and 'pass' Traditions 1 before going on to specialized or technical training. That's right, Disney U.—a multilevel educational institution run on Disney property by a full-time staff. In addition to several basic Disney philosophy courses there are evening classes in Spanish or accounting or drama or disco dancing. All Cast Members are eligible to attend and college credits are given for many courses.

Traditions 1 is an all-day experience wherein the new hire gets a constant offering of Disney philosophy and operational methodology. Every audio-visual and static presentation method is used. And no one is exempt from the course, from VP to entry-level part-timer. All must matriculate at Disney U. before any time is spent on a job, backstage or onstage.

Here is where banks so often fail to take advantage of a marvelous opportunity. We don't have our policies in writing. We tell the new people to "report on Monday." That's it. When they show up, we so often hand them benefits booklets that are out of date and expect them to decipher the material. If a briefing is given, it is boring, ill-produced, lacks imagination and is usually way over the heads of those forced to sit through it. Our principal method of indoctrinating a new hire resembles handing a new recruit a gun and showing him which end to hold, and then walking off, leaving the person to load, aim and fire the best he can.

Disney expects the new CM to know something about the company, its history and success, its management style before he actually goes to work. Every person is shown, during Traditions 1, how each division relates to other divisions, and how each division—Operations, Resorts, Food and Beverage, Marketing, Finance, Merchandising, Entertainment, etc.—relates to "the show." In other words, here's how all of us work together to make things happen. Here's your part in the big picture.

Are you listening?

The new CM shows up his first day at Disney U. He is ushered into a room with round tables, four to the table. Coffee and juice and a Danish are offered. It is 8:30 a.m. A name tag is given each person, but we'll get into that later. The "instructor" is with that group for the next eight hours.

Everyone is introduced—not by the instructor, or by himself. The four people at the table are asked to get to know each other and then all of them will introduce each other. Immediately you know three other people by name, face, where they came from and their future jobs. You are a part of a group now, not alone—one of the crowd.

All of you gather for a picture. You smile. When your Traditions 1 day is over at 4:30 p.m., you are given a copy of the weekly Disney newspaper for the theme park and there on the front page is your group photo, with your name in the caption! Impressed? Certainly.

For about half of your eight hours you're in a classroom setting, watching films or slides or listening to an enthusiastic young lady use magnetic elements to show how the company operates. The other four hours are spent on a guided tour of the park. Onstage, backstage— you are exposed to it all. And at lunchtime you are taken to one of the many company cafeterias and treated to as much lunch as you desire. Free. Impressed? You begin getting the idea this company wants you to be happy on the job, and knowledgeable.

How many banks take their new hires throughout the facility, explaining each department's function and how all relate to the business of the bank? Do we treat our new hires to a lunch? Take their picture, give them the company newspaper, explain the benefits properly?

Sure, your bank isn't Walt Disney World and you don't have the people, the money to do all that. Are you sure you don't? Have you tried?

Remember those name tags? Everyone at a Disney theme park wears one; every person who works for any Disney enterprise wears one. Everybody. From the chairman of the board of Walt Disney Productions to that guy sweeping cigarette butts off Main Street after the parade. The dishwasher few people see, the ticket taker at the entrance, the secretaries, security people—everyone wears a name tag.

With only the first name on it. That's it. President of Disney Productions, director of marketing, popcorn vendor, cook, first name only.

And the rule is that when addressing each other, only first names will be used. No Mr. or Mrs. or Miss or Ms. First names, please. It is part of the "family feeling" Disney advocates. It is part of the oneness, the unity, the "no one is better than anyone else" policy.

Can you imagine the average teller addressing the chairman of the board as "Charlie." Or the janitor calling the VP/commercial loans by his first name? Perhaps banks need to be more formal than entertainment entities. It is probably expected that banks not be too familiar, too folksy, for money and credit is perceived as a more serious business than the attractions business.

Or is it? Have we structured ourselves so stiffly; are we so status-level-position conscious that communication doesn't properly occur? Do we have the feeling that sometimes it is "Them" and "Us"? Do we demand formality, aloofness?

After a day to learn what's what, get the Pixie Dust, the name tag and the photo, the new CM is dispatched to his/her job-training assignment. Very little OJT occurs at WDW—Walt Disney World. On-the-job observing, perhaps, but little training.

Example. My two kids, ages 18 and 16, average intelligence, reasonably quick, are accepted to be Casual Temporaries—summer, Christmas, Easter, etc., employment.

They are to take tickets, either at the main entrance or the Magic Kingdom entrance. Take tickets. That's it. How tough can that be?

Four eight-hour days of instruction are required before they can go "onstage"! They are paid to learn, but before a Disney CM interfaces with a Guest—Disney has no customers at theme parks, only Guests—the management must be absolutely certain that the CM can, and will, perform properly. After all, we are dealing with Guest Satisfaction, they say. Nothing is spared to assure Guest Satisfaction.

"Why," I inquired, "does it take four days to learn how to take tickets?" Waste of time, I thought.

My two Traditions 1 graduates, with his new haircut and her "a-little-lipstick-only" makeup, jump to the defense of 32 hours of education in the fine art of taking tickets.

I was informed there are x varieties of tickets, each having special meaning. What happens if someone wants to know where the restrooms are, when the parade starts, what bus to get back to the campgrounds, what the park's hours are, where do we eat inside, what happens if I lose my child, how many bricks in the castle? Questions ad infinitum.

"We need to know the answers or where to get the correct answers quickly," I am advised. "After all, Dad, we're onstage and help produce the show for our Guests. Our job, every minute, is to help the Guest enjoy the park."

Wow! Can you imagine one of our book-keepers, a proof operator, a secretary, a collector rising to the defense of four days of intensive prejob training so they could better serve our customers? Well, why not?

After four days, they went on the line. First to observe, then to try it under careful supervision. After a few hours, they were put to the task. It is this way in every job throughout the park where some specific training is required and general knowledge demanded. Regardless of the time it takes or the instructional costs, no one interfaces with a Guest until he or she is proved ready to properly serve that Guest.

Stop and examine the average bank's teller training programs. The New Accounts persons. Baptism under fire.

And so I said to my minimum-wage-to-start-with tycoons after the first day, "How does it feel to be ticket takers?"

Again I was berated.

"Ticket takers? Dad, we're WDW Hosts."

I had forgotten. Everyone onstage and backstage in the theme park area itself has a title with the word "host" in it. There is no Policeman. There is a Security Host. There is no monorail driver; there is a Transporta-tion Host. There are no street cleaners, there are Custodial Hosts. No french fries server, but a Food and Beverage Host. Guests have hosts, don't they? Certainly, so everyone at Disney is a Host or Hostess.

And everyone who interfaces with a Guest in the park is "themed"—costumed to fit the job. The world's largest laundry does all those costumes and uniforms every day, or all night, as the case may be. Come to work in the morning and after clocking in go to Wardrobe. Show biz again.

Mike Mescon, the incredibly provocative Georgia State professor/lecturer, says if he headed a bank he would drop almost all bank titles and use instead the term, Salesperson. For, Mr. Mescon emphasizes, that's what it is all about. Selling. Low-key or hard-sell, salesmanship and customer service are two elements that separate banks from one another. The bank that can train its people properly, motivate its people, reward its people and has its people enthusiastically representing that bank on and off the job will win.

Walt Disney was a marketing magician, no doubt. But his keen insight into personnel and customer relations, separately and collectively, enabled him to create the world's most sucessful entertainment conglomerate by starting with a mouse he drew and named Steamboat Willie in 1928.

The next article, also keying on The Disney Way, will highlight Customer Relations and feature several marketing approaches banks might use to sell to their target groups.

More Mickey Mouse Marketing

N. W. (RED) POPE

Nothing I've had published in 30 years prompted more mail or phone calls than "Mickey Mouse Marketing," the first of two articles concentrating on customer and staff relations as practiced by the Walt Disney organizations.

While this could mean all my previous stuff was pretty bad, it might also mean this piece was particularly good. I don't think it was either. What I think prompted the cards and calls was that the gist of the article touched some of banking's exposed nerves.

A banker in New York wrote he had known for years how good Disney was at customer relations, and how bad his bank was at it, but he hadn't been able to get money to do much about the latter. The Denver banker said he knew his bank's training was horrible, but management hadn't given that priority billing. The Pennsylvania banker remarked that until bankers cared as much about how well the customer was served as how well the bank was served, banking would never change its customer relations.

An Ohio banker wrote me stating that odds were pretty long on bankers looking upon their personnel as high priorities. His way of stating that was "human resources inside our banks are yet to be ranked as important as computers, branch offices or, for that matter, the board of directors' annual retreat. In the main, staff morale is not all that big a need to too many bank managers."

The good part about the letters was that people apparently were moved to critical introspection upon reading the piece. The bad part was that almost without exception everyone admitted management apathy or lack of commitment.

Incidentally, Disney does not make its programs or methods or manuals or personnel available, as a rule, to outsiders on a "for sale" or consulting basis.

Now, back to Part Two in the continuing saga of how Walt Disney World, and other Disney entities, look upon their bread (staff) and butter (guests). Remember, please, as you read on, compare how your bank does things with the way Mickey Mouse and his associates do them.

Of the 100 million people who have passed through Walt Disney World's turnstiles since October, 1971, a great many ask seemingly stupid questions about the place. Stupid to us, perhaps, but not to Disney. Like how many bricks are in the Castle, how many lights are there in the theme park, how many boats do you have here, how long did it take to build this place, how much did it cost, how many telephones are there in the whole place, how often do you have to paint the submarines, how many hot dogs do you sell here each year? Ad infinitum.

To many businesses this sort of barrage of trivia inquiry would lead to an abrupt, "How should I know, kid!" To Disney it is the sort of stuff dreams (and attendance) are built on.

Reprinted with permission from *American Banker*, September 12, 1979.

And if any employee (Host or Hostess) cannot give the answer to any question . . . that's right . . . any question, then there is a telephone exchange to call. Immediately. The minute the question is asked and the Disney staffer can't answer it, call that number and ask!

Twenty-four hours a day a cadre of switchboard operators with factbooks to rival the largest phone books in America are standing by to answer those "very stupid" questions, on the spot. Like, the most meals served in a single day was 220,500 (12/31/75). And 13 million ketchup packets are given out annually and 24 tons of french fries are sold every week, and 3½ million pounds of hot dogs were sold to the guests last year.

And if you add up all the boats and rafts and submarines and ferries and canoes and other floating material throughout the 27,400 acres, you'd have the seventh largest navy in the World, and that's a fact.

The bottom line is: serve the guest. If someone cares about hot dogs, tell 'em the answer. Whatever the guest wants to know, get 'em the facts, now!

Sometime, stand in your lobby and watch your personnel attempt to answer basic, not stupid, questions. How much are your safe deposit boxes? What are your CD rates? How much can I get for a Canadian dollar? Does your bank have a branch office in the south part of town? What's your best rate on an auto loan? What hours are your drive-ins open?

Maybe the person asked doesn't have the answers, or perhaps shouldn't try to give out rates, but how does she, or he, respond? How does he, or she, serve the customer?

One fast rule at Disney theme parks is that no employee will be served before a guest. In fact, Disney provides cafeterias, breakrooms, snack bars and other facilities for its people "backstage." This includes special live and automated teller operations our Sun Bank runs for Disney employees so they can do their banking conveniently.

If you want a soft drink and you work at Disney, go backstage. If you want to buy a Minnie Mouse blouse, do it at the company store. Need a check cashed? Backstage. From toilets to parking, Disney makes sure its guests' needs are not slowed by staff use. While we in banks don't run theme parks, I'll have to admit I've seen our bank employees in teller lines ahead of customers.

Every week Walt Disney World's cast communications division of Disney University produces an eight-page 8½ × 11 newspaper called Eyes and Ears. One glance at its contents and you know it was prepared for Disney people. It is a people publication, featuring all sorts of activities, improved employment opportunities, special benefits, educational offerings and even a complete classified section. The stories are very short, newsy, punchy. Lots of pictures of cast members. A brief feature perhaps. And I've never, never seen a single photo in that newspaper in seven years that showed anyone not smiling. Contrived? Maybe, but it got to me, didn't it?

Banks produce some of the worst employee publications possible. Poor writing, inadequate story selection, not enough photos, and often those published are poor quality, and too much about the brass or the home office. And the reason is, I think, that we expect people in marketing or personnel or some other division to take on the paper as an additional job. We don't hire newspaper people to produce newspapers. We hire loan officers to make loans, and auditors to audit, and managers to manage, but we feel some obligation to assign the internal communications to someone as an afterthought, an extra job, assuming it is a simple, quick thing.

"Give it to the boss' nephew . . . he used to write for the high school newspaper."

One evening during a BMA conference when some of us were "learning from one another," the subject of company publications, house organs, arose. Most of us agreed poor quality was a standard. One member of the group admitted, blushingly, that his personnel director had decreed the bank would have some sort of newspaper to appease all the EEOC types, and to show some union that his bank "talked" with its people, regardless of content or quality. He said the bank president wanted to prove, if the need arose, that his bank had an ongoing communications vehicle, content notwithstanding.

Disney feels, on the other hand, that informed people are happier, less confused, more aware of benefits and opportunities, and more cognizant that management genuinely wants and strives to communicate. In addition to the weekly newspaper, Disney produces on a regular basis single-page bulletins for management, two-page "hot news" bulletins with promotions and transfers on a regular basis and, less frequently, an eight-page standard-size newspaper for all cast members.

The written word is most important to employees of any company. But it must be professionally done to properly communicate. A cheap, shoddy and poorly-constructed publication will be obvious to the intended readers. Perhaps they will take that to mean management isn't all that interested in doing any better. And that publication is an extension of the bank. How we are perceived by those that see it, inside or out, is cause for concern.

Disney also cares what its staff members think about the theme park as a place to work. When your reputation and continuation in business depends upon how well employees serve paying customers, then per-haps some attention should be given to the "care and feeding" of the employees. (Hear that, banks?)

There are several types of employees at a Disney theme park, from the permanent year-'round types, to what Mickey terms "the casual temporary cast member." This means summers and holidays and maybe weekends, when the attendance is greatest and staff needs are highest. Like my two kids taking tickets during peak seasons. Disney is a master at being able to use part-timers, keeping the higher paid group at a minimum, a trick many banks are beginning to pick up, especially in the teller area.

As the summer ends and some 3,000 casual temporaries are returning to school, Disney asks each to complete a simple questionnaire, anonymously. My job was, my division or department was, my age is, my formal education is, I live __ miles from the park, etc. I am a: man-woman. Notice it didn't say male, female. They find out some basics first.

Then they ask the respondent to check one of five applicable answers, from very good to poor, to these:

• I think the reputation Walt Disney World has with the public is . . .
• Looking at Walt Disney World compared with other companies, I would say it is managed . . .
• How did you feel when you told people what company you worked for?
• How did you feel your wage (salary) compared with wages (salaries) paid for similar jobs outside Walt Disney World?
• Inside Walt Disney World?

Then there are questions about hiring practices and procedures, the orientation program, the initial training given. Did you feel satisfied with your job? How important did you feel it was? Was it interesting?

For eight pages and eighty-four questions the Disney management wants to know, from those in the less glamour jobs all the way to the more outstanding positions, if its people are happy, treated fairly, trained properly and communicated with. Why? because the basis for operating a theme park dedicated to the happiness of all sorts of people must be . . . happy people. Inside. People with pride, respect for the employer. And to get those kids back next summer, Disney knows it has to offer the best surroundings, training and opportunities.

Banks are beginning to pay some heed to what its employees think about working conditions and opportunities, too. Next to interest paid on time deposits, salaries and wages are the second highest cost in most banks. The cost of turnover is exorbitant. Our training has been inadequate. We have not been competitive in the personnel marketplace. And, like Disney, a bank is a service business which requires people to interface with the customer in so many transactions.

When the energy business hit Florida, and California, and gasoline became as precious as glass slippers, Disney realized its large contingent of people, working literally around the clock, might be hardpressed to get gas to come to work. Mobilization occurred. First, in all publications car pools were encouraged and, via computer, actually designed for everyone on the payroll. Large buses were contracted to run regular schedules from the largest neighborhood areas to the park, for 90 cents. And if eight or more cast members arranged a car pool and would agree to pay for gas, oil and maintenance, Disney would provide a van! Free! Finally, to assure some gas for work-oriented travel, Disney put in its own cast gas station!

Many banks have opted to reduce the lighting, raise the thermostat, or permit removal of jackets. But Disney, keying to employee needs, went further. It did the analysis, it made the decisions to lease vans, work out car pool schedules and set up bus routes, before it asked for employee cooperation. Many banks I'm aware of asked every employee interested in a car pool to contact personnel.

The obvious happened. Both people contacted personnel. Perhaps had the banks leased vans, set up the routes, put the thing into service and said: "Okay, we've committed and set it up, now you take advantage of it," more people would have done just that. Waiting for enough volunteers to come forth will seldom provide sufficient personnel to fight the battle, much less win the war.

I hope all bank vice presidents (and above) are sitting down to read these next two items.

Annually all the "white collar" types at Walt Disney World, the management if you will, undertake a week-long program called cross-utilization. In essence it means giving up the desk, the secretary and the white collar and donning a themed costume or an apron and heading for the frontline action. For a week the "bosses" sell tickets or popcorn, dish out ice cream or hot dogs, load and unload rides, park cars, drive the monorail or trains, or take on any of the 100 "onstage" jobs that make the park come alive to guests.

According to my sources at Disney, the cross-utilization concept is designed to give management a better "hands on" view of how the guests need to be served and, at the same time, management gets a better understanding of what the cast member must go through to properly serve the guests. And assignments are made for Cross U, not selections offered. You take the job given you and head for wardrobe, and a long eight hours on your feet with a smile on your face, ready or not.

Now, all the time you've been reading this you have been envisioning the VP/installment credit in a drive-in teller cubicle, the VP/trust holding down a collector's job, perhaps the VP/marketing working in the proof department, the president of the bank handling the new accounts desk and all those dumb questions. There's the commercial loan VP operating the mailroom, and somehow our operations VP is in marketing trying to handle a newspaper reporter's persistent questions about why the "little man" is being charged so much interest while, at the same time, attempting to compute market share for 15 branch offices manually.

Kind of makes you smile, doesn't it?

Secondly, and I quote from a recent Eyes and Ears: "As many of you are aware, our vice presidents and directors (Note: a director at Disney is a level below a VP, in a management function such as director of marketing, director of finance, director of food and beverage, etc.) have been scheduling themselves to visit the Magic Kingdom to increase their awareness of both the guest experience and the work experience of our cast members. So don't be surprised if you're stopped during your workday to chat with one of our VPs or directors. He's genuinely anxious to see your operation and what you do each day!"

Following that statement to the troops there is a schedule showing what day which VP or director will be in the park. Both day and night shifts are covered. And wouldn't you know . . . those VPs and directors are supposed to write a report on their findings!

What is all this mingling about? What is this orchestrated entry into the trenches with the folks doing the dirty jobs going to achieve? Well, for my money it is going to tell one heck'uva lot of hardworking people that "somebody up there cares."

How can you spend eight hours shoving out those fries, alongside a couple of sweatin' and smilin' kids making $3.20 an hour, and not be learning something positive about personnel relations, and management?

How can you stand there for eight hours, smiling and saying "Howdy" to 60,000 people, trying to answer their questions in Spanish, direct them to the nearest restrooms, look at their faces of anticipation, and not learn something about the consumer public?

Perhaps periodically it would be most revealing, and educational, if the bank's brass, and some of our board members for that matter, came down to the lobby on a Monday morning. Or meandered out into the drive-in lanes on a Friday afternoon. Talked to the people in line. Or took the place of that person in the teller window. Chances are it wouldn't take many such trips for improved communications to come about, for some improved benefits to be put in, for some staff morale to improve and for productivity on both ends to get even better.

Mutual understanding for each other's needs and problems. Mutual respect for each other, as people, and as fellow bankers.

To all those who say they are too busy, whose schedules won't permit them to idle away a couple of hours doing such things, I'd suggest the demands upon senior executives at Walt Disney World at peak season are at least as compelling as those of most bankers. It is, I submit, a matter of priorities. He who sees the need, who wants to fill it, will. Case closed.

Disney has a private recreating area with lake, rec hall, picnic areas, boating and fishing and volleyball and family-outing opportunities ad infinitum for its cast members' exclusive use—professionally staffed.

There is a library, staffed, with everything from "How To Do It" books to the latest fiction best sellers, for the benefit of the cast members.

There is a division of Disney University called cast activities. Its sole purpose is to provide educational, recreational, entertainment and cost-saving opportunities to the employees.

Several women from casting make the rounds of all work areas, offices, backstage and onstage, daily to check cast members' hair lengths, make-up, general appearance. Disney has rules about how to dress. You understand them when you report to work. You get one warning. The public sees fresh-faced, neatly-attired people serving them, but that didn't happen by accident.

There is no question that much of Disney's success with people, inside and out, stems from quite a bit of regimentation. Some say it is militaristic in fact. And, in spite of all those smiling faces out there in Fantasyland, there are more than a few sour attitudes behind the braces.

But in spite of the rules, the regulations, the demand that everyone do everything The Disney Way, there is no question the people who work there have a special feeling for that 50-year-old mouse. They know the man-agement overtly works at employee relations. They are cognizant that if they want a lifetime career, or a summer's employment, there is a cornucopia of possibilities within the organization. They know all this because the company management puts employee relations just under guest relations as a top priority, and not far under.

And that is, of course, the real answer.

When a company's customers are happy with the service and the product, and find enthusiastic and knowledgeable personnel who are anxious to help, chances are that company will continue to enjoy the lucrative patronage of those customers for a long, long time.

When a company's employees know, and are continually reminded, that their employer is genuinely concerned with and has interest in their personal well-being, and undertakes meaningful programs to manifest that interest, chances are things are alive and well inside the shop.

Hark! Could that be your bank's employees whistling as they arrive for the day's toil? Listen . . .

"Hi ho, hi ho, it's off to work we go. . . ."

How to Initiate a Marketing Perspective in a Health Services Organization

WILLAM R. GEORGE • FRAN COMPTON

Recognizing employees as the initial market of a health services organization epitomizes the internal marketing concept in action. A training module is presented to focus on the marketing role of all personnel and to involve many employee groups as active participants in the marketing process.

INTRODUCTION

The introduction of sophisticated business techniques and practices into the not-for-profit organization may create unanticipated, negative consequences. Two possibilities are: (1) considerable internal hostility, disassociation and barrier erection; and, (2) an endowment of the new approach with almost mystical powers that become the special province of one group within the organization. New language and new approaches to old problems and changes in the "tried and true" ways may seem too strange and threatening to be considered. Marketing, with its unfamiliar buzz words (e.g., bundle of benefits, differential advantage, etc.), the focus on specific groups rather than on the community as a whole and the requirement of a user, rather than a provider, orientation has

often been viewed suspiciously by health professionals. To lessen such suspicion and possible negative consequences, internal marketing is suggested as a prerequisite to implementing a marketing approach with the other publics of the health service organization.

The internal marketing concept holds that employees precede other publics as the initial market of an organization. The objective of the internal marketing function is to develop motivated personnel within an environment which supports customer consciousness (Gronroos, 1981). This objective is especially relevant for organizations providing services such as health care because production and consumption occur simultaneously (Sasser and Arbeit, 1976; George, 1977; Berry, 1981; Fisk and Freshley, 1981; Hafer and Joiner, 1984). Thus, *all* health

William R. George and Fran Compton, "How to Initiate a Marketing Perspective in a Health Services Organization," *Journal of Health Care Marketing*, Vol. 5, No. 1 (Winter 1985), pp. 29–37.

Reprinted from *Journal of Health Care Marketing*, published by the American Marketing Association.

service personnel must perform as producers *and* sellers of the specific service and organization. This means that internal exchanges between the organization and its employee groups must be operating successfully before the health service organization can be successful with its external markets.

The purpose of this article is to examine a successful approach in order to provide a marketing orientation for health service personnel who traditionally have not viewed themselves as part of the marketing process. It also provides an example of how to establish the important customer-consciousness component of an internal marketing strategy.

BACKGROUND

Traditionally, social service organizations, in general, and blood collection agencies, in particular, have concentrated their efforts in communicating *their* needs to the public at large. Their needs have been paramount in all communications, i.e., "We need money"; "We need blood"; "We need volunteers." The expectation was that the public would respond favorably simply because the blood collection agencies articulated *their* needs.

In recent decades, however, our society has undergone some dramatic changes in perspective—from self-denial to self-fulfillment (Yankelovich, 1981). These changes have impacted on the effectiveness of historic blood collection efforts as the age of "What's in it for me?" has made it increasingly difficult to get the desired results out of the "goodness of your heart" approach. Just as commercial firms have sensed the changing needs of society and responded to a more self-aware, even self-centered, consumer, so must the not-for-profit organization. In this sense, marketing must function as the organization's change agent to assure that the

organization is kept in synchronization with its ever-changing external environment (Cardinal, Sanderson and Wingenter, 1977). Introducing the marketing process as an instrument of change can be a slow and difficult undertaking. Kotler (1980) describes this movement toward a marketing enlightenment as the "law of slow learning." Many profit and nonprofit organizations have had to proceed through all stages of slow learning to achieve a marketing orientation.

Blood Services

The American Red Cross organizes its blood collections regionally through the Blood Services division. Within Blood Services, it is the Donor Resources Development (DRD) department which has the responsibility for planning and implementing growth strategies for blood collection. Historically, education and persuasion have been the most frequently used techniques to encourage more blood donations, and the needs of the agency were paramount. The needs of the donor, as part of an exchange process for collecting blood, were not recognized.

The formal recognition of the role marketing could play in collecting blood finally became evident. A seminar on marketing for the DRD and public relations personnel of Blood Services was first sponsored in 1979 by the Blood Services national headquarters. By 1981, the Training and Education Department of Blood Services had contracted with an outside marketing consultant to conduct a two-part intensive seminar on the marketing of management techniques for Donor Resources Development, and this two-part seminar has been repeated several times. As a result, these and other marketing activities fermented within the DRD and, gradually, a movement toward a marketing orientation evolved.

It has been a considerable challenge to introduce marketing as a new operating philosophy for the DRD and as a consideration for all other departments of Blood Services. Within some blood centers, the negative possibilities as noted above have happened in varying degrees. However, in many cases, a crucial impediment has been the internal barriers between the DRD and other departments. Thirty-five DRD personnel from 20 states identified such barriers which may result from any of the following: (1) a perceived prima donna status of DRD representatives (e.g., company cars, higher average starting salaries in many cases, flexible schedules that include travel, etc.); (2) inconsistent collection levels; (3) lack of commitment by upper management to professional donor recruitment approaches (i.e., many managers still prefer the "volunteer" approaches of the past); (4) a sense of not having any input to the DRD effort; (5) a feeling of not being a part of the DRD effort; and, (6) a past history of ill will. Clearly, an internal marketing approach which would facilitate exchanges within the Blood Center was needed before any external marketing could be effective.

CUSTOMER CONSCIOUSNESS FOR ALL PERSONNEL

A number of blood centers have initiated specific programs to achieve a customer consciousness within their organizations. One was the DRD department for the Central Ohio Region of Blood Services which has been confronted with the task of obtaining a six to eight percent increase in blood units per year. Adoption of a marketing approach was desirable because of the potential for long-term improvements in donor recruitment and blood collections. However, this had to be done without erecting barriers with

other Blood Services departments as well as attempting to eliminate any barriers that may have already existed. The Blood Center's tradition of emphasizing team effort would further show that the other departments had roles in meeting consumer needs.

The initial focus was on several Blood Center departments which interact with external publics of Blood Services. Training for the DRD staff had to be upgraded and reoriented toward a customer consciousness. Public Relations has always been a vital resource for the DRD, and that department needed to understand its new role in adopting a marketing approach. Other internal publics with a need for an early understanding of marketing were directors of the personnel, volunteers and laboratory departments. Especially critical to the success of this new approach to the donors was the nursing staff. These are the only Blood Services personnel who always have direct contact with donors. Yet, Blood Services nursing orientation seldom, if ever, had included training to encourage repeat donations throughout the year or to inspire first-time donors to donate in the future. Indeed, nurses, doctors and many other health care personnel sometimes feel that marketing is "crass" and unprofessional. All of these internal publics needed to be educated about their crucial role in marketing the Blood Services program.

Training Presentation

A simple training presentation was needed to communicate the essence of a marketing orientation to staff that, for the most part, did not see themselves as part of the marketing process. It was necessary to get their attention, to build awareness and to tear down any barriers which the DRD might have inadvertently produced. All staff had to switch their thinking from "we need" to "they (consumers) need/we have," and to realize that this new approach required the conscious involvement of everyone in Blood Services.

The presentation was designed to last 30 minutes, with additional time allocated for questions and the perusal of specific items. Most participants were stimulated to ask many questions during the 1½-hour sessions. Overheads were used to keep the presentation on track, and handouts provided participants with specific marketing concepts and techniques for later review. These included a list of basic terms and definitions, the use of a blank chart to identify competitors and differential advantages and two blank worksheets for analyzing benefits sought and delivered.

The five specific goals of the orientation were:

a. to clarify the *basics* of marketing in order to dispel myths about the marketing mystery;
b. to illustrate how marketing concepts include everyone in an organization in everyday activities;
c. to present basic marketing terms to those who were unfamiliar with them;
d. to provide exercise materials concerning basic marketing techniques; and
e. to build awareness/appreciation/acceptance.

To remove marketing from specific "departmental pigeon holes," the presentation began with the clarification of marketing as more than just:

• a buzz word (as "communications" was 10 years ago);
• PR/advertising (although it does include activities from those disciplines);
• sales/DRD (although these disciplines are heavily committed to it);

• a management tool (although management, too, must be committed to it).

Marketing was then defined and simplified in terms of its most fundamental ingredients: *Marketing is a way of thinking and acting about what we do based on the concept of exchange.* Although a gross simplification of the most sophisticated inclusive definitions, this definition was understandable by the initiates and acceptable to the more experienced.

To illustrate what is involved in the exchange process, a worksheet was designed with five headings and made into a transparency: "they / want / exchange / we / have." Under the heading "they" were five terms: *publics, markets, consumers/donors, research* and *actual/potential.* This procedure allowed the use of marketing terms under an easily recognized neutral heading. In this sequence, it was possible to show how the DRD can fine-tune publics from the 2.1 million people in central Ohio to female donors, age 21–35, who are not employed outside the home and who live in communities of 1,000 to 15,000 people, etc. It was noted that research would help to understand what was special about the "they's," whether they be donors or potential donors. The illustration was targeted so far down that a small "they" resulted as an illustration of how one must keep practicality in mind and not let the concept override the purpose. The group was asked to help identify characteristics of a possible target market so that from the start the group was involved in a marketing experience. As a result, nonmarketing personnel were learning market segmentation skills, while the group dynamics added zest to the lecture-style presentation.

Next, "want" was covered based on the concept of benefits sought. It was pointed out that research on donors is the most reliable way to determine benefits sought. However, communication with donors can give us intuitive knowledge until verifiable facts are available through appropriate research.

Skipping over "exchange" for the moment, the "we" component was examined. After a few minutes of discussion, participants readily agreed that "we" is both the entire organization as well as each department and/or activity. Everyone in Blood Services has some role in the exchange process—from recruitment, through collection and processing, to distribution. The fact that everyone is included in the process would be reemphasized later in the presentation.

Next, the offer, or "have," part of the exchange process was considered. Identification of what Blood Services offers the donor replaced the old emphasis on "we need." Participants suggested that the offering might include: (1) benefits of a good feeling about helping others; (2) a mini-physical; (3) cookies in the canteen; (4) time off from work; and, (5) a safe unit of blood at the hospital should the donors or their families ever need it. Perhaps this presentation portion was the first enlightenment for the majority of the participants. Clearly, Blood Services does indeed offer a lot of benefits for donors; it is not just "taking" and never "giving." Exchanges are being made even if the benefits given are mostly intangible and subtle.

Finally, it was illustrated that the "exchange" can be made—*they want, we have.* This is a fundamental shift in thinking away from the old "we need your blood, money and time." The components of exchange considered were: (1) competition; (2) differential advantage; (3) delivery of benefits; (4) marketing mix variables of product, price, place and promotion; and, ultimately, (5) a marketing plan. At first, most participants thought that the Blood Center was spared

competition since it operates under a "total supply" contract with all health facilities using blood. To their surprise, a number of competitive distractions were identified such as apathy, company picnics, layoffs, a slow economy and other solicitation drives.

Once competition was recognized, it was possible to raise the question of how the Blood Center could best overcome the identified competitors. This transition to considering differential advantage was smooth and logical and led directly into delivery of the benefits which provide the Blood Center's differential advantage. Once again, all participants recognized that everyone—from the greeter at the door to the delivery volunteer who processes the order for blood to treat an injured child—is involved in the exchange process between Blood Services and its publics. They were beginning to see their part in the marketing process.

It took some stretching of minds to reach a consensus that Blood Services' product is the "opportunity to share life"; but once agreed to, the other marketing variables fell into place. For example, price involves the cost to the donor in time, inconvenience, fear, etc. Place concerns where and when the exchange occurs, and whether the facilities are conducive to a pleasant donating experience. Promotion entails how the offering is symbolized and how the donor is stimulated to make the exchange with Blood Services. It was emphasized that the organization is in charge of the above marketing variables within specified limits. For example, donating blood cannot take less than 30 minutes under optimum, one donor at a time, conditions. This is the base price (i.e., time = cost). However, inefficient collections that "cost" two or three hours—a price that is too high to pay for the benefits offered—is not permissible.

By the end of the discussion on the marketing exchange process, participants under-

FIGURE 1: Blood services benefit matrix

Features Offered[a]

A. Benefits Sought[b]

	Efficiency	Mobility	Health Education	Mini-Physical	Recognition	Community Service	Product Availability	Cost Efficiency	Absolution	Camaraderie	Opportunity to do Good	Food	Blood Pressure Check	Lab Work (Hep. test, etc.)	System	Subtotal
Self-Esteem					B/F	B/F			B/F		B/F					4
Convenience	B/F	B/F		B/F		B/F									B/F	5
Time Away From Job	B/F	B/F														2
Belongingness						B/F				B/F						2
Affirmation of Health			B/F	B/F									B/F	B/F		4
Semi-Tangible Items				B/F		B/F			B/F			B/F	B/F		B/F	⑥
Psychosecurity			B/F			B/F	B/F									3
Importance						B/F										1
Relief from Guilt/Fulfillment of Obligation						B/F	B/F				B/F					③
Total:	2	2	2	3	⑥	3	①		2	①	2	①	2	①	2	

B. Those Delivering and/or Communicating Benefits

	Efficiency	Mobility	Health Education	Mini-Physical	Recognition	Community Service	Product Availability	Cost Efficiency	Absolution	Camaraderie	Opportunity to do Good	Food	Blood Pressure Check	Lab Work (Hep. test, etc.)	System	Subtotal
Employer/Sponsor		D/C	D/C		D/C	D/C				D/C	D/C	?				6
Nurses	D/C	D/C	D/C	D/C	D/C	D/C			D/C		D/C			D/C	D/C	10
Volunteers	D/C	D/C	D/C	D/C	D/C	D/C	?		D/C	D/C	D/C	D/C		D/C	D/C	12
Media			D/C		D/C	D/C			D/C		D/C				D/C	6
Public Relations			D/C	D/C	D/C	D/C		D/C	D/C		D/C				D/C	8
Donor Resources Department	D/C	D/C	D/C		D/C				D/C		D/C				D/C	7
Other Donors	D/C	D/C	D/C		D/C	D/C						D/C				6
Lab/Distribution		?					D/C	D/C							D/C	3
Coordinator	D/C	D/C	D/C	D/C	D/C	D/C	D/C	D/C	D/C	D/C	D/C	D/C	D/C	D/C	D/C	⑮
Chapter Personnel			D/C		D/C	D/C					D/C				D/C	5
Doctors/Non-ARC Medical Personnel			D/C													①+
Total:	5	6	⑩	4	9	8	2	5	6	4	6	3	2	①	8	

[a] B/F = Benefits/Features; D/C = Delivering/Communicating.
[b] Marketing research should be used to determine benefits sought by target group.

stood why a marketing plan is important. They are now supportive of the need to specify how Blood Services plans to manage its exchanges and they understand the need for a formal marketing plan.

Benefits Analysis

A final exercise involved matching features of the Blood Services program to benefits sought by potential donors. Two other worksheets developed by the entire DRD staff during a staff retreat were shared with participants for this exercise. The first one (Part A) identified what the experienced staff believe are the benefits sought by donors and the features of the blood service program which fulfill these desires (see Figure 1). Obviously, the most scientific method for establishing the benefits sought would be to conduct carefully designed marketing research studies of donors, potential donors and nondonors in central Ohio (Sands and Warwick, 1981; Akaah and Becherer, 1983; Neslin, 1983). For the exercise, however, reliance was placed on knowledge of other research, readings, contact with donors and intuition. The staff quickly suggested benefits such as self-esteem, convenience, time away from job, belongingness, affirmation of health and semi-tangible items (e.g., snacks, pins, stickers, etc.). Then, more subtle benefits were considered such as psychosecurity (i.e., pride in overcoming the fear of giving blood and a secure feeling about oneself) and importance (i.e., if one takes the time and makes the effort to do something, it should be important and worthwhile—the act itself counts). A final benefit to be included was relief from guilt by fulfillment of a social obligation, based on the idea that most people know they should give blood and feel guilty about not doing so. "Absolution" is a relevant program feature to communicate that "you don't need to feel guilty now." It is also an important assurance for those who are deferred, which recognizes that at least they tried to give.

The first part of the matrix facilitates analysis of the relationship between benefits sought and program features. It focuses management consideration on issues such as benefits which may require more attention or features which provide the most and the fewest benefits sought, etc. Rows or columns with many notations highlight items of current significance. For example, the effectiveness of the program's recognition component may warrant further study. Those rows or columns with few notations may indicate items of greater potential or of possible elimination. For example, what additional features can be added by the Blood Center to meet the donor's need of "importance"? It enables participants to see more easily the relationship between the features offered by

Blood Services and the benefits sought by donors.

The second worksheet developed by the DRD staff (Part B) extends the analysis by examining who delivers these promised features/benefits of the Blood Services program (see Figure 1). Usually it is the DRD department personnel who make the promises, but others within the Blood Center are expected to deliver them. This worksheet highlights all of those persons directly involved in the exchange process. The impact of the quality and quantity of their delivery greatly affects DRD's ability to mobilize and extend the donor base. The more those who "deliver" the promises of the Blood Services program understand and acknowledge their roles in the exchange process, the more likely it is that the Blood Center will attract more donors, and more units per donor, during a specified time period.

The "delivery of benefits" part of the matrix highlights many of the essential marketing factors that must be considered in developing, or revising, the marketing mix. For example, based on the analysis illustrated in Figure 1, Part B, blood drive coordinators are a vital force in delivering the benefits of the Blood Center's program. Management may decide to audit the entire exchange process between coordinators and the Blood Center. More effective exchanges with this target group (coordinators) should enhance the level of donor satisfaction because of their better delivery of the organization's benefits. Since health education benefits can be delivered by every one of the organization's communicators, an audit here could determine which communicator groups need additional training to become more motivated to deliver the Blood Center's health education services. Focused management scrutiny of the most important marketing factors is facilitated by the "delivery of benefits" part of the matrix. This matrix provides direction for initiating quality control check points and systems within the delivery process.

By this point in the presentation, nearly everyone acknowledged his/her role in marketing the Blood Services program. They recognized the validity of a customer-consciousness approach for all Blood Services personnel and the great importance of their own role in achieving it. The marketing mystique was dispelled; it was not seen as the prerogative of only one department. Agreement was established that good marketing in a service organization directly involves all personnel.

Throughout, the presentation was built on group involvement, simple terms and familiar ingredients. It was not an abstract, academic or obtuse lecture on marketing theory, and it exemplified good marketing in that it was developed around the needs of the internal audience.

Another Setting

The benefits analysis exercise was undertaken by the planning staff at Medical Center Hospital, Chillicothe, Ohio, a 284-bed general community hospital. Empirical data available from earlier marketing surveys were helpful in determining the benefits sought which were then compared to the features offered by the hospital. Figure 2, Part A, is an example of an overall analysis of general community benefits sought and features offered. It is not a comprehensive illustration because of the wide array of services available. When focusing on specific areas of service delivery to specific target markets, the entries are selected for the relevant needs of the particular group under consideration. According to Roberta Stewart, Director of Planning at Medical Center

Hospital, hospital inpatient surgery consumers seek different benefits than do patient visitor consumers in the hospital. She believes, however, that the overall analysis of the general community is useful because the needs and wants of the total hospital environment must be attended to by the hospital staff. Figure 2, Part B, illustrates the great variety of hospital personnel involved in communicating and delivering the benefits and features of the hospital. Clearly, all staff play a part in marketing a hospital's services. Analysis of benefits via these two matrices increases the likelihood of more efficient and effective marketing of the hospital's services.

EVALUATION

This training evoked positive feedback to the presentation; but was this a perception based on the excitement of the moment? Six months after the training, a brief survey was conducted on a sample of the participants to measure their perceptions about marketing and the training they had received (see Table 1). Responses to the 15 Likert-type statements indicated the existence of a very positive feeling on the part of the participants to the marketing training (see statements #7, #12, #13 and #14) and to the usefulness of the marketing ideas they have been exposed to (see statements #2, #5 and #15). Most felt they were now using the marketing concepts (see statements #3 and #4) and understood their role in the marketing process (see statements #8 and #11). Yet, in the key marketing areas of all personnel as deliverers of the service (statement #6), the donor as consumer (statement #9) and recognition of competitors (statement #10), the high level of uncertainty points to a need for additional marketing training. Indeed, the uncertain responses on these last three statements may

FIGURE 2: Hospital benefits analysis matrix illustration

A. Benefits Sought[b]

Benefits Sought[b]	Health Education	Medical Care	Basic Needs (Food/Shelter)	Amenities	Counseling	Efficiency	Confidentiality	Lab Work	Specializing/Testing	Training Opportunities	Medication and Med. Supplies	Therapy	Safety and Security	Subtotal
Rest/Recuperation		B/F	B/F									B/F		3
Affirmation of Health Services	B/F	B/F						B/F	B/F					4
Relief from Pain		B/F									B/F			2
Relief from Guilt	B/F				B/F								B/F	3
Physical Comfort			B/F										B/F	2
Cost Efficiency					B/F									1
Convenience				B/F		B/F								2
Cure for Disease or Illness	B/F	B/F						B/F	B/F		B/F	B/F		6
Professional Advice	B/F				B/F		B/F							3
Emotional Support					B/F		B/F							2
Tangible Items			B/F									B/F		2
Efficacy		B/F	B/F						B/F		B/F			4
Fulfillment of Educational Requirements										B/F				1
Total:	4	5	4	1	4	1	2	2	3	1	3	3	2	

B. Those Delivering and/or Communicating Benefits

	Health Education	Medical Care	Basic Needs (Food/Shelter)	Amenities	Counseling	Efficiency	Confidentiality	Lab Work	Specializing/Testing	Training Opportunities	Medication and Med. Supplies	Therapy	Safety and Security	Subtotal
Physicians	D/C	D/C					D/C			D/C	D/C	D/C	D/C	7
Nurses	D/C				D/C	D/C	D/C			D/C	D/C		D/C	7
Chaplains					D/C		D/C						D/C	3
Volunteers				D/C		D/C								2
Community/Professional Relations	D/C												D/C	2
Finance/Business Office						D/C	D/C							2
EMTs		D/C				D/C					D/C		D/C	4
Housekeeping			D/C											1
Laundry			D/C											1
Food Service			D/C	D/C										2
Pharmacist	D/C										D/C			2
Administration	D/C													1
Nutritionist	D/C		D/C											2
Educational Coordinator	D/C													1
Purchasing			D/C	D/C		D/C								3
Board of Trustees	D/C	D/C	D/C	D/C	D/C	D/C	D/C	D/C	D/C	D/C	D/C	D/C	D/C	13
Total:	8	3	6	4	3	6	5	1	1	3	5	2	6	

[a] B/F = Benefits/Features; D/C = Delivering/Communicating.

[b] Marketing research should be used to determine benefits sought by target group.

confirm Kotler's (1980) "law of fast forgetting" and his warning that managers must always fight a strong tendency to forget basic marketing principles.

The participants were asked, in an open-ended question, to describe briefly at least one way they had used the marketing concepts gained from the training. All but one were able to do so, with the responses from the nurses being especially noteworthy of

TABLE 1: Marketing training presentation evaluation[a]

Statements	Strongly agree/ agree (%)	Uncertain (%)	Disagree/ strongly disagree (%)	Not applicable (No.)
1. These marketing concepts were new to me.	59	14	36	0
2. These marketing concepts are not usable in my position/role in Blood Services.	0	5	95	0
3. I am using marketing concepts to assist me in conversations with potential blood donors.	90	10	0	3
4. I incorporate marketing concepts when encouraging donors to give blood again.	84	16	0	3
5. Marketing training did not increase my understanding of the benefits sought by donors.	0	5	95	0
6. I have a better understanding of my contribution in the delivery of features/ benefits to the donors.	59	35	6	2
7. The marketing training presentation is not worth the amount of time involved.	5	0	95	0
8. I am more aware of the impact my department has on the delivery of benefits to the donor.	84	16	0	3
9. Most of my peers still do not visualize the donor as the user/consumer of our services.	48	36	16	4
10. Most of my peers now better recognize the potential competitors for blood donors.	56	33	11	4
11. I now understand my role in promoting American Red Cross differential advantages.	85	5	10	2
12. I do not feel this marketing training would be appropriate for all Blood Services staff.	14	9	77	0
13. I would like to attend programs that would further develop my understanding of marketing.	81	9	10	1
14. I have not seen evidence that my peers have benefitted from the marketing training.	25	44	31	6
15. I feel marketing concepts/practices are relevant to other Blood Services activities besides donor recruitment.	90	0	10	0

[a] n = 22 respondents.

their shift in thinking to that of customer consciousness. The response to the open-ended question on whether to recommend this marketing training to other Blood Centers was very positive, with more than three-fourths giving specific comments as to why they felt it would be good for others to undertake such training.

CONCLUSIONS

Internal marketing, especially in its emphasis on customer consciousness, asserts that to serve the needs of the market the organization must first serve the needs of its own personnel. This is especially true for service firms because for customers who are purchasing services, the personnel *are* the service. George (1977) explains the crucial role of staff in a service firm in this way:

> First, public contact personnel are a key element in an image development program. Second, they can provide vital service differentiation for the firm. Third, since visible and tangible reinforcement is missing in a service offering (as compared to a good), the customer's uncertainty can be most effectively reduced by public contact personnel. They can reassure customers that the best choice was made and stimulate them to buy again and to tell others of their satisfaction. In addition to reducing cognitive dissonance, such human and personal dimensions of the service will add materially to its perceived value (and) will encourage repeat sales. . . (p. 92).

Thus, managers of health care organizations must explicitly and continuously reinforce a marketing perspective to all personnel.

The training presentation described above is an effective way to initiate a marketing perspective within the health care organization. It can be adapted easily to any health care setting for training purposes. It is essentially timeless and can be used as an orientation program for new staff as well as for initial training when a market approach is adopted. A matrix with another delivery system could readily be made to reflect an entirely different set of benefits sought and features offered, as illustrated by comparing Figure 1, Part A, to Figure 2, Part A. Similarly, another set of deliverers/communicators could be substituted in the second matrix (compare Figure 1, Part B, to Figure 2, Part B). What will remain the same, however, is that all personnel from the various departments will be able to understand that good marketing includes everyone within the health care organization.

REFERENCES

Akaah, Ishmael P., and Richard C. Becherer (1983), "Integrating a Consumer Orientation into the Planning of HMO Programs: An Application of Conjoint Segmentation," *Journal of Health Care Marketing*, 3 (Spring), 9–18.

Berry, Leonard L. (1981), "The Employee as Customer," *Journal of Retail Banking*, 3 (March), 33–40.

Cardinal, Robert J., Ronald Sanderson, and George J. Wingenter (1977), "The Changing Private Market System," *Journal of Advertising* (Summer), 34–40.

Fisk, Raymond P., and Carol Freshley (1981), "Marketing Applications for Hospital Laboratory Services," *Journal of Health Care Marketing*, 1 (Spring), 33–39.

George, William R. (1977), "The Retailing of Services—A Challenging Future," *Journal of Retailing*, 53 (Fall), 85–98.

Gronroos, Christian (1981), "Internal Marketing—An Integral Part of Marketing Theory" in *Marketing of Services*, James H. Donnelly and William R. George, eds. Chicago: American Marketing Association, 236–38.

Hafer, John C., and Carl Joiner (1984), "Nurses as Image Emissaries: Are Role Conflicts Impinging on a Potential Asset for an Internal

Marketing Strategy?'' *Journal of Health Care Marketing*, 4 (Winter), 25–35.

Kotler, Philip (1980), *Marketing Management*. Englewood Cliffs, NJ: Prentice-Hall, Inc., 11–13.

Neslin, Scott A. (1983), ''Designing New Outpatient Health Services: Linking Service Features to Subjective Consumer Perceptions,'' *Journal of Health Care Marketing*, 3 (Summer), 8–21.

Sands, Saul, and Kenneth Warwick (1981), ''What Product Benefits to Offer to Whom—An Application of Conjoint Segmentation,'' *California Management Review*, XXVI (Fall), 69–74.

Sasser, Earl W., and Stephen P. Arbeit (1976), ''Selling Jobs in the Service Sector,'' *Business Horizons* (June), 61–65.

Yankelovich, Daniel (1981), *New Rules*. New York: Random House.

Marketing: One YMCA Attacks the Problems

JACQUELINE JANDERS

One of the earliest examples of marketing in the YMCA took place in New York City right after the Civil War. The original concept of the YMCA was a simple Association of young men united in Christ. Men used to meet regularly in religious reading rooms usually located above shops and stores.

The city was teeming with saloons and theatres and dance halls from which the Association wanted to attract the young men. One evening, as a group of YMCA members sat discussing how they could get more young men to join the Association, one of their number, businessman J. Pierpont Morgan, said, ''If you want to attract the young men of today, you'll have to bring the YMCA down out of these upper rooms.''

That is just what they did and the first YMCA building was constructed in 1869.

Ever since the YMCA came down out of the upper rooms and began providing services for which dues and fees are charged, the YMCA has been in the ''marketplace.''

At its most elementary level a market exists whenever a buyer and a seller come together for a mutually beneficial exchange of a product, a service, an idea. Usually it is an exchange involving money. Now, the YMCA has not thought in terms of buying and selling, but we do provide programs and services for which people pay dues and fees. Therefore in a sense there is a buyer and a seller and we have created a market.

As in the story above there is much more

Reprinted with permission from *Perspective Magazine*/Journal of Professional YMCA Directors in the United States. Copyright © May 1975, pp. 23–26.

to marketing than that which takes place at the point of exchange. This article is about the value and the process of marketing in today's multi-service YMCA.

If we are indeed concerned with "being about our Father's business" and enriching the lives of people, we should use every management skill available to us. The most successful YMCAs are those which have truly thought they were in the "People Business" and have focused on satisfying the needs of people. Modern marketing can facilitate this process.

MORE THAN SEMANTIC

The problem with most discussions of marketing is that what gets emphasized is *promotion and selling*, not marketing. The difference is more than semantic. Selling focuses on the needs of the seller; the YMCA's need to enroll members and sign up participants. While selling is a part of marketing, marketing moves far back from the point of sale and focuses on the needs of the buyer; the potential member, the customer.

Marketing asks the questions: Who is the customer? Where is the customer? What are the customer's needs and wants? . . . And what value-satisfying programs and services can we provide that the customer will want to buy? I do not mean to imply that selling is unimportant. It is very important and I shall have more to say about selling later. But because marketing is a more complex and sophisticated management process, it often gets ignored.

Marketing is concerned with the identification of the needs and wants of potential members and the whole series of activities associated with the creation and delivery of programs and services which satisfy these needs. It is a concept which starts with top management and must become a way of thinking in every nook and cranny of the organization. YMCA directors are very program- and operations-oriented. Sometimes we think and act as if we were in the program business instead of the people business. Marketing is a management approach which is customer-oriented. The program or product is the consequence of the marketing effort, not the starting point.

The Milwaukee YMCA initiated an in-depth Marketing Training Project in Fall 1973 for all professional management staff. President M. Brutus Baker; Dick Protzmann, Vice President for Branch Operations; Larry Smith, Director of Manpower Development; and I were the Marketing Training Project Team for planning and implementation of the program. Professor Dick Berry, Management Specialist in Marketing from the School of Business and Management of the University of Wisconsin, was our co-planner, consultant and trainer.

The Marketing Training Project had two objectives:

- A professional staff trained in the application of marketing principles and techniques to the end that these will be applied to the planning, development, packaging and promotion of YMCA programs . . . And because we are a results-oriented organization we established a measurable objective. . . .
- Six useful marketing proposals for new or improved programs and creation of new markets to help achieve our corporate operating goals.

Briefly, the design of the training project was:

- Selected readings, prepared by Berry to introduce us to the study of marketing as a modern management discipline
- A series of seminars and workshops for

additional input, exploration and training in the many aspects of the marketing function

- Establishment of task teams to help internalize and put into practice learnings about marketing

The content of the several workshops and seminars included:

- Marketing strategy and the marketing-mix concept
- Marketing planning
- Customer orientation at contact point of front desk and telephone inquiry
- The role of the public relations program in marketing
- The application of counsellor selling techniques
- Telephone contact and sales
- Corporate planning and setting Branch unit objectives

There were so many components to the Marketing Training Project that time and space here will not permit me to adequately report on all of them. Perhaps the concept of marketing and its dynamic implications for the YMCA can best be demonstrated by sharing with you the work of the marketing planning task forces and some of the results of their work.

ESTABLISHING THE MARKETING PLANNING TASK FORCES

As I have already suggested in the statement of objectives and the design of the training project the task forces had two purposes:

1. Training: to be a vehicle for practicing and internalizing marketing principles and techniques
2. Results: preparation of 6 useful marketing proposals that could be made operational in the Milwaukee YMCA

The function of the task forces was Marketing Planning. The project team selected six program areas which we believed would best lend themselves to the experience; either because they were operated Association-wide and would be familiar to most staff, or because they were recognized problem areas, or because they were considered to be key market areas. It was decided to establish a marketing task force to develop a marketing plan for each of the following:

- Health Clubs
- Tot Time Preschool Education Program
- Y-Indian Guides—Parent–Child Program
- Family Program and Membership
- Camping
- Food Service

Six professional marketing directors, laymen from business and industry, were recruited to serve as marketing consultants to the task teams. Each of these people agreed to meet with one of the task forces. Their function was to bring marketing expertise to the planning and an objective point of view to the program area. A Staff Chairman for each group was appointed to work with the various consultants and trainers, and to present the final marketing proposal.

Each of the 43 professional staff people in the Milwaukee YMCA was assigned to one of these task forces. Ideally, members of a marketing planning group should be selected for their creative ability, expertise in the program area, commitment to the task and influence in carrying out the resulting marketing program.

However, in this case because the primary purpose was training, *all staff were assigned*, across organizational lines, selected only partly for their interest, commitment or expertise in the particular program area.

After the task forces had met several times I was assigned to work with them. Obviously the success of each group depended upon the degree to which full group interaction could be generated and sustained. My job was to help them pull together as a single creative unit building on each other's ideas and working toward a common goal.

At the same time I needed to keep before the groups all of the marketing concepts and methods Berry had given us in the initial 2-day seminar.

MARKETING MIX

One of the most helpful tools provided during the first workshop was the concept of the "Marketing Mix." The marketing mix is the idea that there is a pattern of important elements or ingredients in every marketing plan. These elements are the 4-Ps . . . product, place, price and promotion.

The mixing of these factors, which management controls, with external forces bearing upon the market, results in the formula for success which becomes the marketing plan. The external force with which the 4-Ps must be considered are consumer buying behavior, life styles, competition, the law, etc., which management does not control, but about which it must be thoroughly knowledgeable.

In order for the planning groups to properly mix all of the ingredients, Berry had stressed the importance of situation analysis and focusing on objectives. Roughly, the thought process and discussion from which ideas will flow and plans will evolve looks something like this:

Focus on objectives:

- What segments of the market are we dealing with?
- What are the needs of the customer?
- How can we satisfy these needs?
- What do we really want to do?
- Program or service objectives.

Situation analysis:

- Consider broad strategies.
- Consider corporate operating goals.
- Consider the customer viewpoint.
- Analyze strengths and weaknesses.
- What are the problems and opportunities?
- Consider the product.
- Consider the organization's resources.
- Consider competition.

Mix all of the above . . . explore the resulting ideas . . . build on the best ideas . . . assess the minimum requirements to meet customer needs . . . identify features and benefits that will have the greatest customer impact . . . apply resources of time, money, staff and facilities. If workable, develop the idea and document the plan. If *not* workable, keep mixing alternative ideas.

The examples I will use to reveal the marketing planning process are taken from the experiences of the task forces. We were a-borning something new for the YMCA and there is no shame in suffering birth pains.

OVERCOMING ROAD BLOCKS

One of the problems all of the task forces initially encountered was the shift from marketing theory to practice. For example, the matter of setting objectives.

It was at first difficult for the groups to distinguish between identifying the objectives of the task team itself and the objectives of the program area they were assigned. In other words: What was indeed the task of the group and what was expected of them? And what were the objectives of the program category they were assigned? And again, what were the objectives of the marketing plan they would develop?

As you may imagine, some task force members wanted to set dollar and enrollment objectives similar to those they had already identified in the Branch budgets. These were the operators. Others who thought marketing means promotion leaped immediately to set promotion and advertising objectives. Others dealt with the ideal philosophical purposes of the YMCA and still others with the individual curriculum, program or fitness objectives.

The truth of the matter is that all of these are legitimate considerations in the marketing mix, but the group had another obstacle to overcome first. It was that of understanding and believing in their mission. A marketing planning group is essentially an invention or idea group. Our purpose was to identify new market segments, create a new program or improve an old one based on the needs of the market segment and to devise ways and means, including new promotion techniques, to deliver the program. Considerable time was spent in each group clarifying the above.

As each group began to analyze its marketing opportunities and group members were beginning to build on each other's ideas the following road blocks would also appear: "We're already doing all we can." "We can't attract any more people until we get a new building." "It's really the price that's too high." "We tried that in my former Association and it didn't work." "No YMCA program should be self-sustaining." "People don't really want what they need." "That's P.R.'s job!"

Participatory management, in the involvement of line managers in corporate planning and decision making, always sounds like a grand idea. However, the additional effort and responsibility it demands require a lot of extra hard work. And who needs that?

If the work of the task forces was ever to get off the ground and become productive we had to clarify our mission and find a positive focus. It occurred to me that if the groups could picture the total corporate planning process and realize that they had been given the opportunity to participate in strategic planning for the Association it would clarify what we were doing.

They would see that this was a serious assignment, the results of which would greatly influence the future of the Milwaukee YMCA. A brief blackboard outline helped the groups see how strategic marketing planning fits into the total planning processes of the Association.

Further, they began to see that the kind of planning now required of them could serve their own interests later in the establishment and achievement of Branch unit objectives. These insights helped the groups gain confidence in their function as planners and we were able to move on.

IDENTIFYING THE PROGRAM AND MARKET AREA OF EXPLORATION

The next step was to define and agree upon the program and market area in which the task force was to work. This may seem like a simple step in view of the assignments given. It really was not so obvious. For example, my first meeting with the family program and membership task force went something like this:

Minutes of three previous meetings were distributed which revealed that the group had done some homework. They had researched and discussed the philosophy of family program in the Milwaukee YMCA. They had compiled a list of physical and educational program offerings and membership statistics on the two family serving Branches in operation at the time. They had also identified membership enrollment objectives for these two Branches for the coming year.

I asked the group which specific market they were interested in programming for.

"Well, what do you mean? We're interested in selling memberships. We need to program for men, women, boys and girls . . . all of them, of course!"

This response demonstrated that we needed to get a better focus on the work of the task force if we were going to create any new markets or develop any new programs (the real work of the task force). We needed to narrow the perimeters of our work or time limitations and frustration would immobilize the team.

I rephrased the question, this time with a program emphasis. "What are the programs that you believe are most needed or wanted by families?" This resulted in some narrowing identification, mostly of physical programs, youth activities and health club services. Then one group member said, "Look, it's a package. Only Family Memberships are available, so when you buy a membership you get it all for the whole family— Mom, Dad and all the kids."

We were getting nearer to answering the original question so I asked, "Can we identify a YMCA family? Is it just any old combination of men, women, boys and girls?" There followed some discussion about how the young couple in the high-rise could be considered a "family," and that the teenager whose parents buy him a membership is certainly "part" of a family. Well, after several more hours and the aid of a "life cycle" chart and a close look at the characteristics of the families already enrolled, the group identified that the specific market segment we were most interested in was "young families, fathers and mothers with children between the ages of 6 and 12, living together."

At subsequent meetings we further defined the program and market by looking in depth at the needs, desires, problems and capabilities of the target families. We zeroed in on the developmental tasks of children in this age category. We discussed the predominant life style and family income and educational level of the families in the prescribed Branch service areas. We looked at the number and the concentration by neighborhoods of the target families.

We brainstormed about the real needs of families in this life cycle. Many of us personally recalled how we felt as children or parents at these ages. What were our desires, our needs, the normal problems of family life? How did or how could the Y have helped? We looked at how existing programs could help strengthen family life. In short, we conducted a total situation analysis of what we really wanted to do in relation to the needs of the families who were the target market segment we had identified.

By defining the program area in consumer terms and by focusing on the real needs of families the task force became more innovative. We began to deal more with family communications, values and relationships.

These, even more than physical fitness and leisure time activities, were seen as the real needs to be satisfied through family programming. New ways of appealing to couples and involving whole families were explored. New program ideas emerged. Women, with their changing roles, attitudes, self-image and aspirations were identified as a whole new market on which to concentrate.

Outside marketing consultants were helpful. "You have to realize that people do not need the YMCA to exist," one said. "However, as their basic needs are provided for, people begin to realize that man does not live by bread alone. The satisfactions the Y is concerned with are the intangible, though very real needs of most people. We have to first identify and then find ways of helping people recognize these needs; then we can satisfy them."

On another occasion during a heated discussion one of the outside marketing consultants said:

Look, you people act as if you're ashamed to charge a legitimate fee for your programs. If you believe in your basic service you know its value, and you want to make it available to as many folks as possible.

To keep the price of the basic service as reasonable as possible, you have to charge the full cost on the extra services that people want. It's a different market. In our company we know what our basic service is. It has to do with our purpose. Anything extra we offer we charge what we need to . . . so we can continue to provide our basic service to more and more people at a reasonable rate.

Bravo!

COMPILING AND APPLYING BACKGROUND MATERIAL

Adequate preparation of information relative to the program and market subject area is absolutely essential to successful marketing planning.

A narrative description of each program category and some statistical data on existing programs had been prepared for each of the task forces at the time of assignment in order to get them started. To enable us to do a thorough situation analysis, considerably more research and documentation of facts had to be compiled as questions came up.

Most of this data was assembled by the task forces from existing information readily available in our own or other YMCA records or from published sources such as census tracts, etc. Generally no new market studies were undertaken by the task forces. The Health Club task force conducted one small survey to test "felt-needs" of potential members.

The information needed for each of the program areas we were considering included:

• *Market size and trends:* Number of people in the market segment, the number and size of families, were they increasing, decreasing or relocating in the service area? . . . mobility, income, life style, purchasing preferences, etc.
• *Competition:* Who and what is our competition? . . . visit it, collect samples of advertising and literature, compare prices and benefits, observe sales techniques, etc.
• *Technical program information:* Program resources available within the Y or in the field. Research or development already underway. Example: Havighurst's "Developmental Tasks and Education" was used by the Camping task force; Milwaukee Area Technical College tested Tot Time teachers' curriculum; National YMCA and other research in the field of family life education was reviewed.
• *YMCA policy or legal controls:* The Tot Time task force considered State of Wisconsin standards for preschool programs. The Camping task force considered YMCA and American Camping Association standards.

Here are other examples of how the above information was secured and its usefulness to the task forces.

Market-Size and Trends. The Tot Time task force compiled statistical population data on children under five years of age for each Branch service area.

This information helped us identify that in some instances we were operating preschool programs in locations determined by where the facilities or teachers were available and primarily counting on these outside sources to provide enrollment. An examination of the statistics, by neighborhoods, revealed that the concentrations of very young families with children of this age were actually located elsewhere in the service area. These facts were certainly important in our "Place" considerations.

The statistics also revealed that the population under 5 years of age in the Greater Milwaukee area is approximately 100,000. Further, that of this number only 4,400 were enrolled in any kind of nursery program.

From the compiled information the Tot Time task force was able to identify and locate its target market segment and conclude that the growth potential for Tot Time programs was extensive for the next two to five years, based on the size and trend of the market.

On Competition. The Health Club task force members individually visited and filed reports on seven private and commercial competitive health clubs in the Greater Milwaukee area, and three successful YMCA health clubs in other cities. The most valuable learnings from these visits were:

- The importance of quality: clean, comfortable, attractive, even posh facilities commensurate with the tastes of the market segment most likely to pay for these services.
- Complete customer-orientation . . . use of counsellor selling. In every instance the potential customer was asked, "What do you want to accomplish?" Then the sales counsellor concentrated on showing how the health club membership could help the member achieve his personal goals.

The strength in the commercial clubs was the emphasis on sales.

Research indicated that their weakness is that there is only the most superficial attention to health and fitness programs and almost no expertise in this area. Whereas the YMCA has the expertise and the programs, our greatest weakness was in not having any kind of focus on sales.

An example of this fact came out in one of our counsellor selling workshops. During a role-playing exercise the professional YMCA director, upon meeting the prospect, conducted a tour of the facilities. The overwhelming tendency was to talk only about the facilities. "This is our beautiful pool." "Here's our exercise room." "We have massage available, too."

Obviously most of these facilities when they are seen speak for themselves as to what they are. We must translate our knowledge of the facilities into customer needs. An illustration:

> With an electric drill in one hand and a block of wood with a hole in it in the other hand our trainer said, "Nobody has a need for this electric drill." Holding up the block of wood with the hole in it, he said, "What there is a tremendous need for is holes! We market the drill because it satisfies the customer's need for holes."

We market gyms and pools and exercise rooms to satisfy the customer's need for health, fitness, fun, fellowship, weight control, relaxation, etc.

Far more important in a tour of facilities is the communication with the prospect about who he/she is . . . how they happened to come to the Y . . . what it is they would like to accomplish . . . where they live . . . the family's interests . . . what kind of work they do.

All of these give us clues as to how a health club or Y membership can help satisfy the prospect's needs . . . but only if we do more listening than talking. When we talk about our program and facilities it must be in terms of benefits to the prospect.

If we have designed our program to meet customer needs instead of our own ego needs for a marvelous and highly technical program, and if we relate to the potential member in terms of his needs, it will become clear what he wants to hear about and what benefits and features to talk about.

IMPLEMENTING THE MARKETING PLANS

One of my favorite pragmatic friends holds a theory that "idea people" are great but ideas are a dime a dozen. "It's the implementors of the world who count," he says. "They get the job done." The Marketing Task Force approach is a way of getting the new ideas originated by the people who will be responsible for implementing them. Obviously, follow-through is essential.

RESULTS

There is no doubt that the first objective for the formation of the task forces was achieved—that of training. The learnings which took place during the Marketing Training Project are evidenced in attitudinal changes that have influenced management decisions up and down the organization. The conscious application of marketing principles has affected manpower planning, training, program development and allocation of resources.

Customer-orientation and a focus on satisfying the needs of people has influenced volunteer involvement and support as well as enrollments. The marketing approach has subtly influenced day to day judgments. The staff have become better planners.

There is less resistance to charging appropriate fees. Better pricing and improved promotion efforts have resulted in increased earned income in 1974. Tot time enrollments increased from 585 students in the fall of '73 to 704 today. Health club membership has increased from 689 to 1228. The number of families enrolled in family serving Branches has increased from 2,199 to 2,960.

There is a growing awareness of what happens in the non-profit market. For instance: You have designed a program and you have budgeted it with all the overhead to break even with an enrollment of 20 people.

If, because you have overestimated the need, or inadequately promoted it, only ten participants are enrolled you not only have a no profit situation, you have a deficit . . . to which you must apply donor subsidy. This is poor management, not philanthropy.

Now on the other hand if we deliberately plan to subsidize a program, it is a different matter. Suppose we provide a program to meet a specific need and it is purposely planned, with a maximum enrollment, to be a deficit operation.

To increase the number of these programs is of course to increase the overall deficit . . . a point not often thought about outside of non-profit management. If the reasons for operating this program at a deficit are sound, then this is where contributed dollars belong.

The YMCA is a non-profit organization. It should be non-profit by intent and good management, not by accident and poor management!

The second objective for the formation of the task forces was substantially achieved with the completion and acceptance of four of the six marketing proposals. Each of the four complete proposals received a "go" decision from top management.

Within the framework of the organizational structure and the corporate planning system of the Milwaukee YMCA, the marketing plans are largely being implemented in the branches. This means that branch staff and boards of managers set branch unit objectives in the program area and develop action plans from the recommendations of the marketing proposals. Action plans include designation of staff responsibility, time schedules and budget requirements.

Several of the marketing proposals called for increased corporate staff and general office support in the form of more centralized direction or coordination of the program. Additional resources have been mustered to help implement the marketing plans. Examples:

- Maintenance Reserve funds have been allocated to renovate the Central Branch Health Club entrance as recommended.
- A highly skilled professional Health Club director has been employed for this unit. Fifty percent of his responsibilities include conducting a training school for health club personnel for all branches with emphasis on massage and sales.
- The Public Relations staff of the General Offices has been increased with the employment of a Director of Communications to aid in the development of interpretive materials and promotion of programs.
- Increased coordination of the Tot Time program and the addition of YMCA Movement Education to the program were recommended by the Tot Time Task Force. One Branch Executive has taken the responsibility to get all Tot Time teachers, from across the Association, together on a regular basis for review of objectives, study, discussion and coordination of the recommended curriculum. Training in YMCA Movement Education has been added to the program under the direction of the Assistant Vice President for Physical Education. Standards for teacher credentials and salary ranges have been established.
- Recruitment of a professional staff person to coordinate Y-Indian Guide programs for 3 or 4 Branches in a geographic district is underway. The revving up of an Association-wide Y-Indian Guide lay organization is being considered. The possibility of the Milwaukee Association hosting the 1979 National Longhouse Convention, 20 years after its last convention in Milwaukee in 1959, is under consideration.
- A market study and analysis of population data for the Greater Milwaukee area, segmented by Branch service areas and neighborhoods was conducted. This information reinforced the decision to merge two Branches and helped gain acceptance of the merger. This information is also available to staff for planning in the Branches.

Because marketing is a management approach that grew out of the profit motivation of a free enterprise system many people have not seen what it has to do with the YMCA, a non-profit organization. I believe that marketing is a way of thinking and a management discipline that is as applicable to the YMCA as other management tools adopted from business and industry . . . from business office practices to Management by Objectives.

In business, the motivation for marketing planning is to satisfy customers and to make a profit. In the Milwaukee YMCA the motivation is to attract people to the Association to have an influence for good upon their lives . . . and to break even.

I believe that a marketing approach can help us achieve YMCA purposes. It is a new way of thinking about how to manage the People Business.

Predictors of Attendance at the Performing Arts

ALAN R. ANDREASEN • RUSSELL W. BELK

The present study differs from earlier efforts by its consideration of (1) future attendance intentions of potential arts-goers, (2) life-style, attitudinal, and experiential predictor variables, and (3) multiple market segments, and by its use of multivariate methods. With such differences, socioeconomic variables that were best predictors of arts attendance in prior work become nonsignificant. Implications for arts management are discussed.

PAST FINDINGS

A large and growing number of arts audience studies were conducted in the United States within the last ten years, many of which are unpublished. In general, these studies have concluded the obvious: attendance at the performing arts is strongly positively associated with income, educational and occupational attainment, and white racial status. A recent review of 270 studies of audiences for museums and performing arts also found, not surprisingly, that heavy attenders at one live performing art (except theater) tended to be heavy attenders at other live performing arts (DiMaggio, Useem, and Brown, 1978). In addition to confirming findings that were already well-known to arts managers, these past studies exhibited other deficiencies that the study reported here sought to remedy.

1. Much of the past research on arts audiences has tended either to profile current audiences or to contrast attenders and nonattenders. It has not sought meaningful subsegments within either group. The study reported here divides the population into subsegments based on their leisure-time use patterns, and then observes their likelihood of future attendance. In addition to developing these leisure life-style groupings, this study also develops a richer array of data on respondents' general life-style tendencies. To meaningfully examine the role of arts attendance in life-style patterns, the study considers a broader group of people than present arts attenders, but excludes those most likely to be "hardcore nonattenders" of the performing arts.

2. As DiMaggio, Useem, and Brown (1978) have noted: "Another issue about which little is known and much curiosity exists is the process of socialization into arts attendance: How early does it begin, how important is the family, and how impor-

Reprinted with permission from *The Journal of Consumer Research* (September 1980), Vol. 7, pp. 112–20.

tant is the school?'' (p. 73). The present study adds to the standard set of socioeconomic variables two new sets of questions asking about (a) the extent to which respondents were interested in classical music or live theater when they were growing up, and (b) the extent to which their parents were also interested in the same performing arts. In addition to these new questions, the study also asked whether receptivity to the performing arts is higher or lower as one moves through the family life cycle.

3. Past studies have had relatively little success in linking attendance or nonattendance to individual perceptions of the performing arts. Thus, the present study has included a substantial battery of questions about consumer attitudes, i.e., their expectations when attending theater and symphony, and the importance of those expectations to them.

4. Finally, past research has failed to employ sophisticated analytic techniques to look at the interactions among variables. Instead, the tendency has been to observe (and make recommendations from) relationships between arts attendance and standard socioeconomic variables, examined one at a time (DiMaggio, Useem, and Brown, 1978). Although such studies could benefit from greater use of the relatively simple technique of cross-tabulation analysis, the present study suggests that a much higher payoff is possible from the use of more sophisticated techniques, namely, factor analysis and multiple regression.

Thus, in summary, the present study attempts to introduce more advanced analytic techniques as well as several new audience measures in an attempt to learn whether these innovations will yield better predictions of future attendance at theater and symphony performances than have been possible in the past. It is, however, recognized that the associational approach described here is not without its faults. A complementary approach based on presenting respondents with possible new offerings is described elsewhere [Andreasen and Belk].

METHODOLOGY

The study was carried out in four southern cities—Atlanta, Georgia; Baton Rouge, Louisiana; Columbia, South Carolina; and Memphis, Tennessee. The four cities were chosen from among a list of several dozen southern cities with both a symphony and regular theater presentations. Southern cities were chosen by the study sponsor because of lower attendance in this region (National Center for the Arts, Inc., 1975).

Data were gathered by means of telephone interviews with respondents 14 years of age or older, systematically selected from households with telephones. At the outset, it was decided that a major focus would be on marginal attenders—those who do not now go frequently to the theater or symphony, but who might be enticed to do so. For this reason, those judged to have virtually zero probability of attending the theater or symphony were screened out. At the same time, heavy attenders were intentionally undersampled because our main concern was not with audiences already heavily involved in the arts. Therefore, we interviewed only one-half of those who had attended three or more theater performances or three or more symphony performances in the previous year.

Screening questions defined potential users as:

1. Those who did one of the following in the last 12 months:

- Went to a live popular or rock concert
- Listened at least ten times to classical music on radio, television, record, or tapes
- Visited an art gallery or museum
- Went to a live classical music performance other than a symphony concert
- Saw a ballet either live or on television
- Saw one or two plays
- Went to a symphony orchestra concert once or twice.

2. And/or those who met one of the following qualifications:

- Play a musical instrument
- Have worked for or in a theater, music, or dance production
- Attended three or more live plays sometime in their lives, but not in the past year
- Attended three or more symphony orchestra concerts sometime in their lives, but not in the past year.

A total of 3,956 residential telephone numbers were selected for screening, using telephone directories and supplementary random digit dialing. Of these, 44 percent were not screened because the numbers were no longer in service or the residents were not at home after five callbacks, or refused to participate. Of those screened, 15 percent were heavy attenders; by sample design, one-half of them were dropped from the main sample.[1] Only 14 percent of those reached were dropped because their probability of attending was deemed to be zero, according to the criteria discussed above. After screening, a total of 1,733 households were designated for

complete interviews. A systematic selection table was used to determine the household member to be interviewed. Of the remaining respondents, an additional 14 percent were unavailable or refused to participate in the main interview, yielding a final sample of 1,491.

Comparisons of respondent characteristics with census data suggest that the sample population is younger, better educated, has higher incomes, and is substantially more often female than the general population of the four areas. These differences are consistent with those found in other studies using telephone interviewing and our procedure for screening out those with zero probability of attending arts events.

PREDICTOR VARIABLES

Respondents in the study were asked extensive questions about their attitudes and behavior toward theater and symphony, aspects of their leisure and general life-styles, and their socioeconomic characteristics. The questions were developed from other research studies, from introspection, and from several focus-group interviews with heavy and light arts attenders.

Life-style measures offer profiles of consumer purchases that are greater in depth and clarity than those provided by simpler demographic information about the consumer (Wells, 1975). In addition, there is some evidence that "cultural activities" are important to the leisure component of certain life-styles (Hawes, Talarzyk, and Blackwell, 1975; Holbrook and Lehmann, 1980). In the present study, consumer life-style was measured at two different levels. The first level was the individual's use of leisure time, the second level was the individual's more general activities, interests, and opinions re-

[1] Of the heavy attenders, 77 percent were heavy attenders of theater only, five percent were heavy attenders of symphony only, and 15 percent were heavy attenders of both.

flecting the general life-styles in which the leisure activities are imbedded.

Leisure Life-Style Characteristics

The first type of life-style analyzed was based on responses to a set of 50 questions about leisure-time activities, interests, and opinions. These data were then used to group respondents into leisure-specific life-style categories. Unlike the analysis of the general life-style characteristics to be discussed below, a *Q* factor analysis was performed on the answers to the 50 leisure life-style questions to place respondents into unique groups, each with similar leisure-time use patterns (Stephenson, 1953). The objective of this analysis was to find types of life-styles, i.e., types of people rather than types of life-style characteristics or traits.

A *Q* factor analysis program (Johnson, 1970) was employed for this task. Several groupings were tested for stability between two randomly chosen halves of the respondents. A solution was selected that partitioned the population into six unique clusters. Group means for major variables are reported elsewhere [Andreasen and Belk]. The results suggest the following characterization of the six groups:

- *The Passive Homebody* (n = 295). This group prefers family- and home-oriented activities. They are heavy watchers of television, have essentially negative attitudes toward cultural organizations and activities, and tend to avoid nearly any activity outside the home, such as bowling, eating out, or seeing a movie. These people recognize that their days are routine and filled with unused leisure time.
- *The Active Sports Enthusiast* (n = 285). This group is the antithesis of the previous group. They take part in active sports, such as tennis and bowling, and engage in

other outgoing activities, such as movies, parties, and spectator sports. They strongly disagree that they are homebodies or like to spend a quiet evening at home. On the other hand, they are like the homebodies, but more extreme, in their negative attitudes toward theater, symphony, and other cultural activities.

- *The Inner-Directed Self-Sufficient* (n = 216). Members of this group are best characterized by their participation in a number of industrious home-oriented activities, such as gardening, reading, and craft projects. They are family-oriented and prone to undertake outdoor activities, such as hiking and picnics. They are inactive and uninformed when it comes to cultural activities, although they are not negative toward these activities as are the Passive Homebody and Active Sports Enthusiast groups. They are not overburdened with leisure time as is the Passive Homebody. Instead, it appears that their leisure interests keep them busy, either alone or with their family.
- *The Culture Patron* (n = 295). This group would be expected to be the best market for theater and symphony, because they are involved with these activities. This is a reflection of their favorable attitude toward the arts. They lack the orientation toward home and family of the Passive Homebody and the Inner-Directed Self-Sufficient and the sports orientation of the Active Sports Enthusiast. They rely very little on television for entertainment or relaxation.
- *The Active Homebody* (n = 190). Members of this group resemble the Passive Homebody group in their home- and family-orientation, but replace that group's non-active TV-watching with such activities as golf, working on the car, and gardening. They have a generally negative attitude toward the arts, and do little reading, par-

tying, or radio-listening. In other words, they are not very socially active or media-oriented, but fill their time with what might be called productive "tinkering" activities.

• *The Socially Active* (n = 210). This last group is also active, but in a more social vein. They give and attend parties, eat out often, and participate in clubs and other meetings. They are aware of theater and symphony offerings, and have friends who are interested in these activities. Nevertheless, their own patronage is infrequent. They are busy and cannot abide leisurely pursuits such as golf, reading, or spending a quiet evening at home.

In the present context, then, the Culture Patron and Socially Active groups have leisure life-styles conducive to attending the performing arts. On the other hand, the Passive Homebody, Active Homebody, and Active Sports Enthusiast groups are negatively predisposed toward attendance. Finally, the Inner-Directed Self-Sufficient group is generally uninformed, and possibly neutral, about the arts.

General Life-Style Characteristics

The *R* type factor analysis of general life-style items sought meaningful composites of 43 activity, interest, and opinion questions through principal axes factor analyses with iterative estimation of communalities and varimax rotations. On the basis of eigenvalue plots and interpretations of various solutions using 2 through 15 factors, it was decided to retain 6 factors that together account for 33 percent of the variance in the original questions. Factor loadings and interpretations for these 6 rotated factors are reported elsewhere [Andreasen and Belk]. To examine the stability of these factors all solutions using 5 through 8 factors were derived sepa-

rately for randomly selected halves of the data, and then examined for comparability. Five- and six-factor solutions were the most stable, and allowed derivation of nearly identical factors in both halves of the data. These two solutions were also tested separately with the data from each of the four cities in which samples were obtained. Again both solutions proved to be stable. The six-factor solution was selected on the basis of its superior interpretability.

The final step in the *R* factor analysis was to develop a set of factor scores for each individual. These factor scores, developed by least-squares regression estimates, served as the representation of the amount of each general life-style dimension possessed by each individual. The six dimensions may be characterized as follows:

• *Traditionalism.* This characteristic is associated with church-going, old-fashioned tastes, a feeling that things are moving too fast, and a wish for the good old days. It is also related to preferences for a traditional child- and family-centered home where the man is in charge and the woman is home-oriented. Finally, it includes a preference for security and an unwillingness to take chances.

• *Hedonism/Optimism.* This characteristic involves wanting to look attractive and perhaps a little different, wanting to travel around the world or live for a time abroad, and living to eat. It is associated with the positive view that one's greatest achievements lie ahead.

• *Defeatism.* This characteristic is marked by a depressed outlook due to a belief that things have not turned out so well. One's present life is thought undesirable; if given the chance, one would do things differently. It is also associated with wishing for the good old days, thinking things are changing too fast, spending for today, and dreading the future.

- *Self-Confidence/Opinion Leadership.* Two characteristics seem to best describe this dimension—a feeling of self-confidence and liking to be considered a leader.
- *Urbanism.* This factor involves a preference for big cities and support for progressive issues, such as Women's Liberation.
- *Outdoorsiness.* This dimension involves a predilection for outdoor activities, such as picnics and hiking.

ATTITUDES TOWARD THEATER AND SYMPHONY

The life-style approach to explaining arts behavior examines how various arts behaviors fit into more general life patterns. Attitude measurements focus, instead, on predicting behavior by understanding the nature and value of the various outcomes that an individual expects from engaging in a behavior, e.g., attending the theater or symphony. Behaviors that yield positive outcomes on important dimensions will be adopted; those that do not yield positive outcomes or that yield positive outcomes only on unimportant dimensions will not be adopted (Ryan and Bonfield, 1975).

In the present investigation, subsamples of consumers were asked about their attitudes toward attending the two performing arts under study. Because of the length of the overall questionnaire, attitudes about theater attendance were asked of one-third of the sample only, and attitudes about symphony attendance were asked of another third. Focus groups and pretests helped to define salient attributes of arts attendance. Each participating respondent was asked (a) how likely it would be (on a 4-point scale) that they would obtain each of 17 different outcomes (e.g., get exactly the seats you wanted, find friends there, or understand what was going on) and (b) how important it was (on a 4-point scale) to achieve these outcomes. In addition, as Fishbein recommends in his extended attitude model (Fishbein and Ajzen, 1975), respondents were asked about their perceptions of what significant others expected of the respondent's arts-going behavior. The resulting model was therefore of the following form:

$$BI_{jk} = \sum_{i=1}^{n} I_{ij}B_{ijk} + NB_{jk},$$

where:

BI = likelihood of respondent k attending performing art j,

I_{ik} = the importance weight given to consequence i by respondent k,

B_{ijk} = the respondent k's belief about the extent to which attending performing art j will result in consequence i, and

NB_{jk} = normative belief; the extent to which respondent k perceives that significant others believe he or she should attend performing art j.

Other Questions

In addition to these life-style and attitude items, respondents were asked about childhood socialization into the arts. Specifically, they were asked:

1. How interested were you in live theater (classical music) when you were growing up?
2. How interested were *your parents* in live theater (classical music) when you were growing up?

Further, any background in theater, music, or dance was ascertained as well as any ability to play a musical instrument.

RESULTS

The key questions that stimulated the present analysis were:

1. Which individual variables best predict likely future attendance at symphony and theater? We also wished to assess whether our findings paralleled those reported by others.
2. Which *set* of variables best predicts future attendance at symphony and theater? This analysis considers all the variables together, taking account of interdependencies among these predictors.
3. What contribution does the addition of life-style, attitude, and socialization variables make to predictive ability compared to the traditional age, income, and education measures?

Simple Correlations

As the interest of the study was in predicting future attendance at theater and symphony, the dependent variable in the analysis was the individual's responses to the question: How likely (on a 4-point scale) are you to attend theater/symphony "in the next year or two?" Although responses to this question were significantly related to prior attendance at such events (Table 1), these relationships were far from perfect. However, in view of the emphasis on marginal attenders in the sample (those who attended two or fewer performances in the past year), the likely attendance variables became the most relevant focus for the study.

Univariate correlations of 56 independent variables with the likelihood of attending theater and symphony are reported in Table 1. Note that several key variables, such as family life cycle and income, are treated as sets of dummy variables to detect possible curvi-linearities. In these cases, point biserial correlation coefficients are reported.

Correlation coefficients greater than ± 0.045 can be considered statistically significant at the 0.05 level, given the sample size. Here, one observes findings agreeing with earlier studies:

1. Sex is not significantly related to attendance likelihood.
2. Education of respondent is positively correlated with attendance likelihood (as is education of each parent).

Elaborating on earlier findings, the present sample indicates that:

3. Age is negatively correlated with attendance. The family life-cycle measures suggest that this may be because of high attendance among (a) single adults and (b) young adults with no children, and low attendance among older adults with no children ("empty-nest" stage).
4. Only membership in the highest income category (over $25,000) is positively related to attendance.
5. Race is not significantly related to likely attendance. This marks the only significant exception to prior research, and may suggest that the screening procedures eliminated more potential respondents who were black than those who were white.

In addition to these variables, attendance was also found to be positively related to years living in the area, living in Atlanta, and number of cars owned (symphony only), and negatively related to number of children over 14 years (the life-cycle factor again), being a homemaker, and living in Columbia, South Carolina.

However, what is striking in Table 1 is not that we have confirmed or elaborated the traditional predictor variables, but that variables unique to this study generally have much higher correlation coefficients. All of the variables with simple correlations equal

TABLE 1: Simple correlations of selected respondent characteristics and likelihood of attending symphony and theater

Variable	Correlation with likelihood of attending		Variable	Correlation with likelihood of attending	
	Symphony	Theater		Symphony	Theater
Interest in classical music when growing up	.35	.23	Years in area	−.09	−.12
			Defeatism[b]	.08	.11
Culture Patron[a]	.34	.32	Lives in Atlanta	.08	.08
Attendance at symphony in last 12 months	.34	.20	Inner-Directed, Self-Sufficient[b]	−.08	−.04
Attitude toward symphony	.33	.19	Age of respondent	−.07	−.12
Attitude toward theater	.29	.38	Empty-nest life-cycle stage	−.07	−.07
Parents' interest in classical music	.28	.19	Young-married with no children life-cycle stage	.06	.09
Attendance at theater in last 12 months	.25	.32	Homemaker	−.06	−.06
Interest in theater when growing up	.24	.28	Number of children over 14	−.06	−.07
Parents' interest in live theater	.23	.20	Young-children life-cycle stage	−.05	−.03
Hedonism/Optimism[b]	.20	.20	Income over $25,000	.05	.08
Urbanism	.19	.21	Employed full-time	.04	.06
Number of cars owned	.18	.02	Employed part-time	.04	.08
Listened to 10+ classic records last year	.17	.14	Retired	−.04	−.11
			Lives in Memphis	.04	.06
Active Sports Enthusiast[a]	−.16	−.13	Income $7,000–$9,999	.03	.01
Education of respondent	.16	.19	Income $10,000–$11,999	−.03	−.05
Education of father	.14	.11	Income $15,000–$19,999	.03	.05
Plays musical instrument	.14	.12	Income $20,000–$25,000	.03	.02
Ever worked for theater/music/dance production	.14	.18	Not employed	−.03	−.03
Lives in Columbia	−.13	−.15	Amount of leisure time available	−.02	.02
Ever attended three plays (but none last year)	−.13	−.19	Older-children life-cycle stage	−.02	.00
Traditionalism[b]	−.12	−.15	Income under $7,000	−.02	−.05
Education of mother	.12	.12	White	−.02	.01
Passive Homebody[a]	−.12	−.15	Outdoorsiness[b]	.02	.05
Self-Confidence/Opinion Leadership[b]	−.11	−.20	Female	−.01	−.02
			Widowed life-cycle stage	−.01	−.06
Single adult life-cycle stage	.11	.13	Spouse employed	.00	.07
Socially Active[a]	.10	.08	Teenage life-cycle stage	.00	−.04
Active Homebody[a]	−.09	−.09	Income $12,000–$14,999	.00	.03
			Temporarily unemployed	.00	.01

[a] Leisure life-style group.

[b] General life-style dimension.

to or above 0.20 for either theater or symphony were measures of (a) leisure life-style group membership, (b) general life-style dimensions, (c) past attendance, (d) attitudes, or (e) childhood socialization influences; all newly introduced to arts studies in this project.

Multiple Regression

A problem with total prediction from these correlations is that many of the variables are related. For example, as income increases so does the number of cars in the family ($r = 0.46$) and the likelihood that the spouse is employed ($r = 0.36$). The importance of several variables must then be assessed in explaining the likelihood of attendance while taking account of their interrelationships. The technique chosen was stepwise regression using "step-up" procedures in which predictors were selected one at a time, starting with the single best predictor and adding that one variable at each "step" that increases predictive accuracy the most. This continued until the best remaining predictor that could be added produced no significant improvement in overall predictive accuracy.

Theater. Of the 58 variables examined in the stepwise regression, 6 were found to add to the prediction of theater attendance at the 0.05 level of significance. The 6 predictors were jointly able to account for 28 percent of the variability in the reported likelihoods of theater attendance using an adjusted R^2 measure. Although this R^2 leaves most of the variability in these likelihoods "unexplained" (and potentially related to factors not examined in the study), it is double the "predictive" ability of the best single variable.

Table 2 shows by quite a substantial margin that the best predictor of the likelihood of future attendance is attitude toward going to the theater. Not surprisingly, the more one thinks the outcomes of attendance will be favorable, the more these outcomes are im-

TABLE 2: Standardized beta weights for variables predicting likelihood of attending symphony and theater[a]

Variable	Standardized beta weight	
	Symphony	Theater
Attitude toward attending theater	NS	.31
Attitude toward attending symphony	.21	NS
Culture Patron[b]	.25	.15
Socially Active[b]	.12	NS
Interest in live theater when growing up	NS	.15
Interest in classical music when growing up	.20	NS
Theater attendance during past year	NS	.14
Symphony attendance during past year	.20	NS
Traditionalism[c]	NS	−.13
Self-Confidence/Opinion Leadership[c]	NS	−.12
Number of cases	(232)	(222)
Adjusted R^2	.289	.279

[a] Significant at the 0.05 level.
[b] Leisure life-style group.
[c] General life-style dimension.
Note: NS = not significant.

portant, and the more significant others are seen as favoring attendance, the more likely one will be to plan future attendance.

Three variables of approximately equal importance are the next best predictors. All three are measures of positive past experiences with the arts. One variable is the respondent's interest in live theater when growing up. Being favorably socialized to the theater as a child seems to have a strong and lasting effect on future attendance independent of whether one presently has favorable prospects for attendance. Also in this predictor group is theater attendance during the past year; past behavior is a good predictor of likely future behavior. A third variable in this set is membership in the Culture Patron leisure life-style group. Here we see that past attendance, not only at the theater, but at several other of the arts, as well as having other interests and opinions reflecting an arts-centered leisure life-style, make significant contributions to likelihood of theater attendance. This finding also lends support to our contention that performing arts attendance can profitably be seen from its perspective within particular life-styles. It also supports the contention of DiMaggio, Useem, and Brown that "aficionados of one art form also attend others" (1978, p. 73).

Following the three "experiences" variables, at a slightly reduced level of importance, are two general life-style dimensions, Traditionalism and Self-Confidence/Opinion Leadership. Both dimensions are negatively related to future attendance.

Symphony. Five variables explain about 29 percent of the variance in likely attendance at symphony concerts (Table 2). Most striking is the fact that, although this is an entirely different sample of respondents, the first four variables—those with the most weight in this equation—are the variables that are the most important in the theater analysis. Again, attitudes are significant. Also, the three experience dimensions—past attendance, interest in the art form when growing up, and membership in the Culture Patron life-style group—are included in this set of most important predictors.

The single new variable in this equation is membership in the Socially Active leisure life-style group. This group also was predisposed toward the arts, which may lend credence to the suspicion that symphony attendance for some patrons serves social needs beyond any cultural needs it may fulfill.

Nonuseful Potential Predictors. The fact that a particular set of variables entered the

equations in the preceding two regression analyses does not mean that other variables do not have substantial simple correlations with likely attendance. Table 1 attests to this. What the equations do is capture the best linear combinations of predictors. In this light, it is informative to consider which variables did *not* enter the equations.

First, all the socioeconomic variables used in other studies—education, sex, income, occupation, and so forth—are not significant predictors of likely attendance when the attitude and general and specific life-style factors that we have included here are entered into the analysis. This finding suggests that socioeconomic variables are significant only when the richer set of variables added here are not included.

The second factor that does not show up is variation across cities. Columbia was generally less responsive to the performing arts at the time of our study; however, even this apparent difference does not produce a significant effect on likely attendance when other variables are considered. This finding gives us some confidence that the results reported here are generalizable across cities of different sizes and different cultural opportunities—at least in the South.

IMPLICATIONS

If we can overlook the limitations of drawing directional causal inferences from correlational data, and the likely imperfection of intentions data as a surrogate for behavioral data, this study suggests a segmentation strategy that has rather clear implications for building arts audiences. It suggests that one should take the factors now leading to likely attendance and use them to identify target audiences. There may also be some opportunity to motivate attendance in present nonattenders. In the present analysis, three factors show through in both analyses.

Attitudes

Expectation of positive outcome clearly affects whether one will attend theater or symphony. Although static and cross-sectional, the data suggest that future attendance may be increased and arts audiences broadened by one of three approaches.

Improving Expectations. Nonattenders are significantly less positive than attenders on twelve expected outcomes of going to the theater; there are nine such dimensions for symphony. Further, seven dimensions show high average importance scores for nonattenders for both theater and symphony. At the intersection of these two groups, where expectations are significantly low although the importance weight for nonattenders is high, four dimensions for theater and five for symphony merit attention. Improved attendance for both theater and symphony, thus, may result if nonattenders become more positive in their perceptions of the following:

The likelihood that they would like the particular program
The likelihood that they would understand what is going on
The likelihood that those with whom they attended would have a good time
The likelihood that the evening would prove stimulating.

In addition, theater attendance might be enhanced if nonattenders felt that the performers were better, and symphony attendance might be increased if nonattenders would come to believe that they were not going to waste their time.

Increasing Importance. Increasing importance weights is generally a much more difficult task than changing perceptions, and often takes many years. The analysis here suggests that the problem in the arts is even more difficult, because in only two cases nonattenders reported lower importance than attenders, as well as high expectations. Both

of these cases are for theater: one is understanding what was going on; the other is feeling that those with whom they were attending were having a good time. The fact that these are both dimensions where expectations are also significantly lower for nonattenders suggests that these dimensions may be susceptible to short-range as well as long-range promotional strategies.

Increasing the Impact of Significant Others. Attenders are substantially more likely than nonattenders to agree that significant others expect them to attend theater and symphony. This factor may be used to induce more attendance through promotions aimed at stimulating personal influence, possibly by encouraging present attenders to bring nonattenders to performances.

Leisure Life-Style Groups

Most arts marketers feel that Culture Patrons are excellent prospects for attendance at arts events. However, several studies suggest that theater audiences are isolated from other cultural event audiences, and that the "core" cultural audience is composed of heavy attenders, with marginal attenders failing to show such cross-patronage (Baumol and Bowen, 1964; Ford Foundation, 1974; National Research Center of the Arts, 1975). This study contradicts both conclusions. Even though the sample was largely composed of marginal attenders, membership in the Cultural Patrons life-style group was the best predictor for symphony and the second best predictor for theater attendance intentions. The use of mailing lists, programs, and posters for one performing art to encourage attendance at another should be commonplace in the arts. However, reluctance to share mailing lists seems surprisingly high among administrators in this field.

Even more intriguing is the indication that likely attendance at symphony concerts is high among the Socially Active group. This finding would suggest that promotions emphasizing the social dimensions of symphony attendance may bear considerable fruit among this group. Analysis of correlates with membership in the Socially Active group suggests that if symphony marketers wish to promote to Socially Active respondents, they should aim their messages toward older, retired people who are active in giving and going to dinners and parties, possibly portraying a visit to the symphony with other mature, socially active people as a natural complement to their active, social life-style. The fact that this group has more leisure time and fewer family responsibilities leads to the speculation that they may be good workers as well as attenders for the symphony, if working on a fund drive or a related activity can be seen as part of an active social life-style.

Interest in the Arts as a Child

It is still true, as Ryans and Weinberg (1978) point out, that we know little about how people learn to attend arts events over time, but it seems clear from this study that early exposure is a major determinant of arts attendance. It appears reasonable to suggest, therefore, that if they have not already done so, both theater and symphony organizations should develop active youth programs, young people's concerts or plays, in-school programs, youth discounts, and the like. Bradley Morison, a marketing consultant to many arts organizations, recently stated his belief that the development of an active children's theater program at the Guthrie Theater in Minneapolis was largely responsible for a drop of five years in the average age of attenders at the Guthrie between 1963 and 1973.[2] This infusion of youthful attendees is, Morison argues, a source of continuing vitality to such established organizations. Teachers of music and theater to young people (in as well as out of school) should be viewed as key gatekeepers, and courted and aided accordingly.

It should be commonplace to develop mailing lists of participants in school or youth programs, if this early exposure is to be turned into active adult patronage of symphony and theater. It may also be useful to consider longer-term series discount programs (perhaps billed as "learners' discounts") to encourage young people to continue their patronage through adulthood.

CONCLUSION

The present data strongly suggest that life-style, attitudes, and developmental experiences are both more conceptually useful variables with which to understand consumer behavior regarding the performing arts, and more empirically predictive than socioeconomic variables. This suggests that prior studies and conclusions may be short-sighted, and that to increase attendance, at least for theater and symphony in the South, concentration on children and limited life-style segments of the adult population may be most fruitful. Criteria for measuring the success of such efforts should focus on attitudes and attendance by these same segments. The specific implications discussed illustrate some of the ways in which these strategies might be pursued.

[Received October 1979. Revised April 1980.]

REFERENCES

Andreasen, Alan R., and Russell W. Belk, *Consumer Response to Arts Offerings: A Study of Theater and Symphony in Four Southern Cities*. Washington, D.C.: National Endowment for the Arts.

Baumol, William J., and William G. Bowen (1966), *Performing Arts—The Economic Dilemma*. Cambridge: MIT Press.

---

[2] Comments at a Conference on Planning for the Arts, University of Illinois, January 16, 1978.

DiMaggio, Paul, Michael Useem, and Paul Brown (1978), *Audience Studies of the Performing Arts and Museums: A Critical Review*. Washington, D.C.: National Endowment for the Arts.

Fishbein, Martin, and Icek Ajzen (1975), *Belief, Attitude Intentions and Behavior: An Introduction to Theory and Research*. Reading, PA: Addison-Wesley Publishing Co.

Ford Foundation (1974), *The Finances of the Performing Arts*. New York: Ford Foundation.

Johnson, Richard M. (1970), "*Q*-Analysis of Large Samples," *Journal of Marketing Research*, 7, 104–5.

Hawes, Douglass, Wayne Talarzyk, and Roger Blackwell (1975), "Consumer Satisfaction from Leisure Time Pursuits," *Advances in Consumer Research, Vol. 2*, ed. Mary Jane Schlinger. Ann Arbor: Association for Consumer Research.

Holbrook, Morris, and Donald Lehmann (1980), "Patterns of Allocating Discretionary Time: Some Issues in Assessing Complimentarity Among Activities," unpublished paper, Columbia University.

National Research Center for the Arts, Inc. (1975), *Americans and the Arts*. New York: National Committee for Cultural Resources.

Ryan, Michael J., and E. H. Bonfield (1975), "The Fishbein Extended Model and Consumer Behavior," *Journal of Consumer Research*, 2, 18–36.

Ryans, Adrian, and Charles Weinberg (1978), "Consumer Dynamics in Non-Profit Organizations," *Journal of Consumer Research*, 5, 89–95.

Stephenson, W. (1953), *The Study of Behavior*. Chicago: University of Chicago Press.

Wells, William D. (1975), "Psychographics: A Critical Review," *Journal of Marketing Research*, 12, 196–213.

A Market Segmentation Approach to Transit Planning, Modeling, and Management

CHRISTOPHER H. LOVELOCK

The importance of marketing for public transportation has received increasing attention in the ten years since Schneider's seminal work on this issue was first published [23]. Recently, it has provided the topic of an entire Transit Marketing Conference, co-sponsored by the Urban Mass Transportation Administration and the American Public Transit Association.

There is a risk that marketing may be seen simply as a managerial activity designed to maximize transit ridership, and as having

Reprinted from *Proceedings of the Sixteenth Annual Meeting of the Transportation Research Forum*, 1975, pp. 247–58. By permission of The Richard B. Cross Company, Oxford, Indiana 47971.

little relevance for transportation planners and researchers. As emphasized by Kotler, marketing involves analysis, planning, implementation, and control, manifesting itself in carefully formulated programs designed to achieve specific objectives [14]. In most instances, it involves the careful selection of a limited number of target markets, rather than a quixotic attempt to win every market and be all things to all people. As part of this process, marketing requires understanding the needs of each different target market and developing products or services which attempt to meet these needs.

This article will focus on a key marketing concept, market segmentation, and discuss its relevance for planning and modeling as well as for management. First, it looks at what is implied by the concept of market segmentation, at the potential value of dividing a mass market into smaller groups, and at the criteria which must be satisfied if meaningful segments are to be developed for use in a specific operational context.

Alternative methods of segmenting the transit market are then evaluated in the context of relating modal choice behavior to both the characteristics of individual travelers and the types of trip that they make.

Finally, findings are presented from a survey of a specific subsegment, namely, adults in middle-income, surburban, car-owning households, located within a short distance of local transit routes. This study showed that nontransit users perceived public transportation very differently from regular users and were also less well informed about the specifics of local services.

SEGMENTING THE MARKET FOR "MASS TRANSIT"

It is sometimes observed that the term "mass transit" is an unfortunate one, since it implies a mass market with undifferentiated needs and characteristics [24]. In practice, as will be shown, the demand for public transportation is made up of many submarkets (or market segments) representing people of different ages, sexes, occupations, and income levels, traveling for various purposes, with varying degrees of frequency, at different times of day, and between different locations. Certain segments may be much more important than others from the standpoint of defining and achieving transit objectives.

Although every transit operation is likely to have somewhat different priorities, the objectives for transit tend to fall into two broad categories. The first concerns the diversion of travelers from private automobiles, with a view to achieving such goals as reducing traffic congestion, noise and air pollution, energy consumption, and traffic accidents, as well as avoiding the need for new highways and parking facilities. The second is concerned with improving mobility for those who presently lack access to adequate transportation, either because they do not own a car or lack access to one on a regular basis, or else are unable to drive.

If these goals are to be achieved, it is immediately apparent that planners must set objectives for managers of planned or existing transit systems in terms of encouraging ridership among specific segments of the population, rather than in vague terms of "maximizing ridership" for the overall system.

Various researchers, including Smerk, Lovelock, Reed, and Watson and Stopher, have emphasized the importance of developing transit services which are responsible to the needs of different market segments [16, 22, 25, 30]. This is especially necessary when attempting to encourage a modal shift from autos to transit. Failure to take these varying needs into account and failure to adopt communications and pricing strategies which are tailored to the characteristics of specific segments can only weaken transit's prospects for competing successfully against private automobiles.

Transportation models, too, need to reflect the structure of the market. If transportation objectives focus on specific segments of the travel market, then it is important that models be developed which can predict (and perhaps explain) the behavior of these segments.

Pointing to the limited explanatory power of highly aggregative models based upon economic analysis, a number of transportation researchers have stressed the need to develop a better understanding of the ways in which consumers arrive at modal choice decisions [12, 15, 26]. Particular interest has been shown in learning more about how behavioral variables such as attitudes relate to modal choice [1, 11].

DEFINING MARKET SEGMENTATION

In the context of the private firm, market segmentation may be defined as the two-stage process of first dividing the consumer market into meaningful buyer groups, and then creating specific marketing programs for each group such that financial profits will be maximized. In the case of urban public transportation (which has largely ceased to be profitable financially), the objective function theoretically centers on attaining specified social goals (e.g., helping achieve new air pollution standards) which can justify a defined level of deficit spending on transit. Unfortunately, transit's success or failure is all too often measured simply in terms of gross ridership statistics.

In evaluating a market and developing appropriate programs, one of three broad alternative strategies can be followed. The first is *market aggregation*, treating all consumers as similar and offering a standard product for everyone. Historically, "mass transit" has tended to fall into this category.

At the opposite end of the scale is *total market disaggregation*, where each consumer is treated uniquely. In the last analysis, each individual may be thought of as a separate market segment, on the grounds that each person is slightly different from everybody else in personal characteristics, behavior patterns, needs, values, and attitudes [29]. Total disaggregation of the population has particular appeal for the modeler, in as much as it can be argued that the best way to develop an understanding of how travel decisions are made and how they may be influenced is to study individual consumers.

Recognizing the dangers inherent in taking an undifferentiated, mass market approach to transportation planning and management, interest has been shown in developing disaggregative behavioral models of modal choice [28]. I believe that understanding the behavior of individual travelers can yield valuable insights for model builders, and also assist transit managers in developing strategies for influencing modal choice decisions. However, there are limits as to how far disaggregation can be carried. Planners have to develop transportation systems for populations which may run into the millions, total disaggregation can quickly become a complex and expensive procedure when running large simulation models, and there are limits to the ability of transit managers to provide personalized service in buses designed to seat fifty people and trains which may carry as many as fifteen hundred at a time.

Obviously, there has to be a happy medium between complete aggregation of the population on the one hand and total disaggregation on the other. This is where the third strategy, that of *market segmentation*, promises to be of value. It calls for grouping consumers into segments on the basis of intra-group similarities and inter-group differences. Wilkie notes that market segmentation may be viewed as a descriptive process, in that it recognizes both individual differences and group similarities [31]. Segments can be developed either by dividing a large, amorphous group into smaller groups with certain characteristics in common, or "built from the ground up" by assigning individuals to one of several groups according to certain specific characteristics which each person possesses.

The concept of market segmentation is based upon the propositions that (1) consumers are different, (2) differences in consumers are related to differences in market behavior, and (3) segments of consumers can be isolated within the overall market. Engel, Fiorillo and Cayley summarize a number of benefits which may be expected to result from a segmentation approach [8], including:

1. A more precise definition of the market in terms of the needs of specific groups, why they behave as they do, and possible ways of influencing behavior
2. A better ability to identify competitive strengths and weaknesses, and opportunities for winning specific segments from the competition
3. More efficient allocation of limited resources to the development of programs that will satisfy the needs of target segments
4. Clarification of objectives and definition of performance standards

The basic problem is to select segmentation variables which are likely to prove useful in a specific operational context. Kotler proposes three criteria [13], each of which must be satisfied if meaningful market segments are to be developed:

Measurability: It must be possible to obtain information on the specific characteristics of interest.

Accessibility: Management must be able to identify chosen segments within the overall market and effectively focus marketing efforts on these segments.

Substantiality: The segments must be large enough (and/or sufficiently important) to merit the time and cost of separate attention.

Wilkie stresses the importance of choosing segmentation variables which are useful as correlates of behavior and can be related to strategic considerations [31]. He also argues that the best segments are those which display "homogeneity within and heterogeneity between groups;" in other words, there should be minimal within-group variation and maximal between-group variation.

SELECTION OF SEGMENTATION VARIABLES

How can the transportation market be segmented, and which variables are likely to yield *useful* segmenting descriptors? In order to see how segmentation variables relate to modal choice decisions (and, perhaps, influence the outcome of such decisions), a flowchart of the decision process is shown in Exhibit 1. This illustrates the stages through which an individual traveler is posited to go in selecting a mode for a specific trip and is based upon an earlier, more complex model to which explicit segmentation variables have been added [16, 17].

This diagram helps us categorize *who* is traveling, and also *why, when, where,* and *how* they are making a trip. It serves to indicate some of the many ways in which the travel market can be segmented, as well as providing insights into modal choice behavior patterns and how they may be influenced. The traveler is seen as specifying the modal attributes desired for a particular trip, then evaluating alternative modes to see which is

EXHIBIT 1: Relationship of segmentation variables to modal choice decisions

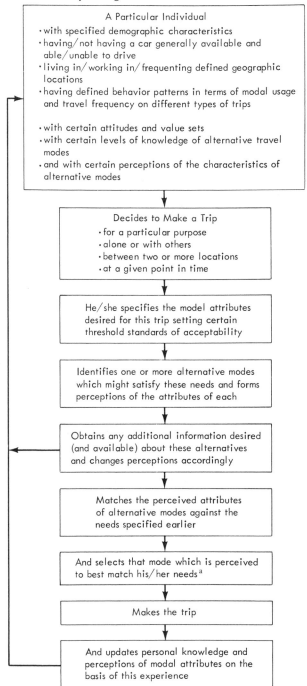

A Particular Individual
- with specified demographic characteristics
- having/not having a car generally available and able/unable to drive
- living in/working in/frequenting defined geographic locations
- having defined behavior patterns in terms of modal usage and travel frequency on different types of trips

- with certain attitudes and value sets
- with certain levels of knowledge of alternative travel modes
- and with certain perceptions of the characteristics of alternative modes

Decides to Make a Trip
- for a particular purpose
- alone or with others
- between two or more locations
- at a given point in time

He/she specifies the model attributes desired for this trip setting certain threshold standards of acceptability

Identifies one or more alternative modes which might satisfy these needs and forms perceptions of the attributes of each

Obtains any additional information desired (and available) about these alternatives and changes perceptions accordingly

Matches the perceived attributes of alternative modes against the needs specified earlier

And selects that mode which is perceived to best match his/her needs[a]

Makes the trip

And updates personal knowledge and perceptions of modal attributes on the basis of this experience

[a]If no acceptable match results, the traveler posited to either change the nature of the trip itself, after his/her requirements, or else not make the trip at all.

perceived as providing the best "match" for this trip, choosing that which is perceived as the optimal mode, and then making the trip.

Two broad categories of potential segmentation variables are represented here: (1) traveler-related variables and (2) trip-related variables.

As shown in Exhibit 1, travelers can be described according to demographic characteristics, such as age, income, sex, etc., which, in turn, may be related to certain lifestyle characteristics such as car ownership and ability to drive. They can also be segmented by locational variables, such as where they live, work, shop, and so forth; by their actual travel behavior patterns; and, finally, by various psychological variables, which may be linked to such behavior as attitudes and values, or perceptions and knowledge of alternative modes.

Trip-related variables are shown as being categorized in four basic ways: the purpose for which they are made; the size of the party making a particular trip; the length and nature of the route linking origins, destinations and any intermediary points; and the time of day, week, month, or season at which the trip is made.

It is immediately evident that many of these variables are interrelated. Thus, car ownership and ability to drive are in large measure a function of age and income characteristics. Other demographic characteristics may be related to home and work locations, as well as to trip-making behavior.

Certain personal characteristics are obviously linked to the type of trips made. People in most full-time jobs have to commute to and from work each weekday, while students have to go to school or college each day during the school year. With a few exceptions (such as traveling salespeople) these journeys are repetitive in nature, being made at approximately the same time each day and between the same two points. In short, they are "committed" trips. Other types of trips, such as shopping or recreational, may be said to be "discretionary" in nature, in that there is usually some flexibility in timing and/or the locations visited.

Exhibit 2 shows the distribution of trip purposes by time of day and week experienced by the GO Transit rail service in Toronto, highlighting variations in the nature and timing of travel demands among existing transit users. The study found that travelers

EXHIBIT 2: Trip purpose of peak, off-peak Saturday and Sunday riders[a]

Trip purpose	Weekdays		Saturdays	Sundays
	Peak	Off-peak		
Work	· · · ·●● ●●●●●●●●	· · · · · ·●	· · · ·●	●●
Business	· ·	· ·	· ·	·
Shopping	· ·	· · · · ·	· · · · ·●	
School	· · · · · · ·	· · · · · · ·	·	·
Entertainment	·	· · · ·	· · · · ·	· ·
Social	·	· · ·	· · ·●	· · · ·●
Personal		· ·	·	
Recreation			· ·	· · ·
Other		·	· · · · ·	· · ·

[a] ● Represents 1,000 trips; · represents 100 trips; · represents fewer than 100 trips.
Source: [20].

at off-peak and weekend periods were less frequent users of the system and that the proportion of the two sexes varied by time of day and week.

Which of all these numerous segmentation variables is likely to prove useful to planners, modelers, and managers? Let's first evaluate them from the standpoint of defining objectives for public transportation.

RELATING TRANSIT OBJECTIVES TO SEGMENTATION VARIABLES

Improving Mobility. It is immediately apparent that objectives relating to improvement of personal mobility tend to be keyed to the needs of specific demographic segments who do not own a car or may not be able to drive one. These groups usually include the elderly, young people, handicapped persons, and low-income groups.

Frequently, transit-related legislation specifically singles out these segments for special attention. Even though some of these segments may be relatively very small (the handicapped, for example), transit planners and managers must still cater to their needs. Ideally, this requires identifying the home origins of as many as possible, the destinations they most need to visit, evaluating their ability to pay, and assessing the extent to which it is necessary and/or feasible to modify vehicle characteristics, promotional strategies, and operating policies to meet their special needs. For example see [4].

Modal Shift. Objectives relating to modal shift are concerned with getting people out of their cars and into public transportation. Here the target may at first appear to be simply the four-fifths of all American households which own automobiles. However, when looking at specific objectives, it becomes apparent that priorities need to be set. For instance, if our concern is with reducing

energy consumption, then we might usefully attempt to group consumers according to quantity of gasoline they consume annually (presumably a function of miles driven, frequency of trips, and ownership of cars yielding poor gas mileage). If relieving congestion is our concern, then it makes sense to focus on people driving along specific routes during defined periods of the day or week.

Planners and researchers can play an important role here in seeking to identify key groups. However, identification is not enough; it is also important to evaluate the factors motivating the choice of automobiles over other modes for individuals within these groups, as well as to discover how susceptible various subcategories of individuals are to switching to public transportation. This is where the consumer research and the model builder may be able to develop useful insights for transit management.

INSIGHTS FROM PAST RESEARCH

Location. Many studies highlight the importance of location as a segmentation variable, indicating that transit's share of the travel market is a function of the accessibility of origins and destinations from stopping points on the transit route. For interurban rail or bus transit, accessibility is perhaps best measured in terms of travel time. A study of the GO Transit rail service in Toronto showed that GO's market share of all "in scope" trips declined from a high of 41.2 percent, when both origin and destination were within ten minutes' walk of the station, to a mere 1.8 percent of trips originating ten to fifteen minutes' drive from the suburban station and terminating fifteen to twenty minutes' transit ride-plus-walk from the downtown station (Exhibit 3). On the basis of other transit research in Toronto, Bonsall has suggested that the effective

EXHIBIT 3: GO transit market share by origin/destination zones

Origin[a] (suburbs)	Destination zones[b] (central Toronto)	GO transit market share (%)
XX2	002	41.2
XX4	002	39.8
XX2	004	22.4
XX4	004	15.8
XX2	005	12.7
XX2	006	9.2
XX6	002	10.5
XX4	005	6.7
XX4	006	5.3
XX6	004	6.5
XX6	005	2.6
XX6	006	1.8
		14.5

[a]*Origin zones* in the two suburban corridors were defined as follows:

XX2: Less than 10 minutes walk from the station (innermost zone)

XX4: 5–10 minutes drive from the station (excluding 10 min. walk area)

XX6: 10–15 minutes drive from the station

[b]*Destination zones* within the Central Toronto area were defined as:

002: Less than 10 minutes walk from Union Station (innermost zone)

004: Up to 10 minutes transit ride plus walk (excluding innermost zone)

005: 10–15 minutes transit ride plus walk

006: 15–20 minutes ride plus walk

Source: [18].

catchment area (or "transit envelope") for local bus service is about one thousand feet [2].

The implications of location as a segmentation variable are twofold. First, if planners want people living or working in a particular geographic location to use transit, they must ensure that transit service provides acceptable access levels to both their origin and principal destination locations. Second, transit marketers are wasting time and money if they try to market their service for trips whose origins and/or destinations lie outside the transit envelope. For this reason, geographically specific media such as direct mail or billboards may be a more cost-effective means of communicating with potential riders than wide-area media such as TV and radio. Another advantage of direct mail is that it can tailor information on routes, fares, and schedules to the needs of a specific location (residents of a local area or employees at a specific plant, for example).

Demographics. How useful are demographic variables (other than geographical location) as a means of segmenting that great bulk of the American population which travels by car? It is known that demographic variables may influence the modal attributes desired by consumers and the relative importance they attach to them. Golob *et al.*, Stopher and Lavender, Dobson and Nicolaidis, and Watson and Stopher have all conducted research which indicates that groups with different socioeconomic variables display different preferences for transportation mode attributes [6, 9, 27, 30]. Often the group which stands out most prominently from the others is the elderly.

However, it is worth noting that business marketers consider demographics as only one of several possible methods of segmentation and not necessarily the most useful at that. Haley cites a number of studies which suggest that demographic variables are, in general, poor predictors of behavior and less than optimum bases for segmentation strategies [10].

Trip Characteristics. A number of researchers have found that people's needs differ according to the type of trip they are making. For instance, Paine, Nash, Hille and Brunner identified the relative importance given to various modal attributes for both work and non-work trips [21]. Their study showed that speed, punctuality, and timing considerations were significantly more important for work trips than for non-work trips. However, for non-work journeys, travelers were noticeably more price sensitive and more concerned about weather protection while waiting and having to walk more than one block; they also placed greater emphasis on clean, comfortable vehicles, on availability of package and baggage space, and on the ability to take along family and friends. Domencich and Kraft, too, have found that demand for shopping trips is much more price elastic than that for work trips [7].

MULTIDIMENSIONAL SEGMENTATION

Thus far, segmentation has been discussed primarily from a unidimensional standpoint. In practice, classification may be more useful if it is undertaken along two or more dimensions simultaneously, to yield a variety of subsegments.

It is my belief that transportation researchers and modelers should be taking a matrix approach to segmentation, with meaningful traveler characteristics along one axis and trip characteristics along the other. In such an approach, each cell would represent a separate subsegment. It might be hypothesized that each subsegment would have somewhat different modal attribute preferences and might therefore be expected to show variations in modal choice behavior from other cells. Moreover, such an analysis could well yield insights into preference and behavior differences that are presently obscured by segmentation along a single dimension.

Little research is known to have been conducted along such lines, although Bucklin found marked differences in modal choice behavior among shoppers according to (1) the size and composition of the shopping party, (2) the shopper's marital status and

stage in life-cycle, and (3) the time of day and/or week at which the shopping was done [3, pp. 59–61].

Whether or not a subsegment merits separate analysis will depend primarily on its size. Some cells will contain insufficient travelers. However, by use of multidimensional scaling and cluster analysis, it should then be possible to group modal attribute requirements for different cells according to their similarities to one another, thus collapsing many small cells into a limited number of larger groups, which will satisfy Wilkie's criterion of minimizing differences within groups and maximizing them between groups.

In a number of urban areas, large-scale transportation censuses have been conducted which correlate travel behavior (including modal choice) with data on personal characteristics. Such censuses can provide the basis for an understanding of the size of different traveler/trip cells as outlined above, and the nature of the data available may in itself help determine which bases of segmentation should be employed.

Transportation and population censuses are also valuable in yielding demographic data by geographic area, enabling transportation researchers and managers to identify both the size and geographic location of the segments. Information may be available for population units as small as a city block. This approach has particular value for marketing urban transit services in that these provide transportation along predefined routes which can be related to the characteristics of populations within the surrounding transit envelope.

AN EXAMPLE OF SEGMENTATION IN TRANSIT RESEARCH

Although transportation censuses may describe modal choice behavior, they cannot necessarily *explain* it. By breaking the market down into a series of progressively smaller groupings, it may be possible for researchers to develop new hypotheses into the behavior of specific subsegments.

Such an approach may be particularly useful when seeking to explain differences in modal choice behavior among individuals who are realistically in a position to choose between either car or transit for specific journeys, and who appear to have similar demographic characteristics. As suggested in Exhibit 1, personal values, attitudes, perceptions, and knowledge of alternatives may all contribute to determining the outcome of modal choice decisions.

To improve our understanding of the different cells in the segmentation matrix described earlier, therefore, it may be necessary to conduct additional research into (1) the modal requirements of specific subsegments, (2) their perceptions of the various attributes of different modes, and (3) the extent of their knowledge of alternative modes. In this way, it may be possible to relate "soft" characteristics like personal preferences to more readily identifiable personal characteristics such as demographics and behavior patterns.

San Francisco Area Study. With a view to determining the relationship between modal choice behavior and travel perceptions and knowledge, a large scale consumer survey was made in the San Francisco area of a carefully defined subsegment of the population [16]. The sample was confined to adults aged 18 to 65 years in middle-income, car-owning households situated in suburban cites 20–30 miles from San Francisco and located within a quarter-mile of a local transit route and one mile of a trunk-line interurban transit route. Various controls were used to exclude any respondents who might be captive transit users, due to inability to drive or lack of access to an automobile.

Using several measures of reported behavior, the 1,328 remaining respondents could be assigned to one of four categories of transit user behavior:

1. Non-user—had never used transit (13.6%)
2. Non-user—but had used transit in the past (49.5%)
3. Occasional transit user (30.1%)
4. Regular transit user by choice (6.9%)

To find out how respondents perceived the characteristics of car, bus and commuter train travel, they were asked to rate the three modes separately on each of twelve attributes, using a seven-point semantic differential scale keyed to polar opposite descriptors. For instance, on the characteristics of punctuality, the favorable pole was labeled "on-time arrivals" and the unfavorable pole "late arrivals." The results are shown in Exhibit 4 and indicate distinctly different profiles for each of the three modes.

When respondents were segmented according to their transit usage category, there was often a significant difference in their perceptions of the characteristics of the three modes (Exhibit 5). As a broad generalization, the more often people used public transportation, the more favorable their ratings of bus and train travel; by contrast, regular transit users tended to rate car travel somewhat less favorably on most characteristics (despite the fact that they were car owners and drivers themselves).

The findings for bus travel are highlighted graphically in Exhibit 6, showing the difference in ratings for non-users and regular users (for clarity, the two non-user groups have been combined and occasional users excluded). As can be seen, the differences are largest for convenience, simplicity ("simple to use"—"complicated to use"), enjoyableness, and comfort. With the exception of cost, non-commute speed, safety and

EXHIBIT 4: Mean ratings for car, bus and train travel[a]

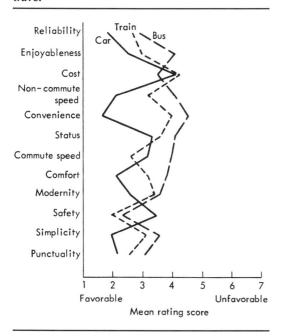

Reliability
Enjoyableness
Cost
Non-commute speed
Convenience
Status
Commute speed
Comfort
Modernity
Safety
Simplicity
Punctuality

1   2   3   4   5   6   7
Favorable   Unfavorable
Mean rating score

[a]All differences between each of the three possible modal pairs were statistically significant at the $p < 0.05$ level except for the Bus-Train difference on "Modernity."

punctuality, all differences in ratings between users and non-users are statistically significant at the $p < .05$ level or better. How should we interpret these findings? Can we infer that one explanation for non-users' failure to ride transit lies in the fact that they perceive transit service as much less competitive with the automobile on many attributes than do regular transit users?

Essentially, this begs the question of whether attitudes cause behavior or vice-versa. Behavioral scientists are divided on this point. A majority hold the view that attitudes (of which perceptions are a subset) are intervening variables which account for behavioral differences. Others, however, argue that attitudes often represent a rationalization for behavior.

I incline towards the view that perceptions are both a cause and an effect of modal choice behavior, with the former the more significant. It is noteworthy that when respondents were asked how confident they were about the ratings they had made of bus travel, non-users showed significantly less confidence in their judgments than users (Exhibit 7).

One of the problems in encouraging car travelers to make use of transit is that many of them are basically unfamiliar with this mode. In the survey, respondents were asked a series of questions designed to test their knowledge of bus services from their community to San Francisco (these questions were phrased in terms of providing information to a new neighbor who had asked for assistance). As can be seen in Exhibit 8, the less respondents used transit, the more ignorant they were about the specifics of the service.

It is entirely possible that two individuals may have the same modal attribute requirements for a given trip, but perceive competing modes in different ways. Essentially, then, it is not the "real" or engineering attributes of a mode which may determine success or failure in attracting travelers, but the *perceived* attributes. An obvious corollary is that a person cannot be expected to use a mode of which he or she is largely ignorant. For these reasons, perceptions of specific attributes and the extent of overall knowledge may constitute important variables in modal choice decision-making.

The findings presented from the San Francisco area study suggest a strong link between perceptions of modal attributes and modal choice behavior, but longitudinal studies are needed to test the hypothesis that perceptions and knowledge levels explain

EXHIBIT 5: Consumer ratings of car, bus and train travel, by transit usage class[a]

	Never used	Past user (not now)	Occasional user	Regular user (by choice)
N:	181	656	399	92
Car travel				
Reliability	1.70	1.76	1.86	1.92*
Cost	4.04	4.02	4.19	4.51
Enjoyableness	2.51	2.54	2.69	2.57
Non-commute speed	2.29	2.10	2.10	2.02
Convenience	1.49	1.52	1.66	1.77*
Status	3.12	3.33	3.36	3.14*
Commute speed	3.12	3.03	3.23	3.49*
Comfort	2.08	2.11	2.27	2.25
Modernity	2.57	2.52	2.75	2.76
Safety	3.30	3.51	3.79	3.69
Simplicity	1.95	1.95	2.16	2.12
Punctuality	2.14	2.01	2.24	2.44*
Bus travel				
Reliability	2.92	2.81	2.73	2.25
Cost	3.65	3.65	3.68	3.35
Enjoyableness	4.37	4.28	4.05	3.41*
Non-commute speed	4.26	4.17	4.15	3.75
Convenience	4.74	4.70	4.39	3.17*
Status	4.13	4.10	4.12	3.79*
Commute speed	4.17	4.00	3.81	3.51
Comfort	3.96	3.98	3.86	3.20*
Modernity	3.60	3.64	3.49	3.07*
Safety	2.35	2.35	2.33	2.02
Simplicity	3.79	3.64	3.55	2.58*
Punctuality	3.31	3.11	3.02	2.72
Train travel				
Reliability	2.82	2.55	2.55	2.15
Cost	4.04	4.19	4.30	4.33
Enjoyableness	3.40	3.12	2.99	2.63
Non-commute speed	3.33	3.26	3.09	3.09
Convenience	4.31	3.86	3.86	2.91*
Status	3.59	3.54	3.50	3.13*
Commute speed	2.95	2.74	2.78	2.34*
Comfort	3.37	3.33	3.30	2.81*
Modernity	3.71	3.55	3.60	2.81*
Safety	2.12	2.08	2.04	1.97*
Simplicity	3.59	3.07	3.06	2.57*
Punctuality	2.84	2.63	2.64	2.12*

[a]Ratings could range from 1 to 7, with a low number constituting a very favorable rating and a high number a very unfavorable one.
*Differences are statistically significant at $p < .05$ level.

EXHIBIT 6: Ratings of bus travel by non-transit users and regular transit users[a]

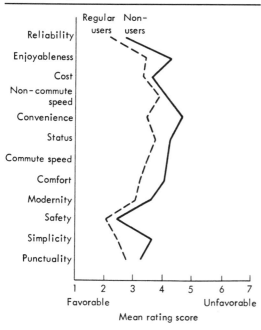

Regular users / Non-users

Reliability
Enjoyableness
Cost
Non-commute speed
Convenience
Status
Commute speed
Comfort
Modernity
Safety
Simplicity
Punctuality

1   2   3   4   5   6   7

Favorable   Unfavorable

Mean rating score

[a] Includes both past and "never used" groups.

behavior, rather than the other way around. If it can be shown that they do, then an attempt should be made to incorporate these variables in future modal choice models, especially when focusing on subsegments of the population which are prime candidates for switching from auto to transit.

Managerial Implications. Clear evidence that perceptions and knowledge levels do influence modal choice behavior among defined segments of the population would have important implications for transit management. If non-users located in transit service areas are deterred from using public transportation because they are either ignorant of the availability and specifics of service or else perceive transit attributes in an unfavorable light, then marketing communications programs designed to correct misperceptions and provide needed information may be able to influence modal choice behavior in many instances.

However, for such an approach to prove effective, it would be most important to tailor

EXHIBIT 7: Confidence in judgments of bus travel by transit usage class

Degree of confidence	Usage class				
	(A) Never used	*(B)* Used in past, but not now	*(C)* Occasional user	*(D)* Regular user	*Total*
Extremely	3.7%	6.7%	3.9%	30.5%	7.1%
Very	16.7	30.2	39.4	43.9	32.1
Somewhat	49.4	40.9	45.2	23.2	42.1
Only slightly	22.2	19.8	11.0	2.4	16.3
Not at all	8.0	2.5	0.6	0.0	2.5
	100.0	100.0	100.0	100.0	100.0

Measure of association	γ	Significance
All usage classes	$-.322$	$<.001$
(A) + (B) and (D) only	$-.677$	$<.001$

EXHIBIT 8: Knowledge of interurban bus service (to San Francisco) by transit usage class

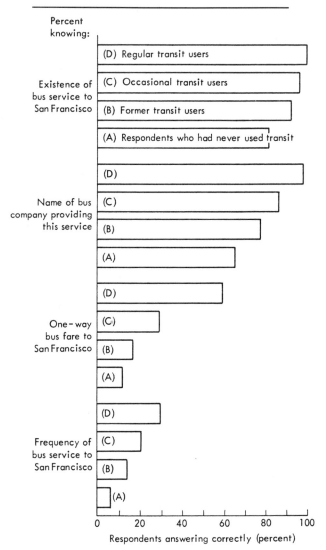

Percent knowing:

Existence of bus service to San Francisco
- (D) Regular transit users
- (C) Occasional transit users
- (B) Former transit users
- (A) Respondents who had never used transit

Name of bus company providing this service
- (D)
- (C)
- (B)
- (A)

One-way bus fare to San Francisco
- (D)
- (C)
- (B)
- (A)

Frequency of bus service to San Francisco
- (D)
- (C)
- (B)
- (A)

0   20   40   60   80   100
Respondents answering correctly (percent)

target segments whom research had shown to be the most likely to change their behavior as a result of (a) obtaining specific needed information and (b) changing their perceptions of specific attributes. A broad based campaign along the lines of "Ride the Bus, It's Nicer than You Think" is unlikely to achieve much.

CONCLUSIONS

This paper has attempted to emphasize both the importance and the benefits of taking a segmentation approach to transportation planning, modeling, and management.

Various bases of segmentation were discussed, including geographic location, other demographic variables, and trip characteristics. It was argued that greater emphasis should be placed on multidimensional segmentation, as opposed to categorizing consumers along only one dimension at a time. By focusing on specific subsegments of the population, it may be possible to obtain new insights into the modal choice behavior of certain groups which have particular significance in terms of achieving transportation objectives.

Although the emphasis in this paper has been directed towards segmentation's application for public transportation, it should be stressed that it is also a potentially valuable concept for a broad range of urban transport services. Issues such as toll road pricing, ramp metering, preferential freeway lanes, parking supply management, and highway safety campaigns all have behavioral implications. Decisions in these areas may benefit from research and analysis which yield a better understanding of the needs and behavior patterns of different highway user segments.

NOTES

1. Summarized in [16], Appendix B.
2. For an overview of this controversy, see [5].

REFERENCES

[1] Allen, W. Bruce, and Andrew Isserman, "Behavior Modal Split," *High Speed Ground Transportation Journal* (Summer 1972), 179–99.

[2] Bonsall, J. A., *Dial-A-Bus: The Bay Riders Experiment*. Toronto: Ontario Department of Transportation and Communications, August 1971.

[3] Bucklin, Louis P., *Shopping Patterns in an Urban Area*. Berkeley: Institute of Business and Economic Research, University of California, 1967.

[4] Cantelli, Edmund J., et al., *Transportation and Aging: Selected Issues*. Washington, D.C.: Supt. of Documents, Stock #1762-0042, 1970.

[5] Day, George S., "Theories of Attitude Structure and Change," in *Consumer Behavior: Theoretical Sources*, S. Ward and T. S. Robertson, eds. Englewood Cliffs, NJ: Prentice-Hall, 1973.

[6] Dobson, Richardo, and Gregory C. Nicolaidis, "Preferences for Transit Service by Homogeneous Groups of Individuals," *Proceedings*. Transportation Research Forum, 1974.

[7] Domencich, Thomas A., and Gerald Kraft, *Free Transit*. Lexington, MA: Lexington Books, 1970.

[8] Engel, James F., Henry F. Fiorillo, and Murray A. Cayley (eds.), *Market Segmentation: Concepts and Applications*. New York: Holt, Rinehart and Winston, 1972.

[9] Golob, Thomas F., Eugene T. Canty, Richard L. Gustafson, and Joseph E. Vitt, "An Analysis of Consumer Preferences for a Public Transportation System," *Transportation Research* 6 (March 1972), 81–102.

[10] Haley, Russell I., "Benefit Segmentation," *Journal of Marketing* 32 (July 1968), 30–5.

[11] Hartgen, David T., and George H. Tanner, "Investigations of the Effect of Traveler Attitudes in a Model of Modal Choice Behavior," *Highway Research Record*, no. 396 (1971), 1–14.

[12] Horton, Frank E., "Behavioral Models in Transportation Planning," *Transportation Engineering Journal*, Proceedings of the ASCE, May 1972, 411–20.

[13] Kotler, Philip, *Marketing Management*, second ed. Englewood Cliffs, NJ: Prentice-Hall, 1972. (See especially chapter 6.)

[14] Kotler, Philip, *Marketing for Nonprofit Organizations*. Englewood Cliffs, NJ: Prentice-Hall, 1975.

[15] Le Boulanger, H., "Research Into the Urban Traveller's Behaviour," *Transportation Research* 5 (1971), 113–25.

[16] Lovelock, Christopher H., *Consumer Oriented Approaches to Marketing Urban Transit*. Ph.D. dissertation, Stanford University.

Springfield, VA: National Technical Information Service, #PB-220 781, 1973.

[17] Lovelock, Christopher H., "Modeling the Modal Choice Decision Process," *Transportation* 4 (1975).

[18] Metropolitan Toronto and Region Transportation Survey (MTARTS), *GO Transit Commuter Rail Project.* Special Report No. 9 (Second Household Survey, 1968).

[19] Oi, Walter Y., and Paul W. Shuldiner, *An Analysis of Urban Travel Demands.* Evanston, IL: Northwestern University Press, 1962.

[20] Ontario, Government of, *People on the GO.* Report C4. Toronto, Ont.: Department of Highways, June 1969.

[21] Paine, Frank T., Allen N. Nash, Stanley J. Hille, and G. Allen Brunner, "Consumer Attitudes Towards Auto vs. Public Transit Alternatives," *Journal of Applied Psychology* (November–December 1969), pp. 472–80.

[22] Reed, Richard R., *Market Segmentation Development for Public Transportation.* Stanford University, 1973. Springfield, VA: National Technical Information Service, #PB-227 178/AS.

[23] Schneider, Lewis M., *Marketing Urban Mass Transit—A Comparative Study of Management Strategies.* Boston, MA: Harvard Business School Division of Research, 1965.

[24] Schneider, Lewis M., "Marketing Urban Transit," Highway Research Record, No. 318, 1970, 16–19.

[25] Smerk, George M., "Mass Transit Management," *Business Horizons* (December 1971), 5–16.

[26] Sommers, Alexis J., "Towards a Theory of Traveler Mode Choice," *High Speed Ground Transportation Journal* (January 1970), 1–8.

[27] Stopher, Peter R., and J. P. Lavender, "Disaggregate Behavioral Travel Demand Models: Empirical Tests of Three Hypotheses," Transportation Research Forum *Proceedings*, 1972.

[28] Stopher, Peter R., Thomas E. Lisco, "Modelling Travel Demand: A Disaggregate Approach, Issues and Applications," Transportation Research Forum *Proceedings*, 1970.

[29] Twedt, Dik Warren, "The Concept of Market Segmentation," in *Handbook of Modern Marketing*, V. P. Buell, ed. New York: McGraw-Hill, 1970.

[30] Watson, Peter L., and Peter R. Stopher, "The Effects of Income on the Usage and Valuation of Transport Modes," Transportation Research Forum *Proceedings*, 1974.

[31] Wilkie, William L., *An Empirical Analysis of Alternative Bases of Market Segmentation.* Unpublished Ph.D. dissertation, Graduate School of Business, Stanford University, 1971.

From "General Audience" to "Quiet Pessimists": Sharpening the Focus in Cancer Audience Segmentation

WILLIAM D. NOVELLI

Just as biomedical and clinical research in the control of cancer has made considerable progress in the last decade, so has cancer control *communication*. Informing, educating, and motivating public audiences about prevention, detection, treatment and rehabilitation issues is moving forward. . . rapidly in some ways, slowly in others . . . but moving forward. Much of the credit for this progress in cancer communication goes to the Cancer Communications Conference of the American Cancer Society.

Research into target audience knowledge, attitudes and practices—so-called KAP studies—has helped pinpoint health consumer audiences. These studies, coupled with an identification of who is at risk, have served as the primary means of selecting target segments for cancer communication initiatives.

We have gone beyond the stage when we thought our messages could be all things to everybody. The words "general audience" are being eliminated from today's cancer communication plans, and *audience segmentation* is more the norm.

This target audience segmentation is based on the fundamental ideas that:

- Health consumers are not all the same . . . there are many important differences among them.
- We can measure these differences . . . especially those differences which are related to health behavior.
- We can isolate and reach key target segments . . . using tailored messages through mediated and interpersonal channels.
- The segments we choose to target are substantial enough in size and in need so that we can make a difference in the nation's public health status if and when we succeed.

By necessity, risk factors coupled with demographic attributes are the primary variables by which cancer communication audience segmentation is now done.

These risk factors have been the most *important* characteristics in terms of the current and future health status of our public audiences. And demographics have been the

Reprinted with permission from William D. Novelli, Needham Porter Novelli, 3240 Prospect Street, NW, Washington, D.C. 20007. Presented at the Fifth National Cancer Communications Conference, February 15–17, 1984.

the *easiest* data to acquire and to use in audience segmentation.

Thus, we direct our efforts to such audiences as:

- Men and women 50 and older—for campaigns to influence the earlier detection of colon and rectum cancer
- Females 40 and above, especially those with a family history of breast cancer, for programs aimed at breast cancer detection
- And people (teens, men and/or women) who smoke—again combining demography and risk—this time risk related to *behavior*

Geographic variables have also been helpful. For instance, research by the Illinois Division of the American Cancer Society . . . which has served as a cornerstone of the ACS Colorectal Health Check Program . . . showed a fairly substantial skew by region of the country for people reportedly predisposed to undertake detection tests.

But despite all the health consumer KAP studies and resulting audience segmentation that's been done, there is a real need to improve this process. A greater understanding of our health consumers is necessary. At this point, we have only a dim, hazy profile of our targets. We must sharpen our focus if we are going to hit the mark with effective, personally relevant, motivating communications.

In marketing research, many attempts have been made to go beyond demographic descriptions of target audiences. These attempts have led into psychology, the same discipline in which so much patient communication is grounded.

Marketing researchers have applied standardized personality inventories to better understand consumer behavior. Another avenue into psychology was called motivation research. This was much in vogue during the 1950s and early 1960s as a means of defining the "real" reasons consumers behave the way they do. Some great revelations came forth, such as the early contention that housewives baking cakes were symbolically enacting childbirth. Today, motivation research has left the psychological field and has turned to small-scale qualitative research studies—such as focus groups, in depth-type interviews, and mini groups—in order to build a context or framework to better understand decision-making and behavior. Many of you routinely use these techniques in your communications planning.

These marketing applications of psychology have also evolved into a quantitative avenue that is used for audience segmentation—called *psychographic* research. All this goes to reinforce the axiom that marketing is truly an eclectic discipline, which is a euphemism for saying that marketers will steal an idea from anywhere and fit it into their toolbox—as long as it works.

Psychographics, also called "lifestyle" or "activity and attitude" research, is based on the idea that people within the same demographic group can be quite different in other ways. Grouping audiences by sex, age, income and education may mask considerable differences about attitudes and living styles. These differences may relate to the behaviors we want to influence, and may be more important for our segmentation purposes than demographic or geographic similarities.

In psychographic analysis, audiences are divided into homogeneous groups on the basis of their social class, lifestyle or personality characteristics.

A typical questionnaire for a psychographic study consists of a battery of activity, interest and opinion (AIO) questions, as well as demographic measures, and questions about media patterns. In addition, most commercial psychographic studies ask about the usage of a variety of products and services.

Here are some examples of typical activity, interest and opinion questions. In the category of health concerns and remedies:

- If I don't feel well, I take a pain reliever or other medication right away.
- I often have difficulty getting to sleep.
- I frequently get indigestion.

In the category of buying behavior:

- Before going shopping, I sit down and make out a complete shopping list.
- I tend to spend for today and let tomorrow bring what it will.

In the category of sex roles:

- Men are better at investing money than women.
- I think the women's liberation movement is a good thing.

Agree/disagree responses to these statements usually apply a scale ranging from "definitely agree" to "definitely disagree."

Some of you may already be applying psychographic studies to your own program planning. The Office of Cancer Communications has been involved in the early stages of lifestyle segmentation with its national survey on breast cancer in 1980 and with the 1982 qualitative phase of a national survey of public knowledge, attitudes and practices. In this series of 16 focus groups, the beginnings of audience segments were postulated, based on attitudes and opinions rather than only on demographics. Audience profiles suggested were labeled "The Fatalist," "The Diligent," "The Avoider," and "The Oblivious."

For example, "The Oblivious" group was described as "healthy and feeling good . . . not concerned about the disease . . . not frequently in contact with people who have cancer . . . do not have much information about what cancer is like . . . tend to be concerned with planning for the future and living for today."

And the ACS national study related to colon and rectum cancer which I mentioned earlier suggested some ideas for possible psychographic follow-up. Two characteristics of respondents who reported that they definitely or probably would undertake detection tests were a sense of personal susceptibility and a belief that early detection works.

Describing several examples of psychographic studies can be helpful in thinking about the application of this segmentation approach to cancer communication.

First, psychographic research can be helpful in a descriptive way—by adding additional dimensions to an audience to make it more alive and more comprehensible. Several years ago the annual Lifestyle Study of Needham, Harper & Steers was used to provide a profile of men 55 and older. Several areas were reported on: changing work status, a decrease in family size, a decrease in household income, and changing health needs. Clearly, all Americans who fall into this category are not the same. There are likely to be a number of psychographic clusters of men 55+. But here is how the entire category was described, as a first step, in the area of changing health needs:

Food and diet are not only a . . . pastime . . . but the cornerstone of maintaining good health for the 55 and older male. Nutritional needs change. Less salt, less sugar, less high cholesterol foods, and a well-balanced diet are primary concerns. He prefers more "natural" foods which really means that he avoids foods having a lot of chemical or natural additives. . . .

The 55+ male is a regular breakfast eater, tends to skip lunch, and feels that dinner is incomplete without dessert. However, he is not a snacker and generally shuns "junk foods." He also is not interested in convenience foods, preferring a "family meal."

Although the numer of 55+ males drinking alcoholic beverages decreases sharply, the frequency of use among those who do drink remains constant compared to younger men. Beer consumption goes down. Soft drinks and juices with high sugar content decrease . . . however, diet soft drinks increase, particularly among males 55 to 64.

Medication use increases for the 55+ male. He finds it difficult to sleep and suffers from digestive problems. However, he complains of fewer headaches and colds than younger men.

The 55+ male does not follow the latest fashion trends, but he likes to look good. He uses more basic cosmetics and grooming aids such as body lotion, hair dressing and mouthwash than younger men.

That was an example of using psychographics to characterize a large category of consumers. Another use of psychographic research is to classify a broad population into smaller groups, such that within these smaller segments, consumers have similar lifestyles. Again, there may be demographic similarities or dissimilarities among the groups, but they are psychographically homogeneous. To illustrate, a representative sample of U.S. men and women received a questionnaire containing general lifestyle items on such topics as family, work, recreation, health, politics, religion and so forth. Through factor analysis, the males and females were segmented into five groups, identified on the basis of their central tendency or the "typical person" in the groups. Here are two female segments which emerged:

Mildred, the militant mother (20 percent of the total female population studied). Mildred married young and had children before she was quite ready to raise a family. Now she is unhappy. She is having trouble making ends meet on her blue collar husband's income.

She is frustrated and she vents her frustrations by rebelling against the system. She finds escape from her unhappy world in soap operas and movies. Television provides an ideal medium for her to live out her fantasies. She watches TV all through the day and into the late night. She likes heavy rock and probably soul music, and she doesn't read much except for escapist magazines such as True Story.

Now consider **Cathy, the contented housewife** (18 percent of the total female population studied). Cathy epitomizes simplicity. Her life is untangled. She is married to a worker in the middle of the socio-economic scale, and they, along with their several pre-teen children, live in a small town. She is devoted to her family and faithfully serves them as mother, housewife and cook. There is a certain tranquility in her life. She enjoys a relaxed pace and avoids anything that might disturb her equilibrium. She does not like news or news-type programs on TV, but she does like wholesome, family TV entertainment.

The Franco-American Division of the Campbell Soup Company recently did a similar study, in which they clustered mothers of children living at home into psychographic segments, including Mother Maturity, Nouveau Mom, Mighty Mom, Sister Superstress, Happy Homemaker and Petticoat Prisoner. These segments made it easier to understand an otherwise broad spectrum of women consumers.

The advantages of segmenting by psychographics are many. It can bring organization to a disordered marketplace. Also, the "Mildreds," "Cathys" and other groups each represent patterns of needs and interests. Having first identified the group and then studied their behaviors which are relevant to what we are promoting, we can better appeal to a given segment or several segments.

Psychographic segmentation can also be built around a specific behavior, such as purchase and usage of a product or service, or performance of a particular disease prevention activity. For example, using vacation preferences and behaviors as the activity, a study was done that yielded a number of segmentation clusters, including those labeled "Nature People" and "Cautious Homebodies."

"Nature People" are said to be young, unmarried and well-educated. They want to go to new and different places, to avoid schedules and routine, and to experience the world generally without the concern about the usual comforts.

"Cautious Homebodies" tend to be older, less-affluent, less-educated and less-concentrated in urban areas. They want safety, security and a perfectly predictable environment on their vacation, without any new experiences.

As you can see, demographic characteristics were combined with psychographic attributes in profiling these vacation-interest segments. This is the kind of research that was done to develop the "I Love New York" tourism campaign, which aims at two different psychographic clusters—the great outdoors lovers and the Manhattan lovers.

One can also use psychographic segmentation to help profile a "typical" person representing a certain behavior. For example, a study of the "accident-prone driver" indicates that this individual is "more likely to be a risk taker, is restless, feels pressured, is likely to be an impulse buyer, has money problems but is optimistic, has a cosmopolitan outlook, is interested in movies, especially x-rated and disaster movies, and is less likely to be socially and politically conservative."

As useful as psychographic segmentation can be, it is not without problems. Reliability is an important consideration. Since psychographic research is relatively new, there are no standardized batteries of activity, interest and opinion scales. A study at Purdue University indicated a wide range in the test–retest reliability of "homemade" AIO items and scales.

Another reliability issue involves the relationship between the behavior being studied and the lifestyle variables. Also, the question must be asked if the groups which emerge are real or if they are merely artifacts of the method of clustering analysis that is used. The question of validity—whether psychographic instruments measure what they are supposed to—is a complex issue. On predictive validity, neither psychographics nor any other approach can predict individual behaviors. However, evidence indicates that psychographic variables do provide sharper contrasts between groups of people than do demographic profiles.

These and other concerns with psychographic research were discussed at the 1982 Attitude Research Conference of the American Marketing Association. Tony Adams, Research Director of the Campbell Soup Company, was given the task of stating the problems with psychographic segmentation. Adams pointed out that what people like and opine may not be very related to what they do. As an example, he cited Real cigarettes, which were based on the psychographic finding that naturalness—an absence of adulterated ingredients and the presence of natural ingredients—was meaningful to a sizable segment of consumers. But positioning a cigarette that way did not translate into product purchase. Real cigarettes did not do well in the marketplace. It's hard to imagine a cigarette being associated with naturalness, which is likely to be a characteristic associated with health, so I find it hard to blame that failure on psychographic research.

Adams also pointed out that lifestyles may predict only a small part of purchase behavior as compared to *benefits* sought by consumers, which does a better job of explaining purchase behavior. He also warned that oversegmentation can result from lifestyle analysis. This fragmentation of audience segments can lead to scattered resources and ineffectiveness.

Adams also said that using lifestyle, or even demographic variables, was not necessarily the best way to study audience media patterns and do media planning. His recommendation was to go directly to the target audience behavior itself as the primary media targeting device.

His final recommendation was to use the desired behavior, not lifestyles, as the independent variable—much like the profile I described earlier of the high-risk driver. This way, Adams said, the potential for taking action with the psychographic data becomes more apparent.

I have talked about what psychographic segmentation is, how it has been utilized, and some of the problems it faces. Now the question arises, how can we apply this technique to better understand health consumers, and better segment audiences for more effective cancer communications?

To explore this issue, we added the agree/disagree statement, "**Cancer is usually fatal,**" to the extensive battery of questions which make up the Needham, Harper & Steers Annual Lifestyle Study. Let's examine the findings for *adult males.* As you know, men are often an extremely tough audience for cancer communication, since they seem to be more inclined to avoid health messages, to have a lower sense of personal susceptibility to disease and to be less likely than women to be in contact with the health care system.

Our first step was to divide the male repondents into two groups: those who were in agreement with the statement that cancer is usually fatal—let's call them the **Male Fatalists** in keeping with the OCC qualitative study; and those who disagreed with the statement—our **Nonfatalists**.

In looking at the demographic characteristics of these two groups, there were no real differences between them in age, in region of the country, population density, or degree of urbanization of their place of residence, or in number of people in their households. There were some demographic differences, however:

- Few Fatalists were college graduates.
- More Fatalists were concentrated in the lowest income category, and fewer were in the higher income categories.
- Fewer Fatalists were professional workers than their Nonfatalist counterparts.

Now, based on the activity, interest and opinion questions of our Lifestyle Study, let's look at the psychographic profile of our Male Fatalist.

In their dietary habits, Fatalists show concern for what they eat. They try to eat natural foods most of the time and would be willing to pay more for products containing all natural ingredients. They feel that they eat more than they should, including snack foods.

The Male Fatalist tends to be on the compulsive side. He is most comfortable when his house is clean; he does not like dirt, and has the urge to empty a full ashtray or wastebasket whenever he sees one.

He feels as though he is under a great deal of pressure most of the time, and wishes he knew how to relax.

While he sees himself as a hard worker, the Male Fatalist despairs of getting ahead, no matter how fast his income rises. Part of this may be that he is not very good at saving money. He sees maximum safety, rather than high interest, as more important in investing, and he feels that the stock market is too risky for most families. When he spends his money, the Fatalist likes to pay cash for what he buys.

Basically, the Male Fatalist tends to be somewhat negative, cautious and conservative. He does not think much of big companies or labor unions, although he is more apt to admire a successful businessperson as compared to someone like an artist or a writer. At the same time, he is not willing to concede that most individuals are honest. He does not favor abortion, he respects law and order, and believes that the police should use force to maintain it. He approves of citizens owning handguns. He sees communism as the greatest peril in the world today. He feels that things are changing too fast, and he often wishes for the good old days. If he had his life to live over, the Fatalist would do things differently.

When it comes to self-confidence, the Male Fatalist has a certain macho attitude. He feels he could handle himself well in a fist fight . . . but at the same time he has got less self-confidence than he sees in his friends. His macho self-image extends to sex roles, also. He is not especially keen on the women's movement, and he is inclined to feel that a woman's real place is in the home (where, incidentally, he believes the father should be the boss). The most important thing in a marriage, as far as the Fatalist is concerned, are the children. But at the same time he thinks that kids today have too many privileges.

The Fatalist prefers a quiet, secure, routine life, both at home and on the job. Television is his primary form of entertainment, although he is disturbed by the amount of sex on prime time TV nowadays.

I think you will agree that we have added a new dimension to our understanding of the adult male who believes that cancer is nearly always fatal. We have gone beyond the skimpy demographic differences between the Fatalist and Nonfatalist. We have put some

flesh on his skeleton, and given ourselves a portrait of the man himself. But several questions come to mind:

1. Does the perception that cancer is fatal actually relate to any health behavior that we want to influence?
2. And now that we have the dimensions of this typical Fatalist, what can we do with them? How can this help us do a better job of cancer communication than when we only had demographic attributes?

Let's hold off for a moment on the second question—how we can use our psychographic profile of the Fatalist. On the first issue—whether an attitude of fatalism is related to cancer *behavior*—I do not think anybody knows. It has been postulated that a sense of fatalism may inhibit positive health behaviors, including early detection. Numerous cancer communication programs have attempted to change this perception of fatalism among public audiences.

As we can see, in profiling our Fatalist, we ignored one of the points I mentioned earlier—that it may be best to have the independent variable center on a **behavior** that we are interested in dealing with, rather than on a lifestyle activity, interest or opinion. We built our segment around a **perception**—that cancer is usually fatal. So let's look at another profile, this one centered on a behavior—or to suit our purposes—a non-behavior; that is, **not** practicing the behavior of breast self-examination (BSE).

In our battery of Needham, Harper & Steers lifestyle questions, we added another behavior question. We asked about BSE as one of the activities which female respondents reported on. We then categorized women into three groups: those who practiced BSE nine or more times per year, those who performed BSE one to eight times, and those who did not perform BSE at all. Demographically, the non-practicers of BSE were similar to the frequent practicers in place of residence, in education and in number of people per household. The non-practicer also tends to be similar to the frequent practicer in age, but is somewhat under-represented in the 45 to 54 year old range, a period in life that is important in breast cancer detection. The non-practicer is more apt to be a clerical worker, and to have pre-teen children living at home. Our non-practicer is also somewhat less likely to be in the higher family income categories.

Now let's look at some psychographic characteristics of the non-practicer in comparison to the frequent practicer of BSE.

The first major area that characterizes our non-practicer is in diet and nutrition. She is relatively *uninterested* in the diet issues that are in the news today—cholesterol, salt, sugar, fried foods, additives, caffeine, fortified foods, low calorie foods, fiber and natural ingredients. She is not all that careful about keeping her weight under control, and she is less concerned with nutrition than most of her friends.

The non-BSE practicer wishes she knew better how to relax, and she prefers a quiet lifestyle. Traveling abroad is not especially appealing to her. She does not see herself as a leader, nor is she particularly self-confident. She is not all that interested in dressing well or in browsing through fashion magazines. She is not necessarily in the happiest time of her life, nor does she feel that her greatest personal achievements lie ahead. She is not particularly satisfied that her family income is high enough to afford important desires, but neither does she pride herself on her ability to save money. Basically, the non-BSE practicer might be considered one of life's **quiet pessimists**.

Now let's return to an earlier question. Once we have the psychographic research in hand, how can we use it in cancer communication? The first use of this technique is obvious—to help us better understand diverse, shadowy groups of consumers. The segmentation insights we obtain from profile analysis add to the demographics we may already have. Psychographics help bring our consumer to life.

Second, lifestyle dimensions may help us select media vehicles to better reach our target audiences. To reach "Mildred, the militant housewife," whom I described earlier, it would be particularly futile to use print vehicles. Daytime television and rock radio appear to be virtually the only media windows into her life.

Third, psychographics can help in the creation and production of more effective, more motivating appeals. A knowledge of the attitudes, opinions and activities of target consumers can result in messages with greater believability, heightened interest and increased personal relevance. The clearer the picture we have, the better our chances to appeal to the Male Fatalist or the BSE Non-Practicer.

Another opportunity for using psychographic research may be in the development or refinement of prevention and detection offerings, such as smoking cessation programs and diet and nutrition recommendations.

Finally, psychographics can be useful in charting target audience trends over periods of time. The profiles of Male Fatalists and BSE Non-Practicers I drew for you this morning are based on a single data collection point. But tracking these segments from year to year can identify changes in these health consumer groups. Also, psychographics can pinpoint other important consumer lifestyle clusters, especially when we combine psychographic attributes with cancer risk factors and audience demographics.

This research technique is not the end of the line for health consumer target segmentation, but psychographics can give us new insights to sharpen our cancer communication efforts and increase our effectiveness.

FAMILY SERVICE, INC.

INTRODUCTION

Family Service was established in 1941 as a private nonprofit organization. In 1942, the agency obtained United Way funding for the addition of a school lunch program. Since that time the agency has undergone a series of name changes in an attempt to reflect changes in service offerings. In 1983 the agency once again operated under the name of Family Service, Inc., and its services included counseling, family life education, and home health care.

During 1983, Ann Marek, director of Community Affairs, became concerned about the community's lack of knowledge regarding available services. Before embarking on an awareness campaign, however, she felt it necessary first to assess the community's attitudes and perceptions toward Family Service as well as attitudes and perceptions toward other agencies offering similar services.

Ann arranged for a local graduate student in marketing to assist with the project. It was determined that the project would involve a market research survey of the general public with emphasis on home health services since the home health market was extremely competitive. Ann felt it was important also to survey physicians because many of Family Service's home health clients were referred by their doctors.

GENERAL PUBLIC SURVEY

Telephone interviewing yielded 184 completed interviews from a random sample of 400 names, drawn from the residence pages of the telephone directory. Respondents were first asked how they would rate the services provided by voluntary organizations in general. Ratings were on a scale of 1 to 5, where 5 was high and 1 was low. The results are shown in Table 1.

Respondents were then asked if they were aware of several specific organizations. Awareness did not mean knowledge of services, only that they were aware of the organization's existence. Respondents were then asked to rate (on a scale of 1 to 5) the overall performance of all organizations of which they were aware. The results are shown in Table 2.

The 75 respondents who were aware of Family Service were also asked what they considered to be the most important criteria in selecting a provider of counseling, home health, and educational services. The results are shown in Table 3.

This case was prepared by Donna Legg.

TABLE 1: Overall rating of voluntary organizations

Excellent (5)	38
Good (4)	87
Fair (3)	14
Poor (2)	1
Very poor (1)	1
No rating	43
Mean = 4.13	
Standard deviation = .781	

PHYSICIAN SURVEY

Telephone interviewing produced 102 completed interviews from a random list of 350 physicians (M.D.s and D.O.s). Each doctor was asked first to rate the efforts of home health organizations in general (scale of 1 to 5). The mean response was 3.8250 with a standard deviation of .612 and 80 no responses.

Physicians were then asked if they were aware of several specific organizations. If aware of an organization, he or she was also

TABLE 2: Awareness and ratings of specific organizations

Organization	No. aware	No. rated	Mean rating
United Way	160	128	3.70
North Texas Home Health Services	36	23	4.00
Crisis Intervention	118	79	3.84
Family Service	75	48	3.90
Meals on Wheels	170	138	4.59
Parenting Guidance Center	100	69	4.12
Visiting Nurses Association	107	72	4.31
Mental Health/ Mental Retardation	154	108	4.11
Home Health Services of Tarrant County	69	41	3.93

TABLE 3: Criteria for selecting provider of services

Criteria	No. of responses
Quality	5
Accreditation	3
Cost	5
Recommendations*	23
Image/reputation	8
Credentials/knowledge of staff	9
Supportive staff	1
Success rate	2
Needs/benefits	2
Tradition	1
Confidentiality	1
Communication	1
Christian organization	1
Don't know	13

* Many respondents specified recommendations from doctors, ministers, school counselors, friends, and relatives.

asked to rate the performance of that organization. The results are shown in Table 4.

The interviewer noted that several doctors had heard of an organization but did not

TABLE 4: Awareness and ratings of specific organizations

Organization	No. aware	No. rated	Mean rating
United Way	94	75	3.68
North Texas Home Health Services	52	35	3.86
Crisis Intervention	65	35	4.03
Family Service	50	38	3.71
Meals on Wheels	89	68	4.25
Parenting Guidance Center	50	28	4.00
Visiting Nurses Association	78	61	3.95
Mental Health/Mental Retardation	91	64	3.63
Home Health Services of Tarrant County	57	41	3.76

know enough about it to rate it. Others, however, said they knew of an organization and had actually referred patients to it but were unable to give a rating because they did not know how well the organization had served the patient.

Doctors were also asked to which home health organizations they refer their patients.

Of the 102 interviewed physicians, 15 reported that they never refer to home health agencies. Of the remaining 87, 25 could not name any specific agency. Several of these 25 stated that they do not make the actual referral—they prescribe the needed services but the nurse or the hospital discharge planner actually selects the provider.

LADY INDIAN BASKETBALL

Benny Hollis, Athletic Director at Northeast Louisiana University (NLU), was very interested in the results of a survey he had just received on his desk. The research had been conducted by his staff in response to Hollis' request for information about the women's basketball program at the university. Although the team was becoming very successful, growth in fan attendance was lagging behind. Hollis hoped that the results of a survey to find out what type of person attended women's basketball games might be used to develop a better program for marketing the sport at NLU.

Northeast Louisiana University is a four-year institution, located in Monroe, Louisiana. It has an enrollment of approximately 11,500 students and offers over 150 degree programs at the undergraduate and/or graduate level in such fields as agriculture, business administration, education, fine arts, home economics, liberal arts, nursing, pharmacy, and pure and applied sciences. Students attend from all areas of Louisiana as

well as from 39 other states and 49 foreign countries. Approximately 65 percent of the students commute to the campus.

NLU is located on the eastern edge of Monroe, a city of almost 60,000. Monroe and West Monroe (15,000 population) are known as the "Twin Cities" since they lie on opposite banks of the Ouachita River. The metropolitan area's population is 140,000. The Twin Cities of northeastern Louisana are located approximately midway between Memphis and New Orleans, and Shreveport (LA) and Jackson (MS). Monroe and West Monroe are the center of a trade area containing over 375,000 people. The Twin Cities are an important distribution center in a 13-parish (county) northeast Louisiana market. The area's industry is well-balanced and diversified.

NLU has a varsity athletic program that has grown rapidly in stature with 19 team sports. The school has one of the top-rated 1-AA football teams in the nation, a water ski team that has dominated the national title for

This case was prepared by David Loudon, C. W. McConkey, and Maynard M. Dolecheck, all of Northeast Louisiana University. Copyright © 1986 by David Loudon, C. W. McConkey, and Maynard M. Dolecheck. Reprinted with permission.

years, an outstanding tennis program, and a winning record in both men's and women's basketball.

The Lady Indians began with the 1974–1975 season. They played 20 games the first year and had a record of 9 victories and 11 defeats. The program did not achieve much notoriety until last year (the 1982–1983 season) when two team members (Lisa Ingram and Eun Jung Lee) were named to All-American teams during their freshman year. During that season the Lady Indians became the first NLU varsity team ever to win an NCAA post-season event. They went 23 and 6 for the season, were undefeated in Southland Conference play, were ranked among the top twenty teams in the nation in four of the eight team statistic categories compiled by the NCAA, and were third in the nation in scoring offense.

Although the Lady Indians were gaining much success, Hollis was not sure that they had been adequately marketed to the relevant groups of fans who might be attracted. Not only was this true at NLU, but around the country women's sports were just beginning to grow.

Many athletic administrators viewed intercollegiate women's sports (which were mandated by Title IX of the Education Amendments of 1972 to achieve equality for women) as a necessary evil—at least an unwanted expense. Nevertheless, the expansion of women's sports was continuing, as evidenced by NCAA legislation requiring Division I schools to sponsor eight women's sports by 1987–1988 instead of the four currently required.

Prior to 1977 expenditures for women's intercollegiate sports were insignificant. Most schools made little effort to expand their women's programs until 1976, as official regulations to enforce Title IX were not published until June 1975. In 1977 aggregate expenditures were only $24.7 million, followed by a dramatic increase to $116 million in 1981. As institutions complied with the new rules, expenditures would be increasing dramatically.

While expenditures for women's athletics had risen dramatically, the revenue side of the ledger had not kept pace. For example, among the 187 institutions classified as Division I (in football) in 1980–1981, women's basketball revenues covered only 17 percent of expenses while men's basketball revenues exceeded expenses by 35 percent.

Although men's football and basketball had been the primary source of athletic revenue at NLU as well as at most colleges, Hollis wondered whether they could carry the mounting burden of women's athletics. Trends from around the country showed that men's football and basketball revenue growth was slowing, as reflected in the fact that average men's basketball attendance was up less than one percent over the average of the previous five seasons.

To Hollis and other athletic directors, women's sports appeared to be an untapped source of revenue for their schools. As John Toner, president of the NCAA, stated, "It seems to me that it is time for women leaders to concentrate on how they can stimulate and enlarge the income from women's programs." The NCAA was leading the way by taking an active part in promoting women's sports. Of the $709,000 in its current year's promotion budget, $347,000 (49 percent) was being spent to promote women's athletics.

Therefore, Hollis believed that the greatest return for the cost, at the present time, was to be found in the promotion of women's basketball. The quality of competition and interest had increased to the point that if the sport were effectively marketed, it could have a significant impact on university athletic income. Additionally, most conferences, including the Southland Conference, had now incorporated women's programs into their conference structures, thus enhancing image and interest. Most of these changes had occurred in just the past three to five years.

Hollis knew that increased revenue from women's basketball would come from growth in attendance and contributions. However, the first step would be to increase attendance since only the fans who are interested and enjoy the game will contribute. Thus, the key seemed to be to develop loyal fans and then move into fundraising.

It was also apparent to Hollis that there was tremendous room for attendance growth in women's basketball. For instance, the average attendance during the current year for all NCAA Division I women's basketball games (excluding double headers with men) was only 555—up 9.25 percent over the previous year. Yet, a few teams such as Louisiana Tech (located 30 miles from NLU), Iowa, and Southern California averaged 5285, 3381, and 3159, respectively, during their season. NLU averaged only 2,441 at home for the season. However, as recently as five years ago, a crowd of 200 was considered good.

Athough the potential for increased attendance appeared to be present, Hollis realized that women's basketball had to be properly marketed. Before an effective marketing plan could be developed, however, the market for women's basketball had to be defined and selected. Then a marketing program could be assembled to attract this target market. Thus, the Sports Information Department planned a survey aimed at learning some things about women's collegiate basketball fans to help establish appropriate marketing strategies.

A questionnaire was developed to administer to patrons at one of the well-attended games during the season (see Figure 1). The single-page, two-sided questionnaire was designed to gain general demographic information as well as to gauge what attracts women's fans to the game.

The questionnaire was distributed at the women's game between Northeast Louisiana University and Louisiana Tech University, held on the campus of NLU. Almost everyone entering the game was offered a questionnaire to complete for usher pickup at halftime. To assure maximum participation, a pencil was supplied with each questionnaire. A total of 2200 questionnaires were distributed and 717 were returned. The collection process was twofold: (1) ushers collected them at halftime, and (2) those who had not completed them could deposit them in boxes provided at all exits.

The results were tabulated and summary tables were provided to Hollis as a report of the findings (see Tables 1–35). As Hollis evaluated the responses, he now had the challenging job of interpreting their meaning for the future marketing direction of the Lady Indian basketball program.

FIGURE 1: Women's college basketball survey

Dear Fan:

   To learn more about the growing interest in WOMEN'S college basketball, please help us by completing this questionnaire. It will take you less than 10 minutes to complete. THANK YOU.

SECTION 1

   For EACH of the statements below, CIRCLE the Number that best describes how much you AGREE with that statement. Please give careful thought to each of the statements.

1. WOMEN's basketball should be the preliminary game to the MEN's game so the fans can view two games for a single admission 1   2   3   4   5   (5)
2. Sufficient tax dollars should be spent on athletics to produce a winning program 1   2   3   4   5   (6)
3. WOMEN's basketball is more entertaining than MEN's basketball because it displays more finesse than physical dominance . 1   2   3   4   5   (7)
4. I select basketball games to attend based on the reputation and ranking of the visiting team............................... 1   2   3   4   5   (8)
5. WOMEN's basketball is one of the best entertainment values available 1   2   3   4   5   (9)
6. I attend WOMEN's basketball because of the urging of my spouse or children.. 1   2   3   4   5   (10)
7. I usually attend WOMEN's basketball games with a friend or neighbor 1   2   3   4   5   (11)
8. I am personally acquainted with one or more players in tonight's game... 1   2   3   4   5   (12)
9. I would be inclined to attend more WOMEN's basketball games when my team is ranked nationally........................ 1   2   3   4   5   (13)
10. I listen to the away games on the radio when I am unable to attend... 1   2   3   4   5   (14)
11. I enjoy participation in recreational activity 1   2   3   4   5   (15)
12. Special event nights (such as T-shirt night) are important to my attending WOMEN's basketball.......................... 1   2   3   4   5   (16)
13. Quality education is more important for WOMEN athletes because of the lack of professional sports opportunities....... 1   2   3   4   5   (17)
14. A successful athletic program is important for a positive University image in the community............................. 1   2   3   4   5   (18)

SECTION 2

   Please supply the following information by either filling in the blanks or circling the number of the appropriate reply:

1. SEX: 1. Male 2. Female (18)   2. MARITAL STATUS: 1. Single 2. Married   (19)

3. NUMBER OF CHILDREN: 0   1   2   3   4   5 or more   (20)

4. THE AGE OF MY YOUNGEST CHILD IS _____   (21-22)

5. EDUCATION (highest level of education attained):   (23)

1. Grade   2. High   3. Vo-Tech   4. Attended   5. College
   School   School   College   Graduate

6. MY AGE IS _____. (23-24)   7. RACE: 1. Black   2. White   3. Other   (25)

8. EMPLOYMENT STATUS:
   1. Retired   2. Homemaker   3. Self-employed   (26)
   4. Employed (not self)   5. Student

9. I have attended the following universities: 1. NLU   2. TECH   3. OTHER   (27)

10. I am a graduate of the following university: 1. NLU   2. TECH   3. OTHER   (28)

11. My children have attended the following universities: (29)
    1. NLU   2. TECH   3. OTHER

12. Circle all of the following that describe you: (30-35)
    1. College athletic club member   2. College alumni association member
    3. Civic club member   4. Country/tennis club member
    5. Fitness club member   6. Union member

13. How many miles have you traveled to see tonight's game?   (36)
    1. 10 or less   2. 11-20   3. 21-50   4. More than 50

14. How many WOMEN's basketball games will you attend this season? _____.   (37-38)

15. How many MEN's basketball games will you attend this season? _____.   (39-40)

16. My interest in WOMEN's basketball started when I was exposed via   (41)
    1. Newspaper   3. Radio   5. Discussion with friend
    2. TV   4. Game attendance

17. For sports information, I depend on: (Rank the following based on frequency of use—1 most used
    thru 8 least used)   (42-49)
    _____KTVE-TV   (42)   _____Ouachita Citizen   (46)
    _____KNOE-TV   (43)   _____Ruston News Leader   (47)
    _____KARD-TV   (44)   _____Monroe News-Star World   (48)
    _____KNLU   (45)   _____Word-of-mouth   (49)

18. Which radio format do you listen to most often?   (50)
    1. Country   2. Soft rock   3. Hard rock   4. Easy listening

19. Other than basketball, which WOMEN's sport would you most enjoy viewing?
    1. Softball   2. Tennis   3. Swimming   4. Track   5. Volleyball   (51)

20. Do you plan to attend the NLU vs. TECH MEN's basketball game on Feb. 9?
     1. Yes   2. No   3. Undecided   (52)

21. Which team are you "rooting" for tonight?   1. TECH   2. NLU   (53)

We need your help ! ! ! !
Would you be willing to spend 15-30 minutes to complete an in-depth questionnaire concerning college athletics? If so, please print your name and address below. Those selected will be mailed a questionnaire (No one will call). Upon completion and return of the questionnaire you will receive a coupon worth $10.00 off the purchase price of each 1984-1985 NLU Women's Basketball Season Ticket as an expression of our appreciation.

         NAME:_____
         ADDRESS:_____
         _____

PLEASE PASS THE COMPLETED QUESTIONNAIRE TO THE END OF THE ROW FOR COLLECTION AS INSTRUCTED BY THE PUBLIC ADDRESS ANNOUNCER—————
THANK YOU.

SECTION 1

TABLE 1

		Response to Statement						
No. 1 Statement:	Classification	SD	D	N	A	SA	Total Percent	Total No. Rspndnts.
WOMEN's basketball should be the preliminary game to the MEN's game so the fans can view two games for a single admission.	Non-student	11.5	22.6	11.7	24.4	29.9	100	(532)
	Student	7.7	17.5	14.7	37.1	23.1	100	(143)
	All Respondents	10.8	21.1	11.8	26.8	29.4	100	(701)

TABLE 2

		Response to Statement						
No. 2 Statement:	Classification	SD	D	N	A	SA	Total Percent	Total No. Rspndnts.
Sufficient tax dollars should be spent on athletics to produce a winning program.	Non-student	9.2	14.8	14.4	34.2	27.5	100	(575)
	Student	5.6	14.0	16.1	37.8	26.6	100	(143)
	All Respondents	9.0	14.2	14.8	34.4	27.6	100	(703)

TABLE 3

| No. 3 Statement: | Classification | Response to Statement | | | | | | |
		SD	D	N	A	SA	Total Percent	Total No. Rspndnts.
WOMEN's basketball is more entertaining than MEN's basketball because it displays more finesse than physical dominance.	Non-student	6.8	19.5	33.0	19.9	20.8	100	(533)
	Student	14.7	20.3	27.3	18.2	19.6	100	(142)
	All Respondents	8.5	19.7	31.6	19.2	20.9	100	(702)

TABLE 4

| No. 4 Statement: | Classification | Response to Statement | | | | | | |
		SD	D	N	A	SA	Total Percent	Total No. Rspndnts.
I select basketball games to attend based on the reputation and ranking of the visiting team.	Non-student	11.7	22.1	23.4	30.4	12.5	100	(531)
	Student	12.7	18.3	23.2	30.3	15.5	100	(142)
	All Respondents	12.2	20.8	23.1	30.8	13.1	100	(697)

TABLE 5

| No. 5 Statement: | Classification | Response to Statement | | | | | | |
		SD	D	N	A	SA	Total Percent	Total No. Rspndnts.
WOMEN's basketball is one of the best entertainment values available.	Non-student	2.9	7.3	18.8	45.4	25.6	100	(520)
	Student	1.4	10.0	30.0	35.7	22.9	100	(140)
	All Respondents	2.5	8.0	20.9	42.9	25.7	100	(685)

TABLE 6

| No. 6 Statement: | Classification | Response to Statement | | | | | | |
		SD	D	N	A	SA	Total Percent	Total No. Rspndnts.
I attend WOMEN's basketball because of urging of my spouse or children.	Non-student	24.2	21.9	42.5	7.4	4.0	100	(525)
	Student	36.2	18.2	33.6	5.1	6.6	100	(137)
	All Respondents	27.4	20.8	40.2	7.1	4.4	100	(686)

TABLE 7

No. 7 Statement:	Classification	Response to Statement						
		SD	D	N	A	SA	Total Percent	Total No. Rspndnts.
I usually attend WOMEN's basketball games with a friend or neighbor.	Non-student	6.7	7.0	30.5	38.7	17.1	100	(525)
	Student	4.9	3.5	8.4	42.7	40.6	100	(143)
	All Respondents	6.3	6.2	25.0	39.8	22.7	100	(693)

TABLE 8

No. 8 Statement:	Classification	Response to Statement						
		SD	D	N	A	SA	Total Percent	Total No. Rspndnts.
I am personally acquaint-ed with one or more players in tonight's game.	Non-student	18.6	17.6	38.7	14.7	10.4	100	(519)
	Student	23.4	12.1	29.8	15.6	19.1	100	(141)
	All Respondents	19.2	16.1	36.8	15.5	12.3	100	(682)

TABLE 9

No. 9 Statement:	Classification	Response to Statement						
		SD	D	N	A	SA	Total Percent	Total No. Rspndnts.
I would be inclined to attend more WOM-EN's basketball games when my team is ranked nationally.	Non-student	6.5	14.1	15.0	33.5	31.0	100	(536)
	Student	4.2	9.9	12.0	28.9	45.1	100	(142)
	All Respondents	6.2	13.4	14.1	32.3	33.9	100	(693)

TABLE 10

No. 10 Statement:	Classification	Response to Statement						
		SD	D	N	A	SA	Total Percent	Total No. Rspndnts.
I listen to the away games on the radio when I am unable to attend.	Non-student	9.1	17.1	19.5	34.3	20.0	100	(519)
	Student	15.5	15.5	23.2	27.5	18.3	100	(142)
	All Respondents	10.3	16.6	20.2	32.8	20.1	100	(682)

TABLE 11

| No. 11 Statement: | Classification | Response to Statement | | | | | | |
		SD	D	N	A	SA	Total Percent	Total No. Rspndnts.
I enjoy participation	Non-student	2.9	5.9	8.2	42.2	40.8	100	(510)
in recreational	Student	1.4	2.1	2.9	29.3	64.3	100	(140)
activity.	All Respondents	2.7	5.1	7.0	39.1	45.1	100	(672)

TABLE 12

| No. 12 Statement: | Classification | Response to Statement | | | | | | |
		SD	D	N	A	SA	Total Percent	Total No. Rspndnts.
Special event nights (such as T-shirt night) are important to my at-	Non-student	22.3	29.5	32.6	9.7	5.9	100	(525)
tending WOMEN's	Student	18.2	20.3	33.6	14.0	14.0	100	(143)
basketball.	All Respondents	21.4	26.9	33.1	10.5	8.1	100	(692)

TABLE 13

| No. 13 Statement: | Classification | Response to Statement | | | | | | |
		SD	D	N	A	SA	Total Percent	Total No. Rspndnts.
Quality education is more important for WOMEN athletes be- cause of the lack of	Non-student	7.6	12.7	14.6	34.2	30.8	100	(526)
professional sports op-	Student	9.9	8.5	23.9	33.1	24.6	100	(142)
portunities.	All Respondents	8.4	12.3	16.6	33.2	29.5	100	(692)

TABLE 14

| No. 14 Statement: | Classification | Response to Statement | | | | | | |
		SD	D	N	A	SA	Total Percent	Total No. Rspndnts.
A successful athletic program is important for	Non-student	3.6	5.3	6.8	35.5	49.0	100	(533)
a positive university	Student	2.1	1.4	8.4	46.2	42.0	100	(142)
image in the community.	All Respondents	3.3	5.0	7.1	37.0	47.6	100	(700)

SECTION 2

TABLE 15

Sex	Non-Student	Student	Total
Male	50.1%	50.0%	50.5%
Female	49.9	50.0	49.5
Total	100.0 (529)	100.0 (142)	100.0 (891)

TABLE 16

Marital Status	Non-Student	Student	Total
Single	22.3%	91.0%	38.1%
Married	77.7	9.0	61.9
Total	100.0 (466)	100.0 (133)	100.0 (620)

TABLE 17

Number of Children	Non-Student	Student	Total
0	24.2%	95.1%	39.5%
1	17.7	2.1	10.2
2	37.3	2.1	26.4
3	18.3	0.7	14.1
4	9.2	0.0	7.0
5 or more	3.5	0.0	2.9
Total	100.0 (545)	100.0 (144)	100.0 (717)

TABLE 18

The Age of My Youngest Child Is	Non-Student	Student	Total
6 or under	18.6% (77)	70.0% (7)	19.9% (87)
7–14	25.4 (105)	20.0 (2)	25.1 (110)
15–19	19.1 (79)	0.0 (0)	18.9 (80)
20 or over	36.8 (152)	10.0 (1)	36.1 (159)
Total	100.0 (413)	100.0 (10)	100.0 (438)
Median	16.55	4.28	16.32

TABLE 19

Highest Level of Education Attained	Non-Student	Student	Total
Grade school	0.2%	2.8%	0.7%
High school	20.8	12.1	18.4
Vo-Tech	3.0	0.0	2.3
Attended college	28.5	75.2	38.3
College graduate	47.4	9.9	40.2
Total	100	100	100

TABLE 20

Age	Non-Student	Student	Total
1–24	11.5%	94.2%	29.8%
25–34	21.3	4.3	17.4
35–44	30.2	0.7	23.3
45–54	20.9	0.7	16.8
55–59	5.6	0.0	4.5
60 or over	10.5	0.0	8.1
Total	100	100	100

TABLE 21

Race	Non-Student	Student	Total
Black	3.0%	5.8%	4.1%
White	96.8	93.5	95.2
Other	0.2	0.7	0.7
Total	100.0 (529)	100.0 (139)	100.0 (641)

TABLE 22

Employment Status	Total
Retired	7.0%
Homemaker	8.9
Self-employed	12.3
Employed (not self)	50.9
Student	20.9
Total	100.0 (689)

TABLE 23

Universities Attended	Non-Student	Student	Total
NLU	51.5%	89.8%	60.1%
La Tech	18.3	6.3	15.8
Other	20.8	0.0	16.0
Both	9.4	3.9	8.0
Total	100	100	100

TABLE 24

University Graduated	Non-Student	Student	Total
NLU	47.2%	68.4%	48.8%
La Tech	26.4	21.1	26.1
Other	25.3	10.5	24.1
Both	1.1	0.0	1.0
Total	100	100	100

TABLE 25

My Children Have Attended the Following Universities	Non-Student	Student	Total
NLU	51.7%	33.3%	50.9%
La Tech	17.4	0.0	17.0
Other	20.8	66.7	22.4
Both	10.2	0.0	9.7
Total	100.0 (265)	100.0 (9)	100 .0 (277)

TABLE 26

Member of:	Non-Student	Student	Total
College athletic club	16.7%	9.0%	14.8%
College alumni association	23.7	4.2	19.0
Civic club	21.8	8.3	19.5
Country/tennis club	15.0	13.9	14.5
Fitness club	17.6	18.8	17.3
Union	5.1	1.4	6.5

TABLE 27
Question: How many miles did you travel to see tonight's game?

No. of Miles	Non-Student	Student	Total
10 or less	45.1%	83.1%	52.6%
11–20	11.5	3.7	10.2
21–50	22.9	7.4	19.7
More than 50	20.5	5.9	17.5
Total	100	100	100

TABLE 28
Question: How many women's basketball games will you attend this season?

No. of Games	Non-Student	Student	Total
1	14.6%	11.6%	14.2%
2–5	39.5	35.7	38.2
6–10	21.7	25.6	22.5
11 or more	24.2	27.1	25.2
Total	100	100	100

TABLE 29
Question: How many men's basketball games will you attend this season?

No. of Games	Non-Student	Student	Total
0	27.5%	14.7%	25.2%
1	8.0	10.1	8.4
2–5	29.9	38.0	31.5
6–10	12.4	22.5	14.2
11 or more	22.2	14.7	20.7
Total	100	100	100

TABLE 30
Statement: My interest in women's basketball started when I was exposed via:

	Non-Student	Student	Total
Newspaper	13.5%	4.5%	11.6%
TV	12.9	7.5	11.8
Radio	3.2	2.3	3.3
Game attendance	51.4	66.9	54.6
Discussion with friend	19.0	18.8	18.7
Total	100	100	100

TABLE 31
Sources of information on women's basketball by gender

Source	Male	Female
Television	55.9%	63.7%
Newspapers	40.0	27.7
Word-of-mouth	4.1	8.6
Total	100.0	100.0

TABLE 32
Statement: For sports information I depend on:

	Rank			
	1	*2*	*3*	*4*
KNOE (TV)	51.7%	31.3%	10.4%	5.5%
Monroe News-Star World (newspaper)	29.2	32.5	18.4	11.6
KTVE (TV)	6.2	17.5	25.1	26.0
Word-of-mouth	6.3	9.0	22.1	17.9
KNLU (university radio station)	1.9	2.2	4.5	9.2
KARD (TV)	0.8	2.4	10.2	21.7
Ruston News Leader (newspaper)	2.8	2.2	2.5	1.7
Ouachita Citizen (biweekly paper)	1.1	2.9	6.7	6.4
	100.0	100.0	100.0	100.0

TABLE 33
Question: Which radio format do you listen to most often?

Response	*Non-Student*	*Student*	*Total*
Country	46.1%	10.0%	38.4%
Soft rock	21.4	67.1	31.1
Hard rock	4.4	17.1	7.3
Easy listening	28.1	5.7	23.2
Total	100	100	100

TABLE 34
Question: Other than basketball, which women's sport would you most enjoy viewing?

Sport	*Non-Student*	*Student*	*Total*
Softball	40.0%	38.8%	39.4%
Tennis	23.7	26.4	24.2
Track	13.6	15.5	14.1
Volleyball	12.0	11.6	12.0
Swimming	10.8	7.8	10.3
Total	100	100	100

TABLE 35
Question: Do you plan to attend the NLU vs. Tech men's basketball game?

Response	*Non-Student*	*Student*	*Total*
Yes	41.1%	62.3%	45.3%
No	32.6	9.4	28.2
Undecided	26.2	28.3	26.5
	100	100	100

PART II

STRATEGIC PLANNING AND ORGANIZATION

Strategic planning and organizational aspects of nonprofit decision-making are examined in this part of the book. The importance of a firm commitment to strategic planning in nonprofit organizations is paramount to success in today's changing environment. A strong marketing orientation in the decision process is vital in order to weigh the pros and cons of various decision factors in the competitive environment. This section focuses on the challenges and benefits of such a strategy.

The first article, "Cost-Conscious Marketing Research" by Alan R. Andreasen, examines various myths associated with marketing research as perceived by managers of small businesses and nonprofit organizations. It attempts to show why they are misleading and suggests several approaches to low cost research.

In the second article, "Strategic Planning for Higher Education," Philip Kotler and Patrick E. Murphy stress the importance of planning for the long-run survivability of colleges and universities. Strategic planning is cited as the most appropriate type of planning in terms of adapting to a changing environment. Strategic planning is defined and a strategic planning process model is analyzed.

The third article in Part II is "Strategic Planning for Nonprofit Health Care Organization Funding" by O. C. Ferrell, Charles S. Madden, and Donna Legg. This article addresses the intense competition that nonprofit health care organizations are experi-

encing and their subsequent difficulties in maintaining current funding levels. This paper outlines a general strategic planning framework for constituency support of health care organizations and illustrates the application aspects of the framework through a nonprofit mental health program.

The next article, "The Baptists Want You" written by William Martin, examines how the Baptist General Convention of Texas developed an extensive marketing program to increase the membership of the church. This program included consumer research to help determine the creative strategy for the advertising campaign, a marketing budget of more than $1.5 million, and coordination of the efforts of 4200 Baptist churches, their ministers, and members.

"Non-Profits Need Development Orientation to Survive," by Charles W. Lamb, Jr., stresses the importance of a development orientation to the success of non-profit organizations. The adoption of a development/marketing orientation has been the trend for the most progressive and successful fundraising organizations. This very practical article contrasts a campaign orientation versus a development orientation in terms of fundraising strategy and outlines the important considerations facing managers who attempt to position their institutions in challenging times.

The last article is "Marketing's Application to Fund Raising" by William A. Mindak and H. Malcolm Bybee. The article examines how effective marketing concepts and tools are when applied to a nonbusiness enterprise. The authors try to determine the answer to this question through the application of marketing techniques to a charitable fund drive for the March of Dimes. They found that careful marketing analysis and planning produced the first net increase in donations the fund had experienced in 12 years.

Five cases are included in Part II. "Ozark Saints Hospital (A)" and "(B)" concern a health care organization that is in need of a long-range marketing strategy. In "Ozark Saints Hospital (A)," the director of the hospital expresses a need for a comprehensive survey of the attitudes of physicians and patients. The case focuses on assessing alternative research options.

In "Ozark Saints Hospital (B)," a consultant has been hired and the study has been conducted. The major focus of this case is integrating the results into a long-term competitive strategy.

In "Planned Parenthood of Atlanta," a summer intern is faced with the responsibility of designing a research study. The focus of the case is on developing an appropriate research plan.

"Robert N. Maxwell Memorial Community Hospital" is a well-known major institution serving a large metropolitan area. Top management feels that the present marketing organization is not capable of keeping the hospital competitive in a rapidly changing environment. The case focuses on assessing alternative organization options.

The "League of Catholic Women" is suffering declining membership and financial problems. Information about the organization's structure, how members are recruited, and the results of a survey are presented. The focus is on identifying strengths, weaknesses, opportunities, and possible strategies for arresting and reversing the prevailing trends.

Cost-Conscious Marketing Research

ALAN R. ANDREASEN

Among managers of small businesses and nonprofit organizations, the term marketing research *frequently conjures up images of lengthy surveys, complicated mathematics, and, above all, high price tags. To many, marketing research is something understandable and affordable only to managers of large companies. The author contends that such images spring from five misconceptions. He advises managers to consider alternatives to the full-length, expensive survey as legitimate forms of marketing research—techniques such as test marketing, focus group interviews, visual observations, and the use of secondary sources. More important than the research approach, he contends, is the relationship of the information desired to the decision to be reached. Managers can often get what they want from research without using sophisticated means or going to great expense.*

Many small businesses and nonprofit organizations assiduously avoid more than a cursory flirtation with marketing research because they misunderstand what it is and what it can accomplish. Five misconceptions often dominate managers' thinking about it:

1. *The "big decision" myth*. You turn to marketing research only when you have a major decision to make; otherwise it has little to do with the details of day-to-day decision making.
2. *The "survey myopia" myth*. With its random samples, questionnaires, computer printouts, and statistical analyses, marketing research is synonymous with field survey research.
3. *The "big bucks" myth*. Marketing research is so expensive that it can only be used by the wealthiest organizations, and then only for their major decisions.
4. *The "sophisticated researcher" myth*. Since research involves complex and ad-

vanced technology, only trained experts can and should pursue it.
5. *The "most research is not read" myth*. A very high proportion of marketing research is irrelevant to managers or simply confirms what they already know. Often the research is so poorly designed and written up or so esoteric that it simply ends up in the bottom drawer.

In this article I consider each of the myths and show why they are misleading. Then I suggest several approaches to low-cost research.

THE "BIG DECISION" MYTH

Too often, marketing research is deemed necessary only for decisions involving large financial stakes and in such cases should always be carried out. But research should be viewed from a cost-benefit perspective. Its costs are usually of two types—the expenses for the research itself and the amount

Reprinted by permission of the Harvard Business Review. "Cost-Conscious Marketing Research" by Alan R. Andreasen (July–August 1983). Copyright © 1983 by the President and Fellows of Harvard College; all rights reserved.

of lost sales and lost competitive advantage caused by delaying a decision until the results are in. The benefits result from improving the quality of decisions under consideration. Any improvement, in turn, is a function of the stakes involved and how uncertain you are about the rightness of your course of action. Note that the benefits of research are proportional to the manager's uncertainty about which way to go, not to the uncertainty about the future.

The cost-benefit ratio may often come out against research even when the stakes are high. Take the case of the restaurant manager thinking of adding a line of Mexican dishes to the menu and investing in a series of advertisements to promote this innovation. He called in a research professional to design a study of local food preferences that would show how likely acceptance of the repositioning strategy would be. Although such a study could cost several thousand dollars, the researcher determined in extended discussions with the manager that unless the survey found virtually no interest in Mexican food in the area, the manager was going ahead with the decision to add the line.

The manager was highly uncertain about the market, but he *was* certain that this decision was best. The researcher convinced the manager that the research expenditure was unnecessary and that the money could more productively be used to ensure that the new line got the advertising send-off it needed to have the best chances of succeeding.

On the other hand, research can be justified even when the amount at stake is not very great. This is the case whenever the research can be done inexpensively, will not take very long to complete, and will help clarify which actions to take.

These conditions often accompany advertising copy decisions. While total expenditures are small, managers do usually have two or three candidate ads, each of which seems to have potential worth. Showing the ads to a small but representative set of prospective target customers—very modest research—usually reveals one superior candidate or at least, by pointing out serious defects in one or two candidate ads, allows a narrowing of the choice. This process has a fringe benefit in that once in a while it produces extremely good suggestions for entirely different ads.

Research may also be justifiable when the stakes initially appear modest but later turn out to have been undervalued. In this regard, it is generally useful to think through the monetary consequences of making a poor decision. When one considers the possible side effects of a bad decision on such things as the organization's reputation, its ability to attract funding and staff, and its sales of related products, the costs may be very high indeed. Such is often the case when small businesses or nonprofits venture beyond their national borders and assume that what works in their home countries will work overseas. The international community is replete with horror stories of marketing gaffes with long-term consequences that could have been avoided with a little research.

You may grant the argument thus far but then assert that there is no low-cost research to meet these challenges, that the suggestions for research made previously involve the proverbial quick-and-dirty study that may well be worse than no research at all. The only good research, you say, is a survey carefully done. This contention leads me to the second major misconception about the use of research.

THE "SURVEY MYOPIA" MYTH

Any reliable information that improves marketing decisions can be considered marketing research. If you take this view, many alternatives to formal survey research come to mind. Consider the entrepreneur thinking of introducing a new service but having no idea whether the target market will accept the service or, even with acceptance, how quickly it can be expected to reach break-even. If successful, the new service would yield a contribution to profits of only a few thousand dollars in the first few years. The entrepreneur could conduct a survey to reduce this uncertainty. However, to make the research 95% certain of being within two percentage points of the break-even market share figure of 10%, the entrepreneur must make the sample size 900.

An experienced survey researcher would estimate that, assuming the questionnaire and sampling plan are already designed and ignoring analysis and report preparation costs, simply completing the interviews would cost between $3,000 and $7,000. (The amount would depend on the duration and type of interviews done.)

Clearly, such research would eat up the entrepreneur's initial years' contribution profits. More important is the question whether the research would yield valid data in any case. That is, one should ask whether it is reasonable to expect respondents to be candid about or even to know their likely behavior with respect to this new service, especially if many feel it would not be gracious to disappoint the interviewer or the research sponsor by showing little enthusiasm for the venture.

How else, then, might the survey research objectives be achieved at lower cost? The company can try test marketing in representative markets. This approach has the virtue of not only lowering costs but yielding useful data (that is, it shows what people *will* do, not what they *say* they will do). Testing in a number of markets also allows alternative marketing strategies to be systematically evaluated.

Another low-cost approach is the commissioning of focus group interviews of 8 to 12 members of the target audience at a time. Although the results are not strictly projectable to the larger market because the groups are not randomly selected, these results do cut the cost of interviewing by a quarter or a half. Interviewers can sometimes develop richer data in the relaxed, chatty format of the focus group.

Also, the groups can at least alert management to problems with the new service that would sabotage its introduction, as they might in foreign markets. When a company uses several focus group sessions covering the range of people likely to be target market members for the new venture, officials can spot serious problems mentioned by a modest number of participants and abort a service or product launching. Elaborate probability sampling designs are simply not necessary to satisfy this objective.

THE "BIG BUCKS" MYTH

Marketing research is much more diverse than the inexperienced observer would think. There are many inexpensive alternatives to surveys:

1 Systematic observation. Managers can obtain many kinds of marketing data simply by carefully observing behavior. Retailers have found pedestrian and vehicle traffic counts to be invaluable in assessing the success of competitors' new products or services and in evaluating new outlet locations. To gauge the effectiveness of in-store displays or packages, a staff person can record patrons' reactions. The video cameras now commonly installed for security can also be used for this purpose.

Managers can determine the relative importance of outlet or product features by recording customers' questions and comments in the outlets themselves. Automobile dealers and service station managers have studied their customers' radio station preferences simply be observing the dial settings of cars brought in for service. Salespeople who regularly visit customers can record their reactions to new offers and their future purchase plans as well as take advantage of their knowledge about competitors' plans.

Note that what distinguishes marketing research from casual observation or a "feel" for the market is careful specification of the needed observations, systematic observation, observation at random times and places (where possible, by a variety of observers), and careful recording and analysis of results.

2 Secondary sources. Industry, government, and academic reports and papers often yield data on similar ventures tried elsewhere. Reports of case studies may alert managers to fatal defects.

A medium-sized art museum, for example, learned the value of researching the experience of others when it was planning a program to expose low-income children to the art world. To launch this program, the museum director tried to kill two birds with one stone by inviting government supporters, private sponsors, and influential citizens to observe the first night's "encounter with culture" and see firsthand what a noble enterprise they were associated with. Before proceeding, however, the director conducted an informal telephone survey of museums in other cities to determine if they had staged similar events. What she learned caused her to change her plans drastically.

Another museum that tried the very same approach reported disastrous results. It found that its supporters were horrified to observe children of low-income families hollering and tearing about in the hallowed museum corridors—quite natural behavior for children—and actually touching the statues and other works of art. Mr. and Mrs. Uppercrust, who had given $500,000 for the Jean Tinguely kinetic sculpture, were not at all pleased to see enthusiastic ghetto youths giving the Tinguely kinetics a little help. Donations dropped sharply (although no one ever said anything), and many months and careful countermarketing were needed to overcome the harm.

Secondary data may also provide information about the time needed to gain acceptance. In most cases, entrepreneurs searching through secondary sources can often make effective use of library-based computerized information retrieval systems.

3 Archival research. Valuable marketing research data are already available to many organizations and are simply waiting to be analyzed by the enterprising entrepreneur. For example, owners can glean very good insights into competitors' advertising strategies or pricing practices from a trip to the local newspaper and from scanning past issues of the paper selected at random. Zip code data on existing charge customers can yield much about the geographic dispersion and travel patterns of a store's or a theater's customers and, when supplemented by census data, can indicate income, education, and other household characteristics of these customers.

4 Systematic experimentation. Many regular marketing efforts of small businesses and nonprofit organizations are amenable to experimental manipulation. For example, by varying themes in routine fund-raising mailings, a nonprofit manager can accumulate a great deal of scientifically validated information about which marketing strategies work and which do not. Also, newspaper advertisements can be varied so that the managers will learn the effects of ad size, the ratio of white space to copy, and the use of photographs. Even if a survey must be done, managers can reduce research costs with these approaches:

☐   Convenience samples involving systematic querying of customer contacts, for example. Such samples are often adequate for many exploratory research purposes to identify potential marketing problems or to develop advertising or new product ideas. Indeed, many organizations miss important opportunities for collecting data from those with whom they regularly come in contact. Salespeople can easily query customers coming to an outlet, hospital officials can interview patients, and anyone can ask opinion leaders met at meetings or cocktail parties questions about current managerial concerns.

The success of such surveys depends on careful formulation of the questions in advance, recognition of biases, thoroughness in carrying out the questioning, and systematic recording and analysis of the results.

☐ Snowball sampling, which is the expansion of a convenience sample of present customers by a manager who asks respondents to suggest others to query. Although obviously a biased procedure, snowball sampling has several advantages. If you use the original respondents' names in an introduction to the second set of interviewees, you can significantly improve the chances of getting their cooperation in your research.

Furthermore, the demographics and lifestyle characteristics of the second sample are likely to resemble those of the original respondents. The new sample will differ in one respect only: the respondents will not be regular customers or contacts of the surveying organization.

Snowball sampling is also a unique way to find rare populations. Customers for particular low-volume products and services can often point the way to others who could be surveyed—others who already have these items and services or are thinking of obtaining them from competitors.

☐ Omnibus surveys, which commercial research suppliers conduct regularly. They can often include a few key questions of interest to a marketing manager. The costs per question can be kept low since several clients share them. And, if you are from a legitimate nonprofit organization, some research suppliers may, at little or no cost, include a few questions on an omnibus survey as a public service.

Sometimes volunteers and colleges are willing to help carry out such research. Many nonprofit organizations regularly have access to pools of volunteers—through local service clubs, for instance. You can assign a few such volunteers to routine survey responsibilities, see that they are trained in survey techniques, and closely supervise their work. The volunteers should be treated as professionals, not as unpaid helpers. As noted earlier, bad research is often much worse than no research at all.

Many colleges that have marketing research courses are seeking businesses to serve as field survey research cases for term projects. Again, the key is to make certain that these inexperienced researchers are carefully trained and supervised.

THE "SOPHISTICATED RESEARCHER" MYTH

Just as marketing research need not involve complex sampling and elaborate designs, and indeed often purposely lacks randomization, so a high level of sophistication in sampling techniques, statistics, and computer analysis is not essential. Of course, executives of small businesses and nonprofits planning to undertake programs of research should acquaint themselves with at least the rudimentary principles of random sampling, questionnaire design, and graphic presentation of results.

Even when managers need high levels of

sophistication—for example, if elaborate experiments or careful field study projects are being planned—they can get low-cost assistance on an ad hoc basis. Professors at local colleges are one resource. An alternative particularly appropriate to nonprofit organizations is the voluntary help of local professional researchers. Smaller companies and nonprofits contemplating extended research programs may want to ask marketing research professionals to sit on their boards of directors.

THE "MOST RESEARCH IS NOT READ" MYTH

Unfortunately, executives who would rather not bother with research or who subconsciously fear the results use this rationale for their inaction. Poor research certainly does occur, but when it does it is usually a testimonial to poor planning. In my experience, no piece of well-planned research has ever been rejected as unhelpful, although it may be ignored on other, often political, grounds.

How can one ensure that research will not be wasted effort? The answer rests with both the manager requesting the research and the researcher doing it. Research will be most valuable when:

1. It is undertaken after the manager has made clear to the researcher what the decision alternatives are and what it is about those decisions that necessitates additional information.

2. The relationship between the results and the decision is clearly understood. For the manager, the researcher should prepare hypothetical tables of results indicating likely outcomes for the proposed effort. Depending on the manager's reactions to the tables, revisions can be made to bring the research on target.

3. The results are communicated well. If hypothetical results are presented, the manager should become quite familiar with the intricacies of the research design and be able to appreciate the nuances of the findings when they are finally produced.

Research need not be intimidating. It can play an important role in effective management. While research is not appropriate to all business decisions, it shouldn't be neglected just because managers of small businesses and nonprofits entertain myths about the process. Rather, executives should be prepared to carefully analyze the particular conditions under which research of various kinds is warranted and to consider the wide range of possible low-cost designs. The payoffs from a less myopic approach to the marketing research function can be substantial.

Strategic Planning for Higher Education

PHILIP KOTLER • PATRICK E. MURPHY

At least one demographic impact will be positive. Institutions will be compelled to become more introspective and analytical, to undertake long-range planning, something they did not have to do in good times. They will be forced to set priorities and develop strategies, overcome institutional inertia and make long-overdue choices—for example, to identify areas of growing student interest and create new programs to replace those for which demand may have fallen off. A consumer orientation will benefit higher education. [17, p. 23]

If colleges and universities are to survive in the troubled years ahead, a strong emphasis on planning is essential. The type of planning that appears to be most appropriate for the future is "strategic" market planning. It is one of the most revolutionary commercial sector developments in the last ten years and promises to be a potent tool for use in nonprofit organizations.

Most colleges and universities are not set up with a strategic planning capacity. They are basically good at *operations*, that is, efficiently doing the same things day after day. Patterns of operation were traditionally established to meet the environmental conditions and opportunities; the schools' manner of conducting their affairs are likely to

persist long after these procedures have lost their effectiveness in new environments.

Organizational leaders—boards, major administrators, and faculty representatives—are the only ones who can modify organizations through time as the environments change. Yet few collegiate leaders are able and willing to focus systematically on change. They are largely taken up in today's operations and results. Making changes in the goals, strategies, and organizational systems usually occurs as reactions to crisis events rather than as thoughtful adaptations in advance of crises.

The general notion of planning, however, is not new to higher education. For some time, many institutions have undertaken three major levels of planning. The first level refers to the *budgeting and scheduling process*. All schools are forced to do this level of planning. A second level encompasses *short-range planning*. Major areas of concern here involve recruiting of students, physical plant decisions, development efforts, and program (curricular) modifications. The majority of colleges and universities are engaged, to some degree, in short-range planning. *Long-range planning* represents the third level. This type of planning utilizes both quantitative and qualitative assessments of the exter-

Philip Kotler and Patrick E. Murphy, "Strategic Planning for Higher Education," *Journal of* *Higher Education*, 52 (September–October 1981), 470–89.

FIGURE 1: Strategic planning process model

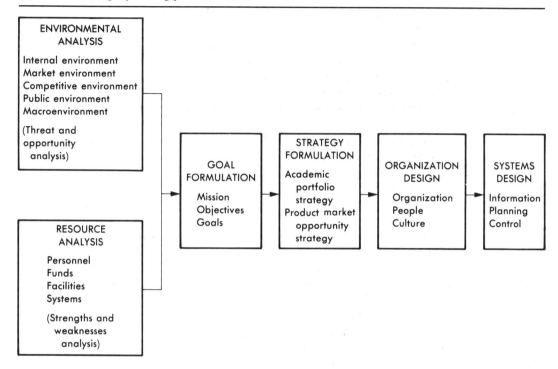

nal environment to determine institutional priorities and strategies. Specifically, devising the school's mission and deciding about long-range program additions or deletions are usually part of the long-range planning process.[1] Other than in the area of "exigency" planning, most planning documents do not serve as a blueprint or become institutionalized [15]. Only a few schools presently seem to be effectively using long-range planning in their organization.

Strategic planning should not be confused with any of the planning levels currently used in higher education. It takes a long-run approach, but the focus is much more comprehensive and strategic than traditional

long-range planning. *Strategic planning is defined as the process of developing and maintaining a strategic fit between the organization and its changing marketing opportunities.*

This definition suggests the appropriate steps that a college or university can take to improve itself (see Figure 1). First, the institution must carry out a careful analysis of its *environment*, both today's and tomorrow's probable one. Then it must review its major *resources* as providing a key to what it can accomplish. The environment and resource analyses allow the organization to formulate new and appropriate *goals* that it wishes to pursue for the planning horizon. Goal formulation is followed by *strategy development* in which the most cost-effective strategy is chosen for reaching the goals. The strategy will

---

[1] For a discussion of the increasing role of the public policymakers in academic planning, see [8].

undoubtedly indicate certain changes that the institution must make in the *organization structure* if it is to implement the strategy. Finally, attention is turned to improving the organization's *systems* of information, planning, and control to permit carrying out the strategy effectively. When these components are aligned, they promise improved performance.

The strategic planning process should be completed at each major institutional level. First, the president and vice-presidents should undertake strategic planning as it affects the college or university as a whole. Then each dean (e.g., liberal arts school, business school, music school) should formulate strategic plans that impact the future of that college. In turn, each department chairperson can carry out strategic planning for the department. If a university operates branches in different locations, each branch should also utilize strategic techniques.

The president should begin the strategic planning process by setting parameters and stating organizational assumptions. This procedure is hierarchical in the context that overall goals are generally set at the top. As mentioned above, each dean and department chairperson would develop a strategic plan and send it up to the high level administrators. Then, the top administrators would examine all plans. There would likely be more than one iteration to this process. In fact, it may take on a negotiation flavor. The strategic planning process is a sequential one where the goals and broad assumptions go from the top down, but the detailed plans come from the bottom up.

Obviously, strategic planning procedures in higher education do not precisely parallel the process in a business setting. Since academic institutions are characterized by a high concentration of professionals and usually a significant amount of organizational

inflexibility, planning is more democratized. The faculty senate or other faculty representatives have a crucial role to play in the planning endeavors of most colleges and universities. Therefore, administrators do not simply select the most cost-effective strategy, as business managers do, because they must consider a variety of organizational and behavioral constraints.

The stages of the strategic planning process for an academic institution will be examined using Beloit College as an example. Beloit is a nine-hundred student liberal arts college situated in southern Wisconsin. Its enrollment dropped substantially in the mid-1970s, and the administrators instituted several major changes at the school that helped to ensure the school's long-term viability. These alterations can be analyzed using the formal strategic planning procedure.[2]

ENVIRONMENTAL ANALYSIS

The first step in strategic planning is to carefully analyze the environment, because the environment keeps changing and calls for new organizational strategies. The major questions in an environmental audit are: (1) What are the major trends in the environment? (2) What are the implications of these trends for the organization? and (3) What are the most significant opportunities and threats? These questions must be examined for each major part of the organization's environment:

- *internal environment* (board of directors, administrators, faculty, and staff)
- *market environment* (traditional students, nontraditional students, alumni, source of funds, employers, and graduate schools)

[2] The authors would like to express their appreciation to Zeddie P. Bowen, provost of Beloit College, for providing information about his school. For more discussion on Beloit's planning, see [14].

- *public environment* (financial, media, government, activist, local, and general public)
- *competitive environment* (direct, type, and generic)
- *macroenvironment* (demographic, economic, technological, political, and cultural).

The aim is to produce a documented picture of the most significant environmental developments around which the organization must formulate its future goals, strategies, structures, and systems. For example, Fox [7] conducted an in-depth analysis of the macroenvironment. She described several key trends, along with their implications for colleges and universities.

For any trend analysis of an environment to be maximally useful, it should be converted into an opportunities-threats audit. A useful exercise for academic planners is to draw out several major opportunities and threats from the trend information. Threat analysis will first be described, then opportunity analysis.

Threat Analysis

Every institution of higher education must establish some early warning system to identify and evaluate threats. A threat is defined as follows: "An *environmental threat* is a challenge posed by an unfavorable trend or specific disturbance in the environment that would lead, in the absence of purposeful action, to the stagnation, decline, or demise of an organization or one of its programs." Not all threats warrant the same attention or concern. Administrators should assess each threat according to two dimensions: (1) its potential *severity* as measured by the amount of money or prestige the organization would lose if the threat materialized and (2) its *probability* of occurrence.

Beloit College detected the following threats in the environmental analysis:

1. In the market environment, they found that most of their student body came from northern and eastern states where the college age population is projected to decline most severely in the future.
2. In the public environment, they determined that the local Beloit community was rather apathetic toward the college and might not support student employment or cooperate with class projects in the future.
3. In the competitive environment, Beloit officials felt that their direct competitors

TABLE 1: Threat and opportunity matrix

A.   Threat matrix

Potential severity	Probability of occurrence	
	High	*Low*
High	1.4	3
Low		2

B.   Opportunity matrix

Potential attractiveness	Probability of success	
	High	*Low*
High	1.3	
Low	2	2

were private, prestigious, well-known institutions such as Carleton (Minnesota), Grinnell (Iowa), and Oberlin (Ohio). It was felt that these institutions might become much more aggressive in recruiting students in the 1980s.
4. In the macroenvironment, Beloit is a private school with a high tuition, and the economic environment represents a threat to them.

Table 1(A) shows an evaluation of these threats. The most serious threats—those that Beloit must monitor and be prepared to effectively respond to—are those with a severe impact and high probability (1 and 4). It can ignore threats that are low in both severity and probability, such as threat 2. Beloit should monitor, but need not prepare contingency plans, for threats such as action by competitors (3). By identifying and classifying threats, this college has a better system for knowing which environmental developments to monitor, plan for, or ignore.

Opportunity Analysis

Opportunity analysis can be potentially more important than threat analysis. By managing its threats successfully, an institution of higher education stays intact, but does not grow. But by managing its opportunities successfully, the school can make great strides forward. A marketing opportunity is defined as follows: "A *marketing opportunity* is an attractive area of relevant action in which a particular organization is likely to enjoy superior competitive advantages." Not all opportunities are equally attractive. An opportunity can be assessed in terms of two basic dimensions: (1) its potential *attractiveness* as measured by the amount of revenue or other results that an organization might value and (2) the *probability* that the institution will be successful in developing the opportunity.

Beloit College officials determined that several marketing opportunities were open to them.

1. In a survey of employers, Beloit found that the demand for liberal arts graduates with some emphasis in applications areas was strong.
2. In the public environment, they detected that there was still strong sentiment on the part of legislators and public officials for public scholarship aid for small colleges.
3. In the competitive environment, Beloit noted that its location was reasonably close to a major metropolitan area (Chicago) and not perceived to be too distant from eastern cities.
4. In the macroenvironment, the school found that there was a local demand for self-improvement courses by the Beloit citizens.

These opportunities can be evaluated using the dimensions of attractiveness and probability shown in Table 1(B). The strongest opportunities seem to be 1 and 3. Opportunity 2 would be helpful to the college but would not make a major difference. Similarly, the school has neither the inclination nor a large enough faculty to move into the self-improvement area (opportunity 4).

RESOURCE ANALYSIS

Following the environmental analysis, the institution should undertake an analysis of its resource position. The purpose is to identify the major resources that the organization has (its *strengths*) and lacks (its *weaknesses*). The theory is that an organization should pursue goals, opportunities, and strategies that are suggested by, or congruent with, its strengths and avoid those where its resources would be too weak.

An institution should conduct a *resources audit* as part of this strategic planning process step. The major resources listed in Figure 1 are people, money, and facilities. The people are the faculty, administrators, and staff of the school. Beloit officials found in the resources audit that the school had an excess of faculty members given their enrollment. Therefore, it was advisable to cut the faculty by one-third, from 120 to 80 members. Although this was an arduous and unpleasant task, the move was necessitated by the severity of the situation. The quality of teaching was recognized as a strength to the institution. The monetary aspect of the resources audit includes financial strength and the ability to gain government, foundation, and alumni support, and funding for daily operations. Beloit found that its monetary situation could not be categorized as a weakness or strength. It fell into a middle range. Facilities and environment encompasses the physical plant and the geographics as well as the social environment of the school. Beloit administrators believe that its size and pleasant small-city campus are definite strengths. However, the location in the snowbelt is perceived as somewhat of a weakness. Of course, Beloit and other schools must more fully catalog internal, tangible as well as intangible strengths and weaknesses.

As a clue to developing goals, the college or university should pay closest attention to its distinctive competencies. *Distinctive competencies* are those *resources and abilities in which the organization is especially strong.* If a small college happens to have a strong foreign language program, it might want to consider such opportunities as starting an international studies program or an evening noncredit language program. Institutions of higher education will find it easiest to work from their strengths, although this carries the risk of overdeveloping their strengths rather than trying to build up a more balanced set of strengths. Furthermore, a distinctive competence may not be enough if the organization's major competitors possess the same distinctive competence. The school should pay attention primarily to those strengths in which it possesses a *differential advantage*, that is, it can outperform competitors on that dimension. For example, Georgetown University not only has an excellent international studies program, but its location in Washington, D.C., gives it a differential advantage in pursuing preeminence in this area of study.

In evaluating its strengths and weaknesses, the administration should not rely exclusively on its own perceptions, but it could initiate an *image study* of how the institution is perceived by its significant publics. For example, the provost may think the college has a fine reputation in the hard sciences, but an image study among high school counselors may reveal that they think the strength of the college is primarily in its humanities offering. A school should study how different key publics—students, parents, business firms, and others—perceive its strengths and weaknesses. The findings may reveal that the college has certain strengths and weaknesses it was not aware of, and others that it has exaggerated.

GOAL FORMULATION

The environment and resource analyses are designed to provide the necessary background and stimulus to administrative thinking about the basic institutional objectives and goals. Every organization at its inception is clear about its objectives. However, as the environment changes and presents new challenges, presidents and boards should review and reassess the basic mission, objectives, and goals. At some schools a review will convince participants in the planning process that the current goal structure is still clear, relevant, and effective. Other colleges and universities will find their goals clear but of diminishing appropriateness to the new environment and resource situation, while some will discover that their goals are no longer clear and that the organization is drifting.

The purpose of developing a clear set of institutional goals is precisely to keep the organization from drifting into an uncertain future. The institution needs to have a clear picture of what kind of organization it wants to look like at the end planning period. It needs to know what it wants to accomplish this year, the next year, and several years after. Goals enable the school officials to determine what they should be doing, develop effective plans, create targets for individuals' performances, and evaluate results. Without goals, whatever the organization does or achieves can be considered acceptable; there is no standard for planning or control.

The issue of institutional goals breaks into two distinct steps, namely, determining (1) what the current goals are and (2) what the goals should be. Even the image of the current goals will differ from person to person and group to group in the organization. The president may see the primary goal as upgrading the quality of the student body, the vice-president of admissions may see the primary goal as increasing the size of the student body, and the vice-president of finance may see the primary goal as increasing the percentage of nonscholarship students. The faculty as a whole may pursue the goal of a reduced teaching load to permit more time for research, whereas the administration may adopt the goal of an increased teaching load to reduce the cost of education. To define the current goals requires interviewing many individuals and groups as to what they think the institution's and their goals are (i.e., goal inventories). The resulting data will show that the school is really a coalition of several groups each giving and seeking different things from the organization.

Determining what the goals of the organization should be is an even harder task. In principle, the president or the board can unilaterally set new goals for the college for the next decade. Increasingly, however, top administrators usually find it appropriate to involve other groups (such as faculty and alumni) in the process of goal formulation. Their insights may not only be valuable, but goals are more likely to be embraced and supported because of their involvement in the process.

In carrying out the process of goal formulation, a useful step is to distinguish among three independent but related concepts, namely mission, objectives, and goals. This procedure involves establishing, first, the mission of the institution; second, the long- and short-run objectives; and third, the specific current goals. The three terms are defined as follows: "Mission is the basic purpose of an organization, that is, what it is trying to accomplish; objective is a major variable that the organization will emphasize, such as student enrollment, alumni giving, reputation; and goal is an organizational objective that is made specific with respect to magnitude, time, and responsibility."

Mission

An institution of higher education exists to accomplish something in the larger environment, that is, its purpose or mission. A useful way to examine a school's mission is to answer the following questions [6]. What is our business? Who is the customer? What is our value to the customer? What will our business be? What should our business be? These simple-sounding questions are among the most difficult the college or university will ever have to answer. Successful organizations continuously raise these questions and try to answer them thoughtfully and thoroughly.

Consider these questions, for example, as they would face Beloit College. What is Beloit's business? The easy answer is that Beloit is in the *educational business*. But so is Harvard, Vassar, Indiana University, Oakton Community College, and Oral Roberts University. Beloit has to define a particular concept or brand of education if it is to stand out. Consider some possibilities. Is Beloit in the *intellectual training business* so that its students are highly knowledgeable and perceptive about the world they live in? Is Beloit in the *personal growth business* where it aims to help its students develop their total personhood—intellectually, emotionally, and socially? Is Beloit in the *college fun and games business* where it aims to give students the "best time of their lives" before becoming adults? Each definition implies a different customer and a different way of rendering value to the customer.

A growing number of schools are deciding to write formal *mission statements* to gain the needed clarity. They realize that defining the mission is critically important because it affects everything else. A well worked out mission statement provides the institution with a shared sense of opportunity, direction, significance, and achievement. The mission statement acts as an "invisible hand" that guides a college or university's diverse personnel to work independently and yet collectively toward the realization of the organization's goals.

Unfortunately, it is not easy to write a meaningful mission statement. The planning committee may have to meet many times and interview many people before it can prepare a meaningful one. The time is not wasted because in the process it may discover much about the institution and its latent opportunities. An effective mission statement should be *market-oriented, feasible, motivating*, and *specific* [13, pp. 75–76].

After evaluating its goals in light of market realities, Beloit's mission statement was altered to include career preparation as well as intellectual training. The key phrase that was added stated: "An awareness of the available career options together with the skills to perceive those options." This addition to Beloit's mission statement should serve it for many years.

Objectives

The mission statement describes the institutional commitments rather than the specific objectives and goals it will pursue in the coming period. Therefore, each institution has to move toward developing major objectives and goals for the coming period separate from but consistent with its mission statement. Ideally, the same type of thoughtful study that led to the mission statements will also characterize the objectives and goals setting process.

For every type of institution, there is always a potential set of relevant objectives, and the task is to make choices among them. For example, the objectives of interest to a college are: increased national reputation, improved classroom teaching, higher enrollment, higher quality students, increased efficiency, larger endowment, improved student social life, improved physical plant, lower operating deficit, and so on. The institution cannot successfully pursue all of these objectives simultaneously because of a limited budget and various tradeoffs, such as between increased cost efficiency and improved classroom teaching. In any given year, therefore, institutions will choose to emphasize certain objectives and either ignore others or treat them as constraints. For example, if Beloit's enrollment were to fall, Beloit would likely make increased enrollment a paramount objective subject to not letting student quality fall below a certain level. Thus, an institution's major objectives can vary from year to year depending on the administration's perception of the major problems, or opportunities, that the school faces at that time.

Goals

Next, an institution's objectives for the coming year should be restated in operational and measurable form, called *goals*. The objective "increased enrollment" must be turned into a goal, such as "increasing enrollment of the next academic year class by 15 percent." A goal statement permits the college or university to think about the planning, programming, and controlling aspects of pursuing that objective. Such questions arise as: Is a 15 percent enrollment increase feasible? What strategy would be used? What resources would it take? What activities would have to be carried out? Who would be responsible and accountable? All of these critical questions must be answered when deciding whether to adopt a proposed goal.

Typically, the institution will be evaluating a large set of potential goals at the same time and examining them for their consistency and priorities. The school may discover that it cannot simultaneously achieve "a 15 percent enrollment increase" and "a 10 percent increase in student quality," given its limited marketing budget. In this case, the planning committee may make adjustments in the tar-

get levels or target dates, or drop certain goals altogether in order to arrive at a meaningful and achievable set of goals.[3]

STRATEGY FORMULATION

After an institution formulates its mission and goals, it must determine strategies that will help it achieve its goals. The college may discover that it cannot find a feasible strategy to deliver an enrollment increase. If so, the planners will have to return to the goal formulation stage to reconsider its goals before determining a final set of strategies.

In developing feasible strategies, the organization should undertake two tasks. First, it should devise an *academic portfolio strategy*, that is, decide what to do with its current major products (programs). Second, it should develop a *product/market opportunity strategy*, that is, decide what new products and markets to add. Although these strategies are discussed sequentially, they probably should be conducted concurrently and evaluated with respect to one another.

Academic Portfolio Strategy

Once institutional and marketing objectives and goals are set, the administration should examine its current academic portfolio. Just as investors review their portfolio periodically, so must a college or university evaluate its academic programs from time to time. In the 1960s colleges and universities continued to add courses and programs to satisfy demand, because there was enough budget to support all departments. However, in the 1970s many schools began to experience a financial crunch. Administrators were forced to identify the stronger programs and

---

[3] For an advanced example of goal setting used at Stanford University, see [11].

TABLE 2: Academic portfolio evaluation tool

Quality	Centrality		
	High	*Medium*	*Low*
High	Psychology (MV-H)* Decision: —Build size —Build quality		Home Economics (MV-H) Decision: —Build size —Hold quality
Medium		Geography (MV-M) Decision: —Hold size —Hold quality	
Low	Philosophy (MV-L) Decision: —Reduce size —Build quality		Classical Languages (MV-L) Decision: —Reduce size or terminate

* (MV-H, M, L) = Market Value—High, Medium, or Low.

maintain full support for them, while taking funds out of their weaker programs.

Industry also experienced financial stringency in recent years, and many companies have examined their product line with a product portfolio tool developed by the Boston Consulting Group. Each product is either classified as a *star* (high market growth, high market share); *cash cow* (low growth, high share); *question mark* (high growth, low share); or *dog* (low growth, low share) [1]. Stars are to be *built*, cash cows *maintained*, questions marks *built or dropped*, and dogs *dropped*. This tool has proven to be quite successful in the corporate setting. These characterizations have been applied to analyze British and U.S. universities [5, 16].

Table 2 suggests an alternative portfolio evaluation tool that we feel academic planners can better utilize. The two primary dimensions of this portfolio are *centrality* to the institutional mission and the *quality level* of the program. The third dimension, *market viability*, is shown in the table in parenthe-

ses. Academic programs were chosen as the unit for analysis in this illustration, but schools in a multiunit system or specific courses could also be utilized. Three levels (high, medium, and low) exist for all three dimensions. High quality is equated with national eminence, medium quality with average national strength, and low quality means that the program is judged to be mediocre or poor. The levels within the centrality dimension are self-explanatory. A judgment on the levels within market viability should be evident from the information collected in the environmental analysis section.

There are many possible ways to judge the quality of an institution's various programs. Outside experts (faculty from other schools) may be asked to evaluate the research productivity of the department and content of the courses. Alternately, the percentage of graduates who go on to graduate school or are employed by national firms may be a surrogate measure of quality. Some independent agency's findings can also be utilized to measure quality.

The school shown in Table 2 has a strong liberal arts tradition. (The school shown in the table is hypothetical.) Psychology and philosophy are judged to be high on the centrality scale, but philosophy is low in quality and market viability. The strategies that the higher education planner can use to deal with the academic programs are to build, hold, reduce, or terminate. Since the home economics department scores high on the quality and market viability dimensions, a plausible strategy would be to hold quality and build size. On the other hand, the philosophy department that is central to the university's mission, but is low in quality and market viability, should probably be reduced in size while building its quality. Because classical languages is low on all scales, it should probably be terminated as a department. Certain courses, though, may remain a part of another program.

A number of institutions have been evaluating their programs in recent years. The academic portfolio evaluation procedure represents a more systematic approach to handling these difficult program decisions. Application of the portfolio analysis resulted in Northwestern University's recent reduction in the size of its geography department.

Product/Market Opportunity Strategy

A formidable challenge facing colleges and universities revolves around how they will maintain enrollment, if not grow, in the future. The strategic planning process formally addresses this issue. Table 3 depicts the opportunity matrix using products (programs) and markets as the variables. (See earlier definition of marketing opportunity.)

Cell number one is labeled market penetration. Under this strategy the institution seeks to gain larger numbers of students similar to those enrolled by relying on existing programs. Possibly, a state university in a large city with a low market share may utilize this strategy. Heavy promotion (i.e., increasing recruiting budget) would be essential to making this strategy work. However, given future demographics, this strategy would be inadequate for most schools.

Geographic expansion of existing programs allows institutions to discover new market opportunities for current courses (cell 2). This strategy is being implemented by many colleges and universities. Some hold classes in grade or high schools in their towns. Southern Methodist University of Dallas is offering courses in their MBA program in Houston. Similarly, Antioch College has established campuses in foreign countries. Significant geographic expansion may not be feasible for many institutions, however, because of resource requirements.

A third possible opportunity exists for schools interested in expanding existing products to new markets. Colleges and universities have been increasing their recruiting of nontraditional student groups, such as senior citizens, homemakers, and ethnic minorities. Women are being more directly served by larger numbers of institutions. Furthermore, educational opportunity programs on many campuses aim to attract more minority students. Finally, large business firms and some social agencies are inviting colleges to present courses on their premises to their employees.

Programs can be modified to appeal to existing markets (cell 4). Addition of evening programs for schools in large cities is an obvious possibility. Weekend programs can attract students not able to attend regular classes. For example, Alverno College, a private women's school in Milwaukee, instituted a weekend college and drew large num-

TABLE 3: Product/market opportunity strategy

Markets	Products		
	Existing	Modified	New
Existing	1. Market Penetration	4. Product Modification —short courses —evening program —weekend program —new delivery system	7. Production Innovation —new courses —new departments —new schools
Geographical	2. Geographic Expansion —new areas of city —new cities —foreign	5. Modification for Dispersed Markets —programs offered on military bases or at U.S. firms based abroad	8. Geographic Innovation
New	3. New Markets A. Individual —senior citizens —homemakers —ethnic minorities B. Institutional —business firms —social agencies	6. Modification for New Markets A. Individual —senior citizens B. Institutional —business —government	10. Total Innovation —new courses —new departments —new schools

bers of housewives and employed women. A fine illustration of a new delivery system is Adelphi University's offering of courses on a commuter train between New York and several suburban locations. Administrators are constrained only by their imagination in developing these potential opportunities.

The fifth cell is named *modification for dispersed markets*. Colleges such as the University of Maryland that offer courses and programs for members of the armed forces both domestically and abroad are examples of this approach. Industrial firms with large pockets of concentrated overseas employment may represent an untapped market.

Product *modification for new markets* (cell 6) may be a more realistic avenue for growth of colleges and universities. It seems that to successfully penetrate the retired market may require a restructuring of courses and registration procedures. Specifically, the time period may need to be shorter, with less reading required, more comfortable seats, and possibly books with larger print. Iowa

State has instituted "Eldercollege" for retired adults. Similarly, business firms and government agencies may be relatively attractive markets for courses in sharpening communications skills. However, the English and speech departments would probably have to develop new courses to meet these particular needs.

The seventh opportunity category shown in Table 3 is labeled *product innovation*. Here, new courses, departments, or schools are developed for existing markets. Realistically, few schools, other than those located in the sunbelt, will be expanding in the future. An example of this strategy, though, was recently employed by the University of Houston, which purchased a downtown junior college and expanded it into a four-year school.

Geographic innovation can be accomplished by using technological breakthroughs. For instance, Illinois Bell has developed an electronic blackboard that allows a professor to write on a blackboard in one location and have it transmitted over telephone lines to a distant city. With the advent of home computers, interactive television, and other new media technologies, it will be possible to offer courses to a national audience.

The final category, *total innovation*, refers to offering new products for new markets. The "university without walls" that offers specialized programs for groups such as government agencies is an example. Competition for traditional higher education may increasingly come from corporate schools modeled after McDonald's Hamburger University. However, the notion of total innovation may not be a viable growth opportunity for most traditional institutions of higher education.

The product/market opportunity matrix essentially helps the administration imagine new options in a systematic way. The hard work then begins when the various opportunities have to be evaluated according to their centrality, cost, market viability, and other appropriate criteria. Once the long-range strategy formulation is complete, the short-term step is to develop a marketing strategy for these market or product opportunities [12].

ORGANIZATION DESIGN

The purpose of strategy formulation is to develop strategies that can be carried out by the institution to achieve its goals. This presumes that the organization is capable of carrying out the strategies. It must have the structure, people, and culture to successfully implement each strategy. For example, if a college plans to build its reputation in the hard sciences, it will need a faculty that is strong in certain disciplines. Clearly, an organization's chosen strategies require certain structures to succeed. Most organization theorists believe that "structure should follow strategy" [3]. However, organizational structures in higher education are often hard to change, and growth opportunities are limited because of the need to satisfy internal constituents.

Under dynamic strategic planning, not only is it necessary to transform the organizational structure if required by the strategic thrust, but it may also be necessary to retrain or change some of the people who occupy sensitive positions in the organization. Thus, if a private college decides to change its fundraising strategy from reliance on wealthy donors to foundations, the vice-president of development who is used to "old-boy-network" fundraising may need retraining in "foundation grantpersonship" or be replaced with a foundation-oriented development vice-president.

In adopting a new strategic posture, the school may also have to develop a plan for changing the "culture" of the organization. Every organization has a culture, that is, its people share a certain way of looking at things. Colleges have an "academic culture," one that prizes academic freedom, highmindedness, abstract theorizing, and so on. The academic culture is often an outspoken critic of the "business culture" (profit as a worthwhile end) and the "marketing culture" (that institutions have to serve and satisfy their publics). College presidents who attempt to have their faculties improve their teaching, spend more time with students, develop new courses for nontraditional markets, and so on, often encounter tremendous resistance. With the growing shortage of students, the challenge facing the president is to develop a marketing orientation with the faculty in which everyone sees his or her job as sensing, serving, and satisfying markets. Changing the culture of an organization is a mammoth task, but one that may be essential if the organization is to survive in the new environment [2].

SYSTEMS DESIGN

The last major step in strategic planning is to design or upgrade the systems that the organization needs to develop and carry out the strategies that will achieve its goals in the new environment. The three principal systems needed by an organization to be effective at strategic market planning are discussed below. They should be viewed as coequal and interacting.

Marketing Information System

The job of effectively running an institution calls for a great amount of information about students, alumni, competitors, publics, and the larger macroenvironmental forces (demography, economy, politics, technology, and culture). This information can be obtained through student enrollment analysis, marketing intelligence, and marketing research. The information, if it is to be useful, must be accurate, timely, and comprehensive.

Marketing Planning System

Many organizations gather information but fail to use it in a disciplined fashion. More and more colleges and universities are becoming convinced of the benefits of operating a formal planning system in which long-term and annual goals, strategies, marketing programs, and budgets are developed at a regular time each year. The planning discipline calls for a planning staff, planning resources, and a planning culture if it is to be successful. It is our contention that discipline is essential if the organization hopes to achieve optimal marketplace results.

Marketing Control System

Plans are only useful if they are going to be implemented and monitored. The purpose of a marketing control system is to measure the ongoing results of a plan against the plan's goals and to make corrective action.[4] The corrective action may be to change the goals or plans or the implementation in light of new circumstances. If strategic planning is to have an impact in institutions of higher education, control systems must be instituted.

CONCLUSION

This article outlined the framework necessary for achieving a strategic planning posture in higher education. However, the implementation of this process was not explicitly addressed. Other authors have provided spe-

[4] For another approach to this subject, see [4].

cific timetables for carrying out this procedure [9, 10].

The most important benefit of strategic planning for higher education decision makers is that it forces them to undertake a more market-oriented and systematic approach to long-range planning. The future that appears to hold many threats for most colleges and universities should become less imposing with the judicious use of strategic planning.

REFERENCES

[1] Abell, D. F., and J. S. Hammond, *Strategic Market Planning: Problems and Analytical Approaches*. Englewood Cliffs, NJ: Prentice-Hall, 1979.

[2] Caren, W. L., and F. R. Kemerer, "The Internal Dimensions of Institutional Marketing," *College and University* (Spring 1979), 173–88.

[3] Chandler, A. D., *Strategy and Structure*. Cambridge, MA: MIT Press, 1962.

[4] Cranton, P. A., and L. H. Legge, "Program Evaluation in Higher Education," *Journal of Higher Education*, 49 (September–October 1978), 464–71.

[5] Doyle, P., and J. E. Lynch, "A Strategic Model for University Planning," *Journal of the Operations Research Society* (July 1979), 603–9.

[6] Drucker, P., *Management: Tasks, Responsibilities, Practices*, Chapter 7. New York: Harper & Row, 1973.

[7] Fox, K. F. A., *Attracting a New Market to Northwestern's Undergraduate Programs: Older Women Living on the North Shore*. Evanston, IL: Program on Women, Northwestern University, 1979.

[8] Fuller, B., "A Framework for Academic Planning," *Journal of Higher Education*, 48 (January–February 1977), 65–77.

[9] Gaither, G. H., "The Imperative to Plan in Higher Education," *North Central Association Quarterly* (Fall 1977), 347–55.

[10] Hollowood, J. R., "College and University Strategic Planning." Working paper. Cambridge, MA: Arthur D. Little, August 1979.

[11] Hopkins, D. P., J-C Larreche, and W. F. Massy, "Constrained Optimization of a University Administrator's Preference Function," *Management Science* (December 1977), 365–77.

[12] Kotler, P., *Marketing for Nonprofit Organizations*. Englewood Cliffs, NJ: Prentice-Hall, 1975.

[13] ———, *Principles of Marketing*. Englewood Cliffs, NJ: Prentice-Hall, 1980.

[14] May, R. B., "One College's Struggle May Aid Other Schools Worried About Slump," *The Wall Street Journal* (January 10, 1979), 1.

[15] Moore, M. A., "On Launching Into Exigency Planning," *Journal of Higher Education*, 49 (November–December 1978), 620–38.

[16] Newbould, G. N., "Product Portfolio Diagnosis for U.S. Universities," *Akron Business and Economic Review* (Spring 1980), 39–45.

[17] Stewart, I. R., and D. G. Dickason, "Hard Times Ahead," *American Demographics* (June 1979).

Strategic Planning for Nonprofit Health Care Organization Funding

O. C. FERRELL • CHARLES S. MADDEN • DONNA LEGG

Nonprofit health care organizations are experiencing intense competition and difficulties in maintaining current funding levels. This article presents a strategic planning model for developing constituency support and funding for nonprofit health care organizations. Too often tactical rather than strategic use of marketing is applied in fundraising efforts.

Today marketing is often viewed as an important tool in improving the operations of nonprofit health care organizations. Too often, however, marketing activities are viewed as "tactical maneuvers" used only to solve a specific problem or deal with an emergency situation. Public relations and, more recently, advertising have been seen as the place to deposit marketing because some administrators view marketing as communications rather than strategic decision variables relating to the process of planning, pricing, promotion and distribution of ideas, goods and services (Steiber, 1985). If marketing is to play a mature role in nonprofit health care goal attainment, then health care marketers (or health care planners that understand marketing) should provide inputs into the health care organization's strategic planning efforts.

This paper presents a general strategic planning framework for constituency support of nonprofit health care organizations and illustrates the application of the framework to a nonprofit mental health program. The framework is not intended to expose all the intricate details which are necessary to undertake formal strategic planning but rather to lay out the general approach to the process. Specific organizational goals and varying roles of functional parts of the organization greatly influence the *processes* involved in the strategic planning effort. This paper describes the benefits of strategic planning and provides enough detail to initiate the strategic planning process.

THE CHANGING NONPROFIT HEALTH CARE ENVIRONMENT

There is not enough illness, disease, injuries and preventive care to support all of the health care organizations competing for patients. Institutions in many nonprofit health care areas are experiencing competition from for-profit organizations and difficulties in

O. C. Ferrell, Charles S. Madden, and Donna Legg, "Strategic Planning for Nonprofit Health Care Organization Funding," Vol. 6, No. 1 (March 1986). Reprinted from *Journal of Health Care Marketing*, published by the American Marketing Association.

funding due to limited reimbursements, changes in government regulations and tax laws. Additional pressure on nonprofits exists because for-profit institutions are often operating at less than full capacity and are embracing marketing at a rapid rate (Goldsmith, 1981, Chapter 1). Survey results indicate that over three-quarters of metropolitan hospital chief administrators now have a marketing department or a person responsible for marketing and only 20 percent of these have been in existence for three or more years (Gardner and Paison, 1985). Therefore, competition due to overcapacity has resulted in aggressive marketing programs by for-profit institutions to attract patients. For nonprofit health care organizations, "uncertainty on how to compete is compounded by ambiguity of the scope and make-up of competition" (Salvatore, 1985). Certainly nonprofit hospitals compete with for-profit hospitals and some traditional nonprofit services in the mental health area are now being performed on a contract basis by for-profit health care organizations.

There is a tendency for nonprofits to plan activities without integrating marketing functions to create an overall marketing strategy to stimulate financial support. Marketing efforts may not be effective in increasing organizational funding if they do not take into account the organization's target public to be served and marketing decision variables. Health care administrators need to understand the larger framework of support constituencies because the differential sources of financial support for health care organizations tend to radically affect the marketing needs of the organization and its strategic planning.

In the typical health care organization, the quality of the service delivered has a direct impact on patient satisfaction as well as indirectly affecting the income stream and profit of the organization. If the patient feels that quality is deteriorating, he/she might respond to that perceived lack of quality by seeking another source of health care. For example, in the case of most nonprofit health care organizations, with limited client fees as part of a multiple funding source base, a number of factors affect the survival of the organization and consequently its ability to deliver quality health services. It is possible, because of the separation of patient care and funding for a facility, for a health care organization that contributes greatly to its community to cease to exist for lack of funds (Lauffer, 1984, p. 10), or for an organization that offers little to its community to prosper because of adequate funding. As a result, external funding and referring physicians, not necessarily the patients' market response to quality health care, tend to determine the success or failure of nonprofit health care institutions.

To understand the funding problems encountered by such nonprofit organizations, environmental factors affecting public opinion, governmental policymaking, and the predisposition of private sources to donate must be evaluated. Changes in cultural, social, political and economic environmental factors can directly or indirectly affect the flow of available funds to nonprofit health care organizations that have a very limited client fee base (Lauffer, 1984, p. 10). For example, the organization may be vulnerable to changes in the economy due to a recession or change in tax laws, or a new market awareness of another "competing" social problem can alter contributions and financial assistance to a particular nonprofit health care organization. Of course, failure to maintain good relations with patients, referring physicians, and other referral agents may be the most important consideration in determining the success or failure of a nonprofit health care organization (Legg and Lamb, 1986; Goldsmith, 1981, pp. 162–63).

In both the public and private sectors, competition exists for funding, and the size of the pool of available funding affects the level of actual fund allocation. It is important to assess the competition and know how to position an organization to maximize its unique attributes. For example, it is harder for a nonprofit hospital to distinguish its services from a for-profit hospital than it is for the nonprofit hospital to distinguish its services from a university-owned teaching hospital. Nonprofit health care organizations depend on tax monies, individual contributions, voluntary organizations such as United Way, foundations, and corporate donations for money to maintain operations. Other sources of funding are patient fees and contract sales to other organizations (Howe, 1985). Patient fees often come from insurance, Medicare, Medicaid, or a transfer payment. Since competition in the fundraising area is intense, the general public is not the largest source of funds for most organizations (Goldsmith, 1981, p. 127).

THE ROLE OF STRATEGIC PLANNING IN CONSTITUENCY SUPPORT

To take a proactive position on constituency support, the organization must establish clear goals and program plans, and understand potential supporters. Health care organizations must understand the needs of the community they serve and why their funds exist. Service roles and funding relationships must be understood before strategic decisions to improve funding can be implemented. It is possible, for example, that political conditions that led to the initial funding of an organization have changed and that the organization may know it is in peril long before funding is actually cut. A redi-

rection of overall mission may be the only solution for survival. To survive in the future "marketers are going to play a key role in researching the community needs for health care and designing and delivering new forms of health care delivery" (Kotler, 1985). Also new forms of funding and support systems will be needed to finance these new programs. Weaknesses, if any, in a constituency support system should be detected and remedied in order to improve funding. The existing communication channels that provide contacts with individual and organizational supporters should be evaluated to understand communication weaknesses. For a nonprofit hospital, the constituency group's view of medical quality, service, food, and overall friendliness may be important. Specific indicators of resources, activities, and the opinion of relevant support groups should be determined through an audit (Crompton and Lamb, 1983). If the nonprofit health organization does not have an adequate support level, then adjustments need to be made in important areas of concern to constituency support groups. Also through an audit, constituency groups that are likely to provide support can be identified. For example, broadening services to appeal to new patients and constituency groups could be the result of an audit.

Once weaknesses have been determined in a funding program, areas of opportunity should be explored. It there *is* public support for the health care organization and long-standing concerns about stigmas affecting support are overcome, then the positions of each support constituency should be examined for policies and/or priorities. For example, probable outcomes of competition for tax monies can be more easily assessed than competition for private funds. At this point there should be an effort to assess the position and strength of competitive organizations. Competitive organizations include generic competitors, service form competitors, and enterprise competitors (Kotler, 1982, p. 55). Enterprise competitors are those organizations who provide identical services. Service form competitors are those organizations that provide differentiated versions of the same service. For example, a hospital emergency room and a free-standing emergency center would be considered service form competitors since they provide differentiated forms of emergency care. Generic competition involves competitors who provide different services meeting the same customer need or demand. In other words, generic competition covers substitute services in the area of health care (Salvatore, 1984). It is essential to assess the competition at all three levels.

STRATEGIC PLANNING FRAMEWORK

Figure 1 illustrates a strategic planning framework for nonprofit health care organizations to manage constituency support and increase funding. The current assessment, which is a diagnosis of the present funding situation, is the first stage in strategic planning. This current assessment includes determining factors and roles affecting funding as well as determining vulnerability to funding withdrawal from present sources. To understand the factors and roles affecting funding, nonprofit health care organizations must first identify all their sources of funding—federal grants, Medicare, Medicaid, private insurance, corporate donations, contract fees, patient fees, United Way allocations, etc. Once identified, each source must be thoroughly analyzed. How much does each source contribute? Why does it contribute? What are the underlying social, political, and economic conditions which affect support? Answers to such questions will not always be

readily available. While the relative contributions of each source can be easily assessed from accounting data, reasons for funding and the underlying environmental conditions will be much more difficult. Consider, for example, Medicare and Medicaid payments. Americans have long held the belief that everyone is entitled to proper health care and that no one should be denied such care. The federal government, through Medicare and Medicaid, has traditionally reimbursed health care providers based on the cost of providing service to the elderly and disabled. Thus, support is founded in cultural and social beliefs. Recently, however, Americans have become concerned over the rapidly rising costs of health care and large national deficits. The government has reacted by limiting reimbursements to specified amounts based upon diagnosis. In other words, by redesigning the reimbursement system, legislators hope to provide incentives for health care providers to control their costs. The point here is that underlying motives and environmental forces may be very broad and may not be specific to a single organization. On the other hand, the motivation behind a large corporate donation may be a tax advantage, the corporation's sincere concern for the health of the community, and/or the CEO's close personal relationship with the director of the health care organization.

Following an in-depth analysis of all funding sources, vulnerability to funding withdrawal must be determined. The bulk of the information for this assessment will come from the previous analysis. However, there is a need to explicitly consider competition at this stage. Consider the home health care organization that provides physical therapy to a local nursing home on a contract basis. Other home health care organizations, hospitals, and the nursing home's own physical

FIGURE 1: Strategic planning framework for funding on nonprofit health care organizations

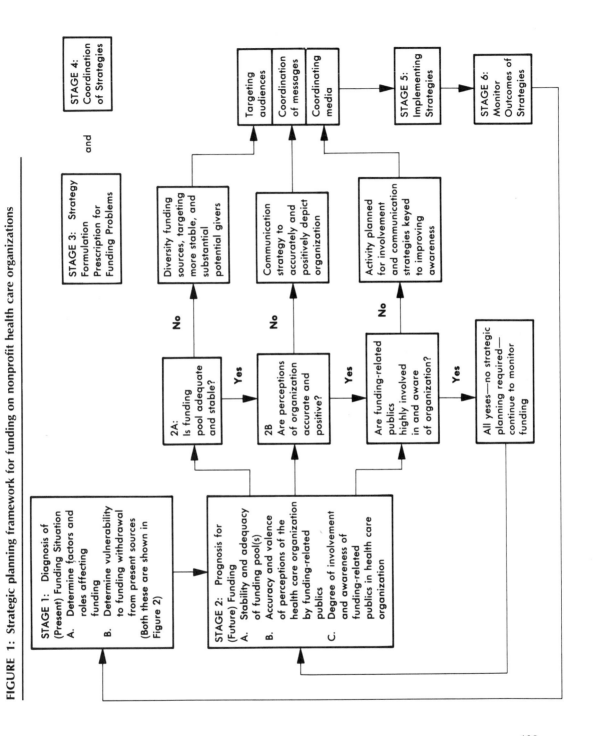

139

therapy staff are all competitors who could impact upon the home health care organization's income stream. As mentioned earlier, competition may also come from other areas of social concern. The corporation who, for public relations purposes, supports the community hospital may be inclined to decrease support in favor of counseling programs due to a highly publicized rash of teenage suicides in the area. In summary, determining vulnerability involves a complete understanding of all funding sources as well as understanding the competitive environment.

Stage 2 in the strategic planning framework is a prognosis for future funding. The three critical issues are (A) the stability and adequacy of funding pools, (B) the accuracy and valence of perceptions held by funding-related publics, and (C) the degree of involvement and awareness of funding-related publics with the health care organization. The first issue, adequacy and stability of the funding pool, can be assessed by aggregating the information provided from stage 1. Specifically, the potential support from each source can be added together to determine the adequacy of potential funding pools. Those funds which are vulnerable to withdrawal can be subsequently subtracted from the total potential funding pool to get an estimate of funding support under adverse conditions. A small difference between the maximum and minimum funding should indicate a fairly stable pool while a very large difference will indicate an unstable pool. Issues two and three, being very organization specific, will necessitate a heavier reliance on survey data. Survey data should address the perceptions of the organization held by each constituency group, their awareness of the organization, and their involvement with the organization. It should be noted that these issues are critical even when adequate funding pools exist. An unheard-of organization cannot hope to attract the support of funding sources nor can a negatively perceived organization hope to maintain its funding sources.

Once the steps of assessing weaknesses and opportunities in the current funding process have been completed, prognoses and prescriptions should be formulated in improving funding for the organization (stage 3). There are a number of possible objectives for funding strategy:

1. Increase total level of support over a period of time.
2. Diversify the sources of funding, e.g., adding private funding to public support or charging client fees to those who can afford to pay for services.
3. Broaden the base of support within a single source of funding, e.g., a larger number of private donors.

More specifically, if the funding pool is determined inadequate and/or unstable, a diversification strategy is called for which focuses on more stable and/or potentially substantial funding sources. When perceptions of the organization are inaccurate and/or unfavorable, a corrective communication strategy should be emphasized. Low awareness and/or low involvement requires activities aimed at increasing the level of involvement and communications which will improve awareness. Of course, if no funding problems are detected in stage 2, corrective strategies are not necessary. The organization must, however, continue to monitor funding sources, the environment, etc.

Stage 4 of the strategic framework consists of coordinating strategies. This means that communication messages and media should be suited to the needs of each target group. Furthermore, the funding strategies should coordinate with other marketing strategies (i.e., strategies for reaching users, the general public, and referral agents, product/service strategies, pricing strategies, and distribution strategies).

Stage 5 in the strategic planning framework involves implementing the strategies developed in stages 3 and 4. Implementation of strategies arising out of this process might include such activities as:

1. Attempting to directly influence public policy on the level at which allocation decisions are made by government;
2. Determining what motivates each support constituency and satisfying its needs, i.e., with tax incentives, chance to participate in the organization, or publicity;
3. Attempting to influence the priorities or policies of private institutional donors;
4. Communicating the organization's activities and results that are consistent with existing priorities or policies (public relations);
5. Communicating with the key individuals in funding institutions and stressing advantages of improved funding to them individually or institutionally (lobbying);
6. Charging other organizations or government agencies that currently obtain services free of charge.

Finally, organizations need to monitor the outcomes of all funding activities and continually assess the funding environment (stage 6). This feedback and evaluation stage is essential to the success of the strategic framework—as it is to all strategic planning efforts. Failure to do so may well result in the destruction of the organization's funding base.

To better understand how the process of constituency development and diversification works, the following case is offered.

THE CASE OF REDUCED AND RESTRUCTURED FUNDING FOR MENTAL HEALTH, MENTAL RETARDATION, AND SUBSTANCE ABUSE PROGRAMS

Mental health and similar programs are facing serious problems in developing constituency support for their programs. Due to recent federal legislation, key policy makers and decision makers who are responsible for resource allocation and operation of the mental health, mental retardation, and substance control programs now have a new environment in which to obtain funding and implement programs. The federal government has demanded that agencies justify their existence at the state level. This demand has created a need for private support of the program. State funded and/or for-profit operated programs receive revenues to support hospital services primarily from three different sources:

1. Federal government—directly or indirectly via a transfer from another state agency
2. State appropriations
3. Other sources—patient fees, sales, contracts, private insurance, estates, etc.

There has been a significant drop in the number of patients or residents served in mental health hospitals compared with previous years. This drop is a function of a national policy on deinstitutionalization, not of funding. The intent is to move clients to the less restrictive, more humane normal community-based settings closer to home rather than housing them in institutions away from home and for long periods of time. The continuing development of alternative community services and resources will make it possible to reduce further the state hospital patient population and to shorten the length of institutional treatment. This illustrates the earlier point that to survive nonprofit hospitals will need to research community needs for health care and test new forms of delivery. Funding must be found to support new services.

Even if deinstitutionalization is successful, without strong constituency support, mental health, mental retardation, and substance abuse programs can be expected to provide even less service to communities because of lack of sufficient funding to cover rising costs.

Based on the probable increase in mental health needs, current levels and sources of funding provide new opportunities and threats for policy makers and program directors. According to Albridge (1982), some of the new directions and issues confronting mental health, mental retardation, and substance abuse programs include:

1. Cutbacks in funding, staffing, management, and services
2. Emphasis from availability and accessibility of services to cost and outcome effectiveness
3. Interagency reorganization and planning, and coordination of services to maintain quality
4. Links between the public and private sectors regarding provision of services to clients
5. Clarification of the respective roles of hospitals and communities, particularly in providing services to indigent clients, emergency services and support for adults, and day and extended employment services for adults

There is opportunity for improved efficiency as a positive result of recent legislation, but overall reduced funding is a negative result and will cause greater dependence on private, foundation, and special state, federal, or local support. The opportunity for effective use of strategic marketing planning has increased sharply.

The immediate reaction of administrators might be the implementation of advertising, public relations, publicity, and personal selling (Brown, 1982). However, it would be a mistake to implement communication tactics without proper strategic planning. Strategic marketing planning is needed to define target publics (patients and constituency support groups) and to develop a marketing mix (product, price, promotion, and distribution). The boundaries of constituency may be expanded as more people become concerned and interested enough to exchange opinions and initiate action about mental health and related programs. The collective opinions and actions of individuals and groups are the main sources and pivots to advocate support of programs (Ferrell and Krugman, 1978).

This discussion makes it clear that several factors impact upon the constituency support system for mental health, mental retardation, and substance abuse programs. Public opinion and advocate support influence legislative support, policy planning, and specific community programs. Additionally, there are numerous competitors for both private and tax monies. A clear understanding of this environment is necessary for strategy formulation.

From a marketing perspective, administrators need to define target publics and develop specific strategies before developing specific action plans. Through marketing research, especially surveys designed to identify awareness and attitudes toward the organization and competing organizations, administrators can assess their current position in the market for constituency support. Research should also provide information regarding the needs and concerns of the various support groups.

FIGURE 2: Strategic planning framework for funding of MH/MR and substance abuse community programs

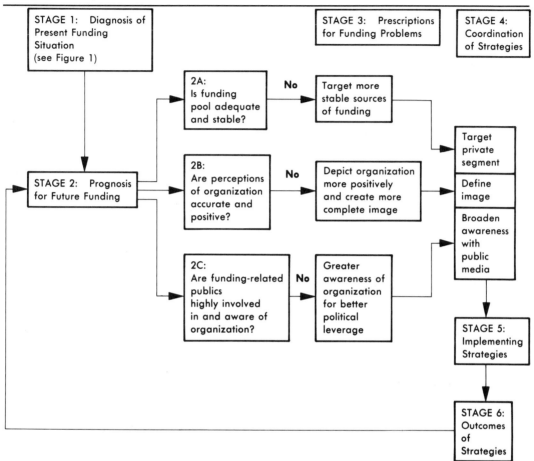

Once the constituency support system is understood, marketing strategies become the key ideas to integrate and achieve desired objectives. It is important to note that a different marketing strategy may be needed for each unique constituency support group. In other words, research may reveal that the various constituency groups view the organization differently, have different relationships with the organization, and may have different needs and concerns. As mentioned previously, the needs and concerns of funding sources may involve an interest in humanity, a tax advantage, a chance to participate, etc. Based on an understanding of these needs, concerns, relationships, and perceptions, the nonprofit health care organization can develop appropriate marketing strategies for the various support groups.

Figure 2 illustrates an application of the general strategic framework shown in Figure 1. The figure shows that MH/MR and substance abuse community programs are facing all three major funding problems. In general, the funding pool is both inadequate and unstable, perceptions are negative, and there is low awareness of such programs. Therefore, organizations need to target more stable sources of funding (namely, the private segment); they need to define their image and broaden awareness through public media.

Such a strategic contingency model could be developed for each possible constituency support group. Possible groups for strategic consideration could be derived from examining the roles of the various constituency groups. Note, however, that this example is relatively general and each program would have to identify their own constituency support groups and relationships. The basic process would work the same regardless of possible funding groups.

CONCLUSIONS

Nonprofit health care organizations are, because of their vulnerability, in need of a strategic approach to constituency development and funding support. With stricter controls on health care costs and a new competitive marketplace, radical changes may be needed to survive. The use of marketing is being embraced as the savior of nonprofit health care organizations. There is a limited scope in viewing marketing as a tactic to quickly improve funding through quick maneuvers that are not a part of a broader plan. Whether public or private funds are sought, the application of a strategic marketing framework can be helpful. Continued reduction of public support for nonprofit health care organizations forces the need to constituency diversification. This diversification should be accomplished through well-defined goals and an integrated effort.

Only through a systematic approach to planning can the organization gain long-term constituency support. Defining the target public (patient and constituency publics) and understanding the benefits they gain from support are necessary to develop a marketing strategy. There is a need to research community health care needs or develop innovative ways of delivering new services. A different marketing strategy is necessary for each public and the organization should focus on those that have the highest probability for providing support.

A strategic planning model was developed to aid nonprofit health care organizations in developing support. Specific issues that should be addressed by nonprofit constituency based health care organizations include the development of concrete, feasible, and hopefully, successful strategies linking service development and constituency support. A vocal and responsive community advocacy group must be built. For example, the mental retardation services system enjoys a very active and powerful advocacy group, and parent groups in substance abuse are growing. However, mental health is still struggling with the stigma issues and the negative public image of state mental health workers.

Important questions that must be considered in strategic planning include: How does one assess the strength of competing organizations or state agencies? When there is keen competition for tax monies and other resources, the question is how to package a program for different audiences and decision makers in order to retain and/or obtain a larger share of the resources. What are some creative and innovative approaches for influencing legislative appropriation decisions? How does one mobilize community advocates and work through existing negative images and failures?

Most important, administrators should be aware of the function and roles affecting support for their organization, and strategic frameworks available to their organizations. Health care administrators that only know how to deliver professional/clinical services for patients/residents may cease to exist due to the separation of patient care and funding. Just as good clinical procedures help the patient get well, good marketing strategies will help nonprofit health care organization survive.

REFERENCES

[1] Albridge, Ulla J. (1982), personal correspondence, Department of Mental Health and Mental Retardation, State of Tennessee.

[2] Brown, Steve (1982), "Health Care Marketing: An Assessment and Look to the Future," *Journal of Health Care Marketing*, 2 (Fall), 5–6.

[3] Bean, Ed (1985), "Doctors Find Dose of Marketing Can Cure Pain of Sluggish Practice," *Wall Street Journal*, March 15, p. 23.

[4] Crompton, Charles L., and Charles W. Lamb, Jr. (1983), "Distributing Public Services: A Strategic Approach," in *Cases and Readings for Marketing for Nonprofit Organizations*, Philip Kotler, O. C. Ferrell, and Charles Lamb, eds. Englewood Cliffs, NJ: Prentice-Hall, Inc., pp. 210–21.

[5] Ferrell, O. C., and D. M. Krugman, (1978), "The Role of Consumers in the Public Policy Process," *Academy of Marketing Science*, 6 (Summer), 167–75.

[6] Gardner, Steven F., and Allen R. Paison (1985), "A Survey on the Current Status of Health Care Marketing," *Health Care Strategic Management*, 3 (January), 26.

[7] Goldsmith, Jeff Charles (1981), *Can Hospitals Survive? The New Competitive Health Care Market*. Homewood, IL: Dow Jones-Irwin.

[8] Howe, Fisher (1985), "What You Need to Know About Fund Raising," *Harvard Business Review*, 63 (March–April), 18, 22–25.

[9] Kotler, Philip (1982), *Marketing for Nonprofit Organizations*, 2nd ed. Englewood Cliffs, NJ: Prentice-Hall, Inc.

[10] ——— (1985), "The Role and Development of Marketing in Today's Health Care Institution," *Health Care Strategic Management*, 3 (January), 24.

[11] Legg, Donna, and Charles W. Lamb, Jr. (1986), "The Role of Referral Agents in the Marketing of Home Health Services," *Journal of Health Care Marketing*, Vol. 6, No. 1.

[12] Lauffer, Armand (1984), *Strategic Marketing for Not-for-Profit Organizations: Program and Resource Development*. New York: The Free Press.

[13] Salvatore, Tony (1984), "Competitor Analysis in Health Care Marketing," *Journal of Health Care Marketing*, Vol. 4, No. 4 (Fall), pp. 11–16.

[14] Steiber, Steven R. (1985), "A New Breed of Marketer Evolves as Hospitals Get Serious About Marketing," *Marketing News*, 19 (January 18), p. 1.

The Baptists Want You!

WILLIAM MARTIN

God, as is His custom, has once again confounded the wise. After listening to a generation of theologians speak bravely of His death, the Almighty has established Himself as the odds-on choice for Comeback of the Decade. Conservative churches are growing, evangelical Christianity has been declared mainstream American religion, and a Southern Baptist Sunday school teacher has become Leader of the Free World. And now, as if that were not enough, the Baptist General Convention of Texas is about to launch a media blitz designed to share the good news of God's love with every man, woman, and child in the state an average of forty times apiece during a four-week period in February and March. The $1.5 million campaign, to be called Good News Texas, will feature commercials for Christ on television and radio, ads in newspapers and other print media, booster spots on billboards, pins on lapels, and an extensive personal visitation program to be run by the local churches. It is going to be pure Baptist. Well, almost pure. To help them do it right, the Baptists have hired one of the largest and most successful advertising firms in the country, the Bloom Advertising Agency of Dallas. Neither Sam nor Bob Bloom has roots in the Christian branch of the Judeo-Christian tradition.

I have mixed feelings about all this. Some of my best friends are Baptists, always have been. Still, I have never been able to shake completely the conviction that Baptists are the Aggies of religion. That in itself is not enough to damn them, but it does sort of set them apart. Part of my problem with Baptists stems from the fact that I grew up in the Church of Christ (Romans 16:16). As you may know, Church of Christ people believe the circle of the saved is rather small, and not many of them would care to sound too certain about their place in it. Baptists, on the other hand, never seem to tire of telling how sure they are they are saved and how good this blessed assurance feels. I thought their "once saved, always saved" doctrine of salvation was unsound—too easy; cheap grace; why, that would mean you could do anything you wanted to—but at least they had some doctrine, which was more than you could say for the Methodists, and at least we all agreed that nothing could send you to Hell faster than kissing the Pope's toe. No, the main problem wasn't doctrine. It was style. No matter what I believed, I could no more have been a Baptist when I was growing up than I could spend every Thursday night at the bowling alley or wear a seafoam-green leisure suit today.

Reprinted with permission from the February issue of *Texas Monthly*, pp. 83–87, 149–157. Copyright © 1977 by *Texas Monthly*. The Appendix to this article was added by the editors.

No part of this article may be reproduced in any form without prior written permission from the publisher.

For one thing, Baptists were so *organized* about inviting people to church. Once I was in the barbershop getting my weekly haircut when Mr. Joy Tilley, who was a big Baptist—I think it says something that the counterpart of "staunch Presbyterian," "devout Catholic," and "pillar in the Methodist Church" is "big Baptist"—stuck his head in and invited the barber to come and sit in his pew at a revival then in progress. That astonished me. We had a few elderly members who sort of had squatter's rights to pews they had occupied for years, but we would never have dreamed of assigning somebody a particular pew and then sending them out to drum up people to pack it.

The contrast carried over to the revivals themselves. The mark of a successful Church of Christ revivalist was his ability to drive the nail of terror into slumbering souls. Though some Baptist revivalists made use of hellfire and brimstone, I always felt that the mark of a successful Baptist preacher was his ability to make you laugh and feel good. That didn't seem much like religion to me.

This difference was further reflected in the Sunday schools, where we gave our classes sensible, functional names—"Preschool," "Elementary," "Junior High," and "Young People"—and encouraged attendance by quoting scriptures, especially Hebrews 10:25 ("Forsake not the assembling of yourselves together."), and threatening slackers with hellfire. Baptists called their classes things like "Sunbeams" and "Pioneers" and "Aviators" and drew crowds by having the youth minister bounce over the church bus from a trampoline.

I used to marvel at what they would do to appeal to young people. Our high school assembly programs fell into two primary categories: magicians, myna birds, and trick-shot artists sent out from the Southern School Assemblies organization and—this was before Ms. O'Hair took God out of the schools—preachers holding revivals over at the Baptist church. They would juggle and tell a few jokes and then talk to us earnestly about taking care of our bodies, which are temples of the Holy Spirit (I Corinthians 6:19). Once a revival team from Baylor entertained us with several hymns and gospel tunes arranged for trumpet trio. Then the leader, a young man with the unforgettable name of Horace Oliver Bilderback, placed a trombone mouthpiece in his trumpet and played "Let the Lower Lights Be Burning," while one of his fellow clerics moved an imaginery trombone slide out in front. That, to me, was the pure essence of the Southern Baptist Church.

At times, to be sure, I envied my Baptist friends and made some effort to be one of them. I went to the Baptist Vacation Bible School several years and made bookends and potholders and whatnot shelves, and did right well at a Bible game called Sword Drill—"Attention! Draw swords! (No thumbs over the edges, now.) John 3:16! Charge!"—and I thought it was keen that their pastor, Brother Rose, illustrated his devotional lessons with magic tricks and showed us slides of his trip to the Holy Land. Once, I joined the Royal Ambassadors (and got elected Ambassador-in-Chief) just to have a chance to go to the summer encampment at Alta Frio, but I lost my nerve before the bus left and stayed home. Later, I longed to go on hayrides and swimming parties with the Training Union and even wished I could go into San Antonio and hear Angel Martinez preach in a white suit. But it was just no use. I was like a lonely traveler watching a group of Shriners cutting up in a hotel lobby; it might be fun for a day or two to wear a fez and ride a little motor scooter down Main Street, but you wouldn't want to go home and still have to be one.

Before all the Baptists walk out on me, I have a confession to make. About four or five years ago, I became sort of a Baptist myself. After spending the better part of the sixties studying religion at Harvard, I grew a bit weak on matters of doctrine and decided I would do more harm than good by sticking with the Church of Christ. When I came back to Texas, I cast around a bit and finally wound up at a church that I suppose could be described as liberal and ecumenical, though even now I find it difficult to identify myself as a theological liberal, so strongly was I taught to believe that few states of being are more pernicious. Still, at least half the people in this chruch grew up as Baptists, a good handful of them are former Baptist preachers, and even though the Union Baptist Association of Houston threw them out for accepting members from other denominations without rebaptizing them, they still persist in calling themselves Baptists. I have had some trouble with it. I am embarrassed when they look at me in amazement because I have never heard of Lottie Moon, and I get a little squirmy when they sing "Do Lord" at the annual retreat up in the woods, and I admit it doesn't make a dime's worth of difference to me whether Baylor wins or loses a football game. Still, we don't have revivals and if we did we wouldn't have trumpets or trombones or jugglers, and nobody checks to see why you haven't been coming to Sunday school and, as far as I can tell, nobody much cares about the details of your belief, so long as you are kind and try to help folk when they need it. It doesn't have anything like the zip of a straight-out evangelical church, but ex-Fundamentalists are some of the best people you'll find anywhere, so I expect I'll keep my letter in a while longer. Besides, if Good News Texas works, we may all be Baptists by summer.

Baptists, of course, have always been ag-gressive. They sought "A Million More in Fifty-Four" and they have sponsored Billy Graham Crusades and hold "Win Clinics" to instruct people in the techniques of personal evangelism. But this is bigger, better, grander than anything they have ever done before.

My immersion in the project came in Dallas at a regional meeting of the Baptist General Convention of Texas (BGCT). The Good News Texas portion of the program was co-chaired by Drs. L. L. Morriss and Lloyd Elder. Morriss, with his smooth gray hair, metal glasses, and high-quality fall woolens, could easily pass for a corporation executive. His speech and manner befit his appearance—one senses he does little by accident. Lloyd Elder's obvious intelligence, warmth, and gentle wit are engaging, but his slightly more rumpled look and apparent unconcern for slickness make it easier to believe he is a seminary professor or church executive.

Morriss declared he was as excited as "an auctioneer at an auction of used furniture," a metaphor I thought fell somewhat short of the mark. He was exicted, he said, about what God had done for Texas in the past and about what He is doing now. He introduced Elder, who was also excited. Good News Texas, Elder said, would have three major targets: (1) the 4.7 million Texans—one third of the state's population—who do not belong to any Christian group, persons "who are completely uninvolved in the things of Christ," (2) inactive and apathetic church members, including 700,000 Baptists, and (3) the active membership of local Baptist churches. He summarized what the Bloom Agency had done so far and sketched out the main lines the media campaign would follow. Then he reminded the assembly that Good News Texas "is not a goodwill campaign for the convention. It is not church advertising. It is going with the best product we have, and that is the gospel of Jesus Christ."

Elder then called on Dr. Jimmy Allen, the pastor of San Antonio's First Baptist Church. Allen is a big man who wears his graying hair rather long for a Baptist preacher and gives off an unmistakable impression of high energy. Working from a few notes scribbled on the back of an envelope, he spoke of "the rhythm in the way God moves in His world, in the tide, in our heartbeat, in the very energy levels of our lives." "There are times," he said, "when God moves in great force and power in our lives, and then there are times of wandering in the wilderness when we begin to appreciate the fact that we cannot live in ecstasy all the time. There must be a hunger before there is filling. There must be thirst before there can be a slaking of thirst. I am convinced we are at the edge of a spiritual awakening in our nation and that some of us are in places where we can already sense the tide of God coming in."

Allen noted that *Newsweek* had carried Charles Colson's testimonial, that the *Fort Worth Star-Telegram* had printed an editorial that told how to be saved, and that CBS had interviewed members of his church for an hour-long documentary on the meaning of salvation. He went on for about twenty minutes, talking about how much we needed revival and how much he hoped God might choose Baptists to be part of the central apparatus by which He moved. Then, in a hushed voice that visibly moved the audience with its intensity, he concluded: "I find myself saying, 'God, could this be the time? Lord, could you be ready now? Is it something that will take our breath away?' I find myself saying, 'O Lord, let it be good news, not just for Texas, not just for Texas Baptists, but for a nation and a world that desperately needs to find out that, indeed, there is good news.'"

Later that afternoon, I sat down with Morriss, Elder, and BGCT executive director Dr. James Landes. Though he was quick to note he is a chemical engineer by training, Dr. Landes' beneficent countenance and rather sermonic manner make it clear he has been around a lot of preachers.

"The rationale of Good News Texas," Landes said, "is the commandment 'Go ye into all the world.' I have seen the heartbreaking conditions so many people are experiencing throughout this state. I had no alternative but to study how to spread the message that there are people in the world who *care*, who are interested in persons just because they are human beings, regardless of race or color or creed, and that the reason these people care is because they believe God *is*, and Christ *is*, and the Scriptures are a mirror of Christ's mind. I realized also that many of our leaders were reaching out for some undergirding arm that could strengthen and help them in their ministry in the local church. So, as I thought and prayed and did a bit of meditating in between fly fishing on the riverbanks of Colorado, I said, 'Lord, if this great big denomination with two million people and forty-two hundred churches and missions will make up its mind to do one thing across a period of a couple of years, there is no telling what good could come of that.' And I thought if we could just plant a seed, maybe it could grow, maybe it could bless a whole state and the nation. I shared that dream with my associates here on the administrative staff and they asked me to share it with the executive board. I came away somewhat shocked but deeply gratified, because men who do not normally react enthusiastically to another evangelistic thrust got to their feet and said, 'This sounds different, get with it!'"

As we talked, Landes and his colleagues echoed what Jimmy Allen had said about the soon-coming revival. Exciting things are happening among our laymen, they said. Signs of awakening are blowing across our nation. But if revival was coming with or without their help, as they seemed to be saying, why didn't Baptists take their $1.5 million and spend it some other way? "Somebody has to be the agent," Landes replied. "God always works through an Abraham, a Moses, an Isaac, a Joseph, a John the Baptist. He doesn't work without working through people. If Texas Baptists have the favorable image the research for this project shows we have, then we've got a *responsibility* commensurate with it. If God wants to use us, we have a responsibility to be available."

I brought up something that had struck me from the moment I saw the first piece of promotional literature about Good News Texas. The logo for the campaign is the Christian fish symbol, with the state of Texas stuffed inside it like Jonah. To accommodate both Amarillo and Laredo, the fish is drawn a bit fat, so that it looks something like a football with a tail or perhaps a Gospel Blimp. Several years ago a mild satire, widely circulated in evangelical circles, described the misadvantures of a Christian group that hired a blimp to broadcast sermons and drop leaflets on the hapless community below. Though it attracted great attention, the townspeople were irritated and offended, and the initial spirit and purpose of the enterprise were lost and perverted. I was curious about whether these men had considered the possibility that Good News Texas might be a Baptist version of the Gospel Blimp.

Elder was aware of the perils. "If we just saturated the media with the gospel message," he said, "and expected something to happen automatically, that would be the Gospel Blimp approach. Just pay your money and send up the blimp. But we are making a real effort to keep that from happening. We are trying to equip ministers and lay people in the local churches to be *witnesses*, so that they don't just let the blimp fly over, but can knock on doors and present the gospel to people as caring, sharing neighbors."

Jimmy Allen had said Baptists would need to remember that "when God comes to town, He doesn't always stay in our house. He moves where He chooses to move and leaps over all kinds of barriers." How would they feel if the Methodists or Presbyterians or Church of Christ picked up some new members on Baptist nickels? The prospect did not seem to dismay them. They were, in fact, informing other denominations in the state about their plans so that if the awakening comes, they can also be ready for it. There is, of course, some confidence that their 4,200 outlets will give Baptists a healthy share of whatever market develops.

This ecumenical talk emboldened me to raise a point I regarded as of at least mild interest. Why had they chosen the Bloom Agency? Granted, it was recognized as one of the best agencies in the country and its Dallas location provided the advantage of close and frequent contact, but was there no sense of incongruity in hiring a Jewish-owned agency to conceive and produce an evangelistic campaign for Southern Baptists? Apparently not. The Baptists chose their agency the same way Procter and Gamble or Exxon might, with a steering committee of seventeen people and a much larger consultation group from across the state that heard presentations by a number of respected firms.

"Bob Bloom is a good salesman," said James Landes. "'When he was through,' I heard a Baptist preacher from East Texas say, 'I don't need to hear anybody else. The man knows where he is going.' When that group voted, they did so with a great feeling of confidence in the ability and desire of the Bloom Agency to help us do what we wanted to do. It was almost unanimous. It was an overwhelming decision.'' Landes admitted to some early personal reservations but insisted things had worked out ''more beautifully and fantastically than we had expected.'' Then he suggested I check out the backgrounds of the men at the agency with primary responsibility for the account.

The Bloom Agency occupies several floors of the Zale Building, which sits alongside Stemmons Freeway like a giant homemaker's misplaced toaster. Instead of the customary rooms and hallways, the agency uses ''action offices,'' work spaces defined by movable partitions about five and a half feet high, which can be shaped to fit needs that change with each new client or campaign. Flexible white hoses bring electrical and telephonic nourishment to each of the modules, so that one can tote up the number of offices currently in use by counting the accordion-pleated umbilici. The occupants of these spaces decorate them as if they are planning to stay for years, so I presume one has a fair chance of hanging onto one's own partitions, but I was told reshuffling is not uncommon.

The furnishings run heavily to chrome, glass, and plastic, with plenty of plants and bright colors. Most of the offices are densely decorated in pop-artifactual chic, with tapestries and macrame hangings and inspirational posters framed in Lucite and fire-alarm boxes and street signs and—everywhere— reminders and remnants of past campaigns. Shelves in the reception area hold symbols of the agency's various clients: Bekins, Southwest Airlines, Owens Sausage, Amalie Motor Oil, Rainbo Bread, Lubriderm Cream, Whataburger, and a score of others. I looked in vain for a New Testament or a Broadman Hymnal, but I guess the display had not yet been brought that far up to date.

Bob Bloom showed me around and talked about the Baptist account. ''We are in the consumer advertising business,'' he explained. ''Our job is to communicate with the general public and get a response from them. That is what we do best. We try to generate retail purchases, to get people to buy motor oil, or a home, or seats on an airplane. We have never been involved in anything like this before, but the thing that stimulated us was the feeling that the BGCT could give us what we want in a partnership role, a sharing of responsibilities as opposed simply to doing what we tell them. They know how to listen, how to guide, how to tell us when we are off base, and they know how to stroke, so we are pleased to have the association from that standpoint. I was impressed that they could not only accept but embrace aspects of our craft that we have difficulty getting business people, including some Harvard MBAs, to accept.''

How did he account for this? ''I'm not really sure,'' Bloom said. ''I guess they are just smart. I had expected a sharp drop-off in intelligence between the leaders of the organization and the men in lower positions. In a business organization like a bank, for example, once you get past the president and a few directors to some of the department heads, you find some terrible prejudices about certain things, a lack of understanding about advertising and research, and an unwillingness to bend. I expected that with the Baptists, but frankly, I found a lot of sharp men at all levels. And they are very flexible. When we got out with the pastors, I expected to confront some prejudice, both from my being Jewish and in their willingness to marry our craft with their pulpit responsibilities. I just didn't find any of that. I found a high degree of comprehension when we went through the various alternatives with them. I kind of expected someone to get up and make an appeal to 'throw all that stuff away and just give people the simple gospel.' It didn't happen. They had smart, agile minds and they really embraced what we were trying to do. If I could get forty rabbis together to do that, I would be terribly surprised. They are also very sincere about the undertaking. It is great to have a client who believes in what he is doing, as opposed to someone who is just grinding out a product.''

Did he have any misgivings about mounting a campaign whose basic premise he, as a Jew, did not believe? ''I never felt any real sensitivity on that issue, except in regard to the terminology, which was very alien to me. Once I became confident they were willing to accept me as a spokesman for the agency and as a craftsman with some expertise, I became very comfortable with it. My role has been much the same as with any client. I feel I am particularly good at organizational work and strategic thinking. I am not concerned with the technological aspects of a motor oil—what it will or won't do for an engine— and I can't comment on the religious aspects of this project. What I am interested in is how we can communicate the selling points to the customer.''

Bob introduced me to his father, Sam Bloom, the agency's founder, who professed an interest in the project that went beyond craftsmanship. He was concerned ''about both the standards and ethics which appear to be declining in politics and business.'' The Baptists, he thought, were on the right track on these matters. Their willingness to lay $1.5 million on the line to bolster the ethics and morality of the state was a courageous act and he was ''terribly enthused'' to have a part in it.

I visited with most of the key personnel working on the account in the agency's new think tank, a tiered and carpeted room with no furniture except for ashtrays and huge pillows covered in plain, madras, batik, and Marimekko. A tray on one of the lower tiers held coffee, Styrofoam cups, little packets of Cremora, Imperial Sugar, Sweet 'n' Low, and a box of those red-and-white plastic sticks that are too skinny to stir anything. On the assumption, I presume, that ideas generated in the room would be too dramatic to jot down on 3 × 5 cards with a ball-point pen, jumbo pads of paper and Magic Markers lay within easy reach. While a person in Faded Glory jeans with stars on the pockets went out to get Frescas and Tabs and Cokes for the non-coffee drinkers, we took our positions, shifted around a bit to look properly relaxed, and began to talk.

Dick Yob, research director for the project, explained that ''the days of doing what we *think* will work are becoming extinct because of the amount of money that is involved. We have to go out and find what really does communicate. Our approach has been to come at this like we would any package goods account, since that is basically what we know how to do.'' The first step had been to see what problems were bothering Texans these days. To accomplish this, Yob hired the Dallas marketing research firm of Louis, Bowles and Grove, Inc., to show a list of problems to approximately 300 Dallas and Austin citizens—divided evenly between active Baptists, inactive Christians, and non-Christians—and ask which most accurately mirrored their own feelings and which were the problems they heard other people discuss. On both counts, all three groups ranked hypocrisy as the number one problem, by agreeing with such statements as ''It's getting harder to trust anybody or anything'' and ''People are not what they pretend to be. They say one thing and do another.''

Survey participants were then offered three possible solutions: (1) reading the Bible, (2) joining a group of active Christians, and (3) entering into a personal relationship with Jesus Christ and following his teachings. All three groups agreed that of the three answers, Christ was the best—though only 27 percent of the inactive Christians and 14 percent of the non-Christians actually felt it was an appropriate solution for them. More than two-thirds of the non-Christians chose none of the three options. In short, despite evidence of considerable spiritual and emotional malaise among backslidden and secular Texans, the field appeared to be something less than white unto harvest. Still, the Baptists and the agency agreed that a personal relation with Jesus was the most commercial of the products they had to offer. The next step was to decide how to package it for wholesale distribution.

At this point, the burden shifted to Bill Hill, the agency's creative director. He did not find the yoke an easy one. What could they say that would communicate effectively to all three target groups? And what vehicle would they use to say it: testimonial? dramatizations? slice of life vignettes? cartoons? jingles? During our first conversation, Hill had a discernible case of advertiser's anxiety. "We are trying to avoid clichés. The men working with us from BGCT are theologians. When they say 'Christ Died for you,' there is a lifetime of knowledge behind it and all sorts of subtleties ripple out of it, but to the people they have singled out as the primary audience—non-Christians—that is a cliché and it may be a turnoff. We want to save the Jesus message to the very end of the TV spots, so we can get people nodding and saying, 'Yes, that is a problem. Yes, I would like to have a solution to that problem.' Then, at the end, we want to say, 'That solution is available to you through Jesus Christ.' We are trying to say, in the simplest form possible, that 'something that happened two thousand years ago is a real force that is relevant to your own individual problems right here and right now. If you are really concerned about your own problems and about what is going on in the world, and you have tried everything else, what have you got to lose?' We are not really trying to say *how* Christ is the answer, but simply *that* he is. We may go into *how* a little more in the other media." The problem of doing justice to the gospel in a brief commercial is tough, Hill admitted: "I keep writing forty-two-second commercials because I just can't boil it all down into thirty seconds. In a thirty-second spot, about all we can say is, 'This aspirin contains more pain relievers than all the others combined.'"

Guy Marble outlined the key public relations aspects of the campaign. His main task would be to bombard local churches throughout the state with newsletters, articles, speeches, posters, lapel buttons, and other communiqués to allow them to take full advantage of the media campaign when it hit their area. The agency people and Baptists both agreed that the world would be barren, like seed on stony ground, unless the local churches were ready not only to urge personal evangelism, but also to accept and nurture those who might be converted. As Jim Goodnight, who has overall responsibility for the account, put it, "We are going to give people the opportunity to respond, but when a guy walks in the back door of a Baptist church some Sunday morning to find what he has been looking for—what happens then will be up to the members of that church. If they are not ready for people who may not share any of their values, then it won't work. If they are ready to accept people 'just as I am,' I believe there will be a tremendous awakening of visible growth in both numbers and spirit." Another promotion task will be to make sure the local churches understand the strategy that will govern the campaign. "When we buy time for these commercials," Goodnight explained, "we are not going to be buying the Sunday Morning Revival Hour. We are going to be buying *Mary Hartmann, Mary Hartmann* and *All in the Family* and *Sonny and Cher.* You can anticipate the kinds of reactions thousands and thousands of Texas Baptists are going to have—'What are we doing supporting that kind of program?' Of course, our purpose is not to support the program. It's where we have to go to reach the people we want to reach."

Despite the frequent comparison of selling the gospel to selling aspirin or motor oil, it seemed clear these men were taking the matter more seriously than that. I recalled what Dr. Landes had said about checking their backgrounds, so I asked each of them to characterize his religious position. The agency didn't exactly turn out to be a collection of Madison Avenue cynics. Dick Yob is a graduate of Catholic University at Marquette, sends his oldest son to parochial school, and is active in the Church. Bill Hill is the son of a Baptist preacher in Amarillo but became so disillusioned with evangelical Christianity by the time he reached high school that for several years he dabbled in Zen, studied Rosicrucian literature, and considered going to live with the Dalai Lama in Tibet. Instead, he got married and became an Episcopalian. For the past seven years, he has participated in Bible class taught by conservative Biblicist Mal Couch, a graduate of fundamentalist Dallas Theological Seminary who specializes in the interpretation of Biblical prophecy. Public relations advisor Guy Marble describes himself as "a lapsed Methodist," but his colleague Frank Demarest is a member of the Northwest Bible Church in Dallas (also aligned with the Dallas Theological Seminary) and admits he

stands a bit to the right of Southern Baptists in his theology. Jim Goodnight grew up in the Park Cities Baptist Church in Dallas but switched to the Church of Christ after he married the granddaughter of G. H. P. Showalter, a Church of Christ patriarch and former editor of one of its most conservative papers, the *Firm Foundation.* Though he locates himself in "the liberal, ecumenical wing of the Church of Christ" (a figure of speech like "virile impotence"), he is still active in the Preston Crest congregation in Dallas and has taught classes in C. S. Lewis' *Mere Christianity*, hardly a radical treatise.

These men, it turns out, are not the only Christians in the Bloom Agency. "You would be amazed," Goodnight said, "at the number of people within the agency who wanted to work on this account. Not only have a number of these closet Christians surfaced, but about twenty-five of us now meet each Wednesday at noon to pray and share our concerns and testimonials." "It's really neat," Demarest said. "All our working lives we have had this separation between our Christian faith and what we do on our jobs. For me, this is the first time to bring the two together."

"There is a terrible intensity among the people on the team," Hill said. "This is not just another piece of package goods. This is something that is going to affect people's lives. I really feel what I am doing. I keep thinking, 'We are going to save Texas!' and that gets to be a bit of a hang-up and causes a mental block." Another problem, Goodnight observed, is that "each of us gets his own theology and beliefs, his own personal slant woven into it. One of the hardest things to do in any advertising is to wash yourself out of it and consider only the people you are trying to write for and what their needs are."

"With most products," Yob pointed out,

"you are selling to people who are already users. It is a matter of getting them to switch brands or buy more of your product. But in this campaign, nonusers are the number one target."

That afternoon I attended a meeting between members of the Bloom team and key staff members at the Baptist Building. Mainly, they were catching each other up on how things were going in their sections of the ball park. Jim Goodnight read the strategy statement that had emerged from their research. "What we are trying to do," he said, "is communicate to people that the frustrations they experience with the hypocrisy and lack of integrity in today's world is the result of misplaced priorities, and that the solution is to place their trust in Jesus Christ who will never fail them, rather than on the imperfect things of the world." The Baptists liked that a lot.

Demarest, Marble, and Mary Colias Carter reviewed PR plans. A steady stream of articles would appear in the *Baptist Standard* to "soften up the terrain," and a piece would appear in the next issue of the *Helper*, BGCT's women's magazine. Pastors would be supplied with information they could use to raise money for the program. Every church would receive materials explaining the nature and scope of the project. Marble reported that he and his associates had done "much agonizing posterwise," but promised the first in a series of posters would be ready in "six weeks max."

They also talked a bit about honorary chairmen. Billy Graham had agreed to serve as national honorary chairman, but both the Baptists and the Bloom representatives wanted to make sure the campaign did not become a Graham affair. "We are not going to be able to use him much in a public way," Marble said. "If he is flying from coast to coast, we may be able to get him to stop off

at DFW airport for a press conference and say how great Good News Texas is. We can do little things like that without much financial or time commitment, but that will be about the extent of it. Right now, we just want to get half a day with him at his place in North Carolina to produce several short items that could be used to stir up enthusiasm in the local churches." In addition to Graham, two state chairmen would be chosen—people who could generate prestige and interest in Jesus just by their association with the campaign. After all, one Baptist executive observed, "Public relations is the name of the game."

Over the next several weeks, Bill Hill and his associates developed four proto-commercials in "animatic" form—a series of still drawings with voice-overs rather than the live action or true animation that would be used in the final product. Each of the four took a different slant and would be tested to see which, if any, might appeal most to the Texas contingent of a lost and dying world. If none clicked, it would be, quite literally, back to the drawing board. If one seemed clearly better than the others, it would become the model for the actual spots to be used in the campaign. On three successive evenings in early October, representatives of Louis, Bowles and Grove showed the spots to "focus groups" drawn from the three target populations. Active Baptists met the first night in three churches scattered around Dallas.

I am not supposed to identify either the church or the people I observed, so I won't, but I promise you it was a real Baptist church, with a poster thermometer in the foyer that showed how the fund drive was going.

Judy Briggs, a market researcher for Louis, Bowles and Grove, told the group they were to give their reactions to some commercials being prepared for television. She did not say they were Baptist commercials or mention Good News Texas. She then showed the commercials on a videotape machine and asked the group to fill out a questionnaire after they viewed each one.

The first commercial, identified as "Promises," offered shots of politicians, automobile dealers, and various businessmen making familiar promises—"You've got my word on it." "It's a sure thing." "You can depend on it." It ended with a note to the effect that Jesus is the only one whose promises can be trusted and "Isn't it time we listened?" The positive responses to "Promises" indicated the Christians held a disillusioned view of humanity: "Everybody is trying to put something over on us." "People will let you down, but if you trust in God, He won't let you down." "You have to put your faith in the Lord and not in other people." I got the message, but I felt sad, and the stark ceiling light illumined other, almost forgotten rooms in my soul, rooms not furnished with warm and reassuring memories, rooms abandoned because the heat had been shut off and the broken panes let in too much damp and cold.

The next example showed a man arising to the sound of a strident alarm and struggling to meet the day as he listened to the depressing litany of the morning news. Then a voice-over announcer asked, "Wouldn't it be a change to wake up one morning without anxiety over what the day might bring? To know that whatever the world throws at you, you'll make it? If that kind of change would be welcome, then get with the one person who can do the changing—Jesus Christ. For a change." This, too, seemed to confirm the experience of the group: "We can't depend on the news being good," they said, "but if we have Jesus Christ with us, it makes no difference. You have to have Him because what problems can you face without Christ?"

The third effort did not lend itself so easily to clichéd response. In this one, a black man told of how he had been a revolutionary, seeking social change by whatever means seemed expedient. But not long ago, he said, he had run across another revolutionary and it had changed his life completely. He can change yours, too, the man promised. Then he said, "My name is Eldridge Cleaver. I'm Living Proof."

Bill Hill had told me one of the commercials would be a testimonial, and I would not have been surprised to have seen Charles Colson or Johnny Cash telling about what God had wrought in their lives. I try to keep up with the box scores on notable conversions, but I had somehow missed the news that the icy soul of Eldridge Cleaver had been warmed with fire from above. I was impressed that Texas Baptists would consider pumping hundreds of thousands of dollars into publicizing the testimony of a man who might still be regarded with skepticism and caution by some of the new white brothers. And I was especially curious about how the members of this largely working-class church might react.

I studied the lone black member of the group, a man about 45. Was he an Uncle Tom who would fear that the sight and sound of this panther in lamb's clothing might stir resentment left over from the sixties and jeopardize his perhaps lately won and still tenuous place in a predominantly white congregation? Would he say of Cleaver, as Peter had said of Christ, "I never knew him"? No, he wouldn't, "This is very beautiful," he said. "It comes from a controversial person a lot of us can identify with. We know Eldridge Cleaver was searching for something he could not find in the world, but only in Jesus Christ. I had much the same problems in my life at one time. It was very hard for me to accept certain things, but now I am able to face these things and accept them." That is not exactly revolution, but it isn't "white folks always been nice to me" either.

A middle-aged woman who had taken much longer than anyone else to fill out her questionnaire spoke next. I sensed she was about to vent a little of the racist spleen we often associate with working-class fundamentalists. "This was also my favorite," she said. "It shows that Christ is a Man for all men. He is not a white man's savior or a black man's savior or a Jew's savior. He is for everyone. I think every minority feels pressures and I think there are times in everybody's life when they feel like they are a minority, even though nobody else may look upon them that way. When you are low man on the totem pole in your office and everybody says, 'You do this' and 'You do that,' and it seems like you do everything for everybody, then you can identify with the feeling of being a little bit left out."

The final commercial depicted a child learning to ice skate with the loving help of a parent-figure in a unisex outfit like the Olympic speed skaters wear. The narrator told how important it is to have someone you can depend on when the going gets a bit hazardous and concluded with the slogan, "Learn to live with Jesus Christ." I liked it best of the four. Its symbolism was aesthetically appealing and I like the way it avoided both the negative connotations about human nature (though I am not especially sanguine about the natural goodness of our kind) and the spurious overgeneralization implicit in any case based on a single testimony. The nine focus groups agreed more strongly than on any other point that "Ice Rink" was clearly the poorest of the four commercials, "It was boring," they said. "It just beat around the bush and didn't really say any-

thing." "I can't ice skate, so I don't identify with that one at all." "A waste of film." I decided not to become a consultant on mass evangelism.

Ms. Briggs asked who they thought might sponsor commercials like these. Oh, the Catholics or SMU or maybe the Dallas Council of Churches. Not one named the Baptists. Baptists have W. A. Criswell; they don't need Eldridge Cleaver.

The meetings with the Baptist groups were designed to see if any of the commercials were likely to run into the kind of opposition that might make funding or other forms of cooperation difficult. But the real test, everyone agreed, would be with those who described themselves as nominal or inactive Christians and those who openly acknowledged they were not religious in any conventional sense. A pool of such people had been obtained by distribution questionnaires in Dallas office buildings; groups representing both sexes and a broad range of ages had been selected from this pool. In keeping with the piety of the groups, we met at a neutral site, the Marriott Inn. Curtiss Grove, a partner in Louis, Bowles and Grove, was moderator for the evening. As we waited for people to assemble, he lamented having to pass up a cocktail party down the hall.

The group looked pretty representative of backsliders I have known: a workingman in his thirties; an overweight balding man who talked knowledgeably about the video equipment; a tall, thin older man who wore a tie with a leisure suit and looked as though he smoked a lot and was perhaps familiar with the taste of liquor; a woman who was pretty in the way that Southwest Airlines stewardesses are pretty, and a thin, serious man who appeared to be with her; a young woman about twenty who wore blue eye shadow and orthodontic braces; a neat woman in her thirties who looked like she was probably in charge of several people where she worked and had a reputation for getting things done on time; one of those ubiquitous, interchangeable young men with a moustache and styled hair and a preference for shiny shirts with sailboats or jockeys on them; a foxy brunette in a suede jacket and lots of bracelets and rings and dark fingernail polish who seemed a poor conversion prospect; and several others I knew then I wouldn't be able to remember. For the most part, they represented a bit higher socioeconomic status than the Baptists I had visited the night before.

Grove is good at his job and easily elicited comments from the group. Interestingly, their reactions were not remarkably different from those of the active Baptists, except that none of them rated the Cleaver commercial highest and four of the twelve designated it their least favorite. (As it turned out, this response was something of an anomaly; the other two groups meeting at the same time felt strongly that the Cleaver spot was the best.) When asked what the commercial sought to accomplish, one man guessed it was trying to stir up pity for Cleaver. Another thought it too controversial even for minority-group people and felt its appeal would be limited to revolutionaries or people "with awful problems."

Each of the other spots got three or four votes as the best of the lot, but what one felt was pungent, another would judge pedantic. The 28-year-old in the shiny shirt said he didn't think any was much better than the others, since they were all about God and the church. A young man about nineteen seemed rather bemused by the whole business, as though he thought his sainted mother had somehow arranged to get him invited to a subtle soulwinning campaign, maybe even paid his way. But all things considered, I think this group uttered more pious clichés

than the dedicated Baptists. Since they did not know they had been chosen because of their shared lukewarmness, they seemed to feel some need to let their colleagues know they were believers. In spite of what may have been a bit of overcompensation, however, I sensed almost none of the assurance I had seen and heard the night before. Several people got sad looks on their faces and lit up cigarettes. I believe they were pretty serious about it all. I had agreed not to ask any questions and I may have misread their reaction, but I had not expected what I sensed and it seemed unmistakable. I wouldn't be surprised to learn that the older man in the leisure suit had started going back to church with his wife.

As before, almost no one perceived the commercials as Baptist in origin. The President's Council on Physical Fitness, the Cerebral Palsy Association, an ice rink, the Department of Health, Education, and Welfare, Channel 39, and Sominex all seemed as likely as the Southern Baptists to sponsor such spots.

On the third night, self-designated unbelievers viewed the spots. This was the crucial test, the people at whom the main thrust of the campaign was aimed, but their preferences turned out to differ little from their more pious predecessors. Neither "Morning News" nor "Promises" struck a responsive chord. One man who at first thought "Morning News" was touting CBS news was irritated when it proved to have a religious theme. Another picked up the religious slant earlier but just thought, "Here we go again." A woman complained that "it doesn't tell me what to do with my problems, except give them to someone else. A little information about how Jesus is going to handle my problems would be helpful."

"Promises" caused even stronger negative reactions—one woman characterized it as "hateful" and said, "It made me want to lock myself in a room and shoot anybody that makes promises"—and "Ice Rink" once again came in as the unanimous last choice. One woman described it as "childish the way they wanted you to put yourself in Jesus' hands with no mention of adult choices." Another took issue with the whole ice-skating metaphor; she didn't feel at all like an ice skater, but rather "a yo-yo, every day I feel like a yo-yo." A man about thirty said he felt a better metaphor would be someone playing poker, or perhaps even solitaire. I doubt seriously the Southern Baptists will pick up on that.

Once again the Cleaver commercial was picked as the best—unanimously by one caucus. A man who freely called himself an agnostic said, "I know what Cleaver's life has been, and if this guy says he can pull it out with Christ, well, I may think there is something to it." He admitted to some doubts whether Cleaver might just be trying to escape a prison sentence by publicly embracing religion, but rejected them: "I have not agreed with Cleaver in the past, but I have respected his integrity." Others did question Cleaver's sincerity, but what carried the day was the feeling that "it gave me a choice. It told me what his opinion was, but it didn't say, 'You take my opinion, buddy, because it is good for you too.'"

The success of the Cleaver spot naturally raised the question of whose testimonials people could accept. The subject shouldn't be an ordinary person, someone from the viewer's own neighborhood ("I would figure someone was just trying to get on television and get some publicity."); it certainly shouldn't be Richard Nixon or Patty Hearst ("It is still too close. With Cleaver you can almost feel the guy has paid his debt and now has a whole new slant on life."). The ideal person, one man thought, would be a non-

criminal figure who still had room for notable repentance—the two names mentioned were Billy Graham and Earl Scheib, the $29.95 auto paint job man.

Interestingly, the non-Christians had no difficulty accepting the idea that Southern Baptists might be behind the commercials. The use of testimonials seemed "more Baptist" than any of the other approaches, even though Eldridge Cleaver seemed like an unlikely star. One woman suggested that if Baptists were indeed the sponsors, they would do well to hide the fact, since "many people are turned off by their extremist actions."

If the consultants were looking for useful criticism, the non-Christians gave them plenty of that, but if they were looking for some signs that Good News Texas was going to send unbelievers flocking to church, the meeting provided little basis for hope. One man quickly deduced that his group contained no practicing Christians and said, "I think people like us tend to rely on ourselves rather than look outside for some kind of placebo. I don't care whether people believe in Jesus or Muhammad or Darrell Royal; just because they believe it and get out and preach it doesn't mean it's true. I just don't buy the idea that you can blindly put your faith and trust in any person, including Jesus."

The bad news for Good News Texas was that the non-Christians didn't like the whole idea of religious commercials. "I am turned off by commercials of this sort," said one. "It cheapens religion to sell it like toothpaste." "There is nothing in these commercials that appeals to me in any way or makes me feel I should investigate Christianity," another said. "They make it sound like Jesus is going to open up a used-car lot." But one man who also had a negative reaction to selling Jesus on TV conceded that "television is such a powerful communications medium that if they use it right, it can help. There are some people whose only way of touching anything outside their home is television.''

It is Bloom's job, then, to see that TV is used right. The hope that any single commercial might provide Baptists with an offer lost Texans could not refuse seemed pretty well dashed. Still, the response to news that the sins of the apostle of Black Power had been washed away had proven sufficiently promising to convince Bloom and the BGCT that testimonials were the route to take. At the state convention in San Antonio two weeks later, L. L. Morriss proclaimed that the theme of Good News Texas would be ''Living Proof'' and would concentrate on ''presenting the testimony of people who have experienced the saving grace of our Lord.'' Dr. Landes announced that Baylor football coach Grant Teaff and actress Jeannette Clift George had agreed to serve as honorary co-chairmen and played a tape from Billy Graham, who said the world was hungry for good news and he was pleased to have a part in the boldest evangelistic venture in the history of Texas Baptists.

By the first of December, some of the top converts in the country had been lined up to add their testimony to Cleaver's. There had been minor problems. Some Christian entertainers had been discouraged from participating by their agents, who feared it might hurt their image with the public. Others had been screened out when their faith was adjudged not yet solid enough to guarantee against an embarrassing relapse during the campaign; no one, for example, would want to take a chance on Jerry Lee Lewis if he were suddenly to go into one of his periodic conversion phases. The final list included country singers Jeannie C. Riley and Connie Smith, Mexican musician Paulino Bernal,

Consul-General of Honduras Rosargentina Pinel-Cordova, Houston Oiler Billy ''White Shoes'' Johnson, and Allan Mayer of Oscar Mayer and Company. A couple of big ones had gotten away. For some reason, Charles Colson had backed out and had to be replaced by Dean Jones, and a former Hell's Angel who conducts a bike ministry on the West Coast didn't leave a forwarding address when he set out on his latest missionary journey. But all the others were ready to go and film crews were heading for Nashville and L.A. to record their stories. We'll see the results soon.

As I wait, I am aware of poignant feelings, I have watched and listened as good, sincere, intelligent men and women groped for a way of making that which stands at the center of their lives plausible and attractive to those who live outside the sacred canopy. Perhaps it will work. I think I could accept that in good grace. I generally feel pretty comfortable around people who take their religion seriously, especially if it is one of the leading brands. But I confess I do not believe historians will remember 1977 as the year the Great Awakening came to Texas. I expect Baptist churches may be stirred up considerably and some wayward Christians may return home like the prodigal. These are the groups that have always responded best to the call of revival. The main work of evangelism in American history—with, it should be noted, some exceptions—has been to keep believers plugged into their systems. That in itself is a significant accomplishment and may well justify the cost and effort involved. Of course, here and there a real scoundrel or a true skeptic may be turned around and set on the Glory Road, but I expect Good News Texas will come and go without making a great deal of difference in the lives of the 4,700,000 sinners at whom it is primarily aimed. That will no doubt discourage a lot of folks, but maybe it shouldn't. After all, even though He knew how to use a bit of dash and sparkle to draw a crowd, Jesus never got anything like a majority, and if the Word of God is anything to go by, He never expected to (Matthew 7:13–14).

APPENDIX: DIGNITY IN CHURCH ADVERTISING [1916]*

O. C. Harn

The church has discovered in advertising, a new force which it believes it can use in furthering its work. There is danger that, in its enthusiasm over its discovery, mistakes may be made. . . .

Dignity is an attribute which should be possessed by all advertising which advertises dignified things. Some advertising men believe that dignity is a handicap to forceful, resultful publicity; but that is because they do not know what dignity is. They confound it with dryness, dullness—old-fogyness.

This is a wrong conception. A dignified man may be the most intensely interesting man in your circle. He may be the best business-getter. He may be the man above all others to whom to look to get things done.

*Excerpt from *Advertising and Selling*, November 1916, p. 15. O. C. Harn was Advertising Manager, National Lead Co., at the time this article was written.

Contrast the dignified methods of . . . advertising success with this sickly attempt found in a collection of church advertisements.

"Don't be a lemon! Tie on to the happy Sunday-nighters."

Or this: A paper wrapper was folded about a piece of pasteboard to imitate chewing gum and the label was printed thus:

Chew this over!	Dr. White's Compound for human ills	The Flavor lasts

This, if you will believe it, was used to advertise the service a church has to offer for the benefit of men!

But, you say, flippant and even vulgar preachers seem to have success in getting serious results. Why will not advertising work similarly?

I would say first that, as it is the exception in the commercial world for trivial advertising to bring the results desired, so is it the exception in the pulpit. . . .

A final caution, do not get the idea that dignity precludes warmth, earnestness, appeal to the emotions, startling effects, and force (or punch, if you like the overworked word—I don't).

The great orator knows well how to use all these means of moving his audience—knows it better than does the clown.

Non-Profits Need Development Orientation to Survive

CHARLES W. LAMB, JR.

Success of non-profit organizations in the future will depend a great deal on how well they adopt a development orientation which includes a marketing strategy, argues this author. He outlines the important considerations faced by management to position their institutions in facing demanding times.

To many people, the term "marketing" connotes crass exploitation; the foistering of unwanted goods and services on unsuspecting people; the superficial glitter of billboards and neon signs; obnoxious television commercials; and aggressive salespeople. This is an inaccurate view, I believe.

The philosophy of marketing is simple and intuitively appealing. The so-called "marketing concept" is a philosophy that states that *the social and economic justification for an organization's existence is the satisfaction of customer wants*. It entails establishing a way for the organization to learn about customer wants, and using that information internally to create marketing programs that will produce mutually satisfying exchanges with target markets (the people served by the organization).

This philosophy has evolved over time as marketing thinking has passed through various stages. Interestingly, Philip Kotler has suggested that the art of fund raising has also passed through various stages that are analogous to the evolution of the marketing concept. He refers to these stages as begging, collecting, campaigning, and development.[1]

Begging is characterized by needy people and organizations pleading with others to give them money or other items of value. The prevailing attitude is that more fortunate people and organizations should take pity on their less fortunate neighbors and give them a helping hand.

Collecting is characterized by organizations regularly accepting donations from individuals and organizations. Sunday church collections, Goodwill Industries, the Salvation Army, and various organizations such as MDA and March of Dimes that place donation containers in convenience stores are examples of collecting.

The prevailing attitude of organizations that rely on collecting is that people should supply them because they are a worthy cause and are making a positive contribution in the

---

[1] Philip Kotler, *Marketing for Nonprofit Organizations*, 2nd ed. (Englewood Cliffs, N.J.: Prentice-Hall, Inc., 1982). p. 425.

Reprinted with permission from *Fund Raising Management* (August 1983), pp. 26–30.

community. This is a passive, inward-looking approach to fund raising.

Campaigning is characterized by organizations appointing individuals and groups to actively solicit donations from the public in general. The goal is normally to canvass every possible source of contributions in a systematic manner.

Most universities, the United Way, and indeed, almost all fund raising organizations are in this stage of evolution. The prevailing attitude in campaign-oriented organizations is that there are many people in the community who owe them, or ought to support them. They view their task as locating these individuals and/or organizations and convincing them to give.

Development is characterized by carefully identifying homogeneous groups or segments within a heterogeneous market, identifying their motivations for giving, and designing marketing programs that will bring about mutually satisfying exchanges over an extended period of time. As Kotler has noted, the prevailing attitude in development-oriented organizations is that:

We must analyze our position in the marketplace, concentrate on those donor sources whose interests are best matched to ours, and design our solicitation programs to supply needed satisfactions to each donor group. This approach involves carefully segmenting the donor markets; measuring the giving potential of each donor market; assigning executive responsibility for developing each market through using research and communication approaches; and developing a plan and budget for each market based upon its potential.[2]

Although the four stages of fund raising evolved sequentially, they all exist today.

[2] Ibid., p. 425.

Some organizations believe that they must beg for support.

Others subscribe to the "better mousetrap theory" and simply assume that support will be forthcoming. Still others believe that if they ring enough doorbells, shake enough hands, mail enough appeals, and generally saturate the market that their fund raising goals will eventually be met.

The most progressive, and most successful, fund raising organizations have moved to the development stage. They have adopted a marketing orientation and have implemented sound, proven, contemporary marketing practices.

CAMPAIGN, DEVELOPMENT ORIENTATIONS

There are four major differences between campaign- and development-oriented organizations. These differences are illustrated by the chart and briefly discussed in the following paragraphs.

Focus

Campaign-oriented organizations may be characterized as "inward-looking," focusing on the needs of the organization and its managers. They typically have a small number of full-time employees and are staffed by large numbers of volunteer workers for short periods of time during the fund raising effort.

Managers often function as separate entities more concerned with defending their status, budget allocation, or role than with how to provide benefits to prospective donors. Volunteer workers have a limited temporal commitment to the organization and are more committed to the needs of the organization than to the needs of prospective donors.

Campaign-oriented organizations fail to recognize that people give their money and time resources with the expectation of providing and/or receiving benefits, not to support the delivery of specific activities, programs, or services. An organization's programs or services are only vehicles that convey benefits to donors and other client groups.

The distinction between focusing on programs and services instead of benefits has enormous implications for the way in which an organization defines its business and its long-term relevance. For example, if an organization defines its business in terms of specific programs or service, it is likely to miss fund raising opportunities, for there is a wide-range of programs and services through which people's wants may be met.

Instead of specific programs or services, the starting point should be meeting donor and client group wants. This may be achieved through a wide variety of programs and services.

For example, university alumni give money for a variety of reasons including the feeling to be part of their alma mater. This benefit can be facilitated through a wide variety of programs and services including newsletters, magazines, alumni clubs, dances, dinners and other events, homecoming receptions, priority status for athletic and cultural event tickets, among others.

Development-oriented organizations are integrated and "outward-looking," focusing on the needs of prospective donors. They are normally staffed by stable numbers of professionals and volunteers who have long-term commitments to the organization.

Integration has two important implications. First, it means that there must be selfless coordination within the organization and willingness to cooperate rather than to compete with other personnel.

Second, the attitude of each employee must be donor-oriented. Any individual professional, support person, staff member, or volunteer may be the only contact that a prospective donor has with the organization.

Hence, in that prospective donor's mind, the contact person represents the organization. A single person that is not donor-oriented weakens the positive contributions of everyone else.

If the person answering the telephone is abrupt or discourteous, for instance, that contact may be taken by the potential donor as being representative of the organization's orientation. For this integrative, outward-looking approach to be successfully implemented, it has to be enthusiastically embraced by senior managers who have the critical task of encouraging its dissemination throughout the organization.

Focusing on prospective donor wants instead of the organization's needs has at least four important implications. First, it ensures that the organization does not become preoccupied with programs, services, or the short-term desires or preferences of individual managers. Second, it encourages innovation and creativity of programs and services by suggesting that there are many ways to service similar donor preferences. Third, it stimulates an awareness of changes in donor preferences as they occur, and hence development efforts are likely to remain relevant. Fourth, it will probably lead to a broader definition of the role of the organization and thus contribute toward keeping its services and programs abreast of society's wants.

Targets

A campaign-oriented organization targets its efforts at "everybody" or the "average donor," while a development-oriented organization aims at "specific somebodies." Historically, many fund raising organizations have employed standardized appeals.

FIGURE 1: Campaign and development orientations contrasted

	Focus	Target	Means	Ends
Campaign Orientation	Inward Upon the Organizations' Needs	Everybody	Intensive Promotion	Money
Development Orientation	Outward Upon Donors' Wants and Preferences	Specific Individuals and Groups	Coordinated Development Strategies	Mutually Satisfying Exchanges

This may be termed the "lowest common denominator" approach to fund raising. It seeks to appeal to the maximum number of people at some minimal level.

The fallacy of developing appeals which are directed at the average donor is that there are relatively few average donors. Typically, populations are characterized by their diversity.

An average donor simply represents a midpoint on some set of characteristics. Development-oriented organizations recognize that potential donors are not homogeneous populations.

They recognize the value of market segmentation to divide heterogeneous populations into smaller homogeneous groups, identifying their motivations for giving, selecting those groups whose interests are most compatible with the organization's, and developing solicitation programs that are specifically designed to match the wants and preferences of each targeted group. As an example, the Brooklyn Academy of Music (BAM) has computerized its mailing list according to what customers bought in the past.

Different subscription literature is sent to those identified as dance subscribers than those identified as music subscribers. A totally different solicitation program is directed at black and Hispanic market segments.

Means

A campaign-oriented organization seeks to generate revenue primarily through intensive, short-term promotional activities. This usually includes some combination of media advertising, direct mail, and personal solicitation.

This once-a-year event approach is analogous to the traveling carnival that comes to town once a year. They come in, set up their tents, aggressively promote their presence, put on the show, pack up their gear, leave, and aren't heard from again until next year.

In contrast, supermarkets, banks, department stores, and most other merchants operate year-round. Their goal is to develop long-term relations with loyal patrons.

Development-oriented organizations also seek long-term loyal patronage from their donors. They achieve this by maintaining ongoing relationships using personal contact, newsletters and magazines, meetings, and other means of keeping in touch.

They perceive their supporters as clients or customers whose long-term interests are compatible with those of the organization. The organization's needs are best met by maintaining an ongoing exchange with its supporters.

Ongoing exchanges are facilitated not only

by communication, but also by carefully blending the other elements of the so-called "marketing mix" (product, collection, and pricing) into a coordinated development strategy.

Product strategy is concerned with specifically defining what benefits contributors receive in exchange for their donations. Examples include self-esteem, recognition, fear reduction, fulfillment of obligations or responsibilities, tax advantages, etc.

Collection strategy facilitates the delivery of contributions. It entails establishing how, when, and where prospective donors can make contributions.

The Jerry Lewis MDA telethon, for example, has been extremely successful in recent years due in part to its collection strategy. Viewers are constantly reminded to call a local telephone number to make their pledge.

Volunteer workers record their names, addresses, and the amount pledged so that collection envelopes can be mailed out immediately. Contrast this to the normal "*Support. . .*" appeal that fails to tell people when, where, or how to send their donations. Collection strategy should make it easy for potential supporters to contribute.

Pricing strategy represents how much the organization would like members of selected target markets to contribute. This strategy is inextricably linked to the exchange process.

Donors must be convinced that the tangible or intangible benefits that they receive in an exchange are equal to or greater than the price that they pay. Establishing the proper price is not easy and often requires empirical research.

The Brooklyn Academy of Music, for example, routinely sends test mailings offering the same series at different prices. A comparison of responses sometimes reveals that the lower price is more effective and some-

times the higher price produces more subscriptions. Asking for too little is as grave an error as asking for too much.

Ends

The ultimate objective of a campaign is to raise money to support the organization's activities, including the delivery of services. The objective of development is to satisfy donor groups in exchange for support.

This difference is extremely important because the desired end result substantially influences the focus, target, and means employed in the fund raising effort. A desired end of raising money will likely lead to a campaign orientation with an internal focus, targeted at everyone, using intensive, short-term promotional means as opposed to an integrated outward-looking effort focusing on the wants and preferences of identified target markets, and using a coordinated development strategy.

The actual tasks involved in moving from a campaign to a development orientation are fairly simple and straightforward. The first task entails restructuring the organization and educating all personnel regarding development philosophy.

All individuals within the organization must learn to become integrated and outward-looking, focusing on the needs of prospective donors as opposed to inward-looking, focusing on the needs of the organization and its managers. The organization's activities must reflect this orientation.

Second, an information system must be established to identify potential donors' wants and preferences. This information is necessary in order to segment heterogeneous populations into homogeneous groups that have common needs, preferences, willingness, and/or ability to support the organization.

Once the heterogeneous population has been segmented, the most attractive groups, or those whose interests best match those of the organization, can be targeted for specific solicitation programs designed to produce mutually satisfying exchange relationships over an extended period of time. These programs include product, collection, pricing, and communication dimensions that must be carefully blended together to form a cohesive development strategy.

Finally, long-range strategic planning is an integral part of implementing a development orientation. Strategic planning requires that the organization look objectively at where it has been in the past, where it is now, where it is headed in the future, and how it is going to get there. It focuses attention upon long-term objectives rather than upon short-term expediencies, thus providing direction for action and a correct perspective in times of crisis. It also forces management to continually realign its resources with the changing environmental situation and changing donor want priorities.

Fund raising has clearly entered the development era. The basic proposition of this paper is that the survival and success of fund raising organizations in the 1980s and beyond will depend upon the extent to which they adopt a development orientation. Responsibility for this task rests with top management, whose support, encouragement, and sometimes insistence is necessary for fund raising organizations to move to development stage thinking.

Marketing's Application to Fund Raising

WILLIAM A. MINDAK • H. MALCOLM BYBEE

In a recent issue of the *Journal of Marketing*, Professors Kotler and Levy maintained that marketing is a societal activity which goes considerably beyond the selling of toothpaste, soap, and steel [1]. They suggested that the basic concepts of product development, pricing, distribution, and communication also apply to nonbusiness organizations interested in services, persons, and ideas. Further, they challenged marketing people to expand their thinking and to apply their skills to an increasing range of social activity rather than to a narrowly defined business activity.

This article is in part a response to that challenge. It discusses a specific case study

William A. Mindak and H. Malcolm Bybee, "Marketing's Application to Fund Raising," *Journal of Marketing* (July 1971), pp. 13-18. Reprinted from *Journal of Marketing*, published by the American Marketing Association.

which applied marketing concepts to a March of Dimes fund raising campaign. The concepts utilized in the study include many of those suggested by Kotler and Levy, plus some additional systematic factors (which are often peculiar to the marketing of ideas and causes). In addition, the article provides some specific examples of communication factors.

THE CASE STUDY

This particular case concerns a March of Dimes fund raising drive held in Travis County, Texas, in January 1970. Despite limited funds and facilities, or perhaps *because* of these limits, the authors had an opportunity to experiment with marketing concepts in an area not traditionally considered a business enterprise.

Anyone who has worked with charitable or volunteer organizations probably is well aware that very few of these organizations have a formally established plan. If they do have a "handbook," it is usually filled with anecdotes, success stories, or invocations to positive thinking. This was not the case for the March of Dimes Foundation, which has pioneered many solicitation techniques that are widely copied by other associations and agencies. However, the perspective of the handbook seemed curiously dated as if one were inspecting the organizational chart of a sales-oriented company back in the 1950s rather than a marketing-oriented company of the 1970s. Despite these difficulties, the authors attempted to translate the Foundation's handbook into a meaningful marketing plan, utilizing recent contributions from systems analyses as well as flow diagrams.

MARKETING ANALYSIS

The first handicap the authors encountered in conducting the marketing analysis was the lack of primary research data about the "heavy giver," his demographic characteristics, the location and size of this particular market, and his basic motivations for giving or not giving. In view of the fact that since its inception in 1934 through 1960 the National Foundation had raised $618.5 million, and that in 1967 it was the fourth largest public health agency in terms of contributions (some $22 million), one would expect a wealth of primary marketing data. However, the policy of the National Foundation of the March of Dimes has been to spend money on medical research rather than on consumer or marketing research. A review of past Chapter records data, in addition to exploratory investigations in the local community, did indicate the following problems:

1. *An apathetic and uninformed public who still considered the major aim of the organization to be the prevention of polio.*

With the advent of the Salk (1955) and later the Sabin (1962) vaccine, an effective prevention for polio was achieved. Although the National Foundation had announced interests in other related diseases, particularly birth defects, as early as 1958, relatively few people had changed their "image" of the March of Dimes.

A preliminary telephone survey conducted in Travis County indicated that only *17.5%* of the respondents volunteered birth defects for the March of Dimes on the unaided recall basis. When aided, only another 13.4% made the association. Thus, 30.9% of those surveyed realized that the March of Dimes was becoming concerned with birth defects.

Therefore, although the product had been redefined, the Travis County public was not aware of this "redefinition."

2. *Decreasing interest in the organization and a subsequent decline in involvement by volunteers.*

This was attributed to a general deemphasis in the importance of birth and child-rearing by women, with subsequent lessened interest in the birth process, and increasing competition from other "causes" needing volunteers.

3. *Declining returns from each campaign in Travis County.*
4. *Lack of primary marketing research data on the composition of donors and the location of prime market segments for the current year or for the previous year.*
5. *Evidence that nationally prepared campaign materials did not apply to the local situation.*

There was a feeling that the national campaign was too organization-centered and not benefit-centered. The use of such themes as "250,000 defective babies are born each year with birth defects" was not personally involving, and the shock effect of a single poster child with missing and disfigured limbs seemed too negative and too removed to be effective.

In addition to the problems, a market analysis indicated several potential opportunities:

1. *A long public association of the March of Dimes Organization with the area of public health.*

A nationwide opinion survey conducted by the American Institute of Public Opinion found that 83% of the population in the U.S. could identify the March of Dimes.

2. *Recent breakthroughs in the area of birth-defect prevention and detection coupled with a high number of people exposed to the problem.*
3. *The organization and structure of the March of Dimes, with a nucleus of dedicated individuals.*
4. *Receptivity at the local level to experi-*

ment with new marketing and communication techniques.

APPLICATION OF MARKETING TECHNIQUES

Once a marketing plan had been instituted and the problems and opportunities analyzed, various marketing techniques were applied using Kotler and Levy's classification.

Target Group Definition—Market Segmentation. In general, the National Foundation's fund raising strategy was to view its potential market as basically undifferentiated. Although the standard March of Dimes fund drive had attempted to contact business and industry, and conducted a mother's march, and had instituted teenage and school programs, the concept of locating the "heavy donor" or "user" was not used nationally or locally. Thus, very little market segmentation information was available.

However, in the marketing of consumer products, the "heavy-user" concept has been widely accepted as a truism. Several authors have indicated disproportionate consumption skews for several product lines. For instance, fewer than 4% of the male population make 90% of the car rentals; 8% take 98% of the air trips in a year; and 26% of the population used 81% of the instant coffee [2]. What about fund raising? Common sense would indicate that the market for the March of Dimes and birth defects is also segmented, and this was validated by research conducted during the study. The prime market for the March of Dimes was felt to consist of parents. Past research had ascertained that 48.5% of the population could be placed into this category [3]. More realistically, however, it was estimated that only 31.4% (young married, no children; young married, youngest child under six; and young married, youngest child six and over) would comprise the prime target for the campaign.

Another indication that the market could be segmented was provided by an analysis of contributions from the direct-mail campaign. It indicated that five of the 24 census tracts in the Travis County area (containing 19.8% of the population) had made 41.3% of the contributions.

Therefore, the key to a successful March of Dimes campaign appeared to be isolating the "heavy user" rather than marketing to an undifferentiated population.

The Search for a Differential Advantage. Despite more than 10 years of promotion efforts, the "top-of-mind awareness" to the March of Dimes and birth defects was relatively low as shown by the initial telephone survey. It was felt that a thematic apperception test would aid in determining which type of appeal would best differentiate the March of Dimes "new" birth defects' image from both the established image of polio as well as from the other charitable causes. The strategy utilized many current and past March of Dimes' slogans and a number of newly created themes. A trivariant analysis [4] test was then conducted on the various thematic appeals.

Twenty-four themes in three specific categories were rated on the three factors of *distinctiveness* (or exclusiveness), *interest* (rather than desirability), and *believability*. The first category of themes included the ones used by the March of Dimes during the last five years:

- Keep our future bright by fighting birth defects today.
- Give for a brighter tomorrow.
- Help make a child whole again.
- Shut the door on birth defects.
- Fight the great destroyer, birth defects.
- Give to the March of Dimes.
- Join the fight against birth defects.

- Where there's help, there's hope.
- Prevent birth defects.

The second category contained locally created themes that were largely centered around the emotional fear technique:

- Your next baby could be born with a birth defect.
- 500,000 unborn babies die each year from birth defects.
- Dying children can be helped.
- Birth-defect babies can't be sent back to the factory.
- Help tomorrow's birth-defect child live.
- Protect your family's health.
- God made you whole. Give to help those He didn't.

The third category also contained locally created themes, but their appeals were more rational:

- 700 children are born each day with a birth defect.
- A birth-defect baby is born every other minute in the U.S.
- Birth defects are: cleft palate, club foot, open spine—curable.
- The March of Dimes has given you: Polio Vaccine, German Measles Vaccine, 110 birth-defects' counseling centers.
- Your gift to the March of Dimes is like money in the bank.
- You owe it to your children to contribute to the March of Dimes.
- Insure your family's health by giving to the March of Dimes.

In trivariant analysis a representative sample rates various themes randomly on three factors. The mean scores for the themes are calculated on each of the factors, and are then plotted on a two-dimensional chart (the mean of the theme on the third factor, believability, is shown in parentheses). Figure 1

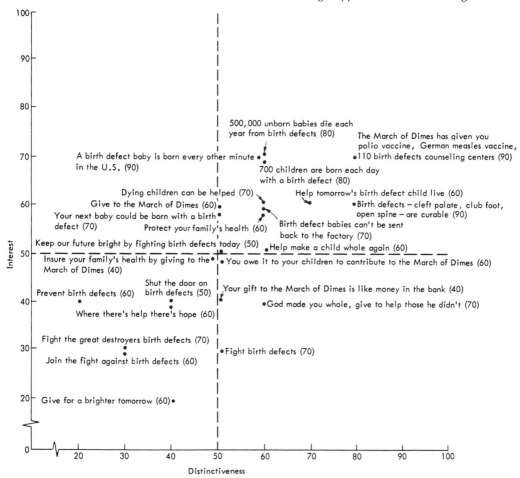

charts the results achieved by each of the March of Dimes' themes on the interest and distinctiveness factors, with the believability mean in parentheses. It is conceded that although the test is an efficient means of testing probable effectiveness of factual claims, it seems less applicable to advertising approaches that depend heavily on emotion or upon graphics. Despite these limitations, Figure 1 provides some interesting insights:

1. The majority of the March of Dimes' themes did not score in Quadrant I where the most interesting and most distinctive themes are found.

2. Themes dealing with *positive, active* aspects of giving, the *results of giving*, or a description of what March of Dimes had done with contributions in the past did well in creating interest, in being distinctive, and in being believable.

3. Some of the emotional appeals showed potential in being interesting, but they would need to be altered in order to achieve higher levels of distinctiveness and believability.

In any event, data were available and used to create strategies for finding a differential advantage.

Multiple Marketing Tools. One of the keys to the success of the March of Dimes' campaign was the "mothers' march," a day set aside for personal solicitations in the prospects' homes. Informal interviews with teams of marchers indicated a basic insecurity on the part of the soliciting mother concerning her behavior when confronting a potential donor at the door. Since these women were the key "salesmen," informational and motivational meetings were held. In addition, a detailed fact sheet was designed to explain the method of requesting funds and the use of prepared materials. Also, a brochure was designed to leave at the door in case the prospect was not at home.

Localized publicity materials which related to the other aspects of the promotional mix were prepared for both the print media, with its characteristic of permanence and exposure, and the broadcast news media, with its potential broad impact and visualization. The latter media had not been used with much effectiveness in the past.

Marketing Audit—Continuous Marketing Feedback. Some of the research or feedback techniques used during the campaign such as "top-of-mind awareness" of March of Dimes, pretesting of appeals, and analysis of returns have already been described. The most critical tests concerned the evaluation of the overall impact of the campaign in meeting its objectives.

One of the objectives of the advertising campaign was to increase the association of birth defects with the March of Dimes. A precampaign audit yielded a 30.9% combined aided and unaided recall for the March of Dimes and birth defects. A second audit conducted a week after the direct-mail campaign showed that the figure had risen to 45.3% (a 50% increase). A third audit, conducted a week after the mothers' march, yielded a recall figure of 61.2% (a 100% increase from the pretest). DAGMAR criteria would indicate that the advertising had been effective in achieving penetration.

With respect to "sales," total income realized for the 1970 campaign increased by 33% over the previous year, but the increased expenses of "tailor-making" a direct-mail program, of preparing radio and TV announcements, and of providing handouts for mothers increased expenses by 14% over the previous year. Nevertheless, it was the first time in 12 years that contributions *had* increased.

Based on these results, the major recommendation for next year's campaign was to move even more strongly toward the "heavy-user concept" in direct-mail advertising. The mass campaign suggested by the National Foundation consisting of impersonal "occupant-addressed" pieces did not take advantage of what marketers know about family life cycles and market segments. As many as half of the census tracts in the Travis County area could have been eliminated without substantially reducing net returns.

The same concentration could apply to the business and industry mailing. Although the number of direct-mail pieces sent to this sector was tripled, response actually decreased. This was attributed to the fact that a mass of letters was sent, rather than consecutive, selective mailings with personalized follow-up.

Much doubt was cast on the efficacy of publicity in motivating and stimulating response in the form of donations. The National Organization's primary emphasis in its communication program is to prepare news-release material containing appeals designed to elicit cash donations to the March of

Dimes. It appears that this approach does not generate adequate donations and, in fact, may jeopardize the placement of other communications into the media dealing with the need for volunteers, meetings, and so forth.

CONCLUSIONS AND IMPLICATIONS

The results of the Travis County "test market" clearly suggest that marketing techniques and philosophy can be applied to ideas and social causes. It also seems clear that they could have national application for a foundation such as the March of Dimes.

Associations and their causes, like products, experience a life cycle. Patton suggests that a product will go through graduated intervals of development, beginning with an introduction stage which is followed by stages of growth, maturity, and decline.

> As volume rises and the market becomes increasingly saturated marketing steps to the center of the stage. Generally speaking at this point all competitive products are reliable and there is less and less to choose between them. Improvements in the product tend to be small with selling features or style changes dominant [5].

The charity "market" has become increasingly competitive. Individual fund raising campaigns, exclusive of the United Fund campaign, are again on the upsurge across the country. Health organizations, which at first attempted to integrate with the United Fund approach, are now conducting their own campaigns. Furthermore, some members of the United Fund are even conducting individual campaigns to supplement their United Fund receipts.

The increasing competition plus the problems already mentioned indicate that the National Foundation of the March of Dimes can be placed in the late stages of the "char-

ity" life cycle, characterized by declining growth and campaign receipts. Even its advantage of being a pioneer in solicitation techniques seems to be dissipated by the competition for the volunteers needed in other organizations.

The question, therefore, is how long can basic market research be viewed as an unnecessary, unwanted expense by an organization such as the March of Dimes.

Research information could be translated into selective promotion, in contrast to the "mass" techniques used in the past. Computer data from the Internal Revenue Service are already available containing information on incomes, number of dependents, and taxes paid for each of the 35,000 postal Zip Code areas. These data, plus a regression and correlation analysis of March of Dimes' data from individual chapter records, could identify the means to efficiently reach the "heavy giver."

The need to apply other marketing management concepts is equally obvious. These concepts include redefining the "product" in a meaningful way, developing new marketing tools for the volunteer, and arranging national test markets to test different types and levels of promotional appeals.

Perhaps readers who have been exposed to the frequently high-pressure techniques of charity organizations and professional fundraisers with their "disease-of-the-month-club" solicitations might be "appalled" by the prospect of these organizations becoming marketing-minded. At the same time, the dedicated professionals and volunteers associated with these organizations might be "appalled" by the prospect of applying business and marketing techniques to a nonbusiness area.

Both groups might profit from reviewing Kotler and Levy's definition of what marketing really means: sensitively serving and satisfying human needs [1, p. 15]. Such a definition of marketing challenges organizations which specialize in the marketing of causes and ideas to ask themselves if they are truly consumer-centered and not simply self-serving. It challenges their understanding of the principle that selling follows rather than precedes the organization's drive to collect funds. It also challenges the marketing man himself to understand that he will have to fit his concepts and techniques to the special goals and objectives of the individual organizations. It is hoped that this case study helps in contributing to the satisfactory acceptance of these challenges.

REFERENCES

[1] Kotler, Philip, and Sidney Levy, "Broadening the Concept of Marketing," *Journal of Marketing*, Vol. 33 (January 1969), pp. 10–15.

[2] Sandage, Carl H., and Vernon Fryburger, *Advertising Theory and Practice*. (Homewood, IL: Richard D. Irwin, Inc., 1967), p. 199; Philip Kotler, *Marketing Management* (Englewood Cliffs, NJ: Prentice-Hall, Inc., 1967), p. 51; Daniel Yankelovich, "New Criteria for Market Segmentation," in *Marketing Management and Administrative Action*, Steuart H. Britt and Harper W. Boyd, Jr., eds. New York: McGraw-Hill Book Co., 1968, p. 189.

[3] Lansing, John B., and Leslie Kish, "Family Life Cycle as an Independent Variable," in *Marketing Management and Administrative Action*, Steuart H. Britt and Harper W. Boyd, Jr., eds. New York: McGraw-Hill Book Co., 1968, p. 213.

[4] Twedt, Dik Warren, "New 3-Way Measure of Ad Effectiveness, "*Printer's Ink* (September 6, 1957), pp. 22–23. See also Dik Warren Twedt, "How to Plan New Products, Improve Old Ones and Create Better Advertising," *Journal of Marketing*, Vol. 33 (January 1969), pp. 53–57.

[5] Patton, Arch, "Top Management's Stake in the Product Life Cycle," in *Marketing Management and Administrative Action* Steuart H. Britt and Harper W. Boyd, Jr., eds. New York: McGraw-Hill Book Co., 1968, p. 324.

OZARK SAINTS HOSPITAL (A)

Edward Lofton, hospital administrator of Ozark Saints Hospital, has been a long time proponent of systematic long-range planning and of keeping ahead of the competition. Fifteen years ago he retained the services of a well-known Washington, D.C., health care management consulting firm to develop long-range plans for the hospital. Since that time new pressures and problems have arisen in the health care industry and Mr. Lofton feels that there is now a need to pay greater attention to the marketing aspects of the operation. He feels strongly that a marketing orientation will ensure the successful utilization of expanded facilities and aid other developmental efforts. He has, therefore,

Reprinted from *Cases in Marketing Strategy*, Hise/McDaniel, 1984 with permission of the authors, C.P. Rao and G.E. Kiser of the University of Arkansas and Stephen W. McDaniel of Texas A&M University. Copyrighted © 1981 by C.P. Rao, G.E. Kiser, and Stephen W. McDaniel.

EXHIBIT 1: Comparative admission data, patient origins by county, 1967–1977, Ozark Saints Hospital

County	1967	1977
A*	8.0	10.7
B	2.6	5.7
C	4.0	7.2
D	0.4	2.0
E	1.6	2.6
F**	61.4	54.4
G*	6.2	5.5
H*	9.5	5.1
Other Counties	5.8	5.8
Out of State	0.5	1.0
Totals	100.0%	100.0%

**The city in which Ozark Saints Hospital and Spencer Medical Center are located is in County F.

As noted by the (*) above, the four counties immediately surrounding the city comprise the regional planning area. These are considered the hospital's primary service area.

been taking steps to accomplish more of a marketing orientation for Ozark Saints Hospital.

BACKGROUND

The Hospital

Ozark Saints Hospital is located in a medium-sized city in the southwest region of the United States. In addition to the metropolitan area of the city in which the hospital is located, the hospital's services are included in eight predominantly rural counties. Ozark Saints Hospital is one of the two major hospitals located in the city. The second hospital, Spencer Medical Center, is much larger than Ozark Saints and services the same health care market area. Both Ozark Saints Hospital (OSH) and Spencer Medical Center (SMC) are actively pursuing facility expansion programs and medical staff development programs. OSH management considers SMC a major competitor in the health care market area.

Based on OSH records, over 93 percent of the patients at the hospital listed as their place of residence one of the eight counties in close proximity to the hospital. A complete breakdown of patient residences in these eight counties is shown in Exhibit 1.

Population Growth

According to population growth projections prepared by the U.S. Bureau of the Census and the Regional Planning Commission, the number of residents within the service market area of Ozark Saints Hospital will increase 35.2 percent between 1970 and

EXHIBIT 2: Population projections by county, Ozark Saints Hospital service area constituency, 1977

County	1970*	1975	1980	1985	1990
A	25,677	30,300	33,300	36,200	39,000
B	11,301	12,000	12,750	13,550	14,400
C	16,789	17,700	18,500	19,300	20,100
D	13,297	14,000	14,900	15,850	16,950
E	8,207	9,000	9,900	10,950	12,000
F	79,239	85,300	91,200	97,000	103,600
G	32,137	35,200	38,000	40,600	42,700
H	23,370	26,300	29,400	32,300	35,200
Totals	210,015	229,800	247,950	265,750	283,950

*Actual 1970 U.S. Census.

EXHIBIT 3: Selected market characteristics and market health resources—1977

Market characteristics	County A	County B	County C	County D	County E	County F
Population density per square mile	49.1	19.9	25.2	16.7	9.9	160.5
Percent urban	32.6	22.9	41.0	34.1	—	82.1
Percent rural	67.4	77.1	59.0	65.9	100.0	17.9
Percent of aged	12.7	16.1	17.0	17.5	15.0	11.2
Aged dependency ratio	23.1	29.2	31.0	32.7	27.1	19.0
Percent aged in poverty	48.2	47.8	48.4	46.4	59.5	34.8
Median per capita family income $	5,226	4,259	4,120	4,515	4,132	6,242
Percent unemployed	8.7	10.1	8.1	10.8	10.5	7.0
Market resources						
Hospitals	1	1	1	1	1	2
Beds	99	40	47	57	26	873
% Occupancy	43.6	88.3	52.0	41.2	47.3	82.9
Public Health Clinics	20	N/A	14	14	N/A	17
Ambulance Services	2	2	1	1	1	2
Professionals						
Doctors	10	1	6	8	2	164
R.Ns	33	76	20	13	8	378
L.P.Ns	43	54	25	20	13	334
Other*	31	35	12	16	8	138
Mental Health Services	7	7	9	9	9	11
Detox Facilities	—	—	—	—	—	1

MH and Detox services based in city (serves regional area)

*Includes chiropractors, dentists, optometrists, pharmacists, physical therapists.

1990. This population growth rate by counties is indicated in Exhibit 2.

The factors responsible for this expected growth are an abundant supply of natural gas energy readily available and proportionately inexpensive, and a stable labor market with a good mix of balanced skills ranging from agrarian and industrially unskilled to well-trained, technologically experienced individuals. The climate is mild and has considerable attraction for those seeking Sunbelt living; several resort-type developments for adults are established or in varying stages of the development process in the area.

Market Characteristics and Health Resources

Together, Ozark Saints Hospital and Spencer Medical Center provide some 873 beds, with an additional 150 beds currently under construction at SMC. However, the five counties surrounding F County only have a total of 269 general care beds in five hospitals varying in size from 26 beds to 99 beds. An additional 22 beds are under construction in County C that will place two community hospitals in C County. Except for the hospitals in F County, presently reported average occupancy in these five hospitals is under 50 percent.

The two hospitals in G County have some 139 general care beds, of which 52 are located at the U.S. Public Health Service Institution. No hospital is reported for H County.

Other market characteristics and health resources are shown in Exhibit 3.

The Market Research Study

As a first step in developing a long-range marketing strategy for the hospital, Mr. Lofton decided that a comprehensive market research study should be carried out as soon as possible. He felt the study should examine the attitudes of local residents toward hospital facilities and services, as well as investigate the behavior of those who would make use of these facilities and services in the local area. To carry out the study, Mr. Lofton procured the services of a local marketing consulting firm. After various and extensive consultations, the marketing consultants submitted a research proposal to Mr. Lofton for his approval. The major parts of this proposal are shown in the Appendix. It includes the consulting firm's statements of the study's objectives and scope, the two questionnaires proposed for the study, and a plan of analysis. The hospital administrator now must sit down, think through the entire situation, and carefully analyze all aspects of the proposal he has just received. He realizes that the cost and time involved in conducting the research makes it imperative that all aspects of the study work to yield the best possible information for making long-term marketing decisions.

APPENDIX: A STUDY OF THE DEMAND FOR MEDICAL SERVICES PROVIDED BY MAJOR HOSPITALS IN THE OSH SERVICE AREA

Objectives and Scope of the Study

The major purpose of the proposed research study is to delineate the "image" profile of OSH among the general public and physicians in the OSH health care market service area. Concurrently the research study will also identify related patient and physician "choice criteria" when making decisions relative to choosing a medical center in the service area. More specifically the study will be concerned with investigating the following research issues:

I. *BACKGROUND INFORMATION*

A. Age (Please circle one)
   30–39   40–49   50–59   60 and over

B. What is your medical specialization?

   _____

   _____

C. Certification (Please circle one)
   Board Certified   Board Eligible   Non-Certified

D. How often, on the average, do you admit patients to the hospital indicated below?

	Spencer Medical Center	Ozark Saints Hospital
Several times a day	_____	_____
Several times a week	_____	_____
Infrequently	_____	_____
Other_____		
(Please specify)		

II. *CHOICE CRITERIA WHEN SELECTING A HOSPITAL*

A. What is the relative importance of the following factors when you choose a hospital for your patients?

Factors	Important	Neutral	Unimportant
Bed availability	_____	_____	_____
Physicians' dining room/lounge	_____	_____	_____
Quality of emergency room	_____	_____	_____
Friendliness of staff	_____	_____	_____
Quality of nursing	_____	_____	_____
Availability of consultants	_____	_____	_____
Quality and type of equipment	_____	_____	_____
Involvement in hospital management	_____	_____	_____
Overall hospital reputation	_____	_____	_____
Patient's choice of hospital	_____	_____	_____
Adequate parking	_____	_____	_____
How well managed the hospital is	_____	_____	_____
Geographical proximity to patient's home	_____	_____	_____
Quality of medical records	_____	_____	_____
Geographical proximity to your office	_____	_____	_____
Availability of operating room time	_____	_____	_____

B. Please rate the two area hospitals in the following areas:

Factors	Spencer Medical Center Superior	Good	Inadequate	Ozark Saints Hospital Superior	Good	Inadequate
Supplies available	_____	_____	_____	_____	_____	_____
Housekeeping	_____	_____	_____	_____	_____	_____

178

Nursing staff						
Physical therapy						
Radiology						
Anesthesiology						
Operating room facilities						
ICU facilities						
Emergency room						
Medical records						
Other _____						

       (Please specify)

C. What, in particular, do you *dislike* most about hospital services and facilities in the service area?

_____

_____

_____

_____

   1. Does your dislike relate more to one hospital than another?
     Yes _____ No _____

   2. If yes, which hospital? _____

D. What, in particular, do you *like* most about hospital services and facilities in the service area?

_____

_____

_____

   1. Does your like relate more to one hospital than another?
     Yes _____ No _____

   2. If yes, which hospital? _____

E. Of the hospitals in the area (Spencer Medical Center and Ozark Saints Hospital), please indicate usage for each hospital.

Hospital	Extensively	Frequently	Infrequently
Spencer Medical Center			
Ozark Saints Hospital			

F. What sources of information do you find most helpful in forming your opinion of a hospital, in general?

	Importance as a Source				
Source	None	Little	Some	Much	Extensive
Direct, personal contact					
Patients					
Fellow physicians					
Professional staff meetings					
Hospital publications					
Salesmen					
News media					
Other _____					

       (Please specify)

G. What service(s) could logically and realistically be offered on a shared basis with other hospitals? Please indicate the service in Column 1 (Service) and the hospital at which the service(s) would be located in the second column (Location):

Service	*Location*
1. _____	_____
2. _____	_____
3. _____	_____
4. _____	_____
5. _____	_____

H. Please circle the group which, in your opinion, generally plays the dominant role in determining to which hospital a patient will be admitted.

Physicians   Patients   Patient's Family   Other _____
                                                          (Please Specify)

NOTE: Additional surveys of the medical staff will be periodically performed. Please make any comments which you believe would serve to increase the value of this survey instrument. Also list those issues which you believe are important, but not specifically addressed in this questionnaire.

_____

_____

_____

_____

_____

_____
Signature (Optional)

CONSUMER HOSPITAL OPINION SURVEY QUESTIONNAIRE:

The purpose of this consumer survey is to get your opinions about hospitals and their services. You may take your past experience, any information you obtained from others, and your general understanding of hospitals in your area as basis for responding to the various questions below. Your household is selected as a part of a carefully developed sampling plan. Hence, your participation in this survey will greatly help us in achieving the objectives of this research study. Any information you may provide will be treated strictly confidentially, and it will not be used in any other form except as a part of a large sample. Please answer all of the following questions.

1. Did someone in your household use the services of any of the *hospitals* in the service area during the past two years?

   Yes _____   No _____

2. If you answered "yes" to Question 1 above, please indicate the name(s) of the hospital(s) utilized by a member of your household.

   _____

   _____

3. If you answered "yes" to Question 1, please indicate the *number of times* members of your household used the hospital services during the last two years. (Please check one.)

Once	*Twice*	*Three times*	*Four times*	*More than four times*
_____	_____	_____	_____	_____

4. If members of your household used hospital services during the past two years, please provide the following information about the visit(s).

Purpose of the Hospitalization	*Length of the Hospitalization (No. of Days Spent)*
1. _____	_____
2. _____	_____
3. _____	_____
4. _____	_____

5. On the basis of your past experience, discussions with relatives, friends, and neighbors, and your general understanding of the hospitals in the service area, please list your preference among the area hospitals.
   (Note: If you choose only *one*, please list under first choice.)

   First Choice: _____

   Second Choice: _____

6. Please indicate your reasons for choosing.

   _____

   _____

   _____

7. In choosing a hospital for the health care needs of your household members, how important are the advice, suggestions, and influence of the following persons? Please check one alternative for each person(s).

	Very Important	*Important*	*Slightly Important*	*Unimportant*	*Very Unimportant*
	Advice, Suggestion and Influence Are:				
Other members of your household	_____	_____	_____	_____	_____
Friends and neighbors	_____	_____	_____	_____	_____
Your physician	_____	_____	_____	_____	_____
Others (Please specify)	_____	_____	_____	_____	_____

8. The following are some characteristics of hospitals in general. In choosing a hospital for health care needs of members of your household how *important* are these characteristics? (Please check one alternative for each aspect.)

	Very Important	*Important*	*Not Very Important*	*Not Important At All*
Good doctors	_____	_____	_____	_____
Good nursing care	_____	_____	_____	_____
Good emergency room	_____	_____	_____	_____
Latest medical equipment	_____	_____	_____	_____
Keeps patients informed about their care	_____	_____	_____	_____
Religious affiliation	_____	_____	_____	_____
Comfortable rooms	_____	_____	_____	_____
Good food	_____	_____	_____	_____
Easy to get to	_____	_____	_____	_____
Adequate parking	_____	_____	_____	_____
Flexible visiting hours	_____	_____	_____	_____
Price of service	_____	_____	_____	_____
Good reputation	_____	_____	_____	_____
Provides rehabilitation	_____	_____	_____	_____
Teaches you to stay well	_____	_____	_____	_____
Has health education programs	_____	_____	_____	_____
Overall hospital management	_____	_____	_____	_____
Other _____ (Please specify)	_____	_____	_____	_____

9. On the following scale, please evaluate the hospitals in the area. Mention the name of two hospitals of your choice and evaluate the same hospital on the basis of the various qualities indicated. If your evaluation is very favorable, please circle 7; if your evaluation is very unfavorable, please circle 1. If your evaluation is in between, please circle one of the numbers between 2, 3, 4, 5, or 6, whichever expresses your opinion accurately.

Your First Choice Hospital							Hospital Aspect	Your Second Choice Hospital						
Name _____								Name _____						
Very Favorable Very Unfavorable								*Very Favorable Very Unfavorable*						
7	6	5	4	3	2	1	Good doctors	7	6	5	4	3	2	1
7	6	5	4	3	2	1	Good nursing care	7	6	5	4	3	2	1
7	6	5	4	3	2	1	Good emergency room	7	6	5	4	3	2	1
7	6	5	4	3	2	1	Latest medical equipment	7	6	5	4	3	2	1
7	6	5	4	3	2	1	Respects your privacy	7	6	5	4	3	2	1
7	6	5	4	3	2	1	Keeps patients informed about their care	7	6	5	4	3	2	1
7	6	5	4	3	2	1	Religious affiliation	7	6	5	4	3	2	1
7	6	5	4	3	2	1	Comfortable rooms	7	6	5	4	3	2	1
7	6	5	4	3	2	1	Good food	7	6	5	4	3	2	1
7	6	5	4	3	2	1	Easy to get to	7	6	5	4	3	2	1
7	6	5	4	3	2	1	Adequate parking	7	6	5	4	3	2	1
7	6	5	4	3	2	1	Flexible visiting hours	7	6	5	4	3	2	1
7	6	5	4	3	2	1	Price of service	7	6	5	4	3	2	1
7	6	5	4	3	2	1	Good reputation	7	6	5	4	3	2	1
7	6	5	4	3	2	1	Provides rehabilitation	7	6	5	4	3	2	1
7	6	5	4	3	2	1	Teaches you to stay well	7	6	5	4	3	2	1
7	6	5	4	3	2	1	Has health education programs	7	6	5	4	3	2	1
7	6	5	4	3	2	1	Overall hospital management	7	6	5	4	3	2	1
7	6	5	4	3	2	1	Other _____	7	6	5	4	3	2	1
							(Please specify)							

10. As measured in driving time how close *should* all area residents be to a hospital? (Please circle one.)

    5 minutes   15 minutes   30 minutes   45 minutes   over 45 minutes

11. In your opinion, should additional hospitals be built in the surrounding area?

    Yes _____   No _____

12. If you answered "yes" to the above question, please indicate where you think a hospital should be built.

    _____

    _____

13. Any other comments you would like to make about hospitals in the area and your household's experience with the hospitals will be greatly appreciated.

    _____

    _____

    _____

    _____

    _____

PLEASE PROVIDE THE FOLLOWING INFORMATION ABOUT YOURSELF AND YOUR HOUSEHOLD:

1. Please check *your* age group on the following:

    _____ Under 20 years   _____ 20–29 years   _____ 30–39 years
    _____ 40–49 years   _____ 50–59 years   _____ Over 60 years

2. Please check the category that applies to the education of the *HEAD OF YOUR HOUSE-HOLD:*

    _____ Grade School   _____ Some High School   _____ High School Graduate
    _____ Some College   _____ College Graduate   _____ Post Graduate Study

3. Which of the following categories applies to your *TOTAL FAMILY INCOME:*

    _____ Under $10,000   _____ $10,001–$12,499   _____ $12,500–$14,999
    _____ $15,000–$20,000   _____ $20,001–$24,999   _____ Over $25,000

4. Please indicate: Your Occupation _____
    Your Spouse's Occupation _____

PLEASE NOTE: ANY INFORMATION YOU PROVIDE WILL BE TREATED STRICTLY CONFIDENTIAL AND WILL NOT BE USED IN ANY OTHER MANNER EXCEPT AS A PART OF A LARGE SAMPLE IN WRITING A GENERALIZED RESEARCH REPORT.
THANK YOU VERY MUCH FOR YOUR COOPERATION.

1. What factors are considered important to the public and to the physicians when selecting a medical center?
2. Considering the various important factors, how do the public and physicians evaluate OSH and Spencer Medical Center (SMC)? These data will enable the researchers to develop the "image" profile of not only OSH but also the other major medical center in the health care market service area.
3. Develop a comparative analysis between OSH and SMC so that OSH's strengths and weaknesses can be compared and contrasted with those pertaining to SMC.
4. Investigate the various dimensions of patient and physician decision-making processes in relation to their choice of a medical center.
5. The data will be analyzed not only for the groups of households and physicians, but also for sub-groups on the basis of demographics for households and some other appropriate basis, such as medical specialization for physicians.

PLAN OF ANALYSIS

Medical Staff Questionnaire

The field research data generated with the use of the medical staff questionnaire will be analyzed on the following lines.

1. Frequency distributions and relative proportions for each response will be generated for the entire sample of medical staff. Such data will provide the following information for the entire sample.
   1. Age distribution of the respondents.
   2. Medical specialization of the respondents.
   3. Type of certification of the respondents.

4. Frequency of admitting patients to the area hospitals.
5. Relative importance of hospital attributes as perceived by the respondents.
6. Respondent evaluation of Spencer and Ozark Saints on the basis of hospital attributes.
7. Respondent preference of one hospital over the others.
8. Relative extent of the use of Spencer and Ozark Saints by the respondents.
9. Relative importance of the various sources of information as perceived by the respondents.
10. Respondent assessment of the "influentials" in hospital selection.

2. Responses to open-ended questions numbers IIC, IID, and IIG will be summarized and reported.
3. A comparative analysis will be performed between Spencer and Ozark Saints. The major purposes of this comparison are:
   1. To identify the strengths and weaknesses of each of the hospitals as evaluated by the respondents.
   2. To identify any significant differences with regard to hospital use-related behaviors between those respondents whose preference is for Ozark Saints vis-a-vis those respondents whose preference is for Spencer.
4. On the various aspects under investigation, a segmentation analysis will be performed on the following bases. The major purposes of these segmentation analyses are to see whether there are any significant differences among the various segments with regard to the behaviors investigated. We propose to use the bases for segmentation analyses.
   1. Geographic areas.
   2. Age of the respondents.
   3. Certification.
   4. Specialization.

Consumer Hospital Opinion Survey

After the field research work is completed the following procedure will be utilized to generate the research data which will form the basis for writing the final report.

1. The data generated through field work will be first computerized by utilizing an appropriate coding scheme.
2. The following types of analyses will be performed to generate useful statistical data.
   A. Frequency distributions and relative proportions for each response will be generated for the entire sample. Such data will provide the following types of information for the entire sample.
      1. Area hospitals utilized by respondents.
      2. Number of times hospital services utilized during the last two years.
      3. Purpose of hospitalization.
      4. Length of hospitalization.
      5. Consumer choice pattern of area hospitals.
      6. Relative importance of "influentials" in the choice of hospital.
      7. Relative importance of hospital attributes as perceived by consumers.
      8. Consumer evaluation of area hospitals on a number of attributes.
      9. Consumer preferences as to the driving distance to a hospital measured in terms of time.
      10. Consumer-perceived need for additional hospitals in the surrounding area.
   B. In addition to generating frequencies and relative proportions on the above ten aspects, data generated through open-ended questions numbers 6, 12, and 13 in the questionnaire will be summarized and reported.
   C. A demographic profile will be drawn on the basis of the responses to questions on demographics of the respondents.
   D. For all those questions where scales have been utilized, means and standard deviations will be computed and reported along with frequencies and percentages.
   E. A comparative analysis will be performed between Spencer and Ozark Saints. The major purposes of this comparative analyses are:
      1. To identify the strengths and weaknesses of each of the hospitals as perceived by consumers.
      2. To identify whether there are any significant differences with regard to demographic characteristics of those respondents whose first choice is Ozark Saints vis-a-vis those whose first choice is Spencer.
      3. To identify any significant differences with regard to hospital use-related behaviors between those respondents whose first choice is Ozark Saints compared to those whose first choice is Spencer.
   F. On the various aspects under investigation, a segmentation analysis will be performed on the following bases. The major purpose of the segmentation analyses is to see whether there are any significant differences among the various segments with regard to the behaviors investigated. We propose to use the following bases for segmentation analyses.
      1. Geographic areas.
      2. Demographic segments based on:
         a) Age
         b) Income
         c) Education
         d) Occupation.

OZARK SAINTS HOSPITAL (B)

Ozark Saints Hospital is one of the two major area hospitals located in a medium-sized city in the southwest region of the United States. Recently, Edward Lofton, hospital administrator, procured the services of a marketing consulting firm in the area for purposes of carrying out customer behavior studies dealing with the area physicians and households. (See Ozark Saints Hospital (A) for details of the health care service market area, research proposal, research instruments and the plan of analysis.) The research findings are expected to be useful for the OSH management to develop an appropriate long-term competitive strategy and generally to impart greater marketing orientation to OSH operations. Eight months after contracting with the local research firm, Mr. Lofton received a copy of the results of the study. The results were presented in tables and divided into two sections: the results of the Physician study and the results of the Consumer study.

PHYSICIAN STUDY

Almost all physicians in the city where OSH was located were sent a questionnaire. Some were screened out initially because they were relatively uninvolved in choosing a hospital for their patients. Out of 159 questionnaires mailed to physicians, 48 were returned. This represents a 30.2 percent response rate of the total and was judged to be above average for these types of surveys. Results from this phase of the study are shown in Exhibits 1–9.

CONSUMER STUDY

The consumer hospital opinion survey questionnaires were mailed to about 1000 randomly selected households in the Ozark Saints service market area. (An additional 200 questionnaires were mailed to the past patients of the hospital.) Through the consumer mail questionnaire survey, 308 responses were generated. After adjusting for undelivered questionnaires, the 308 responses accounted for approximately 33 percent of the mailings. This response rate in a consumer mail questionnaire survey was judged to be highly satisfactory. Results from this phase of the study are shown in Exhibits 10–18.

Reprinted from *Cases in Marketing Strategy*, Hise/McDaniel, 1984 with permission of the authors, C.P. Rao and G.E. Kiser of the University of Arkansas and Stephen W. McDaniel of Texas A&M University. Copyrighted © 1981 by C.P. Rao, G.E. Kiser, and Stephen W. McDaniel.

EXHIBIT 1: Frequency of admission of patients to alternate hospitals in the area

Hospital	Frequency of Admission					
	Several Times a Day		Several Times a Week		Infrequently	
	No.	%	No.	%	No.	%
Spencer	21	43.8	16	33.3	7	14.6
Ozark Saints	5	10.6	17	36.2	20	42.6

EXHIBIT 2: Extent of physician usage of the area hospitals

Hospital	Extent of Usage					
	Extensively		Frequently		Infrequently	
	No.	%	No.	%	No.	%
Spencer	18	42.9	11	26.2	13	30.9
Ozark Saints	14	32.6	14	32.6	15	34.8

EXHIBIT 3: Physician choice criteria in selecting a hospital

Factors	Very Important/ Important		Neutral		Unimportant/ Very Unimportant	
	No.	%	No.	%	No.	%
Bed availability	33	74.9	7	15.9	4	9.1
Physician dining room/lounge	5	11.4	12	27.3	27	61.4
Quality of emergency room	34	75.6	9	20.0	2	4.4
Friendliness of staff	32	71.0	11	24.4	2	4.4
Quality of nursing	43	93.4	1	2.1	2	4.3
Availability of consultants	35	76.0	7	15.2	4	8.6
Quality and type of equipment	42	91.2	3	6.5	1	2.2
Involvement in hospital mgmt.	18	39.9	20	44.4	17	15.6
Overall hospital reputation	25	56.8	14	31.8	5	11.4
Patient's choice of hospital	31	65.9	13	27.7	3	6.4
Adequate parking	20	44.4	14	31.1	11	24.4
How well-managed hospital is	36	79.9	6	13.3	3	4.4
Geographical proximity to patient's home	15	33.3	18	40.0	12	22.2
Quality of medical records	28	60.8	11	23.9	7	15.2
Geographical proximity to your office	31	64.6	9	18.8	8	16.7
Availability of operating room time	25	54.3	10	21.7	11	23.9

EXHIBIT 4: Physicians' evaluation of Spencer and Ozark Saints

	Spencer							
	Superior		Very Good		Poor		Inadequate	
	No.	%	No.	%	No.	%	No.	%
Suppliers available	16	44.5	20	55.5	—	—	—	—
Housekeeping	5	13.8	27	75.0	4	11.1	—	—
Nursing staff	11	30.4	25	69.4	—	—	—	—
Physical therapy	9	28.1	23	71.9	—	—	—	—
Radiology	22	59.4	14	37.8	1	2.7	—	—
Laboratory	16	43.2	19	51.4	2	5.4	—	—
Parking for physicians	6	15.1	22	66.7	4	12.1	1	3.0
Office space in close proximity to hospital	11	40.7	12	44.4	4	14.8	—	—
Anesthesiology	19	63.3	9	30.0	2	6.8	—	—
Operating room facilities	18	59.9	12	40.0	—	—	—	—
ICU facilities	23	63.8	13	36.1	—	—	—	—
Emergency room	18	50.0	18	50.0				
Medical records	8	24.2	24	72.7	1	3.0	—	—

	Ozark Saints							
	Superior		Very Good		Poor		Inadequate	
	No.	%	No.	%	No.	%	No.	%
Suppliers available	6	16.6	23	63.9	6	16.6	1	2.8
Housekeeping	10	28.5	23	65.7	2	5.7	—	—
Nursing staff	8	22.2	23	63.9	3	8.3	2	5.6
Physical therapy	—	—	24	77.4	5	16.1	1	—
Radiology	5	13.9	21	58.3	9	25.4	1	6.4
Laboratory	6	16.2	24	64.9	6	16.2	1	2.8
Parking for physicians	5	13.5	24	64.9	6	16.2	2	2.7
Office space in close proximity to hospital	3	13.0	13	56.5	6	26.1	1	4.3
Anesthesiology	13	41.9	17	54.8	—	—	1	3.2
Operating room facilities	7	23.3	20	66.7	2	6.7	1	3.3
ICU facilities	11	33.3	21	63.7	1	3.3	—	—
Emergency room	6	16.2	25	67.6	5	13.5	1	2.7
Medical records	4	11.4	24	68.6	6	17.1	1	2.8

EXHIBIT 5: Physicians' dislike for the area hospitals

	Yes		No	
	No.	%	No.	%
Is the dislike more for one hospital than another?	19	54.3	16	45.7

	Ozark Saints		Spencer	
	No.	%	No.	%
Which hospital?	11	57.9	7	36.8

EXHIBIT 6: Physician liking for the area hospitals

	Yes		No	
	No.	%	No.	%
Is the liking more for one hospital than another?	18	50.0	18	50.0

	Ozark Saints		Spencer		Other	
	No.	%	No.	%	No.	%
Which hospital?	8	40	10	50	2	10

EXHIBIT 7: Relative importance of the physician sources of information in forming opinions of a hospital

	Relative Importance of Sources of Information									
Source	Extensive		Much		Some		Little		None	
	No.	%	No.	%	No.	%	No.	%	No.	%
Direct, personal contact	30	66.7	12	26.7	2	4.4	1	2.2	—	—
Patients	10	21.7	20	43.5	13	28.3	3	6.5	—	—
Fellow physicians	13	28.9	14	31.1	12	26.7	5	11.1	1	2.2
Professional staff meetings	4	8.9	7	15.6	16	35.6	12	26.6	6	13.3
Hospital publications	—	—	—	—	6	13.6	12	27.3	26	59.1
Salesmen	—	—	—	—	—	—	10	22.7	34	77.3
News media	—	—	—	—	3	6.9	10	23.3	30	69.8

EXHIBIT 8: Physician perception of the dominant role played by various groups in determining patient's admittance to a hospital

Group	No.	%
Physicians	28	65.1
Patients	14	32.6
Patient's family	1	2.3

EXHIBIT 9: Physicians' demographic profile

	No.	%
Age:		
30–39	20	42.5
40–49	14	29.8
50–59	5	10.6
60 and over	8	17.1
Medical Specialization:		
Surgery	14	29.8
Urology	4	8.5
Psychiatry	2	4.3
Ophthalmology	2	4.3
Internal Medicine	6	12.8
Ob–Gyn	3	6.4
Hematology/Oncology	2	4.3
General Practice	7	14.9
Pediatrics	2	4.3
Other (Allergy, Pulmonary Disorders, Cardiology, Otolaryngology, Gastro)	5	10.6
Certification:		
Board Certified	35	79.6
Board Eligible	7	15.9
Non-Certified	2	4.5

EXHIBIT 10: Consumer use of area hospitals

	Yes		No	
	No.	%	No.	%
1. Did the household use any hospital in the past two years?	225	73.1	83	26.9

2. Name of area hospital utilized	Ozark Saints		Spencer		Other	
	No.	%	No.	%	No.	%
	143	48.5	115	39.0	37	12.5

3. Frequency of use in the last two years		No.	%
	Once	96	42.7
	Twice	60	26.7
	Three Times	37	16.4
	Four Times	13	5.8
	More Than Four Times	19	8.4

EXHIBIT 11: Consumer choice pattern of area hospitals

Hospital	1st Choice		2nd Choice	
	No.	%	No.	%
Ozark Saints Hospital	179	60.9	64	33.0
Spencer Medical Center	99	33.7	106	54.6
Other	16	5.4	21	12.4

EXHIBIT 12: Influences of consumer hospital choice behavior

Influences	Importance of Influences					
	Very Important/ Important		Slightly Important		Unimportant/ Very Unimportant	
	No.	%	No.	%	No.	%
Other members of household	229	84.9	26	9.6	15	5.5
Friends and neighbors	121	46.1	84	31.9	58	22.0
Your doctor	271	92.8	13	4.5	8	2.7

EXHIBIT 13: Consumer "choice criteria" in selecting a hospital

Hospital Aspect	Relative Importance of the Aspect							
	Very Important		Important		Not Very Important		Not Important At All	
	No.	%	No.	%	No.	%	No.	%
Good doctors	286	95.7	13	4.3	—	—	—	—
Good nursing care	262	88.2	35	11.8	—	—	—	—
Good emergency room	256	86.5	38	12.8	2	.7	—	—
Latest medical equipment	239	81.3	49	16.7	6	2.0	—	—
Keeps patients informed about their care	207	71.4	75	25.8	6	2.1	2	.7
Religious affiliation	75	26.9	71	25.4	72	25.8	61	21.9
Comfortable rooms	162	55.1	123	41.8	6	2.0	3	1.0
Good food	137	47.0	135	46.2	20	6.8	—	—
Easy to get to	141	48.3	113	38.7	32	11.0	6	2.1
Adequate parking	120	41.5	125	43.3	35	12.1	9	3.1
Flexible visiting hours	110	38.3	124	43.2	45	15.7	8	2.8
Price of service	166	59.1	92	32.7	18	6.4	5	1.8
Good reputation	200	68.7	85	29.2	6	2.1	—	—
Provides rehabilitation	112	40.7	132	48.0	24	8.7	7	2.5
Teaches you to stay well	107	38.8	124	44.9	35	12.7	10	3.6
Has health education programs	85	31.8	115	43.0	49	18.3	18	6.7
Overall hospital management	152	56.3	109	40.4	5	1.8	4	1.5

EXHIBIT 14: Consumer evaluation of their first choice hospital

Hospital Feature	Ozark Saints (164 Total)						Spencer (96 Total)					
	Very Favorable/ Favorable		Somewhat Favorable		Unfavorable/ Very Unfavorable		Very Favorable/ Favorable		Somewhat Favorable		Unfavorable/ Very Unfavorable	
	No.	%	No.	%	No.	%	No.	%	No.	%	No.	%
Good doctors	153	96.8	2	1.2	3	1.8	85	92.4	3	3.3	4	4.3
Good nursing care	145	94.8	7	4.6	1	.6	77	89.5	7	8.1	2	2.3
Good emergency room	132	89.2	14	9.4	2	1.4	66	82.5	8	10.0	6	7.5
Latest medical equipment	140	95.4	8	5.3	2	1.3	75	92.5	4	5.0	1	2.5
Respects your privacy	143	94.7	6	4.0	2	4.3	69	82.1	11	13.1	4	4.7
Keeps patients informed about their care	126	86.9	16	11.0	3	2.1	64	79.0	11	13.6	6	7.4
Religious affiliation	106	74.1	26	18.2	11	7.6	44	59.5	18	24.3	12	16.2
Comfortable rooms	148	96.7	4	2.6	1	.6	67 n	78.8	12	14.1	6	7.1
Good food	117	78.5	26	17.4	6	4.0	60	72.3	16	19.3	7	8.4
Easy to get to	141	92.8	6	3.9	5	3.3	64	75.3	14	16.5	7	8.2
Adequate parking	127	91.4	10	6.6	3	2.0	54	62.8	22	25.6	10	11.6
Flexible visiting hours	133	89.9	13	8.8	2	1.4	72	85.7	9	10.7	3	3.6
Price of service	114	77.6	25	17.0	8	5.4	51	62.2	20	24.4	11	13.4
Good reputation	141	96.0	3	2.0	3	2.0	74	91.4	4	4.9	3	3.7
Provides rehabilitation	105	84.7	14	11.3	5	4.0	52	81.1	9	14.1	3	4.7
Teaches you to stay well	88	72.1	25	20.4	9	7.4	43	65.2	21	31.8	2	3.0
Has health education programs	75	70.8	25	23.6	6	5.7	40	60.6	20	30.3	6	9.1
Overall hospital management	115	90.4	8	6.4	4	3.2	57	81.4	10	14.3	3	4.3

EXHIBIT 15: Consumer evaluation of their second choice hospital

Hospital Feature	Ozark Saints						Spencer					
	Very Favorable/ Favorable		Somewhat Favorable		Unfavorable/ Very Unfavorable		Very Favorable/ Favorable		Somewhat Favorable		Unfavorable/ Very Unfavorable	
	No.	%	No.	%	No.	%	No.	%	No.	%	No.	%
Good doctors	61	89.7	4	5.9	3	4.4	122	91.5	8	6.0	3	2.5
Good nursing care	49	76.6	10	16.6	5	3.1	98	75.4	19	14.6	13	10.0
Good emergency room	49	93.1	4	6.8	6	10.1	92	70.2	25	19.1	14	10.7
Latest medical equipment	45	80.4	7	12.5	4	7.1	124	96.1	5	3.9	—	—
Respects your privacy	47	83.9	3	5.4	6	10.7	86	68.8	28	22.4	11	8.8
Keeps patients informed about their care	39	69.6	12	21.4	5	8.7	78	64.2	32	26.0	12	9.8
Religious affiliation	41	74.5	6	10.9	8	14.5	54	46.5	40	34.5	22	19.0
Comfortable rooms	55	87.4	4	6.3	4	6.3	81	63.3	36	28.1	11	8.6
Good food	44	74.6	13	22.0	2	3.4	73	58.9	38	30.6	13	10.5
Easy to get to	53	81.5	9	13.8	3	4.6	86	65.2	28	21.2	18	13.6
Adequate parking	54	83.0	7	10.8	4	6.2	61	45.5	42	31.3	31	23.1
Flexible visiting hours	57	89.1	2	3.1	5	7.8	89	73.5	26	21.5	6	5.0
Price of service	41	69.5	12	20.3	6	10.2	63	51.2	38	30.9	22	17.9
Good reputation	53	88.4	5	8.3	2	3.3	95	75.4	23	18.3	8	6.3
Provides rehabilitation	32	68.1	11	23.4	4	8.5	82	79.6	16	15.5	5	4.9
Teaches you to stay well	27	56.3	17	35.4	4	8.3	63	61.7	32	31.4	7	6.9
Has health education programs	24	48.0	20	40.0	6	12.0	63	69.2	24	26.4	4	4.4
Overall hospital management	41	80.4	8	15.7	2	3.9	76	73.8	22	21.4	5	4.9

EXHIBIT 16: Consumer preference for the distance to a hospital as measured in driving time

Distance in Driving Time	No.	%
5 minutes	15	5.3
15 minutes	120	42.1
30 minutes	119	41.8
45 minutes	25	8.8
Over 45 minutes	6	2.1

EXHIBIT 17: Consumer opinion as to the need for additional hospitals in the area

	Yes		No	
	No.	%	No.	%
Should additional hospitals be built?	87	31.2	192	68.8

EXHIBIT 18: Demographic profile of the respondents

Age:	No.	%
Under 20 years	4	1.3
20–29 years	47	15.4
30–39 years	49	16.1
40–49 years	33	10.8
50–59 years	50	16.4
60 and over	122	40.0
Education:		
Grade school	34	11.4
Some high school	37	12.4
High school graduate	73	24.4
Some college	91	30.4
College graduate	37	12.4
Post-graduate study	27	9.0
Total Family Income:		
Under $10,000	78	27.5
$10,000 to $12,499	44	15.5
$12,500 to $14,499	35	12.3
$15,000 to $20,000	35	12.3
$20,001 to $24,999	38	13.4
Over $25,000	54	19.0
Respondent's Occupations:		
Professional	48	16.1
White-collar	49	16.5
Self-employed	24	8.1
Blue-collar	61	20.5
Other (retired, student, etc)	115	38.8

ROBERT N. MAXWELL MEMORIAL COMMUNITY HOSPITAL

BACKGROUND AND HISTORY

The Robert N. Maxwell Memorial Community Hospital is a large 400-plus bed hospital serving a city of 842,000 in a county of 1,808,000 people. The hospital is one of eight major ones operating in the county and is ranked second in size in terms of number of beds and number of admissions per year. In addition, several small hospitals also operate in the county, but these are not considered to be major competitors.

The hospital has operated in the community for a number of years and is well known by area physicians and the community. Over 800 physicians are on the hospital's staff, and they provide the hospital with physician expertise in such areas as urology, pediatrics, OB–GYN, orthopedics, general practice, internal medicine, general surgery, neurosurgery, ophthalmology, ENT (ear-nose-throat), plastic surgery, proctology, thoracic medicine, and dental. Many of these 800 physicians are on the staffs of other area hospitals at the same time, but they do admit patients to Maxwell Hospital. It is common practice for many physicians to use more than one hospital, and thus a single physician could be on staff with a number of hospitals at the same time.

Originally the hospital had been called County General Hospital, but it was renamed Robert N. Maxwell Memorial Community Hospital during World War II. Robert N. Maxwell had been the 24-year-old son of a member of the hospital's board of directors, Joshua Maxwell. The younger Maxwell had been an Army Air Corps P-40 fighter pilot who had been killed early in the war in the Philippine Islands. The hospital had been renamed in his memory and was now commonly referred to simply as Maxwell Hospital. Few people in the community actually knew who Robert N. Maxwell had been or the derivation of the hospital's name.

Howard Hartley is the associate director of the hospital and functions in the capacity of its chief operating officer. A graduate of a Midwestern university with an M.B.A. degree, Hartley is a very able and respected administrator. He is responsible for a host of departmental and functional activities, one of which is marketing. He is chairman of the hospital's loosely defined marketing committee and is therefore considered the top marketing officer in the organization. Hartley, however, does not consider himself a marketing authority and in fact is somewhat concerned about this. He has held this position for a number of years, dating back to when the hospital was relatively small. In those days, competition was not as strong as it had become in 1980, and the hospital itself was not as complex. Marketing had not been considered a really important activity. By 1980, the picture had changed—competition was fierce, and the organization was large and sometimes unwieldy. In addition, Hart-

Reprinted from R.W. Haas and T.R. Wotruba, *Marketing Management: Concepts, Practice and* *Cases*, copyright © Business Publications, Inc., 1983, by permission of the publisher.

ley was concerned about his own ability to manage the marketing aspects of the company, since he was responsible for so many other activities at the same time. He did not feel he could give marketing the attention it needed.

THE PRESENT HOSPITAL ORGANIZATION

Figure 1 depicts the present general organization of the hospital. Five individuals make up the organization's top management team.

Paul Cashman holds the position of executive director and is for all purposes the equivalent of the organization's president. Well educated, articulate, and gracious, Cashman is an ideal top officer. He relates well with physician groups, with various hospital association people, with the area's political leaders, and with the community in general. In addition, he is a good buffer between the hospital and its board of directors. He does not, however, take an active interest in the day-to-day operations of the organization but leaves that to his subordinates. He relies heavily on Hartley to keep him informed in this area.

As has been stated, Howard Hartley is the hospital's associate director and acts as the chief operating officer. Cashman looks to Hartley to actually run the hospital. As the organization chart shows, Hartley is involved in many areas, heading up seven departments and chairing five functional committees as well.

Andre Dixon is an assistant director and is considered the hospital's top personnel officer. A college graduate with a degree in personnel management, Dixon has little interest or expertise in marketing. As the chart shows, his primary area of responsibility is in training and personnel development, although he is also involved in the administration of the hospital's rehabilitation division

and its back pain management program. Both of these are medical programs headed by physicians. Dixon works closely with these physicians in the administration of these programs.

Terry Kohler is also an assistant director and is the organization's top financial officer. A recent M.B.A. degree holder from an Ivy League university, Kohler is a financial, statistical, and data processing whiz. As the chart shows, his areas of responsibility are in fiscal control, purchasing, and data processing. He, like Dixon, is also involved in the administration of medical programs and departments, such as pathology and radiology. A very bright and able young administrator, Kohler is also responsible for the hospital's strategic planning program. In view of all his responsibilities, Kohler has little time for marketing activities although he does serve on the hospital's marketing committee.

The fifth top administrator is Nonny Ewart, the nursing administrator. Ms. Ewart has considerable nursing experience and is considered a very able nursing administrator. Well respected by her nurses, Ewart brings stability and professionalism to this important area of hospital administration. Her degree is in nursing, and she acknowledges openly that she has little awareness of what is involved in hospital marketing.

The primary marketing vehicle in the organization is the hospital's marketing committee. This committee is comprised of Dixon, Kohler, Ewart, and Hartley as chairman. Norman Graham, an outside consultant retained by the hospital, also serves on this committee. Graham heads the public affairs department which reports directly to Cashman as the chart indicates. This department is primarily responsible for publicity and public relations. Often, Paul Cashman attends committee meetings which typically take place on the first and third Thursdays of

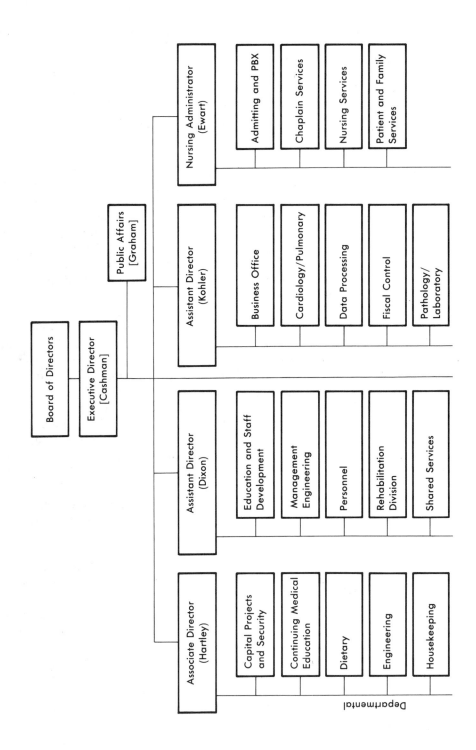

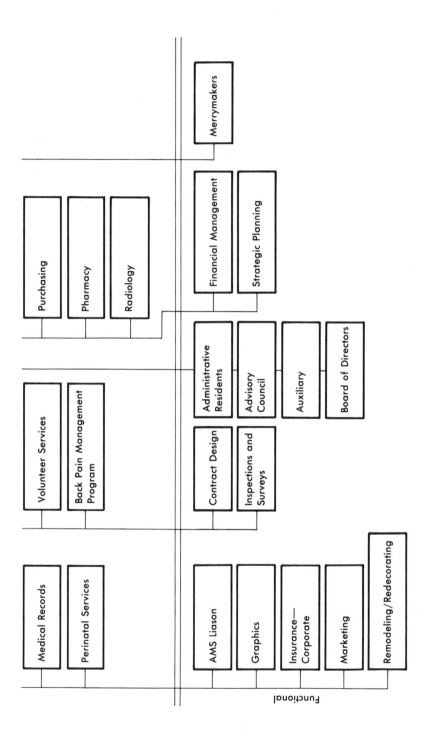

Medical Records
Perinatal Services

Volunteer Services
Back Pain Management Program

Purchasing
Pharmacy
Radiology

Merrymakers

Financial Management
Strategic Planning

Administrative Residents
Advisory Council
Auxiliary
Board of Directors

Contract Design
Inspections and Surveys

AMS Liason
Graphics
Insurance—Corporate
Marketing
Remodeling/Redecorating

Functional

199

every month at 8:00 A.M. In addition, representatives from various departments, such as patient and family services, and public affairs, are often invited to attend. The committee meets to discuss marketing ideas and programs, and Hartley assigns various marketing activities to members when such activities are decided upon. This committee, while stretched thin, has fostered a genuine interest in strengthening the hospital's marketing orientation, which Hartley believes is a positive factor.

THE PROBLEM

A number of things are bothering Hartley regarding the hospital's marketing position.

First, the hospital's market share in terms of beds and admissions appears to be dropping. Hartley has analyzed these data between 1970 and 1980, and the decline is illustrated in Table 1. Hartley is concerned that if these trends continue, Maxwell Hospital could be in trouble in the future.

Second, a study conducted on the staff physicians indicates that the hospital may not be attracting enough young physicians. Reviewing age distributions for general practice and internal medicine physicians between 1970 and 1980. Table 2 shows the data observed. Since both types of physicians are important in generating referrals, Hartley feels that the trends are not favorable.

Third, this same physician study indicates that a definite heavy-user pattern exists with physicians on staff. This is shown in Table 3 which reveals that 12.4 percent of the staff physicians (104 of 835) admitted 61.2 percent of the patients (9,053 of 14,793 in 1980). Hartley believes this statistic is important, but he is unsure of its marketing implications.

Fourth, Hartley is concerned because there is no marketing specialist or profes-

TABLE 1: Robert N. Maxwell Hospital's share of beds and admissions among major hospitals in the county area, 1970 and 1980

Hospital	Beds				Admissions*			
	1970		1980		1970		1980	
	Number	Percent	Number	Percent	Number	Percent	Number	Percent
Maxwell	352	16.0%	401	15.7%	16,679	18.8%	14,793	15.6%
Canyon[†]	175	8.0	195	7.6	1,569	1.8	6,882	7.3
Claybourne	99	4.5	150	5.8	6,057	6.8	4,082	4.3
Greymont	234	10.6	234	9.1	13,175	14.8	12,039	12.7
Mercyhurst	498	22.6	511	20.0	21,599	24.3	21,140	22.3
Peninsula[‡]	150	6.8	150	5.9	4,277	4.8	4,391	4.6
Bayside	240	10.9	363	14.2	10,745	12.1	12,994	13.7
Doctors & Nurses	219	10.0	250	9.8	5,738	6.4	4,387	4.6
North County	232	10.6	306	11.9	9,096	10.2	14,202	14.9
Total	2,199	100.0%	2,560	100.0%	88,935*	100.0%	94,910*	100.0%

*Admission figures do not represent maximum number of patients possible, but rather the number of patients actually admitted in those years.
[†]Opened in mid-1972.
[‡]Opened in 1974.

TABLE 2: Age distributions of staff physicians

Age groups	Percent of general practice physicians		Percent of internal medicine physicians	
	1970	1980	1970	1980
50 and under	69.6%	43.8%	81.3%	66.9%
51 and over	30.4	56.2	18.7	33.1
Total	100.0%	100.0%	100.0%	100.0%

sional on the marketing committee or in the entire hospital. He has read many health-care journal articles whose authors impress the need for hospitals to market more effectively in the changing health-care environment. These same authors also stress the need for hospitals to employ health-care marketing professionals to manage their marketing operations. He is also intrigued by the want ad which he had read in a major metropolitan newspaper. Hartley cannot help but wonder if Maxwell Hospital has arrived at that point where marketing should be handled as a primary as opposed to a secondary activity.

MARKETING OBJECTIVES

A major responsibility of Hartley and the marketing committee had been to develop marketing objectives for the hospital. This was required as part of Kohler's strategic planning program. The committee put in many long hours on this and defined three target markets.

TABLE 3: Heavy-user concept of Maxwell Hospital physicians in 1980

Area	Total number of physicians	Number and percentage of heavy users		Patients admitted by heavy users	
		Number	Percent	Number	Percent
Urology	37	6	16.2	204	61.3
Pediatrics	75	10	13.3	1,541	57.3
OB–GYN	94	16	17.0	2,942	57.1
Orthopedics	68	10	14.7	857	63.8
General practice	148	10	6.8	486	59.6
Internal	142	11	7.7	1,274	60.1
General surgery	93	10	10.8	751	62.9
Neurosurgery	18	6	33.3	256	92.6
Ophthalmology	59	6	10.2	156	88.1
ENT	26	5	19.2	249	83.3
Plastic surgery	16	5	31.2	55	84.4
Proctology	3	2	66.7	64	100.0
Thoracic	26	5	19.2	188	86.4
Dental	30	2	3.3	30	68.6
Total	835	104	12.4%	9,053	61.2%

DIRECTOR OF
HOSPITAL MARKETING

A unique, growth opportunity now exists with our young, rapidly expanding National Health Care Management Company, for a highly motivated individual having a solid record of achieving significant quantifiable results.
The Director's responsibility is to achieve increased utilization and increased revenue for the Emergency Department's ancillary services, and in-patient units of general acute hospitals. The successful candidate would have authority to achieve, with his staff, census improvement results through physician contacts, community relations activity, public service health education programs, open-houses, inter-agency affiliations, and any other suitable techniques with which she or he might be familiar or might innovate. The qualified candidate might come from any of a variety of career backgrounds, but must be thoroughly familiar with hospital procedures and interrelationships. Such a candidate might be a Hospital Administrator, a Registered Nurse Consultant, a Nursing In-Service Director, a Clinic Manager, an Operations Executive of a Hospital Management Company, or an individual who has successfully marketed and developed management contracts for Hospital Ancillary Services.
If you are an ambitious executive seeking an environment where your growth and reward are contingent only upon your own performance, starting with an excellent salary and liberal fringe benefits, this is the unlimited opportunity you have been seeking.
Send your resume and salary requirement to:
BOX D-005NA,   TIMES
An Equal Opportunity Employer M/F

1. *The Physician Market.* Since most hospital patients are admitted by physicians, focusing marketing efforts on physicians in the area seemed most appropriate.
2. *The Patient Market.* Since patients can and do influence physicians in their selection of hospitals, the committee felt some form of patient marketing was needed.
3. *The Community Market.* Since the hospital must operate as a part of its community, marketing effort to promote Maxwell Hospital as a good citizen was logical.

The marketing committee then established objectives in each of these three target markets.

Overall Objective: To increase overall utilization of Robert N. Maxwell Memorial Community Hospital as a major community hospital in the county.

Physician Market Objectives:

• To attract and retain a growing number of heavy-user physicians to the hospital.
• To continue to develop areas of specialization which will in turn attract physicians to the hospital because of the quality of services offered. This is currently being done with cardiovascular services, perinatal services, and rehabilitation services. (These were termed Commitment Level I services.)

- To create an awareness, liking, and preference for Maxwell Hospital among younger physicians and those recently arrived in the county.
- To increase the number of primary physicians (e.g., general practice and internal medicine) and thereby increasing the hospital's referral potential for other physicians.
- To increase the identification by present physicians with Maxwell Hospital and thus foster a closer relationship between the hospital and physicians using the hospital.
- To increase awareness by physicians in the state and surrounding area of the hospital's services, particularly in its areas of specialization.
- To increase awareness of the quality of services provided by Maxwell Hospital to strengthen the preference for Maxwell Hospital among all types of physicians in the county.

Patient Market Objectives:

- To continue to provide the highest quality of patient care possible to foster favorable word-of-mouth promotion by patients to potential patients and to physicians in the marketplace.
- To develop the image of Maxwell Hospital as a quality provider of first-rate acute health care to potential patients in the marketplace.
- To attract health maintenance patients as well as acute health-care patients.
- To develop a file of patients of record so that more of the market has an existing relationship with Maxwell Hospital.
- To establish Maxwell Hospital as a complete source of information on health-care services and their availability in the county area.

Community Market Objectives:

- To increase the level of public awareness in the county, and to broaden the image of Maxwell Hospital as not only a highly specialized hospital but also a total community hospital.
- To provide assistance and services to health-related institutions and to other community organizations.
- To increase the level of public awareness in the state and surrounding region of Maxwell Hospital's Commitment Level I Services.
- To establish the image of Maxwell Hospital as a good corporate citizen that is concerned and involved with community issues and problems.

The committee does not see the three markets as equals but recommends that marketing efforts be devoted toward the three in these proportions: 70 percent to the physician market, 20 percent to the patient market, and 10 percent to the community market.

Hartley believes the committee has done a good job and that the objectives are valid. He doubts, however, that these objectives could be attained with the hospital's existing marketing organization. In particular, he does not believe the hospital possesses the necessary marketing expertise or resources to develop strategies and programs to reach these objectives. He wonders how the hospital might best be organized to attain these objectives and reverse the trends he feels are alarming. Advise Mr. Hartley.

PLANNED PARENTHOOD OF ATLANTA

In early May 1974, Ms. Julie Dallas, a summer intern of Planned Parenthood of Altanta, was trying to determine what actions to take with regard to the increasing problem of unwanted pregnancies among teenagers and the growth of venereal disease for this group. She felt that greater usage of condoms (also called rubbers or prophylactics) by teenagers would help both these problems somewhat and wanted to develop a case to present to condom manufacturers to convince them to initiate a marketing campaign oriented toward teenagers. Several summer interns would be joining the staff in the next two weeks and would be available to help conduct any research that would be beneficial to this effort. Ms. Dallas had to design a program to make use of these interns when they arrived.

BACKGROUND ON THE PLANNED PARENTHOOD OF ATLANTA

The Planned Parenthood of Atlanta (PPA) is one of 190 local affiliates of the Planned Parenthood Federation of America. The first birth control clinic in the United States was opened in 1914 by Margaret Sanger, who later formed the National Birth Control League. Sanger was a nurse by profession, working mainly with underprivileged persons in New York City. Her work stimulated her to become an activist in the early women's rights movement, with emphasis on the right of women to control conception. Although her early concern was with individual rights, the scope of the movement has broadened to include the issue of population control on national and international levels.

In 1939, the League evolved into the Planned Parenthood Federation of America, sometimes also known as Planned Parenthood/World Population. The stated purposes of the federation are:

1. To provide leadership in
   a. Making effective means of voluntary fertility control, including contraception, abortion, and sterilization, available and fully accessible to all.
   b. Achieving a U.S. population of stable size in an optimum environment.
   c. Developing appropriate information, education, and training programs.
2. To support the efforts of others to achieve similar goals in the United States and throughout the world.

Planned Parenthood of Atlanta was formed in 1964 by a group of concerned citizens organized by Mrs. Herbert Taylor. After a period of provisional affiliation, the Atlanta association became a full affiliate of the Federation in 1967. The original intention of PPA was to provide education in the area of birth control for the Metropolitan Atlanta community and to stimulate public health agencies to provide various birth control services. Reducing the number of unwanted pregnancies (among both married and unmarried women) is one of the primary goals of PPA, and they have been using a summer intern program for the past few years to conduct

Prepared by Kenneth L. Bernhardt, Georgia State University, and Danny N. Bellenger, Texas Tech University.

programs in this area oriented toward teenagers.

Early in its existence, Planned Parenthood of Atlanta realized that existing agencies for birth control were handling maximum loads and needs for services were not being met. When federal funds were made available, PPA opened its own clinic in January 1966 at the Bethlehem Community Center. By 1973, seven Planned Parenthood clinics were providing service to approximately 9,000 persons annually. In addition to operating these clinics, they distribute literature and provide speakers throughout the area, mostly directed toward the problem of unwanted pregnancies.

Originally, the PPA operating funds came entirely from membership dues and private donations. By 1974, funding was received from United Way and federal and state government family planning programs.

BACKGROUND ON POPULATION PLANNING

As shown in Exhibit 1, the fertility rate (number of children/woman) in the United States has been on the decline since the late 1950s, and had reached 2.4 by 1970. In 1974, the rate was approximately 2.1 children per woman, considered the theoretical rate whereby zero population growth can be achieved.

The annual birthrate (percent of women of childbearing age who have a child in that year) was declining as shown in Exhibit 2. The rate dropped between 1961 and 1971 in every age category for both whites and nonwhites. Among nonwhite teenagers, however, the rate dropped by only 16% during that period, and dropped by only 3% between 1968 and 1971. The greatest disparity between the birthrates of the two racial groups also occurs among teenagers, with the birthrate of nonwhites almost 2½ times that of whites.

Exhibit 3 presents data concerning unwanted fertility in the United States broken down by education and race. The table shows that the overall expected number of births per each woman is 3.0, with the figure being 2.9 for white women and 3.7 for black women. The figure ranges from a low of 2.3 children for a black woman who is a college graduate to a high of 5.2 children for a black woman who never went to high school. The same relationship between education and number of births is very similar for college-educated blacks and whites, but black women with a low level of education have a much greater number of children than white women of comparable education. The largest portion of this difference can be attributed to the difference in the percent of births that were unwanted for the two groups.

Column 2 in Exhibit 3 presents data concerning the percent of births that were unwanted. Of children born in 1966–1970 to black college graduates, only 3% were unwanted, while over half of those born to black women who never went to high school were unwanted. Column 3 in the table presents data concerning the theoretical births per woman eliminating unwanted births. It shows that if unwanted births were eliminated, black women who never went to high school would only have 41% more children than black married college graduates (instead of the actual figure of 126% more children). Thus it appears that the problem is not so much one of motivation differences among the groups as it is a lack of education about and/or availability of contraceptive methods.

Although the birthrates for teenagers have been decreasing as shown in Exhibit 2, the rates of illegitimacy have been drastically increasing. In 1960, 15% of births to teenage

EXHIBIT 1: Total fertility rate for the United States, 1800–1970[a]

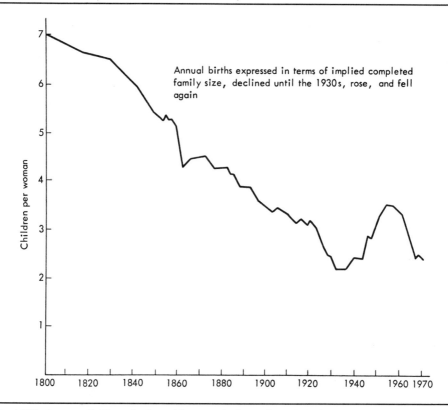

Annual births expressed in terms of implied completed family size, declined until the 1930s, rose, and fell again

[a]Prior to 1917, data available only for white population; after 1917, for total population.
Source: Prior to 1917—Ansley Coale and Melvin Zelnick, *New Estimates of Fertility and Population in the United States* (Princeton, N.J.: Princeton University Press, 1963). 1917 to 1968—U.S. National Center for Health Statistics, *Natality Statistics Analysis,* Series 21, Number 19, 1970. 1969 to 1971—U.S. Bureau of the Census, *Current Population Reports,* Series P-23, No. 36, "Fertility Indicators: 1970," 1971. The figure for 1971 is based on an unpublished Census staff estimate.

mothers were illegitimate, while in 1968, this figure was 27%. For white teenagers, the percentage in 1968 was 16% and for non-white it was 55%.

Exhibit 4 presents details on illegitimate birthrates by race and age. Illegitimate children are usually unwanted. In 1971, among unmarried teenagers who were pregnant, 83% of the white girls and 72% of the black girls reported their pregnancies as unwanted. In 1973, 75% of the abortions in Georgia

were for teenagers, another indicator of the large number of unwanted pregnancies in this age group.

In addition to the problems resulting from unwanted pregnancies, the sexually active person faces the possibility of venereal disease. Over the last decade, the incidence rates of gonorrhea have increased drastically as can be seen from Exhibit 5, particularly for persons under 25. Currently, gonorrhea ranks first among reportable communicable

EXHIBIT 2: Birth rates by age of mother and color in the United States, 1961–1971

	White					Nonwhite				
Age	1961	1965	1968	1971	Percent change 1961–1971	1961	1965	1968	1971	Percent change 1961–1971
15–19	7.9[a]	6.1	5.5	5.4	−32	15.3	13.6	13.3	12.9	−16
20–24	24.8	18.0	16.3	14.5	−42	29.3	24.7	20.1	18.5	−37
25–29	19.4	15.9	14.0	13.5	−30	22.2	18.8	14.5	13.6	−39
30–34	11.0	9.2	7.3	6.6	−45	13.6	11.8	9.1	8.0	−41
35–39	5.3	4.4	3.4	2.7	−49	7.5	6.4	4.9	4.0	−47
40–44	1.5	1.2	0.9	0.6	−60	2.2	1.9	1.5	1.2	−45

[a]Table is read as follows: In 1961, of all white women between 15 and 19 years of age, 7.9% gave birth.

diseases in the United States. During fiscal year 1973, 809,681 cases were reported, while estimates of actual occurrence were around 2,500,000 cases.

While venereal disease is not the specific domain of Planned Parenthood of Atlanta, it is of concern since one of its prime targets— the sexually active teenager—is particularly susceptible. Also, Planned Parenthood of Atlanta is interested in this problem because Atlanta has the highest reported rate of gonorrhea in the United States with incidence

EXHIBIT 3: Unwanted fertility in the United States, 1970[a]

Race and education	Most likely number of births per woman	Percent of births 1966–70 unwanted	Theoretical births per woman without unwanted births
All women	3.0	15	2.7
College 4+	2.5	7	2.4
College 1–3	2.8	11	2.6
High school 4	2.8	14	2.6
High school 1–3	3.4	20	2.9
Less	3.9	31	3.0
White women	2.9	13	2.6
College 4+	2.5	7	2.4
College 1–3	2.8	10	2.6
High school 4	2.8	13	2.6
High school 1–3	3.2	18	2.8
Less	3.5	25	2.9
Black women	3.7	27	2.9
College 4+	2.3	3	2.2
College 1–3	2.6	21	2.3
High school 4	3.3	19	2.8
High school 1–3	4.2	31	3.2
Less	5.2	55	3.1

[a]Based on data from the 1970 National Fertility Study for currently married women under 45 years of age.

EXHIBIT 4: Illegitimate live births expressed as percentage of live births, by age of mother and color, in the United States, 1961–1968

	White			Nonwhite		
Age	*1961*	*1965*	*1968*	*1961*	*1965*	*1968*
Under 15	49.9[a]	57.3	61.0	81.7	86.4	90.8
15–17	12.4	17.3	23.4	56.2	62.5	68.8
18–19	5.9	9.1	12.8	35.6	38.9	44.3
20–24	2.4	3.8	5.1	20.9	23.0	26.4
25–29	1.3	1.9	2.0	14.4	16.3	16.8
30–34	1.1	1.6	2.0	13.2	14.9	15.5
35–39	1.4	1.9	2.5	13.0	14.9	15.7
Over 40	1.7	2.2	2.8	12.7	14.0	15.7

[a]Table is read as follows: In 1961, of all live births to white women under 15 years of age, 49.9% were illegitimate.

rates approximately three times as high as the national figures presented in Exhibit 5.

A major study concerning unwanted fertility among teenagers was conducted in 1971 by the Institute for Survey Research at Temple University as part of the Commission on Population Growth and the American Future which was established by President Nixon in July 1969. Appendix A presents some data from this study concerning sexuality, contraception, and pregnancy among unwed female

EXHIBIT 5: Gonorrhea ratio per 100,000 population by age group, in the United States, 1960–1972

Age	*1960*	*1970*	*1972*	*Percent change, 1960–1972*
15–19	412.7[a]	782.2	1,035.4	151
20–24	859.2	1,541.5	1,813.5	111
25–29	485.5	827.8	921.6	90
30–39	192.1	312.9	347.2	81
40–49	52.1	80.4	84.6	62

[a]Table is read as follows: In 1960, for every 100,000 persons between 15 and 19 years old, 412.7 persons contracted gonorrhea.

teenagers which is based on a national study of 4,611 teenagers.

APPENDIX A:
SEXUALITY, CONTRACEPTION, AND PREGNANCY AMONG YOUNG UNWED FEMALES IN THE UNITED STATES*

The Data. Interviews were completed with females selected in such a way as to represent a national probability sample of the female population, aged 15 to 19, living in households in the United States. In addition to the sample of respondents in housing units, another probability sample was taken of university students living in dormitories. The two samples provided a total of 4,611 interviews, of which 1,479 were with black females and 3,132 were with whites and other races. (Throughout the study, "white" refers to nonblack respondents.) The large proportion of black interviews was the result of a sampling scheme stratified by race.

The sole criterion for eligibility in this study was age, with the provision that only one eligible female could be selected (randomly) from any one household (or any one room in a college dormitory). Women of any marital status were accepted. About 10% of the respondents have even been married; the concern of this paper is with the other 90%, those who have never been married.

The Never Married. For data on prevalence of intercourse, see Table 1.

CURRENT SITUATION

Each summer for the past few years, one or more interns had joined the PPA staff for the summer. The interns were typically un-

*From "Sexuality, Contraception and Pregnancy among Young Unwed Females in the United States," by Melvin Zelnik and John F. Kantner, in Commission on Population Growth and the American Future, *Research Reports, Volume I, Demographic and Social Aspects of Population Growth,* edited by Charles F. Westoff and Robert Parke, Jr., 1972.

TABLE 1: Never-married females who have had intercourse, by age and race (%)

| Age | Percent[a] | | |
	Black	White	Total
15	32.3	10.8	13.8
16	46.4	17.5	21.2
17	57.0	21.7	26.6
18	60.4	33.5	37.1
19	80.8	40.4	46.1
Total	53.6	23.4	27.6

[a]Percentages computed omitting those who have always used contraception, those who gave no answer to the several questions on contraceptive use, and those whose answer to this question was coded other.

dergraduate and graduate students interested in some aspect of public health. The interns during the summers of 1972 and 1973 had concentrated on a program of distributing free condoms to male teenagers in various recreation centers in low-income areas of Atlanta. One purpose of these efforts was to determine how receptive these teens were to this method of contraception.

In May 1974, Ms. Julie Dallas joined the staff of PPA as part of a field internship for her graduate work in Public Health at the University of Michigan. She decided that she wanted to do more with her summer project than had been done in the past. After consultations with top PPA officials, she decided to concentrate on a project that would provide research results useful in convincing condom manufacturers to undertake a marketing education and distribution program oriented toward teenagers.

The immediate problem Ms. Dallas faced concerned what type of research to do to obtain information useful for this objective. She felt that she could obtain the cooperation of the city of Atlanta's Recreation Department, and could conduct interviews with teenagers at various parks during the summer. The summer interns, two black students and one white student, would be available to help gather data for the study.

TABLE 2: Knowledge of onset of fecundity, by age and race, both intercourse statuses (%)

| | "When can a girl first become pregnant?" | | | | | | | |
| | When period begins | | Sometime later | | Don't know or no answer | | Total | |
Age	Black	White	Black	White	Black	White	Black	White
R has had intercourse								
15	45.6	46.2	49.7	51.3	4.7	2.5	100.0	100.0
16	52.4	55.3	45.9	40.2	1.7	4.5	100.0	100.0
17	50.6	64.4	47.7	32.8	1.7	2.8	100.0	100.0
18	55.2	71.2	42.3	27.6	2.5	1.2	100.0	100.0
19	71.6	63.1	27.8	33.5	0.6	3.4	100.0	100.0
Total	56.4	62.4	41.6	34.8	2.0	2.8	100.0	100.0
R has not had intercourse								
15	46.7	48.5	47.4	45.2	5.9	6.3	100.0	100.0
16	53.6	53.6	43.4	40.8	3.0	5.6	100.0	100.0
17	65.1	62.8	30.7	32.9	4.2	4.3	100.0	100.0
18	53.3	64.6	43.7	31.6	3.0	3.8	100.0	100.0
19	64.0	67.1	31.2	29.9	4.8	3.0	100.0	100.0
Total	54.1	57.6	41.5	37.5	4.4	4.9	100.0	100.0

TABLE 3: Knowledge of pregnancy risk within menstrual cycle by age and race, both intercourse statuses (%)

| | *When is a girl most likely to. . . .* | | | | | | | |
| | *Right before, during, or after period* | | *About two weeks after* | | *Any time* | | *Total* | |
Age	*Black*	*White*	*Black*	*White*	*Black*	*White*	*Black*	*White*
R has had intercourse								
15	43.2	44.6	17.5	41.1	39.3	14.3	100.0	100.0
16	53.0	43.8	17.5	43.6	29.5	12.6	100.0	100.0
17	49.5	34.7	18.3	51.3	32.2	14.0	100.0	100.0
18	55.6	24.1	16.1	62.6	28.3	13.3	100.0	100.0
19	34.3	29.6	23.1	59.9	42.6	10.5	100.0	100.0
Total	46.7	33.0	18.8	54.4	34.5	12.6	100.0	100.0
R has not had intercourse								
15	51.0	48.8	17.7	30.6	31.3	20.6	100.0	100.0
16	46.9	47.0	16.7	36.6	36.4	16.4	100.0	100.0
17	44.2	48.2	17.6	40.3	38.2	11.5	100.0	100.0
18	49.4	37.0	17.9	49.9	32.7	13.1	100.0	100.0
19	47.9	33.1	20.0	55.3	32.1	11.6	100.0	100.0
Total	48.2	44.3	17.6	40.3	34.2	15.4	100.0	100.0

*Planned Parenthood Association, 118 Marietta Street, N.W., Atlanta, Georgia 30303.

In addition to providing information useful to their campaign to convince condom manufacturers to promote to this target group, PPA wanted to develop information from the study which would help them develop a strategy to increase their services to best meet the needs of the teenagers. For example, they wondered whether they should

TABLE 4: Percent that had first intercourse at each age, by current age and race[a]

| | *Current age* | | | | | | | | | |
| | *15* | | *16* | | *17* | | *18* | | *19* | |
Age at first intercourse	*Black*	*White*	*Black*	*White*	*Black*	*White*	*Black*	*White*	*Black*	*White*
<12	17.3[a]	8.0	3.0	5.5	5.0	1.1	3.3	6.0	0.9	1.4
13	14.2	17.5	6.0	3.7	4.6	1.3	3.7	4.3	2.6	1.2
14	34.7	30.8	21.8	10.4	7.2	6.9	6.6	2.8	4.2	0.6
15	33.8	43.7	31.9	29.8	30.3	14.4	10.8	6.8	8.2	1.3
16	—	—	37.3	50.6	36.9	51.4	29.5	16.6	25.0	11.7
17	—	—	—	—	16.0	24.9	32.8	30.3	34.0	23.7
18	—	—	—	—	—	—	13.3	33.2	23.3	35.7
19	—	—	—	—	—	—	—	—	1.8	24.4
Total	100.0	100.0	100.0	100.0	100.0	100.0	100.0	100.0	100.0	100.0

[a]Table is read as follows: Of black girls currently 15 years old who have had intercourse, 17.3% first had intercourse before age 13.

TABLE 5: Percent distribution of frequency of intercourse in "last month" by age and race[a]

	Frequency in last month									
	None		1–2		3–5		6 or more		Total	
Age	Black	White	Black	White	Black	White	Black	White	Black	White
15	45.3[a]	49.6	34.4	27.4	14.6	13.3	5.7	9.7	100.0	100.0
16	46.4	45.2	30.4	37.1	16.2	2.6	7.0	4.1	100.0	100.0
17	38.6	32.1	40.2	35.4	15.7	18.0	5.5	14.5	100.0	100.0
18	44.6	35.0	33.8	24.9	13.2	21.4	8.4	18.7	100.0	100.0
19	33.6	33.8	25.1	23.1	31.1	18.9	10.2	24.2	100.0	100.0
Total	41.0	37.3	32.6	28.6	18.8	18.0	7.6	16.1	100.0	100.0

[a]Table is read as follows: 45.3% of 15-year-old nonvirgins did not have intercourse in the last month.

open more clinics, distribute more free samples, offer more counseling services, create and distribute more brochures (an example of a PPA information sheet is included in Appendix B), or what else they could do to help reduce the large number of unwanted pregnancies among this age group.

Two professors at a leading local business school had agreed to help analyze the data they collected from their research and advise them on the study design. A meeting was scheduled for the following week. Among the questions which she [Ms. Dallas] needed to answer before that meeting were the following: (1) what the objectives of the research should be; (2) how she should define the sample population for the study; (3) what type of research to conduct—group interviews, a survey study, an experimental study, or some other type; and (4) what specific questions concerning attitudes and behavior should be asked in the research. As the interns would be arriving shortly, it was imperative that she be well prepared for the meeting so that any adjustments necessary could be made quickly.

For data on basic biological knowledge, see Tables 2 and 3.

The Sexually Active. For data on the sexually active, see Tables 4, 5, and 6.

Table 7 attempts to show what conjunction there is between first use of contraception

TABLE 6: Percent distribution of contraceptive use status, by age and race[a]

	Contraceptive use status									
	Never		Sometimes		Always		No answer		Total	
Age	Black	White	Black	White	Black	White	Black	White	Black	White
15	27.3[a]	34.1	49.5	44.2	19.6	18.8	3.6	2.9	100.0	100.0
16	21.4	19.5	59.6	56.5	15.2	21.9	3.8	2.1	100.0	100.0
17	10.6	12.4	69.1	68.7	19.5	15.8	0.8	3.1	100.0	100.0
18	10.6	13.1	72.0	68.0	16.4	17.7	1.0	1.2	100.0	100.0
19	10.6	12.1	76.1	59.1	8.6	26.4	4.7	2.4	100.0	100.0
Total	14.9	16.0	67.0	61.3	15.4	20.5	2.7	2.2	100.0	100.0

[a]Table is read as follows: 27.3% of 15-year-old black nonvirgins never use any method of contraception.

TABLE 7: **Age at first intercourse by age at first use of contraception, for blacks and whites (%)[a]**

	Age at first intercourse									
Age at first use	<12	13	14	15	16	17	18	19	N.A.	Total
					Black					
<12	18.8[a]									0.9
13		33.6								2.3
14			39.9							5.0
15				44.1						12.5
16					54.1					20.1
17						63.8				18.3
18							71.2			9.1
19								52.0		1.4
N.A. (age)										13.3
N.A. (use)/never used										17.1
Total	4.8	5.3	12.3	20.7	26.2	18.3	7.3	0.4	3.2	100.0
					White					
<12	31.0									1.2
13		34.2								1.5
14			51.3							4.2
15				58.3						8.8
16					65.0					18.6
17						69.1				16.0
18							72.9			16.6
19								83.6		6.8
N.A. (age)										8.7
N.A. (use)/never used										17.6
Total	3.8	4.0	6.9	13.9	25.1	18.8	18.2	6.5	2.8	100.0

[a]Table is read as follows: 18.8% of black teenagers who had intercourse before age 13 began using contraceptives before age 13.

and the beginning of sexuality. Although there is a looseness of the data since age in years is the only increment, the results do give a clear indication of what percentage do not begin using contraceptives immediately. The summary statistics show that 50% of the blacks and about 64% of the whites begin using contraceptives at the same age as they become sexually active.

Tables 8, 9, and 10 present additional data on contraception.

The relative unimportance of commercial sources other than drugstores may appear surprising in view of the importance of the condom. In cases where the condoms were obtained by the male, there is undoubtedly a considerable amount of doubt about the source.

APPENDIX B:
PPA INFORMATION SHEET
ON CONDOMS*

It is wise to know about MORE THAN ONE METHOD OF BIRTH CONTROL in case you stop using the one you are using now.

*Planned Parenthood Association, 118 Marietta Street, N.W., Atlanta, Georgia 30303.

TABLE 8: Percent distribution of most recently used contraception method, by age and race[a]

Method recently used	15 Black	15 White	16 Black	16 White	17 Black	17 White	18 Black	18 White	19 Black	19 White	All ages Black	All ages White
Pills	9.6[a]	2.3	29.4	8.8	21.0	21.4	31.6	25.9	33.4	41.9	26.5	25.0
Foam, jelly, or cream	3.6	2.0	1.8	1.6	3.0	2.7	3.6	4.8	5.0	1.6	3.5	2.7
IUD	3.0	0.0	0.7	0.0	3.4	0.0	4.7	1.3	4.8	0.9	3.6	0.6
Diaphragm	1.0	0.0	0.7	0.0	0.2	0.0	3.0	2.0	1.0	3.9	1.2	1.7
Condom	38.8	25.9	33.4	41.8	32.2	20.1	26.4	16.1	34.3	16.3	32.5	21.8
Douche	7.8	4.3	15.4	4.5	17.7	1.2	7.8	4.0	10.3	1.5	12.1	2.9
Withdrawal	18.5	48.2	5.4	25.3	10.5	41.2	8.6	34.3	4.0	26.2	8.5	33.0
Rhythm	0.0	0.0	0.0	6.2	0.0	2.8	2.2	1.3	0.0	2.5	0.5	2.6
Douche and withdrawal	1.7	7.8	0.7	2.0	3.6	1.9	2.6	2.5	2.4	0.7	2.3	2.2
Condom and other	16.0	9.5	12.5	9.8	8.4	8.7	9.5	7.8	4.8	4.5	9.3	7.5
Total	100.0	100.0	100.0	100.0	100.0	100.0	100.0	100.0	100.0	100.0	100.0	100.0

[a]Table is read as follows: 9.6% of black 15-year-olds who use contraceptives used the "pill" most recently.

TABLE 9: Percent giving specified reason for not using contraception, by race[a]

Reason	Black		White	
Trying to have baby; didn't mind if pregnant	24.2[b]		12.1	
Too young; infrequent sex; didn't think could get pregnant	27.8		16.4	
Time of month which couldn't get pregnant	21.4	49.1	42.5	58.9
Hedonism—heedlessness[c]	7.2		9.6	
Knowledge—logistic[d]	12.7		14.2	
Partner objects; wrong to use	3.0		4.5	
Other[e]	3.8		0.7	
Total	100.0		100.0	

[a]Refers to first reason given. Percentages computed omitting those who have always used contraception, those who gave no answer to the several questions on contraceptive use, and those whose answer to this question was coded "other."

[b]Table is read as follows: 24.2% of the black teenagers who specified a reason for not using contraceptives said they were trying to have a baby or didn't mind if they got pregnant.

[c]"No fun to use"; too "inconvenient"; "didn't want to use"; "just didn't."

[d]Didn't have contraception available; didn't know where to obtain; didn't know about contraception.

[e]"Dangerous"; medical reason for believing to be infecund; "too expensive."

TABLE 10: Percent distribution of sources of contraception, by age and race[a]

Source	15 Black	15 White	16 Black	16 White	17 Black	17 White	18 Black	18 White	19 Black	19 White	Total Black	Total White
Private physician	7.5	0.0	10.6	6.1	8.5	7.6	8.9	12.2	5.2	21.2	7.8	12.7
Drugstore[b]	60.3	78.1	57.2	67.8	64.0	67.4	61.5	64.6	66.1	58.5	62.8	64.3
Hospital clinic	22.7	0.0	24.6	0.0	17.3	4.2	20.3	5.4	18.5	9.7	19.8	5.5
Other type of clinic[c]	6.4	7.0	7.6	8.1	7.2	13.0	8.8	10.6	9.7	9.0	8.3	10.0
Other[d]	3.1	14.9	0.0	18.0	3.0	7.8	0.5	7.2	0.5	1.6	1.3	7.5
Total	100.0	100.0	100.0	100.0	100.0	100.0	100.0	100.0	100.0	100.0	100.0	100.0

[a]Excludes those who never used contraception, who did not answer the general question on use of contraception, who claimed never to have obtained contraception, and those who provided no answer on source.
[b]Includes those who responded private physician and drugstore.
[c]Includes those who responded hospital clinic and other type of clinic.
[d]Includes "friends," "relatives," and "commercial establishments other than drugstores."

The CONDOM, or rubber, is a method of birth control which many couples have used. It is a good method of birth control. It is also a good way to protect against the spread of infection (V.D.) from a man to a woman or from woman to a man.

How to Avoid Mistakes

1. The CONDOM will work if it is used EVERY TIME!
2. To check for holes you can blow the condom up like a balloon.
3. When the man removes his penis from the woman's birth canal, he should hold the condom so that it does not slip off.
4. If a condom is used several times, be sure to check EACH TIME that it has no holes.

Some men do not like to use the condom because they have to stop the loveplay leading up to intercourse to put it on. If the woman puts the condom on for the man, it can become a part of the loveplay and may make the man more willing to use this method of birth control.

Couples should discuss a method of birth control TOGETHER before they use the method. Since we are giving you condoms which you may take home, you may want to show them to your teenagers. It's simple to explain to them how this important method of birth control works.

Condoms can be purchased at any drugstore for nominal costs without a prescription or can be secured from the Planned Parenthood Clinics.

No method of birth control is guaranteed 100% effective. To increase protection foam may be used by the female partner when the man is using the condom.

A nurse is always available at the Downtown Clinic for supplies or telephone help. Daily from 2:00 p.m. until 8:00 p.m. and from 9:00 a.m. until 4:30 p.m. Saturdays. *Phone:* 688-9300

LEAGUE OF CATHOLIC WOMEN

During the summer of 1975 Mary Lynn Landis, the president of the League of Catholic Women, faced a tightening financial situation. In this period of inflation the League's troubles were compounded by the increased number of Detroiters who needed the League's assistance and by the increased administrative complexity of the social service programs established to administer aid. While the League's budget was approaching $1.5 million annually, most support was in the form of federal or foundation grants earmarked for particular social service programs. In the past, membership contributions had been relied upon to defray administrative expenses, but presently membership in the League was on a sharp decline. Mrs. Landis faced the problem of developing a marketing plan to increase membership without appreciably increasing costs by the beginning of the next membership drive in March of 1976.

FOUNDING, PHILOSOPHY, HISTORY

In 1906 a small group of Catholic women formed the Weinman Center to teach English and religion to foreign-born persons who had settled in Detroit, Michigan. The Weinman Center also functioned as a day nursery and became the first Michigan organization to assist immigrants in establishing themselves. This group of women became the Catholic Settlement Association of Detroit in 1911.

The League of Catholic Women was incorporated out of the Catholic Settlement Association of Detroit in 1915. The League's purpose as originally stated was: "To unite Catholic women for the promotion of religious, intellectual, and charitable work." The charitable work continued the settlement work including family visiting, health care, religious instruction, and maintaining a representative at the juvenile court. The services were directed at women, in particular adolescent and minority adult women, rather than toward families. At the time of incorporation the Weinman Center's program was expanded to include the classes in domestic science, sewing, dramatics, dance, manual training, Girl Scouts, athletics, kindergarten, and social clubs. All these classes were taught by volunteers. The Weinman Center program became a model for other League community centers established in 1919 and 1920 in other Detroit neighborhoods.

In the early days of the League's existence there was no ongoing fund-raising mechanism. It was then, and remains today, independent of the Catholic Church and as such received no direct aid from the Archdiocese of Detroit. Activities were supported by the personal financing of its members. An example of this financing is the sale of a $30,000 bond issue in 1916 to League members.

The proceeds of that first bond issue established the Watson Street Club House, a residence for homeless girls. In 1925 the League expanded its residence home program by opening the Madeleine Sophie Training Home for Girls. It served primarily delinquent girls and is still operating today as

Reprinted from K.L. Bernhardt and T.C. Kinnear, *Cases in Marketing Management*, copyright © Business Publications, Inc., 1985, by permission of the publisher.

Barat House. The Watson Street Club and the Madeleine Sophie Home created the League's first payroll obligations. While they were staffed primarily by volunteers they had professional social and child care workers on their staffs.

As the League's programs expanded the women began to plan for a headquarters building to house many activities and to provide ample residence rooms for working women and girls living away from their families. The first organized membership drive, held in the early 1920s, netted $11,771.47. This first drive was the kickoff for the Building Fund which resulted in the completion of Casgrain Hall by January of 1928. Casgrain Hall, which still serves as the League's headquarters, was heavily mortgaged and faced foreclosure in its first year. To rescue their building, League members "bought" bricks in the building and avoided foreclosure. The building was paid off by 1940.

In the 1940s the League expanded its services to provide day-care facilities and recreational programs to the black and Latin communities of Detroit. The 1950s and early 1960s saw little change in the League's activities. In the late 1960s the League moved into a new area of rehabilitation programs for women convicts.

PRESENT

Today the League of Catholic Women is the oldest and largest volunteer social service organization operating in Detroit. It is now administered by a 48-member board of trustees, a president (Mrs. Landis), two vice presidents, a secretary, and a treasurer elected annually by the general membership. All officers and board members serve without pay. The League administration is no longer involved in day-to-day operations of social services. In the past 10 years an agency structure (see Exhibit 1) has been created whereby each League agency has responsibility for a particular area of social service (see Exhibit 2). Each agency has a paid professional executive director and staff, responsibility for planning and executing its own budget, and an autonomous board of directors. The agency boards are chaired by a person appointed by the president of the League of Catholic Women but operate independent of League control. Persons selected to fill agency boards are usually concerned citizens from the neighborhood the agency serves, or professional persons with expertise in social work, health care, or administration. All agency board members serve without pay.

The League is in effect the umbrella administration for the agencies. The agencies operate independently, with supervision from the League board only in areas of general policy and fiscal matters. The League bookkeeping office handles all bookkeeping for the agencies. All federal, state, and foundation grants for agency programs are channeled through the League office and all payables the agencies incur are billed directly to the League.

Casgrain Hall is the one agency that is handled differently. While it has its own board of directors, it is included in the League budget because it does not receive outside aid. In an effort to maintain low-cost housing in the face of rising operating costs, Casgrain Hall has incurred a deficit each of the past four years. The past year it approached $80,000. The problem has been compounded by an environment that has changed drastically since the widespread civil disturbances of 1967. Since then, the 194-room residence hall has experienced an occupancy rate rarely above 60 percent.

The Casgrain Hall deficit consumes more of the League's surplus funds each year. In

EXHIBIT 1: Administrative structure

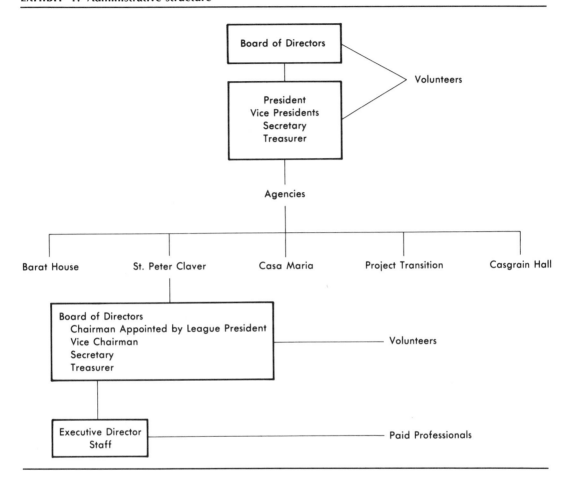

the past three years the League has been unable to provide any direct financial aid to its other agencies because of the Casgrain drain. The only money that could be applied to the deficit was the unrestricted public support (see Exhibits 3 and 4). The survival of the League seemed to depend on increasing the unrestricted public support.

MEMBERSHIP

In the early days of the League activity, membership was a loosely defined concept. Any Catholic woman who was in sympathy with League goals and volunteered some of her time to settlement work was considered a member. It wasn't until the early 1920s that membership lists were compiled and an annual dues of $1 was instituted. Early membership rosters indicate that members were drawn primarily from Detroit's upper socio-economic strata. The lists contain many names from families prominent in the blossoming auto and auto-related industry.

It is evident from records of financial contributions that the early members were not important for their $1 membership dues but

EXHIBIT 2: Synopsis of agency services and funding sources

BARAT HOUSE

An "open" residence treatment center for up to 20 emotionally disturbed teenage girls, offering psychiatric treatment and educational development. Funded by the United Foundation and the State Department of Social Services.

CASA MARIA

Community center in Tiger Stadium area, serving Latinos, blacks, Maltese, and Appalachian whites. It incorporates a nursery school, recreation, crafts, and counseling for youngsters and adult community programs. Funded by Archdiocese Development Fund and federal grants through the Juvenile Facilities Network.

ST. PETER CLAVER

Community center on the lower east side, predominately serving blacks. It incorporates a day-care center, recreation, crafts, and counseling for youngsters and adult community programs. Funded by the United Foundation.

PROJECT TRANSITION

Job training, residence, counseling, and employment assistance for 25 women from the Detroit House of Corrections and other disadvantaged backgrounds. A pilot program initiated by the League in 1971 aimed at offering total rehabilitation for women offenders; it is housed on the fourth floor of Casgrain Hall. Funded by state and federal grants and the Board of Education of the city of Detroit, with some assistance from the League.

CASGRAIN HALL

Eight-story League building near Wayne State University which provides low-cost residence for women of all ages; offers meeting rooms, ballroom, and conference facilities for community activities; and serves as League administration headquarters. Funded by rent receipts; currently carrying a large deficit.

---

for the larger personal resources they could bring to bear on the League's projects. For many years the League operated in a social service sphere in which its programs could be financed almost solely by its members' wealth. This situation changed in the 1930s and 1940s when League programs became more vigorous and the tax laws were changed to place social service more squarely in government hands. Today, large contributions by individual members are rare. The largest component of membership support is now the annual dues.

Today, membership is open to any woman in sympathy with the object of the League. Membership is offered in five classes. Dues are payable annually, charged as follows:

Sustaining	$ 10
Contributing	5
General	2
Life	100
Memorial	100

The bylaws of the League make no distinction between membership classes as to privileges or obligations. Exhibit 5 shows the costs incurred in connection with membership. The League bookkeeping office has always separated these costs into "Membership" and "Communication." Membership consists of those costs incurred in communicating solely with members. Communication costs are primarily the cost of quarterly newsletters.

EXHIBIT 3

LEAGUE OF CATHOLIC WOMEN OF DETROIT, MICHIGAN
Balance Sheets
December 31, 1974,
with Comparative Figures for 1973

Assets	*1974*	*1973*
Cash	$ 26,020	$ 55,582
Short-term commercial notes	54,945	—
Total	80,965	55,582
Accounts receivable:		
Residence (less allowance for doubtful accounts of $1,200 in 1974 and $500 in 1973)	6,199	2,414
Sponsored agencies	9,729	8,222
Related nonprofit corporation	1,544	3,304
Other	117	199
Total	17,589	14,139
Accrued interest receivable	847	151
Prepaid expense	5,255	7,174
Due from restricted fund	8,955	22,693
Total	15,057	30,018
Cash	—	22,340
Grants receivable	216,633	78,629
Total	216,633	100,969
Land, buildings, and equipment fund:		
Land, buildings, and equipment	1,927,586	1,926,413
Less accumulated depreciation	(737,296)	(665,278)
Total assets	$1,520,534	$1,461,843

Liabilities and Fund Balances

	1974	1973
Current funds		
Unrestricted:		
Accounts payable	$ 5,622	$ 6,653
Advance rentals and security	3,098	2,641
Withheld from employees	1,827	2,004
Loan payable	25,000	—
Total liabilities	35,547	11,298
Fund balance	78,064	88,441
Total	113,611	99,739

	8,955	22,693
Restricted:		
Due to unrestricted fund	8,955	22,693
Deferred support	202,629	55,936
Total liabilities and deferred support	211,584	78,629
Fund balance	5,049	22,340
Total	216,633	100,969
Land, buildings, and equipment fund:		
Fund balance	1,190,290	1,261,135
Total liabilities and fund balances	$1,520,534	$1,461,843

EXHIBIT 4
LEAGUE OF CATHOLIC WOMEN OF DETROIT, MICHIGAN
Statement of Support, Revenue, and Expenses,
and Changes in Fund Balances
Year Ended December 31, 1974,
with Comparative Totals for 1973

	1974				
	Current funds		Land, buildings, and equipment fund	Total all funds	
	Unrestricted	Restricted		1974	1973
Public support and revenue:					
Public support:					
Contributions	$ 16,884	$ 7,220	—	$ 24,104	$ 63,811
Memberships and fund raising	29,749	—	—	29,749	27,781
Grants		91,889	—	91,889	61,674
Total public support	46,633	99,109	—	145,742	153,266
Revenue:					
Residence rents	$171,430	—	—	$171,430	$163,876
Bargain counter sales	56,505	—	—	56,505	49,086
Nursery service fees	96,632	—	—	96,632	96,200
Activities and cafeteria rentals	8,609	—	—	8,609	7,345
Investment income	5,497	—	—	5,497	4,397
Miscellaneous	5,034	—	—	5,034	8,354
Total revenue	343,707	—	—	343,707	329,258
Total public support and revenue .	390,340	99,109	—	489,449	482,524

EXHIBIT 4—(Cont.)

| | 1974 | | | | |
| | Current funds | | Land, buildings, and equipment fund | Total all funds | |
	Unre-stricted	Re-stricted		1974	1973
Expenses:					
Program services:					
Residence	255,725	2,697	42,509	300,931	288,067
Nursery	97,426	—	5,409	102,835	112,089
Project transition 1973–1974	171	53,866	2,270	56,307	50,725
Project transition 1974–1975	109	50,019	2,270	52,398	35,993
Contributions to sponsored agencies ...	10,000	—	—	10,000	—
Depreciation of facilities used by sponsored agency and related nonprofit corporation	—	—	17,018	17,018	17,018
Total program service	363,431	$106,582	69,476	539,489	503,892
Supporting services:					
Management and general	16,584	—	3,249	19,833	20,740
Membership and communication	6,669	—	168	6,837	8,917
Bargain counters	21,803	—	—	21,803	15,541
Total supporting services	45,056	—	3,417	48,473	45,198
Total expenses	408,487	106,582	72,893	$587,962	$549,090
Excess (deficiency) of public support and revenue over expense	(18,147)	(7,473)	(72,893)		
Other changes in fund balance:					
Current funds used for the purchase of equipment	(1,130)	(918)	2,048		
Transfer—donor release of restriction ...	8,900	(8,900)	—		
Fund balances, January 1, 1974	88,441	$ 22,340	1,261,135		
Fund balances, December 31, 1974	$ 78,064	$ 5,049	$1,190,290		

MEMBERSHIP DRIVE STRUCTURE

Membership drives at the League of Catholic Women are conducted on an annual basis during the designated membership month of March. The drives are coordinated by a central committee consisting of a membership chairwoman and up to 17 membership coordinators (see Exhibit 6). Each coordinator directs the activities in a geographical region called a vicariate. Vicariates are composed of groups of individual churches or parishes in approximately the same geographical area (see Exhibit 7). Vicariates were formed in the Archdiocese of Detroit to foster closer ties and better communication among the member parishes and the central Archdiocese offices. Thus, it be-

EXHIBIT 5: Costs associated with membership

Membership:

Salaries	$1,933.30
FICA taxes	113.04
Employment tax	21.03
Worker's Compensation	16.93
Equipment and maintenance	29.94
Office supplies	965.62
Postage	518.53
Telephone	130.00
Mileage	15.72
Printing	588.00
Administrative expense	1,921.07
	$6,253.18

Communications:

Salaries	$1,933.30
FICA taxes	113.04
Employment tax	21.03
Worker's Compensation	16.93
Equipment and maintenance	29.93
Office supplies	87.49
Postage	34.95
Printing	95.00
Administrative expense	1,097.76
	$3,429.43

came a set of natural regions within which the League could conduct the annual membership drive.

Under each vicariate coordinator in the structure are the parish membership directors (see Exhibit 6). These directors formed the backbone of the general membership structure. It is at this level that much of the major work of the membership drive was conducted. Each parish director had the responsibility for conducting the drive at her own parish in a manner that she deemed appropriate for her parish. Because each parish differed in important characteristics like physical age, and location of the neighborhood, racial and ethnic composition, and accessibility to members, many different methods were employed during the membership drive. The League did not discourage this heterogeneity of technique but in fact encouraged each director to pursue the most appropriate method that the parish director felt would be the most successful during the membership drive.

EXHIBIT 6: Membership drive structure

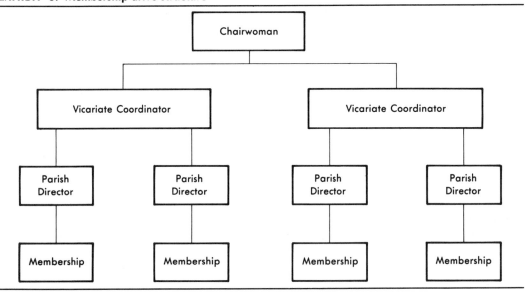

EXHIBIT 7: Map of vicariates

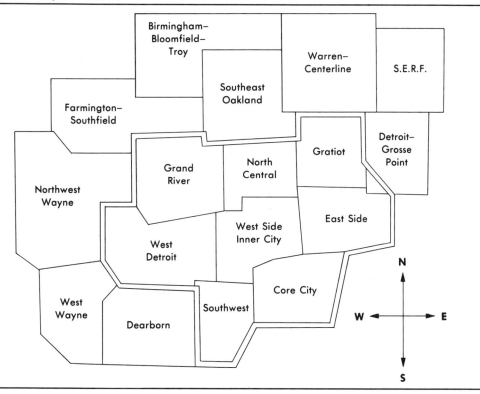

Note: Area enclosed by double line represents city of Detroit limits—outside area: suburbs.

For the past few years the League has held a luncheon at Casgrain Hall in February for parish directors as a kickoff for the membership drive. This luncheon has been poorly attended in the past. The League officers believe poor attendance is attributable to the fact that suburban directors fear Casgrain's neighborhood or find the distance prohibitive.

After the kickoff luncheon, and during the activities each March, the League supplied each parish director with materials to be used to accomplish the membership objectives. These materials included the preprinted membership envelopes containing a blank membership card and a preprinted "Dear Parishioner" letter signed by the re-

spective parish director. These letters detailed the activities of the League and contained other facts and information which would be of interest to prospective League members. In addition to the above, postage paid envelopes addressed to the League and an information brochure suitable for inserting into the parish newspaper were available. These materials are made accessible to the parish directors if they use the convenient order form the League sends to them. Exhibit 8 is an example of League promotional material.

At the beginning of the membership drive each director is issued this publicity information along with a listing of members in her

EXHIBIT 8: Sample promotional materials

Dear Parishioner,

A distraught teenage girl acting out her frustrations; a Chicano preschooler learning the alphabet; families being given emergency food supplies; a black grandmother taking sewing lessons; a lonely woman finding a pleasant residence and meals; a woman parolee being counseled in employment skills—these are some of the people you would meet every day in the agencies operated by the League of Catholic Women.

Christ has told us that when we offer food, clothing, refuge, and counseling in His name to His needy ones, we offer it to Him. Since 1906, the League has sought to offer immediate help and a brighter tomorrow to those who have been caught up in the web of poverty, misfortune, or despair—and always in the name of Christ and His Blessed Mother Mary. At the same time it has offered the opportunity for thousands of women across the Archdiocese to unite their hands and prayers in this service.

Yes, membership in the League of Catholic Women makes you a personal participant in these countless daily acts of love and service, as well as a participant in the monthly Mass said for all League members.

The annual drive for memberships is now in progress. Will you join with me and with fellow parishioners in giving your moral and financial support so that the League can continue being a very visible sign of Christian Service and an extension of your hands to the needy?

Most sincerely yours,

Helen Garbo
League Parish Director, St. Johns

DID YOU KNOW THAT . . .

The League is the oldest and largest social service agency in Detroit?

Membership does not require regular meetings or volunteer work?

The League agencies and operations are financed by over $1.5 million annually from memberships, government grants, United Fund giving, private donations, and rental receipts?

Last year, each dollar given through membership was magnified by $50 from the larger funding sources?

The League is dedicated to services to those in need, regardless of race, color, or creed? You don't have to be Catholic to belong or to be served?

---

parish from the previous year which are for renewals and a report form used to tabulate the results of the membership drive. Names, addresses, dollar amounts of the donations, and summary totals are the responsibility of each director on the report forms.

Parish directors forward their results and problems to the vicariate coordinators so that the central membership committee is advised of the results. In addition to overseeing the parish directors, the vicariate coordinators are responsible for ensuring that each parish of the vicariate has a director to conduct the membership drive. In the areas of the Archdiocese of Detroit in which the League is active there are 17 vicariates.

Contained in these vicariates are 232 parishes of various sizes.

MEMBERSHIP PROBLEM

In the summer of 1975 shortly after the conclusion of the March membership drive the League studied the results, comparing them to those of previous campaigns. In June of 1975 the League had 10,145 members that contributed $26,530. But this was a decline of 43 percent from the 1970 total of 17,913 and a decline of 51 percent from the 1965 total of 21,000. Faced with the alarming decline in membership over a 10-year period, a closer examination was conducted. Exhibit 9 presents membership data by vicariates used in examining the problem.

In summary, the results showed that 74 of the 232 parishes did not include at least one member of the League and that the vicariate coordinators had solicited a total of 108 parish directors, leaving 124 parishes without directors in 1975. In addition 2,508 members from 1974 did not renew their membership, a total of 25 percent of all the previous year's members.

EXECUTIVE REACTION

Faced with the data on membership, an executive committee consisting of Mary Lynn Landis (president), Marie Mathers (treasurer), and Christine Viceroy (membership chairwoman) discussed the situation in an attempt to rectify it as soon as possible.

During the discussion each executive felt that the major difficulty was finding women

EXHIBIT 9: Membership statistics

Vicariate	Number of parishes	Number without members	Number of directors	Number of 1975 members	Percent change during 1970–75	Percent change during 1974–75	Number not renewed in 1975
Birmingham–Bloomfield–Troy	9	1	7	754	+571%	+10%	178
Warren–Centerline	12	2	4	62	−50	−15	14
S.E.R.F.	15	10	5	155	−58	−36	120
Farmington–Southfield	13	2	10	508	−9	−18	87
Southeast Oakland	11	3	6	555	−27	−16	217
Northwest Wayne	16	4	6	377	−44	−24	149
West Wayne	16	10	3	44	n.a.	+25	9
Dearborn	15	3	11	1,091	−12	+4	177
Detroit–Grosse Pointe	11	0	9	2,168	−29	−12	585
Core City–Downtown	19	6	7	598	−9	+7	111
East Side	16	10	5	151	−78	−20	36
Grand River	15	0	7	1,159	−72	+4	260
Gratiot	15	2	9	1,578	−51	−8	294
North Central	16	13	2	49	−82	−49	38
Southwest	13	7	6	210	+14	+14	54
West Detroit	12	1	7	445	−59	+4	111
West Side Inner City	8	0	4	241	−64	−33	68
	232	74	108	10,145			2,508

n.a. = not available.

EXHIBIT 10: Total population shifts, 1970–1974

	1970	1974	Percent change
City vicariates:			
Core City—Downtown			
East Side			
Grand River			
Gratiot			
North Central	1,586,383	1,428,250	−9.9%
Southwest			
West Detroit			
West Side Inner City			
Suburban vicariates:			
Birmingham–Bloomfield–Troy	112,049	127,060	+13.4
Dearborn	184,268	173,600	−5.7
Detroit–Grosse Pointe	68,657	64,710	−6.0
Farmington–Southfield	128,321	141,000	+9.8
Northwest Wayne	213,728	211,575	−1.0
S.E.R.F.	206,410	201,500	−2.3
Southeast Oakland	274,580	253,850	−7.5
Warren–Centerline	189,639	183,800	−3.0
West Wayne	213,547	223,600	+4.7
Total	1,591,199	1,580,695	−0.7

Note: Catholic population is estimated at 32 percent of aggregate totals.
Source: Figures obtained from U.S. Census figures, U.S. Department of Commerce, Detroit office.

to work at the parish level and that the major reason revolved around the notion that these women were mostly employed and unable to devote their energy faithfully to the membership drives. In the same vein the executive committee also hypothesized that the large decline in membership in the last 10 years and especially in the last 5 years has occurred concurrently with the "white flight" from the city to the suburbs. They felt that with the decline of certain inner Detroit neighborhoods along with the threat of court-ordered busing looming in the city, Catholic families had moved to the suburbs where League activity was not well established. They believed that the decline of the once strong city vicariates would be counterbalanced by the increase in the membership roles of the suburban vicariates.

They reasoned that the number of city Catholics had decreased a great deal and that the remaining numbers would be attributed to Catholics in the older age brackets who found it financially impossible to move. (See Exhibit 10.) In conjunction with changing neighborhoods, League officers noted that as the neighborhoods in the city changed composition from predominately white to racially mixed and as the crime rate increased in the city much personal contact was lost, personal contact which was extremely necessary for soliciting memberships for the League.

Additionally the three officers cited a continuing problem of handling the membership renewal. Often communication among the parish directors, the vicariate coordinators, and central office was inadequate. Lag time between reports had increased which invariably led to duplication of efforts and burdensome bookkeeping errors. The errors were admittedly disturbing to workers at all levels but caused the greatest consternation at the membership level. This generated a good deal of ill will from the members that was directed toward the central membership office.

Last, Landis, Mathers, and Viceroy felt that the League had become increasingly confused with an organization called the Council of Catholic Women (CCW). The CCW is an umbrella federation which encompasses all women's groups and is funded by the Archdiocese of Detroit. They stated that the League is the oldest and largest participant of the CCW and that many Catholic women were under the mistaken impression that being a member of the CCW automatically included membership in the League. They thought this confusion had hurt the membership drive in the past.

At this point the officers felt that further study of the membership situation was required in order to reshape and restructure their marketing strategy to increase the number of League members. To do this they desired to know more about the population shifts and more about the women who conducted the membership drives at the parish level.

RESEARCH RESULTS

Obtaining reliable information on just where the Catholic population was located was a major source of concern since it was vitally important to know where the major market centered. The League discovered that the 1970 census did not include a question on religious preference; therefore, it would have to get reliable estimates from a different source.

Turning to the central offices of the Archdiocese of Detroit, the League hoped that individual parish censuses had been tabulated but it quickly found out that the only centralized population data was collected in 1970 and had been discarded as incomplete and useless.

The director of financial planning at the Archdiocese, Harvey Crane, indicated that the Archdiocese used a reasonably accurate estimate for its financial planning. He told the League that historically the percentage of Catholics within its boundaries was approximately 32 percent of total population in the area. Through sample testing the percentage had been found to change little in recent years and was considered reliable by the financial planners.

So assuming that any population shifts retained the characteristic 32 percent Catholic identity (that is, for every 100 people to move, 32 would be Catholic), the League felt that census data on the changing population might prove helpful to see if the increases and declines in area memberships occurred concurrently and in the same proportion as the changes in population. Exhibit 10 represents this tabulated data. It shows that the vicariates with the greatest shifts in population were Birmingham–Bloomfield–Troy with an increase of 13.4 percent and the city of Detroit with a decrease of 9.9 percent.

In addition to the census information a telephone survey of 47 parish directors was taken in order to study several aspects of the membership drive to determine the importance of their performance on the success of the drive. (The questions and tabulated results are presented in Exhibit 11.)

Close examination of the results reveals

1. What is your method of operation during the drive?
   - *a*. Use church bulletin 33
   - *b*. Announcements at Mass 9
   - *c*. Appeal after Mass at church 10
   - *d*. Use membership envelopes in church 4
   - *e*. Solicit at Ladies' Clubs 26
   - *f*. Use personal contact 11
   - *g*. Go door to door 9
   - *h*. Corps of helpers used 14
   - *i*. Send out letters 18
   - *j*. Phone calls 20
   - *k*. Invite members to luncheon 1
   - *l*. Use League speaker 1
   - *m*. File system of parish women 1

2. What problems do you encounter during the drive?
   - *a*. No support from parish priest 10
   - *b*. No response to appeal 13
   - *c*. Lack of publicity 9
   - *d*. Lack of knowledge of League activities 7
   - *e*. Catholics moving out 13
   - *f*. Young women not interested 9
   - *g*. Retirement 3
   - *h*. Competition with other charities 7
   - *i*. No helpers 7
   - *j*. Lack of coordination with League office 5
   - *k*. Director has conflict with other activity 1
   - *l*. Director no longer wishes to serve 10
   - *m*. No longer serves as director 4
   - *n*. Director is no longer a member 4
   - *o*. Membership implies duties 6
   - *p*. Membership cards 2
   - *q*. Cannot go door to door 5
   - *r*. Unemployment 7

3. Do you incur personal expenses?
   - *a*. No 26
   - *b*. Postage 18
   - *c*. Use of car 5
   - *d*. Printing 1
   - *e*. Phone 4
   - *f*. Luncheon 1
   - *g*. Pay for some members 2

4. Do you believe new membership can be increased?
   - *a*. Possible 24
   - *b*. Impossible 19
   - *c*. Will only decline 1
   - *d*. Don't know 4

5. Do you think you are successful?
   a. Yes   29
   b. No   14
   c. Don't know   4

6. What are the ages of your members?
   a. 20–30   0
   b. 30–40   6
   c. 40–50   13
   d. 50–60   32
   e. 60 +   35
   f. Mixed   9

7. What amount of time do you spend on new memberships?
   a. Equal   7
   b. Mostly on new   7
   c. Mostly on old   32
   d. Don't know   7
   e. Neither   2

8. What information are you able to provide?
   a. League pamphlets   37
   b. Personal knowledge   10

9. Is there a best time of day to solicit memberships?
   a. Morning   12
   b. Afternoon   8
   c. Dinner   5
   d. Evening   10
   e. Anytime   8

10. Are you employed?
   a. Yes   7
   b. No   40

Note: Many questions may total more than 47 because multiple responses were recorded to most questions.

several trends. As expected the League learned that the parish directors pursued a wide variety of methods during the membership drive with suitability dependent on the particular parish. But in the area of problems, parish directors indicated largely that lack of response and understanding of the League appeal had become a major diffi-culty. Many parish directors felt that the market for charitable donations had become increasingly more competitive. More groups were appealing to their parish communities for aid. Directors felt that the number of groups seeking help severely restricted their appeal. There was also a tendency on the part of their parish priests to channel charitable dollars to only their own parish projects. In addition many directors noted that it seemed that Catholics were indeed moving out of their parishes. And last the most startling of the tabulations showed that of the 47 directors interviewed, 18 of them no longer served or wished to serve the League as a director while at the same time 29 felt that they were successful as directors.

The League also found through the survey that the membership roles were predominated by members who were over 50 years of age, that it was very possible to increase new membership in future drives, that very little time was in fact delegated to obtaining new members, and that very few of the directors were employed which could have hindered their effect at the parish level.

While conducting the phone survey the researchers discovered another critical problem. The most current list of 1975 parish directors contained many inaccuracies. It appeared that the League would have great difficulty in communicating with its parish directors. This was particularly alarming to the officers because parish directors are the only League salespersons who directly con-

EXHIBIT 12: Telephone survey statistics

Parish directors	108
Surveys completed	47
No answer	30
Not home	6
On vacation	5
No longer director	7
Wrong phone number	9
Disconnected phone	5
No phone number listed	8
Director with no members	3

tact the membership. Also this list may possibly reflect the present condition of the membership list. Exhibit 12 displays the results of the attempt to contact parish directors by telephone.

After reviewing this information the League directors were searching for solid solutions to the problems they faced. They wondered how to increase memberships without increasing costs appreciably and what changes in procedure and strategy were needed to accomplish the goal. In effect they pondered what changes in their marketing plan were necessary in light of their present information.

PART III

DESIGNING THE MARKETING MIX

Part III examines the planning and blending of specific marketing variables into a program of action to reach marketing objectives. The nonprofit organization must find the best combination of marketing decision variables. Marketing programming and budgeting are necessary to coordinate product decisions, advertising, sales promotion, and public relations decisions. These marketing mix decision variables must be carefully coordinated to maximize the attainment of objectives.

The first article in Part III is "Classifying Services to Gain Strategic Marketing Insights," by Christopher H. Lovelock. This article emphasizes the widespread diversity that exists in the service sector and highlights the difficulty of coming up with managerially useful generalizations concerning service organizations. The author stresses the need for dividing the service sector into specific categories. He proposes five schemes for classifying services that will transcend the existing narrow industrial boundaries.

In the second article, "Establishing a Price for Government Services," John L. Crompton and Charles W. Lamb emphasize the extremely delicate nature of establishing a price for government services. They suggest a three stage approach that includes positioning services on the cost recovery continuum, considering going-rate price, and examining the appropriateness of differential pricing. The intent of this paper is to establish a logical basis for determining price.

The third article, "Distribution Decisions for Public Services" by Charles W. Lamb and John L. Crompton, identifies the different elements of the public service distri-

bution decision process and their many interrelationships are addressed. The article stresses the need for public sector managers to be aware of the differences between the public and private sectors and to develop marketing strategies and programs accordingly.

The fourth article is "Marketing Communications in Nonbusiness Situations or Why It's so Hard to Sell Brotherhood Like Soap" by Michael L. Rothschild. In order to use marketing communications techniques effectively for public and nonprofit sector problems, one must consider the extreme differences between these and private-sector problems. Major differences may include the presence of very high or very low involvement, issues offering few perceivable benefits to individuals, and high monetary prices. A framework for considering cases of very high and very low involvement is considered and options for marketers are presented.

The fifth article "Special Events in the 80's: A Case for Marketing Approach" by Joan Loykovich, highlights the need for nonprofit organizations to use as many different approaches as possible to generate interest in their cause. Strategic planning in conjunction with a marketing orientation are deemed vital to success. Special events and their many benefits are discussed and related to the marketing concept.

The sixth article in Part III, by Susan W. Hayes, is "How to Package and Market Major Donor Club Benefits." This article follows the step-by-step account of how a public broadcasting station (WCNY-TV/FM) established and marketed their donor club

231

and its benefits. She also describes the close interaction between the use of direct mail and telemarketing to accomplish this goal.

In the last article, "The ABCs of Implementing Library Marketing," Andrea C. Dragon and Tony Leisner discuss the general awakening of library professionals to marketing activities and the related controversies associated with the initial adoption of marketing practices. They also outline the concepts of responding to the market, achieving a position, balancing demand with resources, and compensating for performance.

Four cases are included in Part III. The first, "Rayana Family Planning Program," illustrates the growth of many nonprofit organizations primarily through line extensions with little planning. This case emphasizes the need for nonprofit managers to think strategically rather than considering only their immediate needs.

"Amtrak" is the national rail passenger system which was established to rejuvenate a mature product. A series of specific questions are identified; including equipment purchases and other investments, pricing, services to be offered, and an advertising budget.

The "Tuesday Evening Concert Series" case focuses on a pricing decision facing the organization's board of directors. In addition to three pricing proposals that have been advanced, three related policy decisions are under consideration.

The "Kent State University: Coping with an Image Crisis" case describes the recurring problems that the university has encountered since four students were killed during an anti-war protest several years ago. The university's promotion strategy for improving its image and curtailing enrollment declines is presented.

Classifying Services to Gain Strategic Marketing Insights

CHRISTOPHER H. LOVELOCK

The diversity of the service sector makes it difficult to come up with managerially useful generalizations concerning marketing practice in service organizations. This article argues for a focus on specific categories of services and proposes five schemes for classifying services in ways that transcend narrow industry boundaries. In each instance insights are offered into how the nature of the service might affect the marketing task.

INTRODUCTION

Developing professional skills in marketing management requires the ability to look across a broad cross-section of marketing situations, to understand their differences and commonalities, and to identify appropriate marketing strategies in each instance. In the manufacturing sector many experienced marketers have worked for a variety of companies in several different industries, often including both consumer goods and industrial firms. As a result, they have a perspective that transcends narrow industry boundaries.

But exposure to marketing problems and strategies in different industries is still quite rare among managers in the service sector. Not only is the concept of a formalized marketing function still relatively new to most service firms, but service industries have historically been somewhat inbred. The majority of railroad managers, for instance, have spent their entire working lives within the railroad industry—even within a single company. Most hoteliers have grown up in the hotel industry. And most hospital or college administrators have remained within the confines of health care or higher education, respectively. The net result of such narrow exposure is that it restricts a manager's ability to identify and learn from the experience of organizations facing parallel situations in other service industries—and, of course, from marketing experience in the manufacturing sector. Conversely, marketers from the manufacturing sector who take positions in service businesses often find that their past experience has not prepared them well for working on some of the problems that regularly challenge service marketers (Knisely, 1979; Lovelock, 1981; Shostack, 1977).

This article argues that development of greater sophistication in services marketing will be aided if we can find new ways to group services other than by current industry classifications. A more useful approach may be to segment services into clusters that share certain relevant marketing characteristics—such as the nature of the relationship between the service organization and its cus-

Christopher H. Lovelock, "Classifying Services to Gain Strategic Marketing Insights," vol. 47 (Summer 1983), pp. 9–20.

Reprinted from *Journal of Marketing,* published by the American Marketing Association.

tomers or patterns of demand relative to supply—and then to examine the implications for marketing action.

After briefly reviewing the value of classification schemes in marketing, the article summarizes past proposals for classifying services. This is followed by presentation and discussion of five classification schemes based on past proposals or on clinical research. In each instance examples are given of how various services fall into similar or different categories, and an evaluation is made of the resulting marketing insights and what they imply for marketing strategy development.

THE VALUE OF CLASSIFICATION IN MARKETING

Hunt (1976) has emphasized the usefulness of classification schemes in marketing. Various attempts have been made in the past by marketing theorists to classify goods into different categories. One of the most famous and enduring is Copeland's (1923) classification of convenience, shopping and specialty goods. Not only did this help managers obtain a better understanding of consumer needs and behavior, it also provided insights into the management of retail distribution systems. Bucklin (1963) and others have revised and refined Copeland's original classification and thereby been able to provide important strategic guidelines for retailers. Another major classification has been between durable and nondurable goods. Durability is closely associated with purchase frequency, which has important implications for development of both distribution and communications strategy. Yet another classification is consumer goods versus industrial goods; this classification relates both to the type of goods purchased (although there is some overlap) and to product evaluation,

purchasing procedures and usage behavior. Recognition of these distinctions by marketers has led to different types of marketing strategy being directed at each of these groups. Through such classifications the application of marketing management tools and strategies in manufacturing has become a professional skill that transcends industry divisions.

By contrast, service industries remain dominated by an operations orientation that insists that each industry is different. This mind set is often manifested in managerial attitudes that suggest, for example, that the marketing of airlines has nothing at all in common with that of banks, insurance, motels, hospitals or household movers. But if it can be shown that some of these services do share certain marketing relevant characteristics, then the stage may be set for some useful cross-fertilization of concepts and strategies.

How Might Services Be Classified?

Various attempts have been proposed in the past for classifying services and are outlined, with brief commentaries, in Table 1. But developing classification schemes is not enough. If they are to have managerial value, they must offer strategic insights. That is why it is important to develop ways of analyzing services that highlight the characteristics they have in common, and then to examine the implications for marketing management.

This article builds on past research by examining characteristics of services that transcend industry boundaries and are different in degree or kind from the categorization schemes traditionally applied to manufactured goods. Five classification schemes have been selected for presentation and discussion, reflecting their potential for affecting the way marketing management strategies are developed and implemented. Each represents an attempt to answer one of the following questions:

1. What is the nature of the service act?
2. What type of relationship does the service organization have with its customers?
3. How much room is there for customization and judgment on the part of the service provider?
4. What is the nature of demand and supply for the service?
5. How is the service delivered?

Each question will be examined on two dimensions, reflecting my conclusion in an earlier study (Lovelock, 1980) that combining classification schemes in a matrix may yield better marketing insights than classifying service organizations on one variable at a time.

WHAT IS THE NATURE OF THE SERVICE ACT?

A service has been described as a "deed, act or performance" (Berry, 1980). Two fundamental issues are at whom (or what) is the act directed, and is this act tangible or intangible in nature?

As shown in Figure 1, these two questions result in a four-way classification scheme involving (1) tangible actions to people's bodies, such as airline transportation, haircutting and surgery; (2) tangible actions to goods and other physical possessions, such as air freight, lawn mowing and janitorial services; (3) intangible actions directed at people's minds, such as broadcasting and education; and (4) intangible actions directed at people's intangible assets, such as insurance, investment banking and consulting.

Sometimes a service may seem to spill over into two or more categories. For instance, the delivery of educational, religious or entertainment services (directed primarily at the mind) often entails tangible actions such as being in a classroom, church or theater; the delivery of financial services may require a visit to a bank to transform intangible financial assets into hard cash; and the delivery of airline services may affect some travelers' states of mind as well as physically moving their bodies from one airport to another. But in most instances the core service act is confined to one of the four categories, although there may be secondary acts in another category.

Insights and Implications

Why is this categorization scheme useful to service marketers? Basically it helps answer the following questions:

1. Does the customer need to be *physically* present:
   (a) throughout service delivery?
   (b) only to initiate or terminate the service transaction (e.g., dropping off a car for repair and picking it up again afterwards)?
   (c) not at all (the relationship with the service supplier can be at arm's length through the mails, telephone or other electronic media)?
2. Does the customer need to be *mentally* present during service delivery? Can mental presence be maintained across physical distances through mail or electronic communications?
3. In what ways is the target of the service act "modified" by receipt of the service? And how does the customer benefit from these "modifications"?

It's not always obvious what the service is and what it does for the customer because services are ephemeral. By identifying the target of the service and then examining how

TABLE 1: Summary of previously proposed schemes for classifying services

Author	*Proposed classification schemes*	*Comment*
Judd (1964)	(1) Rented goods services (right to own and use a good for a defined time period) (2) Owned goods services (custom creation, repair or improvement of goods owned by the customer) (3) Nongoods services (personal experiences or "experiential possession")	First two are fairly specific, but third category is very broad and ignores services such as insurance, banking, legal advice and accounting.
Rathmell (1974)	(1) Type of seller (2) Type of buyer (3) Buying motives (4) Buying practice (5) Degree of regulation	No specific application to services—could apply equally well to goods.
Shostack (1977)[a] Sasser *et al*[a] (1978)	Proportion of physical goods and intangible services contained within each product "package"	Offers opportunities for multiattribute modeling. Emphasizes that there are few pure goods or pure services.
Hill (1977)	(1) Services affecting persons vs. those affecting goods (2) Permanent vs. temporary effects of the service (3) Reversibility vs. nonreversibility of these effects (4) Physical effects vs. mental effects (5) Individual vs. collective services	Emphasizes nature of service benefits and (in 5) variations in the service delivery/consumption environment.
Thomas (1978)	(1) Primarily equipment-based (a) automated (e.g., car wash) (b) monitored by unskilled operators (e.g., movie theater) (c) operated by skilled personnel (e.g., airline) (2) Primarily people-based (a) unskilled labor (e.g., lawn care) (b) skilled labor (e.g., repair work) (c) professional staff (e.g., lawyers, dentists)	Although operational rather than marketing in orientation, provides a useful way of understanding product attributes.
Chase (1978)	Extent of customer contact required in service delivery (a) high contact (e.g., health care, hotels, restaurants) (b) low contact (e.g., postal service, wholesaling)	Recognizes that product variability is harder to control in high contact services because customers exert more influence on timing of demand and service features, due to their greater involvement in the service process.

236

TABLE 1 (continued)

Author	Proposed classification schemes	Comment
Kotler (1980)	(1) People-based vs. equipment-based (2) Extent to which client's presence is necessary (3) Meets personal needs vs. business needs (4) Public vs. private, for-profit vs. non-profit	Synthesizes previous work, recognizes differences in purpose of service organization.
Lovelock (1980)	(1) Basic demand characteristics —object served (persons vs. property) —extent of demand/supply imbalances —discrete vs. continuous relationships between customers and providers (2) Service content and benefits —extent of physical goods content —extent of personal service content —single service vs. bundle of services —timing and duration of benefits (3) Service delivery procedures —multisite vs. single site delivery —allocation of capacity (reservations vs. first come, first served) —independent vs. collective consumption —time defined vs. task defined transactions —extent to which customers must be present during service delivery	Synthesizes previous classifications and adds several new schemes. Proposes several categories within each classification. Concludes that defining object served is most fundamental classification scheme. Suggests that valuable marketing insights would come from combining two or more classification schemes in a matrix.

[a]These were two independent studies that drew broadly similar conclusions.

it is "modified" or changed by receipt of the service act, we can develop a better understanding of the nature of the service product and the core benefits that it offers. For instance, a haircut leaves the recipient with shorter and presumably more appealingly styled hair, air freight gets the customer's goods speedily and safely between two points, a news radio broadcast updates the listener's mind about recent events, and life insurance protects the future value of the insured person's assets.

If customers need to be physically present during service delivery, then they must enter the service "factory" (whether it be a train, a hairdressing salon, or a hospital at a particular location) and spend time there while the service is performed. Their satisfaction with the service will be influenced by the interactions they have with service personnel, the nature of the service facilities, and also perhaps by the characteristics of other customers using the same service. Questions of location and schedule convenience assume great importance when a customer has to be physically present or must appear in

FIGURE 1: Understanding the nature of the service act

What is the Nature of the Service Act?	Who or What is the Direct Recipient of the Service?	
	People	**Things**
Tangible Actions	Services directed at people's bodies: ● health care ● passenger transportation ● beauty salons ● exercise clinics ● restaurants ● haircutting	Services directed at goods and other physical possessions: ● freight transportation ● industrial equipment repair and maintenance ● janitorial services ● laundry and dry cleaning ● landscaping/lawn care ● veterinary care
Intangible Actions	Services directed at people's minds: ● education ● broadcasting ● information services ● theaters ● museums	Services directed at intangible assets: ● banking ● legal services ● accounting ● securities ● insurance

person to initiate and terminate the transaction.

Dealing with a service organization at arm's length, by contrast, may mean that a customer never sees the service facilities at all and may not even meet the service personnel face-to-face. In this sort of situation, the outcome of the service act remains very important, but the process of service delivery may be of little interest, since the customer never goes near the "factory." For instance, credit cards and many types of insurance can be obtained by mail or telephone.

For operational reasons it may be very desirable to get the customer out of the factory and to transform a "high-contact" service into a "low-contact" one (Chase 1978). The chances of success in such an endeavor will be enhanced when the new

procedures also offer customers greater convenience. Many services directed at *things* rather than at people formerly required the customer's presence but are now delivered at arm's length. Certain financial services have long used the mails to save customers the inconvenience of personal visits to a specific office location. Today, new electronic distribution channels have made it possible to offer instantaneous delivery of financial services to a wide array of alternative locations. Retail banking provides a good example, with its growing use of such electronic delivery systems as automatic teller machines in airports or shopping centers, pay-by-phone bill paying, or on-line banking facilities in retail stores.

By thinking creatively about the nature of their services, managers of service organizations may be able to identify opportunities for alternative, more convenient forms of service delivery or even for transformation of the service into a manufactured good. For instance, services to the mind such as education do not necessarily require attendance in person since they can be delivered through the mails or electronic media (Britain's Open University, which makes extensive use of television and radio broadcasts, is a prime example). Two-way communication hook-ups can make it possible for a physically distant teacher and students to interact directly where this is necessary to the educational process (one recent Bell System advertisement featured a chamber music class in a small town being taught by an instructor several hundred miles away). Alternatively, lectures can be packaged and sold as books, records or videotapes. And programmed learning exercises can be developed in computerized form, with the terminal serving as a Socratic surrogate.

WHAT TYPE OF RELATIONSHIP DOES THE SERVICE ORGANIZATION HAVE WITH ITS CUSTOMERS?

With very few exceptions, consumers buy manufactured goods at discrete intervals, paying for each purchase separately and rarely entering into a formal relationship with the manufacturer. (Industrial purchasers, by contrast, often enter into long-term relationships with suppliers and sometimes receive almost continuous delivery of certain supplies.)

In the service sector both household and institutional purchasers may enter into ongoing relationships with service suppliers and may receive service on a continuing basis. This offers a way of categorizing services. We can ask, does the service organization enter into a "membership" relationship with its customers—as in telephone subscrip-

tions, banking and the family doctor—or is there no formal relationship? And is service delivered on a continuous basis—as in insurance, broadcasting and police protection—or is each transaction recorded and charged separately? Figure 2 shows the 2×2 matrix resulting from this categorization, with some additional examples in each category.

Insights and Implications

The advantage to the service organization of a membership relationship is that it knows who its current customers are and, usually, what use they make of the services offered. This can be valuable for segmentation purposes if good records are kept and the data are readily accessible in a format that lends itself to computerized analysis. Knowing the identities and addresses of current customers enables the organization to make effective use of direct mail, telephone selling and personal sales calls—all highly targeted marketing communication media.

The nature of service relationships also has important implications for pricing. In situations where service is offered on an ongoing basis, there is often just a single periodic charge covering all services contracted for. Most insurance policies fall in this category, as do tuition and board fees at a residential college. The big advantage of this package approach is its simplicity. Some memberships, however, entail a series of separate and identifiable transactions with the price paid being tied explicitly to the number and type of such transactions. While more complex to administer, such an approach is fairer to customers (whose usage patterns may vary widely) and may discourage wasteful use of what are perceived as "free" services. In such instances, members may be offered advantages over casual users, such as discounted rates (telephone sub-

FIGURE 2: Relationships with customers

Nature of Service Delivery	Type of Relationship between the Service Organization and Its Customers	
	"Membership" Relationship	**No Formal Relationship**
Continuous Delivery of Service	insurance telephone subscription college enrollment banking American Automobile Association	radio station police protection lighthouse public highway
Discrete Transactions	long-distance phone calls theater series subscription commuter ticket or transit pass	car rental mail service toll highway pay phone movie theater public transportation restaurant

scribers pay less for long-distance calls made from their own phones than do pay phone users) or advance notification and priority reservations (as in theater subscriptions). Some membership services offer certain services (such as rental of equipment or connection to a public utility system) for a base fee and then make incremental charges for each separate transaction above a defined minimum.

Profitability and customer convenience are central issues in deciding how to price membership services. Will the organization generate greater long-term profits by tying payment explicitly to consumption, by charging a flat rate regardless of consumption, or by unbundling the components of the service and charging a flat rate for some and an incremental rate for others? Telephone and electricity services, for instance, typically charge a base fee for connection to the system and rental of equipment, plus a variety of incremental charges for consumption

above a defined minimum. On the other hand, Wide Area Telephone Service (WATS) offers the convenience of unlimited long-distance calling for a fixed fee. How important is it to customers to have the convenience of paying a single periodic fee that is known in advance? For instance, members of the American Automobile Association (AAA) can obtain information booklets, travel advice and certain types of emergency road services free of additional charges. Such a package offers elements of both insurance and convenience to customers who may not be able to predict their exact needs in advance.

Where no formal relationship exists between supplier and customer, continuous delivery of the product is normally found only among that class of services that economists term "public goods"—such as broadcasting, police and lighthouse services, and public highways—where no charge is made for use of a service that is continuously available and financed from tax revenues. Discrete transactions, where each usage involves a payment to the service supplier by an essentially "anonymous" consumer, are exemplified by many transportation services, restaurants, movie theaters, shoe repairs and so forth. The problem of such services is that marketers tend to be much less well-informed about who their customers are and what use each customer makes of the service than their counterparts in membership organizations.

Membership relationships usually result in customer loyalty to a particular service supplier (sometimes there is no choice because the supplier has a monopoly). As a marketing strategy, many service businesses seek ways to develop formal, ongoing relations with customers in order to ensure repeat business and/or ongoing financial support. Public radio and television broadcasters, for instance, develop membership clubs for donors and offer monthly program guides in return; performing arts organizations sell subscription series; transit agencies offer monthly passes; airlines create clubs for high mileage fliers; and hotels develop "executive service plans" offering priority reservations and upgraded rooms for frequent guests. The marketing task here is to determine how it might be possible to build sales and revenues through such memberships but to avoid requiring membership when this would result in freezing out a large volume of desirable casual business.

HOW MUCH ROOM IS THERE FOR CUSTOMIZATION AND JUDGMENT?

Relatively few consumer goods nowadays are built to special order; most are purchased "off the shelf." The same is true for a majority of industrial goods, although by permutating options it's possible to give the impression of customization. Once they've purchased their goods, of course, customers are usually free to use them as they see fit.

The situation in the service sector, by contrast, is sharply different. Because services are created as they are consumed, and because the customer is often actually involved in the production process, there is far more scope for tailoring the service to meet the needs of individual customers. As shown in Figure 3, customization can proceed along at least two dimensions. The first concerns the extent to which the characteristics of the service and its delivery system lend themselves to customization; the second relates to how much judgment customer contact personnel are able to exercise in defining the nature of the service received by individual customers.

Some service concepts are quite standardized. Public transportation, for instance, runs over fixed routes on predetermined schedules. Routine appliance repairs typically involve a fixed charge, and the customer is responsible for dropping off the item at a given retail location and picking it up again afterwards. Fast food restaurants have a small, set menu; few offer the customer much choice in how the food will be cooked and served. Movies, entertainment and spectator sports place the audience in a relatively passive role, albeit a sometimes noisy one.

Other services offer customers a wide choice of options. Each telephone subscriber enjoys an individual number and can use the phone to obtain a broad array of different services—from receiving personal calls from a next-door neighbor to calling a business associate on the other side of the world, and from data transmission to dial-a-prayer. Retail bank accounts are also customized, with each check or bank card carrying the customer's name and personal code. Within the constraints set down by the bank, the cus-

FIGURE 3: Customization and judgment in service delivery

Extent to Which Customer Contact Personnel Exercise Judgment in Meeting Individual Customer Needs	Extent to Which Service Characteristics Are Customized	
	High	**Low**
High	legal services health care/surgery architectural design executive search firm real estate agency taxi service beautician plumber education (tutorials)	education (large classes) preventive health programs
Low	telephone service hotel services retail banking (excl. major loans) good restaurant	public transportation routine appliance repair fast food restaurant movie theater spectator sports

tomer enjoys considerable latitude in how and when the account is used and receives a personalized monthly statement. Good hotels and restaurants usually offer their customers an array of service options from which to choose, as well as considerable flexibility in how the service product is delivered to them.

But in each of these instances, the role of the customer contact personnel (if there are any) is somewhat constrained. Other than tailoring their personal manner to the customer and answering straightforward questions, contact personnel have relatively little discretion in altering the characteristics of the service they deliver: their role is basically that of operator or order taker. Judgment and discretion in customer dealings is usually reserved for managers or supervisors who will not normally become involved in service delivery unless a problem arises.

A third category of services gives the customer contact personnel wide latitude in how they deliver the service, yet these individuals do not significantly differentiate the characteristics of their service between one customer and another. For instance, educators who teach courses by lectures and give multiple choice, computer scored exams expose each of their students to a potentially similar experience, yet one professor may elect to teach a specific course in a very different way from a colleague at the same institution.

However, there is a class of services that not only involves a high degree of customization but also requires customer contact personnel to exercise judgment concerning the characteristics of the service and how it is delivered to each customer. Far from being reactive in their dealings with customers, these service personnel are often prescriptive: users (or clients) look to them for advice as well as for customized execution. In this category the locus of control shifts from the user to the supplier—a situation that some customers may find disconcerting. Consumers of surgical services literally place their lives in the surgeon's hands (the same, unfortunately, is also true of taxi services in many cities). Professional services such as law, medicine, accounting and architecture fall within this category. They are all white collar "knowledge industries," requiring extensive training to develop the requisite skills and judgment needed for satisfactory service delivery. Deliverers of such services as taxi drivers, beauticians and plumbers are also found in this category. Their work is customized to the situation at hand and in each instance, the customer purchases the expertise required to devise a tailor-made solution.

Insights and Implications

To a much greater degree than in the manufacturing sector, service products are "custom-made." Yet customization has its costs. Service management often represents an ongoing struggle between the desires of marketing managers to add value and the goals of operations managers to reduce costs through standardization. Resolving such disputes, a task that may require arbitration by the general manager, requires a good understanding of consumer choice criteria, particularly as these relate to price/value trade-offs and competitive positioning strategy. At the present time, most senior managers in service businesses have come up through the operations route; hence, participation in executive education programs may be needed to give them the necessary perspective on marketing to make balanced decisions.

Customization is not necessarily important to success. As Levitt (1972, 1976) has pointed out, industrializing a service to take advantage of the economies of mass production may actually increase consumer satisfaction. Speed, consistency and price savings may be more important to many customers than customized service. In some instances, such as spectator sports and the performing arts, part of the product experience is sharing the service with many other people. In other instances the customer expects to share the service facilities with other consumers, as in hotels or airlines, yet still hopes for some individual recognition and custom treatment. Allowing customers to reserve specific rooms or seats in advance, having contact personnel address them by name (it's on their ticket or reservation slip), and providing some latitude for individual choice (room service and morning calls, drinks and meals) are all ways to create an image of customization.

Generally, customers like to know in advance what they are buying—what the product features are, what the service will do for them. Surprises and uncertainty are not normally popular. Yet when the nature of the service requires a judgment-based, customized solution, as in a professional service, it is not always clear to either the customer or the professional what the outcome will be. Frequently, an important dimension of the professional's role is diagnosing the nature of the situation, then designing a solution.

In such situations those responsible for developing marketing strategy would do well to recognize that customers may be uneasy concerning the prior lack of certainty about the outcome. Customer contact personnel in these instances are not only part of the product but also determine what that product should be.

One solution to this problem is to divide the product into two separate components, diagnosis and implementation of a solution, that are executed and paid for separately. The process of diagnosis can and should be explained to the customer in advance, since the outcome of the diagnosis cannot always be predicted accurately. However, once that diagnosis has been made, the customer need not proceed immediately with the proposed solution; indeed, there is always the option of seeking a second opinion. The solution ''product,'' by contrast, can often be spelled out in detail beforehand, so that the customer has a reasonable idea of what to expect. Although there may still be some uncertainty, as in legal actions or medical treatment, the range of possibilities should be narrower by this point, and it may be feasible to assign probabilities to specified alternative outcomes.

Marketing efforts may need to focus on the process of client-provider interactions. It will help prospective clients make choices between alternative suppliers, especially where professionals are concerned, if they know something of the organization's (or individual's) approach to diagnosis and problem-solving, as well as client-relationship style. These are considerations that transcend mere statements of qualification in an advertisement or brochure. For instance, some pediatricians allow new parents time for a free interview before any commitments are made. Such a trial encounter has the advantage of allowing both parties to decide whether or not a good match exists.

WHAT IS THE NATURE OF DEMAND AND SUPPLY FOR THE SERVICE?

Manufacturing firms can inventory supplies of their products as a hedge against fluctuations in demand. This enables them to enjoy the economies derived from operating plants at a steady level of production. Service businesses can't do this because it's not possible to inventory the finished service.

For instance, the potential income from any empty seat on an airline flight is lost forever once that flight takes off, and each hotel daily room vacancy is equally perishable. Likewise, the productive capacity of an auto repair shop is wasted if no one brings a car for servicing on a day when the shop is open. Conversely, if the demand for a service exceeds supply on a particular day, the excess business may be lost. Thus, if someone can't get a seat on one airline, another carrier gets the business or the trip is cancelled or postponed. If an accounting firm is too busy to accept tax and audit work from a prospective client, another firm will get the assignment.

But demand and supply imbalances are not found in all service situations. A useful way of categorizing services for this purpose is shown in Figure 4. The horizontal axis classifies organizations according to whether demand for the service fluctuates widely or narrowly over time; the vertical axis classifies them according to whether or not capacity is sufficient to meet peak demand.

Organizations in Box 1 could use increases in demand outside peak periods, those in Box 2 must decide whether to seek continued growth in demand and capacity or to continue the status quo, while those in Box 3 represent growing organizations that may need temporary demarketing until capacity can be increased to meet or exceed current demand levels. But service organizations in Box 4 face an ongoing problem of trying to smooth demand to match capacity, involving both stimulation and discouragement of demand.

Insights and Implications

Managing demand is a task faced by nearly all marketers, whether offering goods or services. Even where the fluctuations are sharp, and inventories cannot be used to act as a buffer between supply and demand, it

FIGURE 4: What is the nature of demand for the service relative to supply?

Extent to Which Supply Is Constrained	Extent of Demand Fluctuations over Time	
	Wide	**Narrow**
Peak Demand Can Usually Be Met without a Major Delay	1 electricity natural gas telephone hospital maternity unit police and fire emergencies	2 insurance legal services banking laundry and dry cleaning
Peak Demand Regularly Exceeds Capacity	4 accounting and tax preparation passenger transportation hotels and motels restaurants theaters	3 services similar to those in 2 but which have insufficient capacity for their base level of business

may still be possible to manage capacity in a service business—for instance, by hiring part-time employees or renting extra facilities at peak periods. But for a substantial group of service organizations, successfully managing demand fluctuations through marketing actions is the key to profitability.

To determine the most appropriate strategy in each instance, it's necessary to seek answers to some additional questions:

1. What is the typical cycle period of these demand fluctuations?

    • predictable (i.e., demand varies by hour of the day, day of the week or month, season of the year).

    • random (i.e., no apparent pattern to demand fluctuations).

2. What are the underlying causes of these demand fluctuations?

    • customer habits or preferences (could marketing efforts change these?).

    • actions by third parties (for instance,

employers set working hours, hence marketing efforts might usefully be directed at those employers).

    • nonforecastable events, such as health symptoms, weather conditions, acts of God and so forth—marketing can do only a few things about these, such as offering priority services to members and disseminating information about alternative services to other people.

One way to smooth out the ups and downs of demand is through strategies that encourage customers to change their plans voluntarily, such as offering special discount prices or added product value during periods of low demand. Another approach is to ration demand through a reservation or queuing system (which basically inventories demand rather than supply). Alternatively, to generate demand in periods of excess capacity, new business development efforts might be targeted at prospective customers with a countercyclical demand pattern. For instance, an accounting firm with a surfeit of work at the end of each calendar year might seek new customers whose financial year ended on June 30 or September 30.

Determining what strategy is appropriate requires an understanding of who or what is the target of the service (as discussed in an earlier section of this article). If the service is delivered to customers in person, there are limits to how long a customer will wait in line; hence strategies to inventory or ration demand should focus on adoption of reservation systems (Sasser, 1976). But if the service is delivered to goods or to intangible assets, then a strategy of inventorying demand should be more feasible (unless the good is a vital necessity such as a car, in which case reservations may be the best approach).

HOW IS THE SERVICE DELIVERED?

Understanding distribution issues in service marketing requires that two basic issues be addressed. The first relates to the method of delivery. Is it necessary for the customer to be in direct physical contact with the service organization (customers may have to go to the service organization, or the latter may come to the former), or can transactions be completed at arm's length? And does the service organization maintain just a single outlet or does it serve customers through multiple outlets at different sites? The outcome of this analysis can be seen in Figure 5, which consists of six different cells.

Insights and Implications

The convenience of receiving service is presumably lowest when a customer has to come to the service organization and must use a specific outlet. Offering service through several outlets increases the convenience of access for customers but may start to raise problems of quality control as convenience of access relates to the consistency of the service product delivered. For some types of services the organization will come to the customer. This is, of course, essential when the target of the service is some immovable physical item (such as a building that needs repairs or pest control treatment, or a garden that needs landscaping). But since it's usually more expensive to take service person-

FIGURE 5: Method of service delivery

Nature of Interaction between Customer and Service Organization	Availability of Service Outlets	
	Single Site	**Multiple Site**
Customer Goes to Service Organization	theater barbershop	bus service fast food chain
Service Organization Comes to Customer	lawn care service pest control service taxi	mail delivery AAA emergency repairs
Customer and Service Organization Transact at Arm's Length (mail or electronic communications)	credit card co. local TV station	broadcast network telephone co.

nel and equipment to the customer than vice versa, the trend has been away from this approach to delivering consumer services (e.g., doctors no longer like to make house calls). In many instances, however, direct contact between customers and the service organization is not necessary; instead, transactions can be handled at arm's length by mail or electronic communications. Through the use of 800 numbers many service organizations have found that they can bring their services as close as the nearest telephone, yet obtain important economies from operating out of a single physical location.

Although not all services can be delivered through arm's length transactions, it may be possible to separate certain components of the service from the core product and to handle them separately. This suggests an additional classification scheme: categorizing services according to whether transactions such as obtaining information, making reservations and making payment can be broken out separately from delivery of the core service. If they can be separated, then the question is whether or not it is advantageous to the service firm to allow customers to make these peripheral transactions through an intermediary or broker.

For instance, information about airline flights, reservations for such flights and purchases of tickets can all be made through a travel agent as well as directly through the airline. For those who prefer to visit in person, rather than conduct business by telephoning, this greatly increases the geographic coverage of distribution, since there are usually several travel agencies located more conveniently than the nearest airline office. Added value from using a travel agent comes from the "one-stop shopping" aspect of travel agents; the customer can inquire about several airlines and make car rental and hotel reservations during the same call. Insurance brokers and theater ticket agen-

cies are also examples of specialist intermediaries that represent a number of different service organizations. Consumers sometimes perceive such intermediaries as more objective and more knowledgeable about alternatives than the various service suppliers they represent. The risk to the service firm of working through specialist intermediaries is, of course, that they may recommend use of a competitor's product!

DISCUSSION

Widespread interest in the marketing of services among both academics and practitioners is a relatively recent phenomenon. Possibly this reflects the fact that marketing expertise in the service sector has significantly lagged behind that in the manufacturing sector. Up to now most academic research and discussion has centered on the issue, "How do services differ from goods?" A number of authors including Shostack (1977), Bateson (1979) and Berry (1980) have argued that there are significant distinctions between the two and have proposed several generalizations for management practice. But others such as Enis and Roering (1981) remain unconvinced that these differences have meaningful strategic implications.

Rather than continue to debate the existence of this broad dichotomy, it seems more useful to get on with the task of helping managers in service businesses do a better job of developing and marketing their products. We need to recognize that the service sector, particularly in the United States, is becoming increasingly competitive (Langeard et al., 1981), reflecting such developments as the partial or complete deregulation of several major service industries in recent years, the removal of professional association restrictions on using marketing techniques (particularly advertising), the replacement (or absorption) of independent service units by franchise chains, and the growth of new electronic delivery systems. As competition intensifies within the service sector, the development of more effective marketing efforts becomes essential to survival.

The classification schemes proposed in this article can contribute usefully to management practice in two ways. First, by addressing each of the five questions posed earlier, marketing managers can obtain a better understanding of the nature of their product, of the types of relationships their service organizations have with customers, of the factors underlying any sharp variations in demand, and of the characteristics of their service delivery systems. This understanding should help them identify how these factors shape marketing problems and opportunities and thereby affect the nature of the marketing task. Second, by recognizing which characteristics their own service shares with other services, often in seemingly unrelated industries, managers will learn to look beyond their immediate competitors for new ideas as to how to resolve marketing problems that they share in common with firms in other service industries.

Recognizing that the products of service organizations previously considered as "different" actually face similar problems or share certain characteristics in common can yield valuable managerial insights. Innovation in marketing, after all, often reflects a manager's ability to seek out and learn from analogous situations in other contexts. These classification schemes should also be of value to researchers to whom they offer an alternative to either broad-brush research into services or an industry-by-industry approach. Instead, they suggest a variety of new ways of looking at service businesses, each of which may offer opportunities for focused research efforts. Undoubtedly there is also room for further refinement of the schemes proposed.

REFERENCES

Bateson, John E. G. (1979), "Why We Need Service Marketing," in *Conceptual and Theoretical Developments in Marketing,* O. C. Ferrell, S. W. Brown, and C. W. Lamb, eds. Chicago: American Marketing Association, 131–46.

Berry, Leonard L. (1980), "Services Marketing Is Different," *Business Week* (May–June), 24–29.

Bucklin, Louis (1963), "Retail Strategy and the Classification of Consumer Goods," *Journal of Marketing,* 27 (January), 50.

Chase, Richard B. (1978), "Where Does the Customer Fit in a Service Operation?" *Harvard Business Review,* 56 (November–December), 137–42.

Copeland, Melvin T. (1923), "The Relation of Consumers' Buying Habits to Marketing Methods," *Harvard Business Review,* 1 (April), 282–89.

Enis, Ben M., and Kenneth J. Roering (1981), "Services Marketing: Different Products, Similar Strategies," in *Marketing of Services,* J. H. Donnelly and W. R. George, eds. Chicago: American Marketing Association.

Hill, T. P. (1977), "On Goods and Services," *Review of Income and Wealth,* 23 (December), 315–38.

Hunt, Shelby D. (1976), *Marketing Theory.* Columbus, OH: Grid.

Judd, Robert C. (1964), "The Case for Redefining Services," *Journal of Marketing,* 28 (January), 59.

Knisely, Gary (1979), "Marketing and the Services Industry," *Advertising Age* (January 15), 47–50; (February 19), 54–60; (March 19), 58–62; (May 15), 57–58.

Kotler, Philip (1980), *Principles of Marketing.* Englewood Cliffs, NJ: Prentice-Hall, Inc.

Langeard, Eric, John E. G. Bateson, Christopher H. Lovelock, and Pierre Eiglier (1981), *Services Marketing: New Insights from Consumers and Managers.* Cambridge, MA: Marketing Science Institute.

Levitt, Theodore (1972), "Production Line Approach to Service," *Harvard Business Review,* 50 (September–October), 41.

—— (1976), "The Industrialization of Service," *Harvard Business Review,* 54 (September–October), 63–74.

Lovelock, Christopher H. (1980), "Towards a Classification of Services," in *Theoretical Developments in Marketing,* C. W. Lamb and P. M. Dunne, eds. Chicago: American Marketing Association, 72–76.

_____ (1981), "Why Marketing Management Needs to Be Different for Services," in *Marketing of Services,* J. H. Donnelly and W. R. George, eds. Chicago: American Marketing Association.

Rathmell, John M. (1974), *Marketing in the Service Sector.* Cambridge, MA: Winthrop.

Sasser, W. Earl, Jr. (1976), "Match Supply and Demand in Service Industries," *Harvard Business Review,* 54 (November–December), 133.

_____, R. Paul Olsen, and D. Daryl Wyckoff (1978), *Management of Service Operations: Text and Cases.* Boston: Allyn & Bacon.

Shostack, G. Lynn (1977), "Breaking Free from Product Marketing," *Journal of Marketing,* 41 (April), 73–80.

Thomas, Dan R. E. (1978), "Strategy Is Different in Service Businesses," *Harvard Business Review,* 56 (July–August), 158–65.

Establishing a Price
for Government Services

JOHN L. CROMPTON • CHARLES W. LAMB, JR.

A three stage approach to pricing government and public services is suggested. Stage 1 requires an agency to determine what proportion of the costs incurred in delivering a service should be recovered from direct pricing. The public, merit, private classification of services provides a framework for this decision. This first cost-based stage ignores market considerations but Stages 2 and 3 ensure that the price is market sensitive. Stage 2 adjusts the cost-based price so it is consistent with the going rate, while Stage 3 considers whether price variations to particular groups may achieve more equitable and efficient service delivery.

Pricing is one of the most technically difficult and politically sensitive areas in which public service managers have to make decisions. Pricing decisions are influenced by a myriad of ideological, political, economic, and professional arguments. The debate that accompanies this diversity of perspectives, however, should be focused on some sound

John L. Crompton and Charles W. Lamb, Jr. "Establishing a Price for Government Services," *Journal of Professional Services Marketing* (Summer 1986). © 1986 by The Haworth Press, Inc.

Reprinted with permission from The Haworth Press, Inc., 75 Griswold St., Binghamton, NY 13904.

FIGURE 1: A logical approach to establishing a price

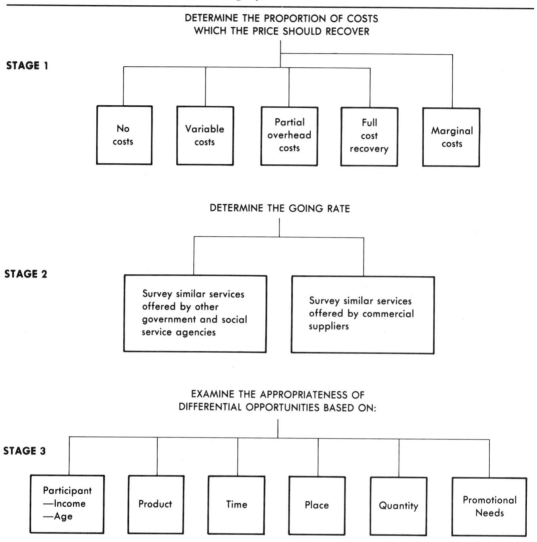

principles. The intent of this paper is to present a logical approach to establishing a price.

The approach suggested here consists of three stages (Figure 1). Stage 1 requires an agency to determine what proportion of the costs incurred in delivering a service should be recovered from direct pricing. Deriving a price based only on the costs of service delivery ignores market considerations. Stages 2 and 3 ensure that the price is market sensitive. Stage 2 considers the going rate charged for similar services by other public agencies and/or the commercial sector, which may add to the cost-based price being adjusted downwards to ensure that it is perceived as "reasonable." In Stage 3, the appropriateness of varying the price for some user groups or in particular contexts is considered.

STAGE 1: POSITIONING SERVICES ON THE COST RECOVERY CONTINUUM

The price setting principle most widely accepted by economists is marginal cost pricing because it maximizes economic efficiency. Marginal cost is defined as the addition to total cost resulting from the addition of the last unit of output. If it is intended to recover marginal costs, then a service is provided at a price equal to the cost of providing an additional unit of service, or the cost of serving the incremental user. Each user pays the additional cost caused by his or her specific use of the service. While the practicing public sector manager may concur that in principle marginal cost pricing is conceptually superior, he or she is likely to argue that it is too difficult to implement and for this reason it is not discussed further in this paper.

Economists classify services into three categories: public, merit, and private services. Much of the debate about whether or not user prices should be levied, and if so at what level, revolves around the classification of the service as one of these types. The differences between these categories are summarized in Figure 2.

This classification provides the economic rationale upon which decisions about user pricing of *public services* should be based. It assumes that the objective is to price each service at a level that is fair to both users and nonusers. It helps the public service manager determine which services lend themselves to monetary pricing, at what basis, on what level, and with what effects.

If a service exhibits the characteristics of a *private service*, its benefits are received exclusively by users rather than by the rest of the community. The case for financing a government service through direct charges to the user is clear-cut when the service is perceived as private. When someone receives a direct benefit from government it seems only fair that he or she should pay for it. If no benefits from a service accrue to other citizens, then it is not reasonable to expect them to subsidize the cost through the tax system.

Government agencies provide a substantial number of essentially private services that, because of historical accident, failure of the private sector to offer a service, the need for quality controls, or where monopolies are necessary to achieve efficient economies of scale (for example, the Postal Service and water and electricity supplies), are provided by government. Water and sewage, public transport, parking spaces, refuse collection, electricity, public marinas, and golf courses are examples of services and facilities that usually exhibit private service characteristics.

Viewing public and private types of services or opposite poles of a continuum is helpful in understanding the essential differences between them, but most government services lie somewhere between the two poles. Such services are called *merit services*. Merit services have been defined in several ways, but fundamentally they are private services that have been endowed with the public interest. In the case of merit services, the individual receives more of a private service than he or she would have purchased on his or her own.

Although it is possible to levy user prices for merit services, it is not reasonable to expect users to cover all costs because the spillover benefits are received by the whole

FIGURE 2: Differences between services with public, merit, and private characteristics

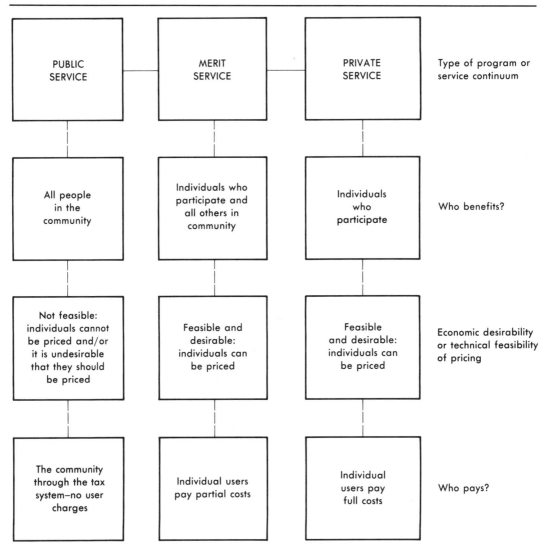

community. Users should be subsidized only to the extent that benefits to the whole community are perceived to occur.

Urban transit services offer an illustration of a merit service. Most urban mass transit systems charge relatively low fees which do not cover the full costs of transit operations. Urban transit is thus recognized as a merit service. The requirement that the users pay some price recognizes that they receive extra increments of benefit that do not accrue to nonusers. However, nonusers subsidize the service since they derive the benefit of reduced traffic congestion. If fares were raised and were successful in recovering full costs, many riders would opt to use automobiles

FIGURE 3: The relationship between type of service and cost recovery strategy

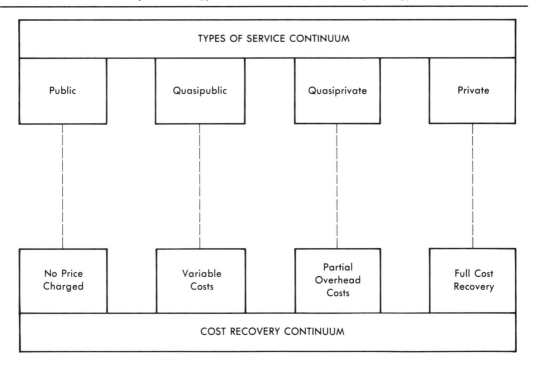

and traffic congestion would be increased, causing a loss of benefits to nonusers.

Most government services for which a user price is charged are not totally self-supporting. Most are partially supported by tax funds, which suggests that such services are perceived as merit rather than private services. However, tax subsidy can only be justified if collective benefits accrue to the majority of the community that subsidizes the service.

Once a jurisdiction has classified each of its services as public, merit, or private, it is in a position to consider the price which should be charged. There are three approaches to establishing a price based on recovering some predetermined proportion of costs: full cost recovery, partial overhead cost recovery, and variable cost recovery. The conceptual relationship between these

three cost recovery methods and the public–private services continuum is shown in Figure 3.

Full Cost Recovery

Full cost recovery is also termed *average cost pricing*. The price of a service is intended to produce sufficient revenue to cover all the fixed and variable costs associated with the service (however these have been defined in the cost accounting system) and enable the breakeven point to be reached. Because the total costs of a service are divided among those who receive it, full cost recovery is sometimes called the "fair price." For example, in the case of a hospital, if patients in need of care pay the full unit costs, the hospital breaks even. This is considered fair because no one has been "taken

FIGURE 4: Pricing to recover full costs

A price which is intended to recover full costs is determined by using the following formula:

$$\text{Average Cost Price} = \text{Average Fixed Cost} + \text{Average Variable Cost}$$

Where:

$$\text{Average Fixed Cost} = \frac{\text{Total Fixed Costs}}{\text{Number of Users}}$$

$$\text{Average Variable Cost} = \frac{\text{Total Variable Costs}}{\text{Number of Users}}$$

If: Total Fixed Costs = \$1000
Total Variable Costs = 500
Projected Number of Users = 100

$$\text{Then: Price} = \frac{1000}{100} + \frac{500}{100}$$

Thus: Price = \$15

advantage of." Figure 4 shows how to determine a price which is intended to recover full costs.

Full cost recovery is an appropriate strategy for those services perceived to exhibit the characteristics of private services which benefit only users and offer no external benefits to the general community. Full cost recovery pricing is most commonly used by government agencies in the pricing of tolls for highways, airports, and bridges, sanitation services, hospital services, and utilities. These are perceived to be private services operating on a self-financing basis.

Partial Overhead Cost Recovery

If the intent is to recover partial overhead costs, then a price is established which meets all direct operation and maintenance costs and some proportion of fixed costs. The remaining proportion of the fixed costs which it is not intended to recover represents the tax subsidy given to the particular service. Figure 5 shows how to determine a price which is intended to recover partial overhead costs.

Conceptually, the proportion of fixed costs which should be subsidized is dependent upon the extent to which nonusers benefit from a user utilizing a service. As the benefits which accrue to nonusers increase, the proportion of fixed costs met by the subsidy should increase (Figure 3).

It is important to note that the anticipated per person subsidy is built into the formula. This is a very different approach to the frequent practice of assigning, say, a 20 percent overhead figure to direct operations and maintenance costs, because this latter approach does not indicate the extent to which individuals are subsidized. If it is decided that a service should be subsidized, then the subsidy should be made explicit in the

FIGURE 5: Pricing to recover partial overhead costs

A price which is intended to recover partial overhead costs is determined by the following formula:

Partial Overhead Recovery Price = Average Fixed Cost + Average Variable Cost − Average Subsidy

Where Average Subsidy represents the amount to which each user is subsidized out of tax funds.

> If: Average Fixed Cost = $8
> Average Variable Cost = $4
> Average Subsidy = $3
> Then: Partial Overhead Recovery Price = $8 + $4 − $3
> Thus: The service would be priced at $9.

budget and built into the authority's financial control system. This is important because managers responsible for services should set performance targets based on costs, subsidies, and targets. Lack of attention to subsidies expressed on a per unit or per capita basis is likely to lead to substantial inefficiency in the allocation of resources and inequities in service delivery. Users of Service A may be receiving much larger subsidies per capita than users of Service B, even though the price they pay is the same, because the costs of operating the two services are substantially different.

Variable Cost Recovery

If variable cost recovery pricing is used, the established price is equal to the average variable cost of providing a service. In this context, variable costs are used synony-mously with direct operating and maintenance expenses. No attempt is made to contribute toward meeting fixed costs. Figure 6 shows how to determine a price which is intended to recover variable costs.

Because direct operating and maintenance expenses can be easily documented, there is a tendency to base price decisions upon them. This is a popular approach with many agency personnel because when fixed costs are omitted, a relatively low price can be charged and a larger client support constituency is likely to emerge. However, it is also argued that the facilities and amenities offered by government agencies add to the quality or life or to the "liveability" of a community. There are benefits to some nonusers from knowing that facilities exist (this "opportunity to acquire" is sometimes called "option demand"), and nonusers should therefore pay the indirect fixed costs

FIGURE 6: Pricing to recover variable costs

$$\text{Variable Cost Recovery Price} = \frac{\text{Total Variable Costs}}{\text{Number of Participants}}$$

If: Total Variable Cost = $500
Projected Number of Participants = 100
Then: Variable Cost Recovery Price = $5

required to make these amenities and facilities available.

STAGE 2: CONSIDER THE GOING RATE PRICE

At the end of Stage 1, a provisional price should have been determined based upon the proportion of costs which it is expected to recover. However, pricing based on costs is not market-oriented because it assumes that service users will pay the suggested price. This may be a false assumption. Stage 2 of the process for establishing a price is intended to ensure that the provisional cost-based price is adjusted, if necessary, so it is responsive to the willingness and ability of users to pay (Figure 1).

Determining the going rate requires that a survey of prices charged by other suppliers of this service be undertaken. Usually this survey will be confined to other government agencies, but in situations where a service is also offered by commercial suppliers they should be included in the price survey. For example, if a jurisdiction offers day care services, it should include private day care suppliers in its going rate survey. The agency may then adjust its cost-based price in order to ensure that the public day care opportunity does not impede the success of private day care suppliers or reduce the range of day care opportunities available. If the public facility charges substantially lower than private suppliers, it might be detrimental to these suppliers and may lead to congestion of the agency's own facilities.

Adjusting a price so it is consistent with the going rate has two major advantages. First, it may be argued that the going rate price range represents the collective wisdom of professionals in the field and elected officials in other jurisdictions as to what constitutes a reasonable price. For this reason, a price within the range will probably avoid

controversy and be regarded by most publics as "fair." For example, if the survey reveals that an agency's prices are lower than those charged by others for a similar service, then it provides strong justification to both user publics and elected representatives for an increase in price.

A second major advantage accruing from comparing existing prices with those charged for similar services elsewhere is that it establishes the *range* of prices which are likely to be acceptable to users of a particular service. It is possible that services may not be exactly the same quality or serve identical types of client groups, but in most cases there are likely to be substantial similarities between services.

Determining the going rate forces an agency to address what potential client groups are willing to pay for a particular service. It is a misconception to believe that costs should necessarily determine price, for often the prices which an agency charges may be used to determine costs. For instance, if a craft program were being priced, a community education agency might first try to find out what prices it can reasonably expect its potential client groups to pay. When it has this information the agency works backwards from this figure to determine the nature of the materials, equipment, and facilities which are suited to such a price.

The going rate price is not "the manager's impression" of what others are charging. It is found by formally surveying what is being charged elsewhere. It may be argued that if the provisional price based on recovery costs in Stage 1 is to be substantially adjusted so it is in accord with the going rate, then Stage 1 may be omitted. This would be a mistake. The going rate often bears little relation to the cost of provision. As a result, if Stage 1 were omitted, sound financial management would not be possible and substantial inequities between services might emerge as some would be more heavily subsidized than others. Without Stage 1 a jurisdiction would not be able to consciously trade-off the opportunity cost of one service compared to another, and would not know whether it should price a service at the high or low end of the range of going rate prices.

STAGE 3: EXAMINE THE APPROPRIATENESS OF DIFFERENTIAL PRICING

At the end of Stage 2 the adjusted price is accepted as the average price which service users should be charged. However, Stage 3 recognizes that there are occasions when offering variations of this price to particular groups may achieve more equitable and efficient service delivery (Figure 1). Price examining the appropriateness of differential opportunities means that an agency considers charging a different price to different groups for the same service, even though there is no directly corresponding difference in the costs of providing the service to each of those groups. Such market-oriented price adjustments assume that the market is segmentable and the segments show different price elasticities of demand. A fundamental requirement for an agency to be able to offer the same service at two or more prices is that it must not arouse resentment from a majority of clients, or else antipathy will be created and goodwill lost.

There are six criteria available for dividing a clientele into distinct user groups within which there may be differential pricing opportunities: participant category, product, place, time, quantity of use, and incentives to try. Although each is discussed separately, there are sometimes opportunities to use some of them together.

Price differentation on the basis of *participant category* is usually related to a perception that some groups may find it difficult to

pay a recommended price. Three groups are frequently identified as less able to pay. They are children, senior citizens, and the economically disadvantaged. Differentials for each of these groups are widely used by government agencies, although the rationale for offering services at a reduced price to senior citizens has been challenged in recent years because of the elderly's substantially improved economic status.[1]

Differential pricing on the basis of *product* may be used to offer client groups extra levels of service, for example, in trash collection, street cleaning, street parking, park maintenance, police patrols, or foreign language instruction. The agency would provide a basic level of service, but those clients who wanted a higher level could receive it by paying a higher price, just as those extra services in some instances are now purchased from private sources. The prices for these added services would be set to cover the incremental costs of providing them.

Differential pricing could also serve as a market test of the public's preferred level of service for it offers a method for trying out and responding to the public's desire for quality changes in public services. The consumer who desires a quality differential could pay for that option—a choice now frequently denied him or her when quality changes must be financed from general revenue.[2] Presumably, if a large proportion of a clientele opted for a higher level of service, then it would become the new norm.

Pricing that differentiates on a *place* basis is commonly practiced at spectator events. For example, at a concert, theater, or sports event, a higher price is charged for front-row than for back-row seats.

The most common use of price differentials based on place relates to higher prices charged to nonresidents. Such differentials are relatively easy to impose since nonresidents are likely to have relatively little political influence outside of their own jurisdiction. For example, state universities charge out-of-state residents a higher price for tuition than residents. The rationale for such pricing is that residents frequently pay at least some of the costs associated with a service through their property taxes, while nonresidents make no such payments. This rationale may not be appropriate if services are paid for from other tax sources, for example, a sales tax. In this case, people living outside the community may legitimately argue that since they purchase a variety of goods from within the community, they have contributed their fair share of sales tax. Hence, there is no rationale for charging them more than residents for use of these services.

At the municipal level, the authority of agencies to impose differential prices based on residence varies between states. As a result, such agencies must be aware of relevant statutes and court decisions in their particular jurisdictions to determine their authority to impose a different price for nonresidents. Generally, if a municipality can demonstrate a reasonable relationship between the differential price and legitimate governmental goals, the price will be upheld in the courts.[3]

If a service is being used to capacity, then a high differential price may be an effective method of discouraging nonresident use. However, if a service has spare capacity, then an agency may want to attract as many outside residents as possible who are willing to pay a price which is higher than the variable cost of servicing them. The revenue accruing from this price will make a contribution to fixed costs and the service will require less subsidy from taxpayers.

In using differential prices on a *time* basis, lower prices are charged for services that are identical except with respect to time of use in order to encourage fuller and more balanced utilization of capacity. The intent is to encourage use of services at off-peak times and to ration use during peak times. Public utilities, computing centers, and parking lots or meters have used this approach, varying their prices according to the time of week (weekend versus weekday) or time of day (charging higher rates for peak periods).

Quantity discounts are deductions from the regular price that reflect economies of purchasing in large quantities. Two primary types of quantity discounts are used by government agencies. The first is declining block rates which often are used in water and utility pricing. Because water delivery involves high fixed costs and low variable costs, the cost of delivering the last gallon of water is less than the cost of delivering the first gallon of water. Water pressure has to be kept high, leaks occur at the same rate, and administration costs remain the same irrespective of whether or not people use the water. The output of water (that is, obtaining it from a source and treating it so that it is fit for human consumption) is subject to decreasing costs over the relevant market size once the plant is in place. For these reasons, as the quantity of water used by a client increases, the price per 1000 gallons decreases.

The second type of quantity discount is the season or multi-use discount pass used in many public recreation facilities such as swimming pools, golf courses, and arts complexes. Their use has been challenged as being inequitable in some situations[4], but in others their use may be an important part of overall marketing strategy. The basic purposes of a quantity discount are (1) to stimulate additional demand, and (2) to reduce the costs of meeting that level of demand. If these two conditions are not met, then an agency should reconsider its use of quantity discounts.

Price discounts can be used as an *incentive*

to persuade people to try a service. New clients may be offered prices lower than those paid by established clients in the hope of encouraging them to be regular users. It is important that such discounts be selective. Those receiving the discounts should recognize that they are for a limited duration or restricted to a particular set of circumstances, and that after a given time period or change of circumstances the regular price will be charged.

CONCLUDING COMMENTS

The systematic approach to deriving a price which has been presented here has to be tempered with a realization that there are two factors which may cause elected officials and potential client groups not always to respond positively to rational pricing decisions. First, a logically derived price may have to be adjusted to accommodate the psychological reactions of targeted client groups. Their reaction to price changes are often irrational, stemming from historical perspectives, analogous experiences, self-interest, or emotion. These psychological dimensions have been addressed by one of the authors elsewhere.[5]

A second qualifying factor is the prevailing political environment which surrounds any pricing decision. Pricing is one of the most technically difficult and politically sensitive areas in which public service managers have to make decisions. Pricing decisions are influenced by a myriad of ideological, political, economic, and professional arguments. However, the debate which accompanies this diversity of perspectives should be founded upon sound principles.

The main failure of existing user price policies is that they have been designed solely or primarily to raise revenue. The prevailing approach is to raise all prices by some arbitrary percentage amount each year. There is little attempt to discover who is benefitting, who is paying, and the level of benefits and payments involved for each service. Even if incremental price increases are based on some acceptable criterion, they assume that the original price was appropriate. If the initial price was arbitrarily derived, then subsequent incremental increases are also likely to result in an arbitrary price.

The reasoned, rational approach discussed here will not always be immediately convincing to decision makers. However, the political and rational approaches to pricing are not mutually exclusive. The introduction of better information is not likely to lead to a weakening of the elected official's vote—indeed, it should strengthen it. If a rational approach is not presented to elected officials, then the approach chosen can only encourage continuation of irrational pricing and imply recognition of elected officials determining those who pay and those who benefit according to whatever personal or arbitrary criteria they care to adopt.

REFERENCES

[1] Crompton, J. L., "The Equitability of Full-Price Policies for Senior Citizens," *Journal of Park and Recreation Administration*, Vol. 2, No. 1 (January 1984), pp. 3–8.

[2] Mushkin, S. J., and R. M. Bird, "Public Prices: An Overview," in S. J. Mushkin, ed., *Public Price for Public Products*. Washington D. C.: The Urban Institute, 1972, pp. 22–23.

[3] Kozlowski, J. C., "Validity of Non-resident and Other Discriminatory Regulations in Municipal Recreation," *Parks and Recreation* (March 1982), pp. 28–34.

[4] Crompton, J. L., "Treating Equals Equally: Some Abuses of a Basic Principle in Pricing Public Recreation and Park Services," *Parks and Recreation* (September 1984).

[5] Crompton, J. L., "Psychological Dimensions of Pricing Leisure Services," *Recreation Research Review* (October 1982).

Distribution Decisions for Public Services

CHARLES W. LAMB, JR. • JOHN L. CROMPTON

DISTRIBUTION DECISIONS FOR PUBLIC SERVICES

It is widely agreed that marketing is an appropriate activity for nonprofit organizations, including government agencies (Kotler, 1982). It is also generally agreed that there are important distinctions between the public and private sectors which affect marketing practices in each of these sectors (Lovelock and Weinberg, 1984). Public sector managers must be cognizant of these significant differences when developing marketing strategies and programs.

This article focuses upon one aspect of public sector marketing—the distribution of public services. The components of the public service distribution decision process are identified, and their interrelationships are illustrated.

OVERVIEW OF THE DISTRIBUTION DECISION PROCESS

Any public service distribution pattern emerges from a series of related tasks. These tasks are illustrated in Figure 1.

The first step in the process is to audit the existing pattern of distribution, if the service is presently being offered. When the existing allocation pattern is known, then objectives may be set to amend or perpetuate this pattern in accordance with the agency's preferred distribution pattern model. After objectives have been set establishing who will get how much of a particular service, then a distribution strategy plan, which establishes how the service will be made available and accessible to citizens, may be developed and implemented.

The distribution plan addresses four questions:

1. Which agency/division will be responsible for delivering the service to target markets? This involves identifying, and in some cases selecting, alternative vertical and horizontal channels of distribution and types of outlets.
2. How many outlets should be used? Concern here is with the appropriate level of distribution intensity.
3. Where should the outlets be located?
4. When will the service be offered?

These four decisions, (1) the channel of distribution decision, (2) the intensity of distribution decision, (3) selection of site locations, and (4) schedule of service delivery,

© 1985. Reprinted with permission of the *Journal of the Academy of Marketing Science*, (Summer 1985), pp. 107-23.

FIGURE 1: A model of the distribution decision process for government and social service agencies

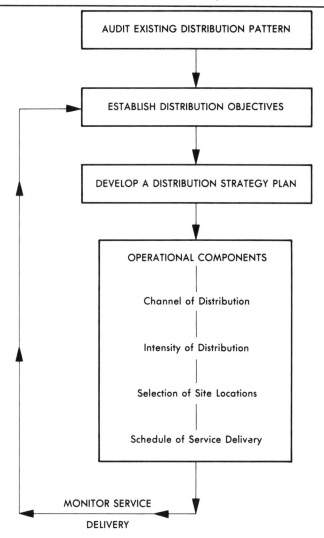

constitute the operational components of a public agency's distribution system.

After these interrelated distribution decisions have been made, the service is delivered and its results and impacts are monitored. These are then evaluated against the established distribution objectives. If the results are not satisfactory, then appropriate adjustments to one, or more, of the four operational components in the distribution system can be made.

AUDITING EXISTING DISTRIBUTION PATTERNS

Both auditing and monitoring require the use of similar evaluation techniques. The main difference is that auditing is periodic and long term, whereas monitoring is on-going and short term. Three major compo-nents of the evaluation process are: (1) de-termining the appropriate unit of analysis, (2) selecting distribution measurement indica-tors, and (3) making comparisons between different services. Following is a review of these components.

UNITS OF ANALYSIS

Evaluation of the equity of service distri-bution involves geographic comparisons. The problem lies in selecting which socio-spatial or geographic units are appropriate, since different neighborhood definitions are likely to produce different analytical results in measuring service equality. Three criteria should guide the unit of analysis decision (Lucy and Mladenka, 1977):

1. It should be feasible to gather data for each unit. For example, are the data al-ready available, or is it possible to gather information on the amount of solid waste collected per household or the weekly number of public transit rides made per household?
2. Population data and physical characteris-tics data (such as housing) should be available for the geographic region of in-terest so it can be related to the service data which are gathered. For example, it may be desirable to relate the service data to the income or race or residents in each geographical unit.
3. The geographical unit should be relevant to decisions that may be made about the service.

The most useful unit of analysis is proba-bly the service district; reallocation of re-sources can then be made between service districts if inequitable service distribution patterns are revealed.

TYPES OF EVALUATION INDICATORS

Relative success in achieving distribution objectives can only be meaningfully evalu-ated if appropriate measurement indicators are developed. Indicators are normally based on either resources, activities, or results (Lucy and Mladenka, 1977). *Resources* are quantitative inputs to the service distribution system which may include money, person-nel, facilities, and equipment. *Activities* are the ways in which the resources are used. For example, the number or frequency of policemen who patrol streets and the number of arrests they make, or the frequency with which sanitation workers collect refuse. *Re-sults* are what happens as a direct conse-quence of the service delivered. For ex-ample, how much stolen property has been recovered, how much refuse has been col-lected. The differences between these three types of indicators can be illustrated with police services. Police distribution may be analyzed in terms of: the number of police patrolmen per 1000 neighborhood residents (a resource indicator); the average response time for each neighborhood, from receipt of a call for service until a police officer's ar-rival at the scene (an activity indicator); or the clearance rate for each neighborhood, that is, the percentage of crimes cleared by the arrest of someone suspected of commit-ing crimes (a results indicator).

No one measurement indicator is neces-sarily better or worse than another. Although they typically produce very different results, the selection of a specific indicator is usually based upon the organization's distribution objectives, the availability of data, and/or the cost of gathering measurement data.

MAKING COMPARISONS BETWEEN SERVICES

In some situations, particularly in discretionary services such as recreation, libraries, parks, and cultural arts, determination of equitable distribution involves trying to assess the benefits offered by very different services. Using recreation as an example, how can the resources in Neighborhood A, comprised of 4 small parks, 1 large swimming pool, 3 ball parks, and a golf course, be compared with those of Neighborhood B which consist of 2 large parks, 3 small swimming pools, and 1 recreation center? These are very different combinations of amenities, and yet they all seek to provide recreational benefits. Clearly, this problem is compounded when comparison between different types of services is attempted.

There appear to be four possible approaches to making such comparisons. First, the visual approach may be used. By mapping the existing outlets for each service, and by developing transparent overlays for each service, visual identification of relatively deprived and relatively well-endowed areas, in terms of the quantity and quality of services, can be identified. The main strength of the visual approach is also its major weakness. The approach is relatively simple, because the use of subjective, normative judgment avoids the difficulty of trying to objectively weigh the value of a recreation center against the value of a park or a swimming pool.

Second, efforts could be made to standardize provisions so each neighborhood has the same number of parks, firehouses, libraries, etc. Provisions could be expressed in such terms as the number and percent of people in a specific geographic area living within a selected travel time or distance from specified facilities or services. However, such standardization is normally inappropriate, since citizens in different neighborhoods often have different service preferences and priorities. Third, an activity indicator, such as participation or visitation, could be used to compare the equality of service distribution among neighborhoods.

A fourth approach is to undertake an investment inventory which measures the current appraised value of all facilities. Thus, dollars invested in libraries, parks, recreation, and cultural facilities could be aggregated to identify the current investment value of quality of life facilities in each neighborhood, and, in this way, identify neighborhood inequities. This investment inventory approach facilitates better budgetary decisions for the allocation of services between different neighborhoods so inequities between neighborhoods are reduced. At the same time, it enables the more detailed decisions, on which particular types of services should receive priority in each neighborhood, to be made flexible, in accordance with the differing wishes of individual neighborhoods.

ESTABLISHING DISTRIBUTION OBJECTIVES

Once an audit of the existing distribution pattern has been completed, it is necessary to establish, revise, or reaffirm distribution objectives. Objectives are the end results which an agency wants to obtain and should guide all the distribution decisions and actions of the agency.

Distribution objectives may be expressed in terms of resources, activities, and results. A resource-based distribution objective for swimming pool provision in a city may be to provide, within a five-year period, adequate recreational swimming opportunities for all citizens by raising the level of public investment in basic swimming facilities in all planning zones to a specified per capital amount, giving priority to those zones which have the lowest current and projected investment. A distribution objective based on an activity approach could be a family counseling department which has an objective of visiting each client family in their home every month. A police department which has an objective of achieving arrest rates of at least 50 percent in every neighborhood within 3 years would be using a results objective.

Distribution objectives should be compatible with the agency's budgetary capacity, so that what is to be attempted in a given time frame is financially feasible. Further, when distribution objectives are being established, other marketing mix decisions, such as prices to be charged, programs to be offered, and promotion, also need to be considered. Distribution objectives should be carefully integrated into the overall marketing plan to achieve an integrated, cohesive strategy.

DEVELOPING A DISTRIBUTION STRATEGY PLAN

The audit of existing distribution patterns establishes "Where we are now"; the objectives project "What we want our distribution pattern to look like in X years' time." The distribution strategy plan provides a blueprint of how to get from where we are now to where we want to be in a specified period of time. There are four main operational components which constitute a public agency's distribution system. They are: channel of distribution, intensity of distribution, selection of site locations, and schedule of service delivery.

CHANNEL OF DISTRIBUTION

A public sector channel of distribution consists of the set of organizations, agencies, and outlets which share in the responsibilities for making a service available and accessible to target populations. Channel of distribution decisions are concerned with whether an agency should attempt to deliver its offerings directly to consumers, or whether it can better deliver selected offerings indirectly through involving other agencies or organizations. The starting point for effective channel decisions is defining target markets and assessing the needs of these target markets. There are three dimensions to channel decisions. The first dimension concerns vertical distribution, and the second dimension concerns horizontal distribution patterns. In both cases, the decision of whether to use a direct or an indirect approach is determined by assessing which approach offers the most effective, efficient, and equitable distribution of a particular service.

An agency is not restricted to using only one particular channel. Indeed, there are instances when it is advantageous to deliver a particular offering through several different types of outlets simultaneously in order to reach different target markets. Thus, the type of outlets to be used constitutes the third dimension of channel decisions.

Vertical Distribution Decisions

Vertical distribution occurs when services are delivered from a higher level of government, through intermediary government levels, to the ultimate target market. This process is somewhat analogous to a manufacturer's decision to sell either directly to customers, or indirectly through retailers or wholesaler/retailer networks. Intermediary government levels should only be included if it is advantageous to deliver some service by using them. If any of the intermediary levels do not increase the effectiveness, efficiency, or equity of the distribution system, then they should be omitted from the delivery system, and a direct approach adopted.

FIGURE 2: Examples of vertical distribution decisions

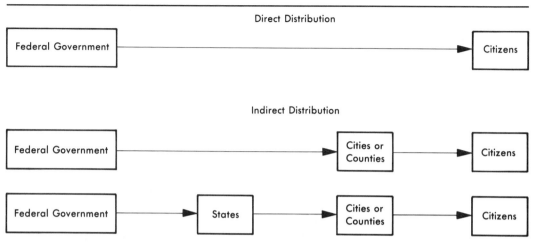

Direct Distribution

Indirect Distribution

Figure 2 illustrates three alternative distribution options the federal government might use to distribute funds to target markets. The first option, direct distribution, entails providing funds directly to those citizens who qualify under the requirements of a program. Social Security payments are an example of this option. Second, the federal government might use one or more indirect distribution alternatives. It might distribute funds to state agencies, for example, and require the state agencies either to allocate the funds to qualified jurisdictions in the state, or to distribute the funds or services directly to qualified citizens or projects. The Land and Water Conservation Fund, which provides matching grants for acquiring or developing outdoor park and recreation facilities, is an example of this alternative. Third, as in the case of general revenue sharing, the federal government may decide it is more efficient for some programs to by-pass states and distribute funds directly to local cities or counties.

Agencies within the vertical channel do not always work in harmony. Sometimes there is conflict, confusion, and duplication of effort. Conflicts often emerge when the objectives at one level of government can only be achieved if another level cooperates. For example, the welfare program Aid to Families with Dependent Children (AFDC) is regularly and partially funded by the federal government, but it is actually delivered by state governments. Conflicts arise because what one level of government intends is not necessarily what another level wants to do or is capable of doing.

Horizontal Distribution Decisions

Horizontal distribution refers to alternate distribution strategies adopted within a single level of government. Three alternate approaches are illustrated in Figure 3. The direct provider role is the model many agencies traditionally have adopted. In this approach, the agency typically assumes exclusive responsibility for planning, organizing, and distributing services and providing facilities.

Two problems associated with exclusive use of the direct provider model have led many agencies to adopt facilitator and/or

FIGURE 3: Alternative horizontal distribution decisions

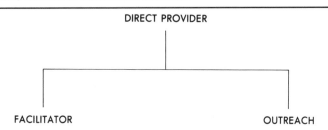

outreach roles as additional modes of service delivery. The first problem is that many citizens are unable, or unwilling for a variety of reasons, to go to distribution outlets to use the services offered. Recognition of this problem has led some agencies to expand their traditional approach to incorporate an outreach role. The second problem is the high cost associated with direct provider and outreach approaches. Services have been subject to more critical cost reviews since the mid 1970s, when funding became less available. This situation caused agencies to examine the potential of serving as a facilitator, encouraging others to deliver selected services, rather than serving as a direct provider.

The facilitative function can include the agency assuming the role of a referral agent. In this situation, the agency acts as a broker, providing a connection between the service needs of community residents and the supply of opportunities available to satisfy them. The facilitation of integrative arrangements and provision of services by others is emerging rapidly as an alternative distribution mode in response to diminishing budgets, rising maintenance and operation costs, and greater service demands.

Type of Outlet Decisions

The selection target markets will influence and directly shape decisions concerning the types of outlets to be used. If an agency adopts a multisegment target market strategy, it must also consider multiple types of distribution outlets.

There is often a tendency to develop standardized uniform distribution systems designed to accommodate common needs shared by all clients. Unfortunately, attempting to accommodate the common needs shared by all often results in the failure to adequately respond to the particular distribution needs of any market segment.

Figure 4 provides an example of how a library might use different types of outlets to reach various market segments effectively. The main library appeals to researchers and others who desire an extensive collection of resources at one location and persons who seek specialized sorts of information and/or services. Most people who use branch libraries seek either leisure reading materials or limited research information. The main appeal of the bookmobile is its convenience to users. Outreach programs have improved library services by offering such programs in association with senior citizen centers, churches, day care centers and headstart programs.

Each of the four target markets has different needs and different distribution preferences. By providing different types of outlets, the library is able to reach a larger portion of its total market and provide services consistent with their needs. All markets appropriate for segmentation should also be

FIGURE 4: Different types of outlets for library services

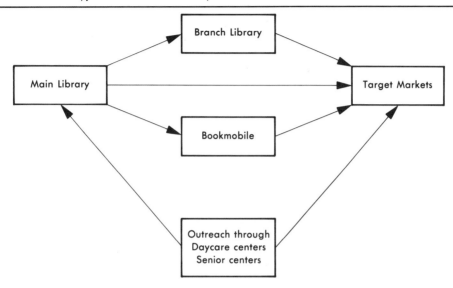

considered candidates for using different types of distribution outlets.

INTENSITY OF DISTRIBUTION

After determining which channels and types of outlets are to be used for distributing a service, the next decision is to identify how many outlets should be provided. Intensity of distribution refers to the relative availability of a service to the consumer.

Generally, the intensity of distribution of a service should meet, but not exceed, the needs and preferences of target markets. Too few outlets may fail to provide a needed level of service, and too many outlets may incur unnecessary costs. The decision regarding intensity of distribution should be guided by the distribution objectives, but will also be influenced by such factors as the financial condition of the agency, degree of dependence upon facilities, the availability and extent of complementary or similar services offered by other agencies, type of outlets desired, and volume of demand expected.

A basic factor influencing intensity decisions is the trade-offs between costs and accessibility. Intensity of distribution, accessibility, and costs are closely interrelated. The greater the intensity of distribution, the greater the accessibility of a service, but the higher the cost.

Intensity of distribution can be viewed in terms of both facilities and services. The intensity of distribution of *facilities* refers to the relative number of physical facilities an agency operates. The intensity of distribution of *services* refers to the relative number of outlets at which a person can receive the service.

Intensive distribution of facilities entails having many physical facilities to serve the target market clientele. At the extreme, intensive distribution of *facilities* would entail facilities adjacent to each potential user's residence, for example: roads, street lights, sidewalks and storm sewers. Alternatively, intensive facility distribution may mean making facilities available in most neighborhoods. Totlots are frequently distributed intensively so that the facilities are within walking distance for all children. Accessibility is maximized. Intensive distribution of *services* entails providing the service directly to clients in their homes, or having it readily available and within easy access.

Selective distribution entails having *facilities* and/or *services* available at several outlets. Selective distribution presumes members of target markets are willing and able to travel some distance to use the facility or receive the service. It also recognizes the inability of agencies to provide some services directly to all users. Selective distribution is a compromise between the economies of scale associated with exclusive distribution and the preference of clients for personalized service delivery. Community centers are typically selectively distributed. Other examples include schools and parks within a community, branch libraries, satellite welfare offices, and family planning clinics. If a selective distribution strategy is adopted, locations should be selected which are most convenient for the target clientele.

Exclusive distribution is the provision of facilities and/or services in only one location within a community or target market area. Immobile facilities offering specialized services, such as hospitals, often use exclusive distribution because they are used relatively infrequently. Exclusive distribution has the advantage of minimized costs and maximized control. The disadvantage, of course, is inconvenience to a large portion of the target market.

By having one large library in a major city, duplication of books, staff, and building costs can be avoided. The citizen will gain to the extent he or she will find an extensive collection of books. Restricting the number of locations forces the client to travel, cost-ing him or her more in terms of time, transportation, convenience and personal energy.

Some state universities employ exclusive distribution. The cost of running the university is minimized by operating only one campus, but the travel costs to clients of attending classes at that institution are likely to be high. If the university decides to distribute its educational product more intensively throughout the state, it will face all the classic distribution questions faced by large business firms: how many branch locations should be established, how large should they be, where should they be located, and what specialization should take place at each branch (Kotler, 1982)?

An agency has nine intensity of distribution alternatives from which to choose. Figure 5 illustrates these alternative intensity of distribution strategies, and suggests possible services that might most appropriately fit into the nine cells.

SELECTING LOCATIONS

After channel and intensity decisions have been made, the agency is confronted with the task of identifying specific site locations through which a service will be delivered.

If the location and size of a facility are not suitable, then no matter how good its subsequent service offerings, management, promotion or pricing strategies, the facility is unlikely to achieve its full potential. Conversely, a well-located facility may be successful in spite of inadequacies in operating management. A good site location requires that two criteria be met. First, it must be accessible to target markets. Second, it should be very visible to target markets.

Access is primarily a function of geographic proximity to potential users. The general conclusion about location and utili-

FIGURE 5: Intensity of distribution alternatives

		SERVICES		
		Intensive	Selective	Exclusive

FACILITIES	Intensive	Street lights
		Storm sewers
		Roads
		Neighborhood
		   playgrounds
			Supervised play at
			   selected neighborhood
			   playgrounds
				Performing arts
				   program in the
				   major city park
				Interpretive na-
				   ture programs

	Selective	Police
		Fire
		Welfare workers
			Community health care
			Parks
			Schools
			Adult education
			   classes
			Libraries
			Community centers
				Blood donor
				   drive
				Public agency day
				   camps

	Exclusive	Garbage collec-
		   tion
		Housing inspectors
		Health inspectors
		College courses
		   via mail or
		   public TV
			Bookmobiles	Hospitals
				Universities
				Judicial courts
				City Hall
				Zoo
				Animal shelter

zation is that use tends to vary directly with distance from the facility. Many studies have illustrated that consumers look upon travel time, transport fare, and so forth, as costs to be paid for obtaining services. Beyond a certain point, consumers are unwilling to pay the cost.

The visibility criterion requires that members of target markets be made aware of a service offering by seeing it. If there is no awareness that a service exists, then obviously it cannot be used. The only ways to learn of the existence of any public service offering are to hear about it, see it, or see a reference to it. Because of the political reluc-tance of elected officials to engage in paid promotional efforts, the major promotional tool which public agencies possess is locating their facilities and services where they are very visible to target markets.

Reasons for Inappropriate Facility Location

Public agencies often have failed to recognize the crucial importance of location. There appear to be at least five reasons why public facilities are located inappropriately.

First, some government and social service agencies have inherited facilities whose locations were selected long ago. These facilities may reflect an orientation toward a target market which has changed considerably since the time the facilities were built. Facilities estabished to serve one socioeconomic group may be serving a very different group of people today. The first group may have left the area and been supplanted by people with different social, racial, or economic characteristics, and hence, different life styles and wants.

Second, donations may be a factor in explaining the distribution of facilities. For example, many cities have acquired over half their parkland from donations. In such cases, the site of a park is dictated by the donor, irrespective of preferred distribution considerations or the desires of the public. In some instances, the source of the donation may have been the federal government. Facilities or services may be offered at a particular location because only that location qualified for a facility under the terms of a particular federal grant program.

Third, local, county, state or federal offices are often centralized in one building or complex because it is administratively convenient for the agencies to be located in close juxtaposition. This expedites bureaucratic procedures, but these offices may not be in the most desirable location from the consumers' perspective.

Fourth, facilities are located in a particular place because a site was available. There are, for example, many areas where parks should be located, and where decision-makers would like to site them, but there is no space available. This problem is particularly acute in central urban areas.

Finally, locations are selected because the land is relatively inexpensive. This is perhaps the most popular criterion currently in use for site selection. This criterion frequently fails to consider the potentially in-

creased benefits of revenues and/or greater utilization accruing to an agency if a facility were located on a more expensive, but more visible and accessible site. Proper site selection entails an analysis not only of cost considerations, but also of revenue and benefit considerations, including accessibility of the location for the target markets it is intended to serve.

Sometimes, public jurisdictions rationalize that they cannot afford to purchase prime locations, because the cost of acquisition is too high, or because the opportunity cost of removing valuable property from the tax roles would adversely affect the jurisdiction's tax base. For these reasons, public facilities are often located at less visible and less accessible sites which are not sought by commercial interests. Decision makers often fail to recognize that a short run decrease in costs may increase long run costs and inhibit the agency from achieving its marketing goals.

SERVICE SCHEDULING

Scheduling is the final operational component to be considered (Figure 1). Scheduling addresses the question "When is the best time to offer a service, for how long, and how often?" There cannot be any generalizable rules, but clearly if a service is not offered at the "right" time, then an exchange is less likely to be consummated. The only firm rule for scheduling is that it should be governed by the needs of target markets. Sometimes, there is a tendency to schedule services at times which are more convenient for the administrators of those services than for target markets.

This is the most flexible of the operational components because it can be adjusted relatively easily. However, it is possible that confusion, loss of support, and loss of goodwill may be incurred by changing well-established schedules. This, together with the expense which may be incurred in communicating changes to target markets, suggests that scheduling changes should be made only after careful deliberation.

CONCLUSION

In this article a systematic approach to formulating public sector distribution decisions has been suggested. Too often, ad hoc decisions are made about locating a facility or delivering a service without the full implications of that decision being recognized. Each element in the distribution system impacts upon the others. The adoption of objectives derived from an audit of the existing distribution pattern, to direct the pattern of facility and service distribution, will facilitate the most appropriate location selections. Periodic evaluations will assess the effectiveness of implementation, given the agreed objectives.

Decisions about the distribution of serv-ices touch the lives of all citizens. A citizen's perception of public officials, or an agency, is often based upon a fairly small number of experiences which have been satisfactory or unsatisfactory. In an era of declining public agency budgets, and accompanying service cuts, the high visibility to citizens of public service delivery systems is likely to make service distribution subject to an increasing amount of critical evaluation.

REFERENCES

Kotler, Philip (1982), *Marketing for Nonprofit Organizations,* 2nd ed. Englewood Cliffs, New Jersey: Prentice-Hall, Inc.

Lovelock, Christopher H., and Charles B. Weinberg (1984), *Marketing For Public and Nonprofit Managers.* New York: John Wiley & Sons.

Lucy, William H., and Kenneth R. Mlandenka (1977), *Equity and Urban Service Distribution.* Washington, D.C.: Department of Housing and Urban Development, National Technical Information Service.

Marketing Communications in Nonbusiness Situations or Why It's So Hard to Sell Brotherhood Like Soap

MICHAEL L. ROTHSCHILD

The use of marketing techniques outside the private sector has increased dramatically in the past few years. Marketing is now utilized by government, education, health and social services, charity and many other types of nonbusiness (public and nonprofit) organizations desiring to communicate a point of view or elicit a particular behavior. One unfortunate similarity in both business and nonbusiness applications of marketing has been a high failure rate due to reasons ranging from poor needs assessment to poor delivery.

Problems more prevalent in nonbusiness cases include the intangibility of nonbusiness products, the nonmonetary price of purchase, the extreme lack of frequency of purchase, the lack of behavioral reinforcers, the need to market to an entire but heterogeneous society/market, and the extreme levels of involvement varying from very low to very high. Because of these factors, the transference of marketing principles from the business to the nonbusiness sector is far more complex than originally had been thought.

The extreme divergence of nonbusiness situations must also be taken into account. One thinks of business as dealing primarily with products and nonbusiness as dealing primarily with services, yet the nonbusiness sector also markets products. One thinks of monetary prices in the private sector and nonmonetary prices in the nonbusiness sectors, yet businesses are very concerned with minimizing time and inconvenience costs for their customers while many nonbusiness organizations charge monetary prices (e.g., the Post Office, universities, charities). This paper deals with emerging tendencies in nonbusiness marketing communications and offers direction to those developing strategy or research. The cases discussed tend to be those which differ from private sector cases; those which are similar to private sector cases can avail themselves of existing work.

By not considering differences associated with nonbusiness products, marketers are neglecting the concept of a systematic situation analysis. This neglect often is coupled with the inexperience of the nonbusiness manager who may think of communications as the essence of marketing. As Weibe (1951) noted, the nonbusiness manager who sees the private sector's use of marketing communications tools asks, "Why can't you sell

Michael L. Rothschild, "Marketing Communications in Nonbusiness Situations or Why It's so Hard to Sell Brotherhood Like Soap," *Journal of Marketing* (Spring 1979), pp. 11-20. Reprinted with permission from *Journal of Marketing*, published by the American Marketing Association.

brotherhood like soap?'' The answer, this paper suggests, is that it is very difficult for marketing communications to have an impact outside the private sector because of the key issues mentioned above. These issues, a framework to present the problems facing nonbusiness marketers, and some options for nonbusiness managers and researchers also are discussed.

COMMUNICATIONS EFFECTIVENESS: ISSUES AND HYPOTHESES

Marketing communications is generally used in conjunction with product, price, and distribution; its potential can be most fully realized when its development follows the other marketing tools. In such a framework, one should consider noncommunications aspects to develop insights into communications issues. There are four major issues which impact on potential communications effectiveness outside of the private sector and lead to several hypotheses:

- Product differences
- Pricing differences
- Involvement differences
- Segmentation differences

Product and Price

Product. The product must first be considered for its benefits so that appropriate behavior can be appropriately reinforced. In nonbusiness situations, traditional communications strategies may be inadequate due to difficulties in communicating a potential benefit to the consumer. Communicators seek out the Unique Selling Proposition to show consumer benefits of appropriate behavior. In the nonprofit area, often only weak personal benefits can be found which do not reinforce or maintain long-term behaviors. In order to establish or maintain a behavior, there must be a positive reinforcer (Rachlin,

1970). In many nonbusiness cases, neither positive nor negative reinforcers are readily perceivable.

Secondly, one must consider the recipients of the product benefits. In the private sector, the purchaser of the product is generally also the consumer or a member of the consuming unit (e.g., the family). In nonbusiness cases, the product often provides little direct measurable benefit to the purchaser. For example, a person who considers purchasing the concept of driving more slowly pays (in time lost) for a product which primarily benefits society (with greater energy reserves). Since the purchaser may not immediately perceive the personal benefit, it must be pointed out more clearly. Many social issue promoters and charities experience this difficulty.

Another product difference between profit and nonprofit markets is that most nonbusiness products, services, or issues are intangible and cannot be shown in advertising. It is considerably more difficult to describe this product to the public/market. Where an object can be shown, it is generally not the product itself, but rather the producer of the product (e.g., an orchestra or university) or some mechanism involved with the product (the potential purchaser of a military experience is shown, for example, a tank).

Finally, one must consider whether there is at least some minimal level of latent demand for the product or issue at hand. In the private sector, a large percentage of new products fail because they do not meet a need or fill a void. Often in nonbusiness cases, there is no latent demand or interest in the product, service, or issue. When there is no voluntarily sought after exchange, it is difficult to elicit behavior.

Price. The underlying theme of price has traditionally been related to monetary issues; price is generally a function of cost and profit or of elasticity of demand constraints. In nonbusiness cases, often there is no monetary cost. Since marketing deals with exchanges of value, one must consider the nonmonetary costs of the product.

One difficulty lies in the diverse nature of nonmonetary costs which include time cost (driving more slowly, joining the military), inconvenience cost (appropriately depositing litter) and psychic cost (the fear of giving blood). Each of these costs may be perceived as greater than monetary costs which dominate the price of consumer products.

The difficulties of nonmonetary pricing also are reflected in the potential perception of the nonmonetary issues as either cost or benefit. For example, the military experience product has attributes of potential danger and separation from family. For some these attributes are seen as costs; for others these are benefits. Monetary costs, in comparison, are rarely perceived as benefits.

While it is generally accepted in the private sector that communications strategies differ as a function of the cost of the product, there are few if any data which report success at overcoming some of the very high nonmonetary prices of nonbusiness products. When nonmonetary (and difficult to measure) prices are combined with intangible (and difficult to measure) product benefits the results may be a staggering communications problem which may not be solvable via traditional strategies. These points lead to the following hypotheses:

H₁: The lower the perceived personal value (positive reinforcement, quid pro quo) to the individual, relative to the cost (monetary and/or nonmonetary), the more difficult the behavior change task, and the lower the likelihood of success of marketing communications.

H₂: The lower the latent or preexisting demand for the object, the more difficult the behavior change task, and the lower the likelihood of success of marketing communications.

Involvement

In the past several years, involvement has emerged as a popular construct which is hypothesized as acting as a mediating variable in learning, information processing, attitude change, and behavior development. While most of the recent involvement work has examined private sector marketing, the major contribution of this construct may lie in its value in nonbusiness situations; here it seems that the range of involvement becomes more extreme in both the very high and very low ranges and therefore information processing, decision making, and communications effects may differ dramatically.

In a recent explication (Houston and Rothschild, 1978), involvement is felt to consist of three component parts:

- Situational Involvement ([SI]: the level of concern generated by an object across a set of individuals at a particular point in time (Hupfer and Gardner, 1971; Rhine and Severence, 1970; Apsler and Sears, 1968).
- Enduring Involvement [EI]: the preexisting relationship between an individual and the object of concern (Sherif, Sherif, and Nebergall, 1965; Sherif and Sherif, 1967; Rhine and Polowniak, 1971).
- Response Involvement [RI]: the complexity of cognitive, affective, and conative development at several points along a sequence of information gathering and decision making activities (Bowen and Chaffee, 1974; Rothschild and Houston, 1977; Park, 1976; Payne, 1976).

SI and EI are felt to interact and impact upon RI so that SI determines the mean level of RI, and EI determines the variance about the mean. Most of the existing involvement research has considered the impact of commu-

FIGURE 1: A hypothetical continuum of response involvement levels

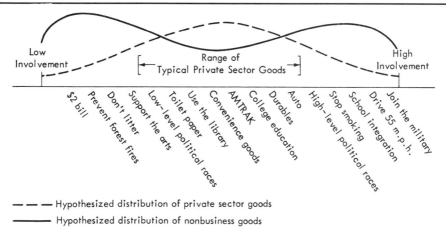

— — — Hypothesized distribution of private sector goods

———— Hypothesized distribution of nonbusiness goods

nications stimuli on response involvement (Krugman, 1965; Ray, et al., 1973; Johnson and Scileppi, 1969).

In Rothschild (1978), two models of affective development are proposed. In the high involvement case, attitude precedes behavior; the main impact of advertising is on the development of awareness and knowledge while additional personal selling is necessary to generate behavior. In the low involvement case, advertising directly affects behavior (at least in the short run) due to the absence of a well-informed attitude structure.

The construct of involvement is a key to understanding the differences, difficulties, and constraints encountered in using marketing communications techniques in the nonbusiness sectors; involvement gives insight into how individuals receive and use information in different situations. These differences need to be considered in developing a communications plan.

The product and price differences discussed above lead to varying levels of SI, and, therefore, ultimately to varying styles of information processing, learning, and decision making. In addition, one's past experience with the issue (EI) will also affect these dependent variables. One can speculate that

levels of RI will be distributed as shown in Figure 1. That is, nonbusiness will, in many cases, generate more extreme levels of involvement than typically found in private sector cases. What has been thought of as high and low involvement in the private sector may only cover the mid-range of possible societal involvement levels. While private sector goods and services seem to be distributed over the middle of the continuum, nonbusiness issues may be slightly bimodal, favoring both extremes.

The marketing issues can be considered from the perspective of intuitively low or high involvement cases. In the low involvement case, the behavior has so little positive value to the individual that any price (in terms of the cost of inconvenience, information processing, or behavior change) will be too high for the value received. Because of the low value placed on any one form of behavior by the individual, only a short-run impact can be made. The change will be at best short-run because there is no reason to integrate the behavior into the belief structure; there is no positive reinforcing stimulus.

This scenario differs from the private sector case in that long-run behavior is established as a result of positive reinforcers. In a stimulus–response sense, one can envision the following:

$$S_1 \to R_1 \to S_2 \to R_2 \ldots n$$

where S_1 = the communications stimulus
R_1 = initial behavior
S_2 = the reinforcer
$R_2 \ldots n$ = repeat behavior

In the typical business sector model, S_1 (advertising) leads to R (purchase) which in turn leads to S_2 (a product or service which is perceived to have a favorable or equitable cost/benefit relationship). S_2 is necessary for long-run behavior; S_1 can only lead to short-run behavior.

In the nonbusiness case, issues of low individual involvement are often brought to the person's attention because there is some value to either society as a whole or some segment of society which is advocating a change in behavior. Often, there is cost to the individual and benefit to a larger group. In such a case, the individual would not consciously choose to be deflected from his/her inertial and apathetic path of least effort. There often is not a sufficiently strong S_2 to maintain behavior.

The issues discussed for low involvement will also hold in high involvement cases. In addition, present behavior may be so strongly related to the individual's central belief structure that most cost/benefit ratios will fall short of giving the individual a reasonable benefit in return for the cost associated with the desired behavior. Past individual behavior will overwhelm a current marketing communications effort.

For the very high involvement case, communications will fail if there is not a perceived benefit of high centrality. There must be a benefit which is both communicable and central to a large segment of the target market. Again, the discussion leads to these hypotheses:

H_3: The greater the involvement level of the object, situation, or issue (due primarily to complexity or price), the more difficult the behavior change task, and the lower the likelihood of success of marketing communications.

H_4: The greater the past involvement level of the individual (due primarily to past experience or the strength of social or cultural values), the more difficult the behavior change task, and the lower the likelihood of success of marketing communications.

Segmentation

Segmentation remains a cornerstone in applying the marketing concept to the practice of private sector marketing. In order to meet needs, one develops products to satisfy one or more distinct market segments and/or communicates the virtues of divergent benefits to divergent segments. Additionally, if a particular segment is felt to be unresponsive or unprofitable, it can be ignored.

In many nonbusiness cases, these options remain feasible and segmentation strategies will be called for, but in many others, all members of society must behave in a certain way and all must purchase the same product. Similarly, if the organization's mandate is to serve all of society, then unappealing segments must also be considered.

Furthermore, there are nonbusiness problems where all members of society must comply for the best interests of society (and themselves). An example occurred when Sweden shifted from driving on the left to driving on the right side of the street. All members of society needed to change behavior simultaneously. Other examples include the decimalization of currency in Great Britain and the metrification of measurement in the United States. All three cases allow segmentation in communications strategies, but do not allow for segmentation in the sense that some members of society can be neglected due to the difficulty in changing behavior.

It has been shown that cumulative response to messages occurs as a function similar to a modified exponential function and approaches an asymptote well below 100% of the potential audience (Kotler, 1971). If nonbusiness communication is charged with gaining a response from all members of society, the cost of raising the asymptotic level of the response function may be quite high. A final hypothesis is offered:

H_5: The greater the level of participation needed within the society, the more difficult the behavior change, and the lower the likelihood of success of marketing communications.

SEVERAL EXEMPLARS

In the absence of a well-developed data set, several historical cases are examined to see the extent to which they fit the hypotheses. Each case should be considered not just for itself, but also as a representative of a class of objects or issues with similar values on the variables discussed above.

Military Enlistment. A review of situational involvement suggests the following difficulties. The product is a complex bundle of intangible attributes which combine as one family of brands in the generic product class of "multiyear experiences." The benefits are intangibles such as personal growth, education, skill training, excitement, adventure, travel, and opportunity to help one's country. The price is also complex, but predominantly is several years of one's life. Additionally, it includes giving up the right to make many independent decisions, changing life style, losing privacy, and the psychic cost related to the uncertainty of such a decision. The complexity of the product and its high cost make it intuitively very high in situational involvement.

Enduring involvement (the sum of past experiences) suggests further difficulties. For most individuals, there will be no prior usage experience from which to draw insights. There also will be limited experience in major issue decision making, since most prospective purchasers are 17- to 21-years of age. Finally, the decision concerning military enlistment has impact from peer, social class, and cultural values. Little prior experience plus great outside pressure suggest high enduring involvement.

On a more positive note, there seems to be a fair level of preexisting or latent demand, since some 400,000 units of product are purchased each year. In addition, the market for this product is highly segmentable; this also helps to ease the task of marketing communications.

Considering the above, response involvement would be extremely high and complex. Marketing theory would suggest here that the potential impact of advertising would be limited and that personal selling would be key to closing sales, as has been the case. The Army has found that advertising aids in attracting walk-in traffic, requests for information, and increasing knowledge, but has little to do with direct impact on behavior. While recruiters are more important than advertising, research has shown that without advertising, the efficiency of recruiters is diminished (Martin, 1978). One should also note that numerous product changes since the inception of the all-volunteer military force have made the product more competitive in its class, thus enabling communications tools to be more effective in discussing potential reinforcers.

55 Mile-per-Hour Speed Limit. The generic issues of fuel consumption and speed of driving have generally had low situational involvement for most people. Even an "energy crisis" and several years of government messages have left many people apathetic regarding a behavior change in these areas. Therefore, the product being marketed can be seen as having little perceived value to many individuals although there is value to society in energy savings and a reduction in fatal accidents. Since most individuals cannot perceive a value, they will consider the costs of time and ego associated with driving at slower speeds.

Enduring involvement is much higher, though, for it is difficult to unlearn a lifetime of behavior, socialization (i.e., large cars with large engines are meant to be driven at high speeds), and values (i.e., time is a scarce commodity to be put to productive use) (Bem, 1970; Rokeach, 1968).

This shows the futility of marketing products with little preexisting or latent demand and no positively reinforcing attributes. There is little that marketing communications, per se, can do in such a case. The burden must fall on developing a more favorable cost/benefit relationship. The marketers of the 55 mile-per-hour speed limit have so far been unable to do this.

The 55-mile-per-hour speed limit case also highlights the difficulty of marketing to an entire society. In addition to the above problems, the behavior of those who comply with the limit is not reinforced when they see the energy conserved at the expense of their time wasted by fellow citizens. It is difficult to accomplish meaningful change when the majority has no incentive to comply.

Anti-Litter. The issue of littering has low situational involvement for most people. Marketing theory would postulate that for low involvement, private sector products, advertising, and promotion could have a strong, short-run impact (Ray, et al., 1973; Rothschild, 1979). This paper makes a similar prediction for low involvement, public sector issues. That is, promotion can elicit short-run behavior with regard to non-business issues as well.

Marketing has been successful in the long run for low involvement, consumer products when the products have a perceived advantage (or at least no disadvantage) for the consumer. In these cases, communications tools can lead to initial behavior and product benefits can lead to repeat behavior. Again, there is little perceived value to the individual in acceding to exhortations to stop littering. Only if one's behavior change led to some reinforcement would one continue with the new behavior. In most cases, an end to one's littering will lead to no perceivable diminution of overall levels of litter and, generally, one's past experiences will have led to such a prior belief. There probably is some latent demand for a clean environment, but without greater societal cooperation, unrewarded efforts will lapse back to old patterns. In isolated, unlittered areas the preserved clean environment does provide a reward.

A cessation of littering behavior offers benefits to society and costs to the individual because it is less convenient than the old behavior. In order for the new behavior to continue (assuming communications can have a short-run impact), there must be a benefit or reinforcement for the individual.

Voting: A Special Case of Short-Run Behavior. This is an area which covers a wide range of involvement with offerings as diverse as presidential races, county clerk races, and referenda. A recent review of voting behavior shows a wide variety of involvement levels and a correspondingly wide range of potential communications impact (Rothschild, 1978).

Over the past 30 years, political science data have consistently shown that political communications have very little impact on voting behavior (Lazarsfeld, Berelson, and

Gaudet, 1948; Campbell, 1966; Campbell, Gurin, and Miller, 1954; Key, 1966; Blumler and McQuail, 1969). In retrospect, one can see that virtually all reported cases have dealt with a race having high situational involvement (generally presidential). This strong pool of data supports the high involvement model.

In the past few years, a new set of studies has shown a significant impact of communication on voting behavior (Palda, 1975; Kline, 1972; Patterson and McClure, 1976; Rothschild and Ray, 1974). These studies have concentrated on lower level, or low situational involvement, races, and the findings are consistent with the low involvement model. Since there are fewer strong beliefs concerning issues in low level races, communications can more easily impact; since there is a strong belief that voting is a desirable behavior, it will take place; since the desired behavior is very short-run (one may vote on election day and then return to apathy), there is no need to develop the types of reinforcement which lead to long-run behavior. Indeed, the mere act of voting is reinforcing; one has been a good citizen, performed one's duty, and met society's expectations.

The impact of both marketing and societal variables in the voting cases can be seen. In all elections, there is a societal pressure to behave. In high level races, there are inputs from more credible news media and peers along with strong enduring involvement based on past voting behavior which outweigh the impact of marketing communications. In low level races, there is less enduring involvement, less interest, less news media, and less peer influence to dissipate the marketing communications influence. In this low involvement case, the above scenario, coupled with no need for long-run behavior, leads to the potential for a strong marketing communications impact.

A summary of the four cases is presented in Table 1.

OPTIONS FOR THE MARKETER

Given a predominance of unfavorable communications situations in the nonbusiness sectors, what options are available to the marketer?

In a study of nonbusiness communications, the point has been made that nonadvertising promotional tools can be very valuable (Mendelsohn, 1973). In the private sector, firms generally rely quite heavily on advertising; in the nonbusiness arena, there is much more likely to be a reliance on public relations, sales force, or other nonadvertising tools since:

- advertising is often frowned upon as an unethical and manipulative tool;
- the organizations often have very limited financial resources to use on communications; and
- when resources are available, they often are controlled by law or charter and cannot be used for advertising.

There are, though, communications tools which circumvent the above constraints and offer the potential of greater credibility and, as a result, more strength as an influencing agent. Mendelsohn (1973) has discussed several of his own studies where nontraditional (to marketing) tools were successfully used. These include:

A television program. "The CBS National Drivers Test" gave drivers a chance to test their knowledge and skills in their home. The program overcame driver indifference to hazards, made them cognizant of their driving problems, and directed them to a mechanism to remedy problems. The program overcame low involvement and generated appropriate behavior (35,000 drivers enrolled in driver education programs as a result).

TABLE 1: Summary of the four cases

Case	Situation involvement	Enduring involvement	Benefits/ reinforcers	Costs	Cost/ benefit	Preexisting demand	Segmentation	Conclusion
Military enlistment	Very complex High cost	Little past experience Cultural values	Personal intangibles	Several years of one's life Personal rights	Very good for some segments	Fairly high	Very specific and limited	Marketing communications can impact
55-mph speed limit	Low Little interest	Central beliefs	Few personal benefits Weak societal benefits	Time Ego/macho	Poor	Virtually none	All drivers	Low likelihood of marketing communications impact
Anti-litter	Low Little interest	Past non-reinforcing experiences	Few personal benefits Moderate societal benefits	Inconvenience	Poor	Low	All members of community	Short-run impact possible Long-run impact difficult
Voting	High to low— depends on race	Central beliefs Pressure to behave	Good citizenship	Time inconvenient Infrequent/ low	Favorable for voting Less favorable for analyzing issues	Moderate	All citizens ≥18 years of age	Short-run impact likely Long-run impact not necessary

A short film. "A Snort History," a cartoon about alcohol and traffic safety, was shown as a short subject in movie theatres. It served to overcome the apathy of low involvement and educate thousands of viewers on a subject of generally low interest.

A television series. "Cancion de la Raza," a soap opera series in Los Angeles, served to provide information to the Chicano community about a number of day-to-day legal and social problems encountered by members of the community. By presenting information in a familiar manner, reach was high and learning took place (although no data were presented to support this reported result).

The three examples are presented to suggest that in nonbusiness areas, marketers need to consider tools which go beyond those traditionally employed in the private sector. In many areas of extreme high and low involvement, the tools to be employed must be even more diverse than those suggested above. For many issues, behavior change or development can only occur as a result of an educational process conducted through the schools or the home. If brotherhood is an issue to be marketed, perhaps it must be done through the schools, the home, or legal channels.

If use of the product has no perceived positive reinforcement associated with it which would make long-run behavior desirable, then the product can be changed so that there is negative reinforcement associated with improper (or lack of) behavior. Bem (1970) discussed this issue in relation to self-perception theory and attitude behavior relationships. He felt that stateways (the law) can change folkways (norms and values). By being forced to behave, people will see that their behavior is not harmful or costly; their attitudes then change to become consistent with their new behavior and long-run behavior results.

Ray et al. (1973) make a similar suggestion in presenting the dissonance-attribution hierarchy of effects model. They posit that a forced initial behavior may be necessary in order to get proper long-run attitudes and behavior in very high involvement cases where there is no individual incentive to behave in a certain way.

Enzensberger (1974) put this legal strategy in proper perspective by suggesting that behavior change acquired through communications is stronger than that which results from any manner of external force. Attribution theory would concur that if the individual could attribute his/her own behavior to an acquiescence to force, it would not be internalized as strongly as if the behavior were attributed to a voluntary judgment. Whenever possible, then, marketing communications would be preferable to legal sanction.

Finally, the role and purpose of marketing communications vis à vis the remainder of the marketing mix should be kept in mind. A very high percentage of business sector products and services fail because they do not meet a need or offer a perceivable benefit to the consumer. This should be kept in mind in nonbusiness cases as well. Communications cannot carry a poor product offering; in too many nonbusiness cases, the offering has little appeal or little benefit to the individual. While this is certainly a *caveat* for marketing in any sector, it is especially noteworthy in the nonbusiness sectors, given the other obstacles to success which exist.

SUMMARY AND CONCLUSIONS

This paper has presented a number of issues which need to be considered in a situation analysis sense before objectives or strategies can be developed in a marketing communications campaign. The tools, techniques, and theories developed in the private sector can be valuable in the public and nonprofit sectors, but their limitations must be recognized.

Before developing a nonbusiness communications campaign, one must consider:

The involvedness of the situation and the relevant segments. Due to the potentially very high and very low levels, traditional promotion tools may be inadequate. Given the current state of the art of marketing communications, one must conclude that what can work reasonably well in private sector consumer goods cases may not work at all for nonbusiness cases. While most consumer goods exist within a broad range of middle level involvement, many nonbusiness issues exist in either very high or very low involvement environments. These environments may call for an enlarged set of communications tools and strategies.

The available positive and negative reinforcers. Since the benefits of nonbusiness issues may be less apparent to the message recipient, it is incumbent upon the sender to consider all possible behavior reinforcers. This especially would be the case where the more apparent benefits are societal rather than individual.

The nonmonetary costs. The costs associated with behavior towards nonbusiness issues may include several nonmonetary costs which raise the cost of behaving beyond the level of the perceived benefit. In such a case, communications tools will be hard pressed to present a convincing case for elicitation of the desired behavior.

The level of latent demand. Many nonbusiness marketing campaigns exist as a result of the efforts of a small group of individuals. When little latent demand exists, then little desired behavior will follow.

The relevant segments. For virtually all issues, there will be at least a small segment of society for whom the issue will have positive value, another segment for whom compliance with the law will be sufficient motivation, and another segment for whom engaging in the socially beneficial act will be sufficient motivation. For many issues, there will remain a large segment for whom a direct personal benefit must be shown if appropriate behavior is to result. This paper has considered issues relating to this last segment. The manager must, of course, consider the trade-offs of using segmentation strategies and whether or not segmentation is a permissible strategy.

The wide range of communications alternatives. Given the limitations of traditional marketing communications tools, one also must consider alternatives such as movies and television programs, or even broader alternatives such as in-school or in-home educational communications. It is generally felt that public service spots are not very effective. Perhaps the money spent on their production could be used more efficiently in one of the nontraditional media suggested above.

As has been noted several times in this paper, nonbusiness marketing problems are generally very different from and often more complex than traditional marketing issues. To improve managers' abilities to deal with these differences, several areas of research which deal with the major issues of the paper should be considered:

- Several researchers are currently considering the measurement of involvement as it pertains to private sector goods. This work should be extended to the nonbusiness arena where potential involvement differences are great.

- The work in behavioral learning theory has had very limited marketing application in both business and nonbusiness areas (Carey, et al., 1976; Deslauriers and Everett, 1977; Everett, Hayward, and Meyers, 1974; Kohlenberg and Philips, 1973; Powers, Osborne, and Anderson, 1973). Research in the use of positive and negative reinforcers, reinforcement schedules, and shaping procedures could be insightful. Given the nature of nonbusiness issues, they may lend themselves to behavioral learning work; transferences could then be made to the private sector.

- Communications alternatives are needed. Testing to be done here could follow established private sector methods used on traditional media.

These areas of research can be further divided into two classes:

- Research to establish the relevant consumer perception with respect to the various dimensions of the model presented above.
- Research to generate and test the effectiveness of various marketing strategies armed at overcoming some of the inherent characteristics which suggest low likelihood of success.

One benefit of examining nonbusiness issues is that the limits of existing private sector techniques are tested. This paper has examined the limits of marketing communications with respect to three variables: (1) extreme levels of involvement, (2) the absence of reinforcers, and (3) the need for highly centralized attributes. By determining limits for existing theories and techniques, the discipline of marketing communications will grow and the potential for strategic success will increase.

REFERENCES

Apsler, R., and D. Sears (1968), "Warning, Personal Involvement and Attitude Change," *Journal of Personality and Social Psychology*, 9 (June), 162–66.

Bem, D. J. (1970), *Beliefs, Attitudes and Human Affairs*. Belmont, CA: Brooks/Cole.

Blumler, J. G., and D. McQuail (1969), *Television and Politics: Its Uses and Influences*. Chicago: University of Chicago Press.

Bowen, L., and S. Chaffee (1974), "Product Involvement and Pertinent Advertising Appeals," *Journalism Quarterly*, 51 (Winter), 613–21.

Campbell, A. (1966), *Elections and the Political Order*. New York: John Wiley and Sons.

———, G. Gurin, and W. E. Miller (1954), *The Voters Decide*. Evanston, IL: Row, Peterson.

Carey, R. J., S. H. Clicque, B. A. Leighton, and F. Milton (1976), "A Test of Positive Reinforcement of Customers," *Journal of Marketing*, 40 (October), 98–100.

Deslauriers, B. C., and P. B. Everett (1977), "The Effects of Intermittent and Continuous Token Reinforcement on Bus Ridership," *Journal of Applied Psychology*, 62 (August), 369–75.

Enzensberger, A. M. (1974), *The Consciousness Industry: On Literature, Politics, and Media*. New York: Seabury.

Everett, P. B., S. C. Hayward, and A. W. Meyers (1974), "The Effects of a Token Reinforcement Procedure on Bus Ridership," *Journal of Applied Behavior Analysis*, 7 (Spring), 1–9.

Houston, M. J., and M. L. Rothschild (1978), "A Paradigm for Research on Consumer Involvement," working paper, 12-77-46. Madison: University of Wisconsin.

Hupfer, N., and D. Gardner (1971), "Differential Involvement with Products and Issues: An Exploratory Study," *Proceedings of the Association for Consumer Research*.

Johnson, H., and J. Scileppi (1969), "Effects of Ego-Involvement Conditions on Attitude Change to High and Low Credibility Communication," *Journal of Personality and Social Psychology*, 13 (September), 31–36.

Key, V. O. (1966), *The Responsible Electorate*. Cambridge, MA: Harvard University Press.

Kline, F. G. (1972), "Mass Media and the General Election Process: Evidence and Speculation," paper presented at the Syracuse University Conference on Mass Media and American Politics, Syracuse, New York.

Kohlenberg, R., and T. Phillips (1973), "Reinforcement and Rate of Litter Depositing,"

Journal of Applied Behavior Analysis, 6 (Fall), 391–96.

Kotler, P. (1971), *Marketing Decision Making: A Model Building Approach.* New York: Holt, Rinehart and Winston.

Krugman, H. (1965), "The Impact of Television Advertising: Learning Without Involvement," *Public Opinion Quarterly,* 29 (Fall), 349–56.

Lazarsfeld, P. F., B. R. Berelson, and H. Gaudet (1948), *The People's Choice.* New York: Columbia University Press.

Martin, A. J. (1978), personal communications.

Mendelsohn, H. (1973), "Some Reasons Why Information Campaigns Can Succeed," *Public Opinion Quarterly,* 37 (Spring), 50–61.

Palda, K. S. (1975), "The Effect of Expenditure on Political Success," *Journal of Law and Economics,* 18 (December), 745–71.

Park, C. (1976), "The Effect of Individual and Situation-Related Factors on Consumer Selection of Judgment Models," *Journal of Marketing Research,* 13 (May), 144–51.

Patterson, T. W., and R. D. McClure (1976), "Television and the Less Interested Voter: The Costs of an Informed Electorate," *The Annals of the American Academy of Political and Social Science,* 425 (May), 88–97.

Payne, J. (1976), "Task Complexity and Contingent Processing in Decision Making: An Information Search and Protocol Analysis," *Organizational Behavior and Human Performance,* 16 (May), 366–87.

Powers, R. B., J. G. Osborne, and E. G. Anderson (1973), "Positive Reinforcement of Litter Removal in the Natural Environment," *Journal of Applied Behavior Analysis,* 6 (Winter), 579–86.

Rachlin, H. (1970), *Introduction to Modern Behaviorism.* San Francisco: W. H. Freeman.

Ray, M. L., A. G. Sawyer, M. L. Rothschild, R. M. Heeler, E. C. Strong, and J. B. Reed (1973), "Marketing Communications and the Hierarchy of Effects," in *New Models for Mass Communications Research, Volume II, Sage Annual Reviews of Communication Research,* P. Clarke, ed. Beverly Hills: Sage.

Rhine, R., and L. Severence (1970), "Ego Involvement, Discrepancy, Source Credibility and Attitude Change," *Journal of Personality and Social Psychology,* 16 (October), 175–90.

———, and W. Polowniak (1971), "Attitude Change, Commitment, and Ego Involvement," *Journal of Personality and Social Psychology,* 19 (February), 247–50.

Rokeach, M. (1968), *Beliefs, Attitudes and Values.* San Francisco: Jossey-Bass.

Rothschild, M. (1978), "Political Advertising: A Neglected Policy Issue in Marketing," *Journal of Marketing Research,* 15 (February), 58–71.

——— (1979), "Advertising Strategies for High and Low Involvement Situations," in *Attitude Research Plays for High Stakes,* J. Maloney, ed. Chicago: American Marketing Association.

———, and M. Houston (1977), "The Consumer Involvement Matrix: Some Preliminary Findings," in *Contemporary Marketing Thought,* B. Greenberg and D. Bellenger, eds. Chicago: American Marketing Association.

———, and M. L. Ray (1974), "Involvement and Political Advertising Effect: An Exploratory Experiment," *Communication Research,* 1 (July), 264–85.

Sherif, M., and C. Sherif (1967), *Attitude, Ego-Involvement and Change.* New York: John Wiley and Sons.

———, ———, and R. Nebergall (1965), *Attitude and Attitude Change.* Philadelphia: Saunders.

Wiebe, G. D. (1951), "Merchandising Commodities and Citizenship on Television," *Public Opinion Quarterly,* 15 (Winter), 679–91.

Special Events in the '80s:
A Case for Marketing Approach

JOAN LOYKOVICH

The 1980s require as many different approaches as possible for cultivating donors and raising funds. How special events can pay off in this decade is discussed as the author explains that the project nature of a special event lends itself to a marketing approach.

Frivolous, leisure-time pursuits were begun to keep the ladies busy, to give their wealthy spouses opportunities to maintain and enlarge their influential business and industrial networks and to make money for favorite local charities—voilà, the special event! They involved lots of time and sometimes didn't make any money or break-even.

Non-profit organizations, however, continue to do special events. They are as much a part of contemporary fund raising as they ever were. During the 1980s they've seen their renaissance and today approach a science as well as an art. The curious stepchild of public relations and development, special events seem destined to be forever with us.

Why are special events such an inescapably integral part of any well-rounded development program, particularly now? How can they be done well—that is, both from an event standpoint and a fund raising standpoint, where can we look for guidance to accomplish them successfully?

Lastly, what part does the invitation play in the life of the special event—what is the invitation and how does it work as the pri-

mary sales tool of the special event, no matter what form the invitation takes?

For purposes of this discussion, a special event is a leisure pursuit involving social participation, occurring within a specific, prescribed time frame[1] and, in non-profit organizations, for the following threefold purpose; *1)* to showcase the organization; *2)* to cultivate, maintain and/or upgrade member (donor) participation; *3)* to make money to support the work of the organization.[2]

Most often—at least in New York—special events take the form of dinners, dances, cocktail receptions or concert performances, or a combination of these formats. Less often they are theatre parties, art exhibit openings, auctions or fashion shows.

The pursuit of leisure implies elements of fun and frivolity. Special events are activities that are to be enjoyed for themselves quite apart from their association with an organi-

[1] Ukman, Lesa. "All the world's a stage for booming events area," *Advertising Age.* April 18, 1983, p. M-31.
[2] Plessner, Gerald M., "A Sound, Well-Rounded Fund Raising Program Includes Special Events," *NSFRE Journal* (Fall 1982), p. 18.

Reprinted with permission from *Fund Raising Management* (January 1985), pp. 26–35.

zation or cause. The social nature of the event is an integral part of its raison d'être for the participants and the sponsoring organization.

The organization wishes to attract donors or members, and participants consider events primary opportunities to build, consolidate or maintain networks of social influence. Well-run events can take from three to 12 months to plan.[3,4]

Events must make the organization look good—hence their public relations component—and particularly in the 1980s, they must attract donors and raise money for the organization—hence their development component.

Until recently, the showcase and cultivational purposes of events were more significant than their fund raising purpose. Organizations produced events more often for their showcase and cultivational values, participants attended because of networking and publicity value, and the professional staff most responsible for their evolution nearly always came from within public relations, not development. Indeed, nearly all the seminal writing in special events was done by public relations professionals, not development experts.[5,6,7]

Because of the public relations history of special events, development professionals have been slow to appreciate their potential fund raising value. The financial return on investment of resources is considerably lower from events than from other forms of fund raising.

For example, an efficient direct mail operation can return dollars for five or six pennies invested, but the efficiently run and profitable special event typically costs 25 to 30 cents for every dollar brought to the organization. Whereas development officers can acquire seven-figure donations by cultivating a few wealthy individuals, corporations or foundations, a much more extensive investment of resources results in much less money from a special event.

MARKETING APPROACH

Why, then, should any non-profit organization be concerned about incorporating special events into their development programs? The answer is simple—they have to. The 1980s require as many different approaches as possible for cultivating donors and raising funds. The really important issue is how special events can pay off for the 1980s.

The field of marketing presents several opportunities for effective strategic planning and is the most dominant and promising approach in the management of development programs today.[8,9] Several aspects of marketing are useful in the strategic planning of special events in particular. The project nature of a special event lends itself to a marketing approach, and events themselves can be viewed as products to be sold.

As noted above, special events combine skills from public relations and development.

[3] Lautman, Kay Partney, and Lynette Teich Caldwell, "Use Precision Planning to Organize Special Dinners." *Fund Raising Management* (August 1982), p. 22.
[4] Watts, William, "The Frank Sinatra Concert for the Benefit of Memorial Sloan-Kettering Cancer Center: A Case Study," unpublished Master's Thesis, New School for Social Research, New York, New York, April 1983, p. 6.
[5] Golden, Hal, and Kitty Hanson, *Special Events* (NY: Oceana Publications, Inc., 1960), Preface [n.p.].
[6] Leibert, Edwin R., and Bernice E. Sheldon, *Handbook of Special Events for Nonprofit Organizations* (NY: Association Press, 1972), p. 16.
[7] Sinoff, Lee, "Special Events: Theory and Practice," in *The Nonprofit Organization Handbook*, Tracy D. Connors, ed. (NY: McGraw-Hill Book Co., 1980), p. 5–90.

[8] Lamb, Charles W., Jr., "Non-Profits Need Development Orientation to Survive," *Fund Raising Management*, Vol. 14, No. 6 (August 1983), p. 26.
[9] Scanlon, Walter, "Non-Business Marketing Becoming Required Strategy," *Fund Raising Management*, Vol. 14, No. 6 (August 1983), p. 42.

It is helpful, therefore, first to examine the relationship between public relations and marketing and then to look at aspects of marketing which lend themselves specifically to a development perspective of special events.

Philip Kotler regards public relations as "primarily a communication tool, whereas marketing also includes need assessment, product development, pricing, and distribution."[10] He cites two other important differences, also.

Whereas public relations seeks to influence attitudes (as in press coverage of an event), marketing seeks to elicit specific behaviors (as in the purchase of variously priced tickets to events). Furthermore, public relations is a support function of the event; marketing sets the goals and defines the customers and benefits to be offered.[11]

Rather than using the traditional campaign approach which focuses on the needs of the organization, a marketing approach focuses on a development strategy which recognizes that "people give their money and time resources with the expectation of providing and/or receiving benefits . . ."[12] This is a much more politically astute and realistic strategy reflecting an exchange of favors between the organization and its customers.

Achieving the proper marketing mix includes three elements: the appropriate product strategy, collection strategy and pricing strategy. In other words, the exchange process of an event involves an attractive benefit exchange, an easily accomplished delivery of money and a price that is convincingly equal to or lower than the benefits received.[13]

PRODUCT MANAGEMENT

As noted above, it is useful to view special events as products to be sold. Within this context. it is also useful to understand the concepts of product life cycle and product portfolio as used in product management.[14]

In the life cycle of a product, one can typically observe four stages: introduction, growth, maturity and decline. To evaluate those events an organization wants to include in its product portfolio, one must assess both the current profitability and the growth potential of each event.[15]

By current profitability is meant the ratio of revenues obtained to resources consumed. By growth potential is meant "the degree to which profitability is expected to grow in successive years."[16]

The growth potential of products at various stages of their life cycle can be described as follows:

1. Cash cows—highly profitable products in the mature stage;
2. Stars—products high in profitability and growth potential that are easy to manage;
3. Question marks—products in the introductory stage, which have star potential;
4. Dogs—former cash cows that have lost their profitability or question marks that never caught on.[17]

APPENDIX A:
THE PRODUCT LIFE CYCLE

In Appendix A, figures 1 and 2 from Gutenberg illustrate these concepts concisely.

[10] Kotler, Philip, *Marketing for Nonprofit Organizations*, 2nd ed. (Englewood Cliffs, NJ: Prentice-Hall, 1982).
[11] Loc. cit.
[12] Lamb, op. cit., p. 26.
[13] Ibid., p. 30.

[14] Gutenberg, Jeffrey S., "Fund Raising Efforts Really Produce Management Strategies," *Fund Raising Management*, Vol. 14, No. 6 (August 1983), p. 22.
[15] Ibid., p. 23.
[16] Loc. cit.
[17] Ibid., p. 24.

APPENDIX A: The product life cycle

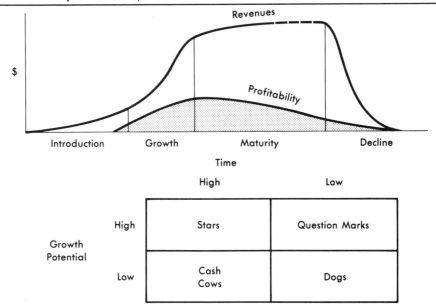

A. Introduction stage
 1. New product/fund raising project
 2. Many "kinks"
 3. Low awareness
 4. Low profitability, etc.

B. Growth stage
 1. Revenues grow rapidly
 2. Refinements are made
 3. Imitations by other organizations
 4. Profitability rises and peaks, etc.

C. Maturity stage
 1. Revenues stabilize
 2. Some imitators drop out
 3. Costs creep upward
 4. Profitability declines, etc.

D. Decline
 1. Fewer customers (donors) respond to marketing efforts
 2. Revenues decline
 3. Revitalization efforts fail, etc.

From a development perspective, the objective of strategic marketing planning in special events is obvious: one wants to acquire highly profitable products with high growth potential. In product life cycle terms, one wants a good supply of cash cows and stars, some question marks and no dogs.

A built-in feature of the product management approach is flexibility in the portfolio evaluation process. The measure of profitability in events for newer and/or younger customers is different from the measure of profitability in events for older and/or wealthier customers.

Hence, informal dances for 450 adults in their twenties or thirties that net the organization $10,000 may be stars, but that same event among adults in their sixties could be considered a dog. The investment of resources may be the same in each case, but the revenues obtained from the older adults should be higher than from the younger adults.

Networking is also different among younger and older customers. Hence, the design of an event is crucial in considering both its profitability and growth potential. Among newer, younger customers, the ability to expand networks of influence is paramount. Among older, wealthier customers, the ability to consolidate and maintain their networks of influence is the determining factor.

Consequently, high-priced dinner-dances or concerts with assigned seating may work well among older, wealthier customers, but newer, younger customers want events allowing high mobility and greater opportunities for networking. Politicians of any kind also prefer high mobility. For these customers, cocktail receptions, buffets and dances with informal seating are usually more successful.

In product life cycle terms a formal dinner-dance may be a cash cow among older, wealthier customers and a dog among younger, more political customers.

Regarding dogs, some anomalies occur regularly in non-profit organizations that don't exist in the private sector. Almost all organizations *must* hold events of some kind on an annual basis.[18] Even if these events are losing propositions financially, they provide the organization with showcase outlets if not cultivational opportunities.

These events are typically boring occasions that no one wants to attend but most people feel obligated to participate in some way. They are dogs that can't be dropped. What to do.

The sound marketing approach is to redesign the event to turn the dog into a star that will attract new customers while holding the regular ones. At the very least, carefully planned changes in the event structure will

turn the dog into a question mark the first year with star possibilities for the second year.

Realistically, then, the carefully managed special events program of the 1980s is one that can recast the traditional elements of case, constituency and leadership into a marketing mix of strategically planned elements of product, collection and pricing to yield a product portfolio of cash cows and stars and dogs that can at least be turned into question marks.

SPECIAL EVENTS LITERATURE

To assist the development professional in strategic marketing planning of special events, Appendix B provides as comprehensive a survey of available related literature as possible.

The literature on special events tends to be appallingly sparse, sketchy, outdated and inaccessible to the learner. Indices and bibliographies are rare, and as explained above, the emphasis in special events has been on their public relations value, not on their fund raising potential.

The practice of special events also integrates skills from various areas: human relations, advertising and promotion, production, graphic arts, organization and management; much important information for the learner is buried in the literature in these areas and must be highlighted even further.

While it is true that the life of a special events professional is primarily an active rather than reflective one, the paucity of literature in the area must be of concern as more and more fund raising programs include special events as a vital source of money. If people can be taught how to give a good party *and* raise money at the same time, the development of fund raising as a

---

[18] Weiner, Harold N., *Making the Most of Special Events,* (NY: Foundation for Public Relations Research and Education, 1977), p. 5.

profession and the development of the fund raising professional will be better served.

Although experts in the area justifiably guard the "secrets" of their trade and safeguard their clients' privacy as closely as possible, more seasoned professionals must be encouraged to publish better organized and more up-to-date information for the 1980s.

THE INVITATION

Within a marketing approach, an invitation is considered an aspect of sales promotion designed to engage the prospective customer in a transaction; a sense of immediacy is explicit.[19]

Regarding a special event, the invitation is most commonly a printed folder/brochure, but it need not be. When planning a cash cow like the six-figure corporate testimonial dinner, the invitation is more effective if in letter form.[20] In the earliest stages of planning an event, this invitation will most probably be preceded by a network of verbal discussions through which invitees will know to watch for the letter.

No matter what form it takes, however, the invitation shows the results of strategic planning. It brings together all the elements of fund raising—case, constituency and leadership—and contains the marketing mix of product, collection and pricing strategies, whether these strategies are simple as in low-budget events or complex as in high-budget events.

As a general rule, folder/brochure invitations should be in the mail six to eight weeks prior to the event.[21] This fact alone has an impact on the timing of planning an event. First, it assumes that all the necessary elements of the event are in place—leadership, benefits to be exchanged, their price to customers, and names and addresses of potential customers.

Second, these elements have been decided at least three weeks prior to mailing to allow sufficient time for the printer to produce a quality product that will showcase the organization and allow the event to "sell itself."

Third, there has been enough time allowed for the leadership to add the all-important and final personal touch of the hand-written personal note to each invitation.[22]

The role of astute leadership is critical in developing a successful invitation. First, the leadership is responsible for all the event elements that go into the invitation. The potential customers are the personal friends, colleagues and supporters, and the leadership knows what will and won't attract attendance and high levels of contribution. The leadership is crucial in weeding out the dogs and in developing the stars.

Moreover, the credibility of the leadership is on the line. The leadership wants an event and an invitation that shows their own growth potential as stars, and what makes them look good varies from constituency to constituency, from market to market.

Astute leaders of non-profit organizations are particularly concerned about the immediacy of impact the invitation will have. The quality of paper stock, appropriateness of typeface, the design, color and coordination of the various components must all be unique and thoroughly professional to attract attention and showcase the organization.

Most astute leaders frown on excessively elaborate, expensive invitations or ones that

[19] Kotler, op. cit., p. 372.
[20] Lautman and Caldwell, op. cit., p. 21.
[21] Sheerin, Mira, *How to Raise Top Dollars from Special Events* (Hartsdale, NY: Public Service Materials Center, 1984), p. 20. (See also Lautman and Caldwell, p.

30, and Leibert and Sheldon, p. 113.)
[22] Lautman and Caldwell, op. cit., p. 21.

require more than one first-class stamp to mail. They will include four colors, die cuts or embossing only if they can find a printer who will give them a lower price. They will want the return package to facilitate the collection of money. They will want only the return address on the back of the mailing envelope. They know that leadership and/or organization names on the front of the envelope are negative cues to wary customers bombarded daily with solicitations.

Astute leaders want their invitation opened, not tossed in the wastebasket. Astute leaders know that their events are ultimately made by the impact of the invitation on their potential customers; they understand that the invitation is probably the most important tool they have for selling a well-planned event.

INNOVATION AND CHANGE

In the increasingly competitive world of contemporary fund raising, it is not easy to write rules for the successful planning and execution of special events because innovation and change are the basic rules that apply.

The field of marketing lends itself to the strategic planning of events. The concepts of product management, profitability and product life cycle must be considered in designing the successful event. A survey of the available literature reveals primarily a public relations orientation to specific organizational details of special events.

The invitation is a good barometer of how well-planned an event is. Astute leadership is crucial to the development of the invitation as the primary sales tool of the event. Astute leaders know how to achieve the proper marketing mix of product, collection and pricing strategies that must be reflected in the invitation, properly timed, if the event is to be successful.

APPENDIX B

Ayer Fund-Raising Dinner Guide, 1st ed. Philadelphia, Pennsylvania: Ayer Press, 1974, 119 pages.

> *Comprehensive guide on necessary printed materials and record-keeping procedures for dinners; explains in detail elements that should be included and/or covered in each area; samples of most forms included; index tabs allow easy access to each section; short on design ideas.*

Berger, Mrs. Miles, "Ten Steps to a Million Dollar Dance," *Grantsmanship Center News,* n.d., pp. 16–22.

> *Case study of "how two volunteers turned Chicago's Crystal Ball into a blueprint for successful direct solicitation"; good reading on successful use of lay leadership in production of event and upgrading of donors; written by one of event co-chairs.*

Droting, Phillip T., *500 Ways for Small Charities to Raise Money.* Hartsdale, New York: Public Service Materials Center, 1979, 177 pages.

> *Community- and volunteer-oriented approach to grassroots organization fund raising; how-to approach designed for beginners; concentrates on designing good event and getting people involved; short on budget and accounting help; includes index.*

Flanagan, Joan, "How the Grass Roots Can Raise Funds in Hard Times," *Fund Raising Management,* Vol. 14, No. 3, May 1983, pp. 28–33.

> *Thirty reminder tips to help community- and volunteer-based organizations overcome fund raising problems peculiar to their organizations in the 1980s; includes imaginative "Never" chart of thirty ways to fail in good use of reverse psychology.*

Flanagan, Joan, *The Grass Roots Fundraising Book.* Chicago: The Swallow Press, Inc., 1977, The Youth Project, 219 pages.

> *Most comprehensive community- and volunteer-oriented guide available; stress on events organized into small-, intermediate- and large-scale projects; nuts-and-bolts approach includes checklists and guidelines for record-keeping; bibliographies and leadership training sources included.*

Fund Raising Handbook: A Guide for Ways and Means Chairmen. New York: The Sperry and Hutchinson Company, 1980, 31 pages.

> *An introductory pamphlet in fund raising for executives and other interested consumers who are beginning lay leaders in the community: designed to offer survey of nine aspects of fund raising: leadership and organization, planning four methods, consultants, publicity and laws.*

Golden, Hal, and Kitty Hanson, *Special Events.* New

York: Oceana Publications, Inc., 1960, 256 pages, out of print.

Early, how-to approach to event design for public relations success; in organizational chart for planning, budget is considered "optional" although stress is given to keeping expenses low and even asking committee to pay for any cost overruns; printed materials discussed but not illustrated; dated.

Gutenberg, Jeffrey S., "Fund Raising Efforts Really Produce Management Strategies," **Fund Raising Management,** Vol. 14, No. 6, August 1983, pp. 22–24.

Short lucid exposition of product management, product portfolio and product life cycle concepts.

Hicks, John, "Hospital Auxiliary Helps with Special Event Aids," **Fund Raising Management,** July–August 1976, pp. 19–23.

In-depth interview with development officer on role of hospital auxiliary in Washington Hospital Center's annual "Race For Life," a horse race in Columbia, Maryland.

Kanner, Bernice, "Guilt Dinners," **New York** magazine, Vol. 16, No. 48, Dec. 5, 1983, pp. 127–141.

Profile of typical testimonial dinner in New York, which produces a six-figure net; strategic tips from top consultants in handling lay leadership and various elements of event design.

Kotler, Philip, **Marketing for Nonprofit Organizations,** 2nd ed. Englewood Cliffs, New Jersey: Prentice-Hall, 1982, 528 pages.

Standard reference work; includes name, topic and subject indices.

Lamb, Charles W., Jr., "Non-Profits Need Development Orientation to Survive," **Fund Raising Management,** Vol. 14, No. 6, August 1983, pp. 26–30.

Comparison of traditional campaign and contemporary development approaches to fund raising.

Lautman, Kay, "Treat VIP Volunteers With Tender Loving Care," **Fund Raising Management,** July–August 1979, pp. 22–25.

Good discussion of relationship of professional staff with lay leadership of event; case statement on strategy for obtaining desired event chair quickly; list of 12 rules for staff to follow in dealing with lay leaders.

Lautman, Kay Partney, and Lynette Teich Caldwell, "Use Precision Planning to Organize Special Dinners," **Fund Raising Management,** August 1982, pp. 20–23.

Short interview with two leading event consultants specializing in testimonial dinners with six-figure nets; do's and don't's checklist included covering 13 different areas of event planning; special "sticky situations" section.

Leibert, Edwin R., and Bernice E. Sheldon, **Handbook**

of Special Events for Nonprofit Organizations. New York: Association Press, 1972, 224 pages.

Early fund raising approach to event design and production; valuable checklists; extensive illustrations of printed materials, record-keeping forms; brainstorming ideas section; dated annotated bibliography; still valuable for inclusion in reference library.

The New York Times

Constant and consistent reporting of significant New York fund raising events, particularly the "Style" section; important information on social and corporate lay leadership (see also The New York Daily News, "Suzy," and The New York Post, "Cindy Adams," and "Around Town With Eugenia Shephard.")

Plessner, Gerald M., **The Encyclopedia of Fund Raising.** Arcadia, California: Fund Raisers, Inc., 3 vols., 1983.

Publication unavailable for review to this writer; advertised as 350 page loose-leaf binder format of "proven practical guidelines" for success in management of charity auctions, golf tournaments, testimonial dinners and luncheons.

Plessner, Gerald M., "A Sound, Well-Rounded Fund Raising Program Includes Special Events," **NSFRE Journal,** Fall 1982, pp. 18–20.

Short discussion of the importance of case and leadership in accomplishing public relations, fund raising and donor cultivation objectives of a special event.

Sainsbury, Jan A., "Put the 'Special' Back in Special Events," **Fund Raising Management,** Vol. 14, No. 3, May 1983, pp. 40–43.

Important reminder to development officers that the content of an event is as important as the design of its structure; example of how to turn a "dog" back into a "star."

Scanlon, Walter, "Non-Business Marketing Becoming Required Strategy," **Fund Raising Management,** Vol. 14, No. 6, August 1983, pp. 42-51.

Discussion of non-business management's adoption of marketing approach as means of survival through increasingly competitive atmosphere affecting non-profit organizations.

Sheerin, Mira, **How to Raise Top Dollars from Special Events.** Hartsdale, New York: Public Service Materials Center, 1984, 123 pages.

Comprehensive, up-to-date guide to producing testimonials, galas, balls, movie premieres, fashion shows, art exhibits, auctions; extensive illustrations of various printed materials and record-keeping forms; combines successful event design with fund raising orientation; basic work with which to begin sound reference library.

Sinoff, Lee, "Special Events: Theory and Practice," in

The Nonprofit Organization Handbook, Tracy D. Connors, ed. New York: McGraw-Hill Book Co., 1980, pp. 5-89 through 5-106.

Short introduction to special event design with extensive checklist covering press relations and event arrangements, especially for outdoor functions.

Skal, David J., ed., and Robert E. Callahon, designer, *Graphic Communications for the Performing Arts.* New York: Theatre Communications Group, Inc:, 1981, 152 pages.

Comprehensive guide to graphic design used successfully for arts organizations; information on institutional design, direct mail, fund raising and institutional promotion transferrable to other types of non-profit organizations; includes section on working with a designer and bibliography of other publications on graphics, plus listing of service organizations.

Special Events Files, Public Relations Society of American Information Center, 845 Third Avenue, New York, New York 10022.

Case studies on specific events; corporately sponsored events with non-profit tie-ins; files are good for brainstorming for ideas on event design; since 1980 have been acquiring more material with fund raising orientation.

Town & Country magazine

Monthly publication of the Hearst Corporation; invaluable information on social leadership in major cities throughout United States; includes corporate leadership involved in charity fund raising; monthly "Chronicle" feature by M. Stannard Doyle is comprehensive national "listing of noteworthy social, cultural, charitable and sporting events."

Ukman, Lesa, "All the world's a stage for booming events area," *Advertising Age,* April 18, 1983, pp. M-29 through M-41 ff.

Lengthy article discussing corporate sponsorship of promotional events in private sector, some of which lends itself to non-profit event design.

Watts, William, *"The Frank Sinatra Concert for the Benefit of Memorial Sloan-Kettering Cancer Center: A Case Study,"* unpublished Master's Thesis, New School for Social Research, New York, New York, April 1983, 30 pages.

Detailed analysis of design and execution of one of New York's largest and most successful annual concert events which raises a seven-figure net annually; detailed information on function of lay leadership; limited bibliography.

Weiner, Harold N. *Making the Most of Special Events.* New York: Foundation for Public Relations Research and Education, 1977, 20 pages.

One of a series of pamphlets in "Managing Your Publications" by the research and education foundation of the Public Relations Society of America; introductory overview emphasizing management approach to event design and production.

Whitcomb, Nike B., "Special Events Integral Part of Fund Raising Plan," *Fund Raising Management,* Vol. 14, No. 1, February 1983, pp. 23–25.

Short discussion of tips for event design to raise money and showcase organization.

Sources of Bibliographic References in the New York Area:

* Public Relations Society of America, 845 Third Avenue, New York, NY 10022—The Society maintains an information center open to staff of member organizations.
* Barnes and Noble Bookstore, Fifth Avenue at 18th Street, New York, NY 10003—Check the sections on management, marketing, and fund raising.
* New York Public Library, Mid-Manhattan Branch, Fifth Avenue at 40th Street, New York, NY 10016—Some periodicals are available, but not all issues in all years published can be found.
* New York University Bobst Library—Some out-of-print materials are available, but you must be a registered student at one of a number of city institutions.

*Special Note: **Places, A Directory of Public Places for Private Events and Private Places for Public Functions*** is available from Tenth House Enterprises, Inc., Caller Box 810 Gracie Station, New York, NY 10028—212/737-7536. This directory is a "guide to environments" for special events and is in its fifth edition (1984–1985); as a basic reference of facilities available for rent, *Places* can be especially helpful in New York City, but it also includes a section of "environments" available elsewhere in the United States (about $21).

How to Package and Market Major Donor Club Benefits

SUSAN W. HAYES

Susan Hayes takes us through a step-by-step account of how WCNY-TV established and marketed their Studio Club and its benefits. She explains the interaction of direct mail and telemarketing.

At WCNY we have found a successful approach to establishing, packaging and marketing the benefits of a major donor club, in our case, the Studio Club.

As we always do when contemplating such a venture, we attempted to arrive at a marketing philosophy. We asked ourselves a series of questions regarding our purpose for establishing such a club, whom it should target and how to evaluate its success. After much discussion, we arrived at our marketing philosophy, consisting of the following:

- An emphasis on the exclusivity of the club
- An effort to capitalize on the television component of what we could offer major donors within the club
- Membership criteria that would permit a growth rate of at least 15 percent per year in club membership. That membership criteria became a minimum annual gift of $300 from an individual or a couple

The next step was to establish a marketing methodology:

- Establishing benefits
- Packaging benefits
- Arriving at an appropriate strategy to market benefits

In terms of establishing benefits, we wanted to differentiate this new category of supporters, to separate them from regular members in ways that would be attractive to them, would be visible and would cost us the least amount of money.

Thus, we arrived at two benefit categories: those that cost us something and—with apologies to Scott Elliot and his love for costing out *everything*—those benefits that didn't cost us anything or at least cost us very little.

ESTABLISHING BENEFITS

An obvious choice for a major benefit was a major donor dinner. But, again, we had to make it *exclusive*, and we had to make it *television*.

Believing it necessary to maintain exclusivity for the long-run viability of the event, and the club, we decided to restrict attendance at the major donor dinner to our Studio Club members. That is, we would not

Reprinted with permission from *Fund Raising Management* (October 1985), pp. 58–65.

sell tickets—ever—and to capitalize on this exclusivity in all our print and promotional material.

We wanted to use the television component of our industry to the hilt, adhering to the strongly held belief—borne out by our experience—that "being TV" was the best thing we had going for us in our market in terms of catching and holding people's attention. Public television stations in general may be regarded as triunes; they are businesses, not-for-profits and media.

Plenty of businesses hold social functions; there seems to be at least one philanthropic dinner event every week at the Hotel Syracuse. During the winter/spring season, the financially well-off in our market eat more hotel dinners per week than they do in their own homes.

We were faced with the problem of establishing a reputation as an annual event that people could enjoy attending. We had to position ourselves against the other longstanding events in the area.

The primary, costly benefit of the Studio Club became this exclusive evening dinner event at *the* luxury hotel in our area. It featured a performance by a noted PBS personality that was taped for a future broadcast over our airwaves.

The final ingredient was an intimate reception for our Studio Club members hosted by a PBS personality. So far, we've been successful in finding PBS personalities who are both well-known enough to pull a crowd and affordable. But, because PBS is less star-studded than most networks, finding the right personality may pose a future obstacle.

We provide an explicit, approved itinerary to our guest speaker well in advance. The guest stays in a lavish suite—donated, of course. We research and work with their preferred foods, drinks and schedules.

Since the Studio Club began, we have successfully hosted Dick Cavett, Mark Russell, Robert MacNeil, Jean Shepherd and Judy Woodruff.

Most important from our standpoint was that the event be perceived as exclusive, and that it be TV. We didn't even care if the cameras were plugged in; the important thing is that they were there.

In preparing for a major donor dinner, we have found no substitute for doing it right: try to achieve that "elegance without opulence" that non-profits have to continually strive for, keep the guest happy and pay close attention to detail.

One such detail is weather. In our first year, we held the event in February—the snowiest season in Syracuse. We decided to hold the event in April the following year in an attempt to increase attendance. On the day of the event, it snowed eight inches, and attendance was lower than we expected. Now, we're back to holding the event in February when people expect snow and are prepared for it.

MAJOR DONOR AWARD

The other costly benefit we incur is a program designed to reinforce the Studio Club membership. It serves as an annual, visible reminder of our major donors' association with us: a major award.

This idea has undergone some changes. At first we issued annual certificates of Studio Club membership. After several years, we concluded that it was impractical. By virtue of their level of community involvement, our Studio Club members generally possessed crates of these kinds of awards—the more prestigious mounted on their office walls but most lining their desk drawers.

We needed a vehicle that reminded the individual of his or her membership in this august body, thereby solidifying that relationship. After the first year, we introduced an item which not only accomplished that purpose, but also reminded the members of the terrific time they had at the dinner event: an autographed copy of the guest's latest book.

This has worked out well so far; every guest we've had has also been a recent author. While our members think we're wasting their money when we print up a rather useless certificate with their name on it, they think it's OK for us to spend twice as much to give them an autographed book.

NO-COST BENEFIT

To flesh out the benefit package, we looked for a body of prerequisites that could be pointed to as benefits and were somewhat attractive as such, but cost us virtually nothing.

We came up with these ''no-cost'' benefits:

- Listing members' names in the program guide
- Inviting members to view—on a first-come, first-served request basis—productions in progress
- Offering to procure transcripts of those programs for which transcripts exist (something we would do anyway)
- Permitting members to purchase high-priced premiums at cost
- Inviting members to WCNY special events, such as the auction volunteer picnic
- Inviting members to serve as auctioneers during the annual television auction.

PACKAGING BENEFITS

Having established the body of Studio Club benefits, we then sought an effective way to package them. Given that the club was relatively small when we started, we looked toward a medium that would enable us to sell the club in a variety of ways. We produced a brochure that could be either mailed or handed out. It was sufficiently generic that it could last for several years at least.

In the brochure, we analyzed Studio Club benefits in a logical fashion, assuming no prior knowledge of public broadcasting.

Part one of the brochure, titled ''Television: The Challenge,'' supplies those powerful yet traditional arguments we all use during membership campaigns: how much television the average American watches and the documented impact of television on adults and children. The conclusion of that section stated that the challenge of television is to ensure that one radio and television station exists with the sole purpose of providing the best quality programming available.

Part two of the brochure, ''Public Television: The Opportunity,'' analyzes benefits by giving the answer to the challenge of television. This section again made the traditional arguments for public television.

Parts three and four of the brochure become a bit more personal by shifting from the impersonal article ''the'' to the personal pronoun ''our.'' Part three became ''PTV: Our Challenge.'' That challenge is to keep public television alive in the face of revenue cuts and rising program prices. Part four became ''Studio Club: Our Opportunity,'' the opportunity to meet that challenge.

The brochure concludes with a call to action by asking the donor to respond to these challenges by becoming a member of Studio Club. The brochures were distributed with a pledge card and return envelope.

With print piece in hand, we had to devise a marketing strategy. We began with a two-pronged approach:

1. We employed our Studio Club Steering Committee to implement a ''friends and

neighbors" approach to solicit those whom we felt and the committee felt should be members—those financially capable and active in the community.

2. In 1983, we began to use our then two-year-old, full-time telemarketing team for new member acquisition for the Studio Club, selling both the club and the event. We have continued with that methodology to the present.

During the month preceding the event, six full-time telemarketers and a telemarketing supervisor call the prospects on a list generated from several sources: patron lists from area arts organizations; a special list of Steering Committee recommendations; and, most importantly, the top three WCNY membership levels.

A mailing prior to the calls provides the setup for the operator. The mail piece informs the recipient of the opportunity to join Studio Club, explains the details of the event and advises the recipient that he or she will also be receiving a phone call.

In the case of existing, upper-level members, who comprised the bulk of those responding to the invitation to join, we used the following pitch: "Are you aware that for only X dollars more per month/year, you, too, can become a member of Studio Club?" This pitch was used in both the letter and the follow-up call.

Key factors in the telemarketing effort are:

• Timing
• Script
• Personal approach
• Coincident public relations effort

The calls had to be sufficiently in advance of the event to allow adequate response time yet sufficiently close to the event to act as a hook and to secure commitments.

The letter and all calls were scripted. Both touted the event, the exclusivity, the benefits of Studio Club membership, and the "only" a few extra dollars per month required for existing, upper-level members to join.

Since we were preaching benefits, and since we were, in large part, preaching to the committed, neither the letter nor the phone call ever referred to need. Follow-up was, as with pledge nights, immediate.

The Studio Club packet goes out first-class the next day. It includes a personal, hand-written note from the operator who had made the call and who had presumably established a first-name personal relationship with the prospect. If the pledge card is not returned within one week, the same operator makes a follow-up call.

The telemarketing campaign and the follow-up proved instrumental in establishing the event's reputation. Since the cost of the event is incorporated in Studio Club membership, a couple who could not attend could send a designated couple in their stead. Often, the designated couple would join the following year.

In many cases, we received calls or notes from contrite "committees" who wanted us to be sure to tell that nice man named "Nick" or lady named "Alma" that they had finally sent their card and check back. The combined effect of the telemarketing effort, reinforced by a simultaneous public relations activity, was an impressive success.

EVALUATIONS

Since our criteria for success was steady annual growth at or around 15 percent, we can look at percentage growth in Studio Club annual memberships as one indicator of success. Studio Club growth was well under that target until we instituted the telemarketing effort.

In fiscal 1982, membership growth was only 6 percent more than 1981. In 1983, the

December 21, 1984

Dear WCNY Member:

We at WCNY are pleased to invite you to join a very important
group of our members. Your current $240.00 annual contribution to
WCNY demonstrates that you already value the programs on Channel 24.
However, are you aware that for an additional contribution of only
$ 60.00 more this year, you can become a member of WCNY's Studio
Club and join us for an exciting evening in February?

Studio Club, composed of those patrons who contribute $300 or
more annually, represents a vital and deeply appreciated source of
WCNY _____. The members of Studio Club derive the satisfaction
that _____, in a tangible way, the very best in
pro_____ ____. In addition, they are invited
to _____ _____.

_____ and humor
of_____
t_____
M_____
_____

> I would like to pledge/renew my membership in
> WCNY's Studio Club for 19____. I/We pledge:
>
> Paid: $ _____ $300
>
> $ _____ herewith and the balance of $ _____
>
> I prefer to charge: ☐ Mastercard   Quarterly
> Card No. _____   ☐ Visa $ _____ to be paid as follows:
>   Semi-Annually
>
> NAME _____
> ADDRESS _____   Exp. Date _____
> CITY _____
> Signed _____   PHONE _____
>
> Make Checks Payable to WCNY Studio Club   ZIP _____
>   Date _____

you__
Public broadca____
support. Won't you jo___
their endorsement of WCNY's exce___
becoming a member of Studio Club? We wou__
with us for a very special evening in February.

Sincerely,

Thomas E. Fanella

Thomas E. Fanella
Vice President for Marketing

TEF/sls

Enc.

*Letter mailed to major donors reminds them of the amount of last year's
contribution and asks them to increase their contribution this year to $300 in
order to qualify for Studio Club membership.*

year telemarketing began, it soared to 75 percent. After that initial surge, we have maintained an annual growth rate of about 38 percent. Since Studio Club began in 1981, membership growth has increased 168 percent and revenue has increased 254 percent.

Overall, the renewal rate for Studio Club is 87 percent, with 84 percent renewal rate for 1984–1985.

A second way to evaluate progress is to factor out the cost of the dinner and awards from the revenue garnered from the club annually, and arrive at a cost-benefit ratio that should show a steady decrease over time. With a slight aberration, that is what has occurred.

In terms of other, more subjective measures, we believe we have a number of ideas in place:

1. We have an event that is affordable, sellable, elegant, profitable, and at this point, on auto-pilot. We know how to execute

Cost-benefit ratio
1981—$1/$4.09
1982—$1/$3.05
1983—$1/$5.10
1984—$1/$4.30
1985—$1/$6.30

the event. Unlike earlier years, it is now relatively unimportant who the guest is. The event has a positive local reputation.

2. We have steady growth among two groups of clientele: the traditional community leaders, financially well-off and predictable members of Studio Club, and a group of individuals who are not community leaders yet began as upper-level or middle-level supporters of the station and were upgraded into Studio Club via the telemarketing effort. After attending their first event, they will most likely continue on as members.

The ABCs of Implementing Library Marketing

ANDREA C. DRAGON • TONY LEISNER

In his excellent review of the literature of marketing for libraries and information services, O. Gene Norman[1] quotes from Ralph M. Gaedeke, "no longer is the issue whether marketing concepts and techniques can be transferred to more effectively manage products and services of nonprofit organizations but, rather, the extent, nature, and effective-

Andrea C. Dragon and Tony Leisner, "The ABCs of Implementing Library Marketing," *Journal of Library Administration*, Vol. 4, No. 4 (Winter 1983), pp. 33–48. © 1984 by The Haworth Press, Inc., 75 Griswold St., Binghamton, NY 13904.

ness of such transfer.''[2] Indeed, the missionary zeal with which articles on marketing are written[3] is indicative of a wide-spread grassroots movement within the profession. This interest in marketing is not the result of a mandate from the leaders of the professional associations nor is it due to any governmental action. This "bottom-up" interest in marketing has grown out of librarians desire to find a more appropriate model for relating their professional activities to their community's needs.

The fact that the library profession has begun to take a keen interest in learning about marketing does not mean that it is universally accepted as an appropriate model for the conduct of library business. Barbara Conroy[4] has written that she believes much of the reluctance to practice marketing in a public service setting is due to a misunderstanding of marketing and its relationship to public service programming. Conroy believes that once librarians understand that marketing and library programs are really quite similar, the hesitancy will diminish.

Another writer voicing criticism of the marketing model is John Dessauer.[5] He states that his misgivings about library marketing stem from his firm belief that libraries are "depositories of civilization" and if a library builds a collection based upon user statistics, then it is not fulfilling its true mission.

John Berry[6] also questions the basic premise of whether libraries need to market themselves. Instead, he argues for libraries to continue to treat information as a "free" resource which should not be subjected to the laws of the marketplace.

Both Dessauer and Berry miss the mark in their attempt to dissuade librarians from adopting marketing. Their arguments fail because they are oversentimentalized. Dessauer speaks of "an amateur scholar devouring volumes on ancient Egypt . . . a reader encountering Plato for the first time . . . the armchair mountain-climber, the sedentary sailor, the supine warrior.''[7] Somehow, Dessauer is unable to connect these idyllic figures with the reality of the librarian who has determined the needs of the market and carefully selected material to satisfy those needs. The patrons using Dessauer's romanticized library are doing so because they have needs or problems that have been recognized by the library staff who then developed a product mix to satisfy those needs.

Understanding patron needs and designing products and services to meet those needs *is* marketing. The librarian who selects books about ancient Egypt for the armchair archeologist is engaging in a marketing activity.

Dessauer questions a library buying materials readily found in bookstores and on newsstands. He would prefer that libraries serve those patrons whose needs cannot easily be met through these channels.

Critics of marketing would have us believe that offering patrons Louis L'Amour is "marketing" but offering them Plato and Voltaire is "professional collection development."

Although much of what Dessauer says is emotionally appealing, he forgets that for too long libraries have attempted to satisfy market segments whose needs closely parallel their own. While this type of marketing can be successful in communities where there are large segments of the population demographically similar to librarians, in other communities the social and demographic characteristics of the market require a different response from the local library.

While some libraries may believe their mission is to continue the tradition of "cultural uplift" associated with 19th century library associations, many other libraries believe their mission is to be responsive to the public needs even if those needs are not for the kind of information and reading material librarians think is appropriate.

Despite the growing interest in and awareness of marketing, we believe that some librarians might continue to be less than enthusiastic about the implementation of marketing even if they were provided a thorough explanation of marketing essentials. They might be so inclined for very good reasons. The ideal of professional librarianship emphasizes the triple role of the librarian as an interpreter of information needs, as a communicator of knowledge about information resources and as a designer of information access systems. These roles are congruent with those described in a recent article on motivation and organizational design by John B. Miner and Norman R. Smith.[8] The authors outline five roles professionals assume in organizations and describe the motivational basis of each. The five roles are:

1. Acquiring further knowledge
2. Abiding by professional behavior standards
3. Accepting status
4. Providing assistance
5. Taking independent action

The authors state:

> In a professional system, the professional is expected to assist the client in achieving desired goals or, in some instances, to do that which is specified by the profession as being in the client's best interest, even if not consciously desired; to function effectively, a professional must want to help others.[9]

In other words, the professional must put his/her interests behind those of the client and society.

Because librarians have become so involved in the process of acquiring professional status by obtaining credentials, i.e.,

the M.L.S., most librarians use the term "professional" as a noun to describe someone who has obtained the M.L.S. and who has achieved a certain "rank" within the library organization enabling the individual to work somewhat independently and without close supervision.

The roles professionals aspire to and the motivational bases for them as described by Miner and Smith may conflict with a marketing orientation as defined by Philip Kotler:

> A marketing orientation holds that the main task of the organization is to determine the needs and wants of target markets and to satisfy them through the design, communication, pricing, and delivery of appropriate and competitively viable products and services.[10]

If the term "professional" is used as an adjective it is almost always used to describe those tasks falling under the purview of the "professional librarian." For example, original cataloging is a "professional" activity but filing is not. Professional librarians, those who possess the M.L.S., carefully guard their rank and its privileges and often refuse to do "non-professional" tasks or allow "non-professionals" to work on professional ones.

Given this almost military concern with degrees, rank and credentials, it is no wonder that many librarians express confusion or perhaps even hostility when faced with the possibility of diminishing their status.

Contrasting with this marketing orientation is a professional (used as a librarian would use the term) orientation which holds that the major task of the organization is to develop programs and products which it believes are satisfying to the public and do not conflict with the professional role to which librarians aspire. In an organization dominated by such an orientation those products and services which enhance the professional's self-esteem will be preferred over those which do not. Any library manager contemplating implementing marketing must be prepared to debate with staff members who perceive marketing as a threat to their personal status. These staff members will question the necessity of acknowledging the primacy of the marketplace in shaping the library's plans, objectives, organizational design and day-to-day operations. To many librarians the term ''professional'' does not describe a way of behaving toward clients, but rather it connotes images of independence, self-direction, freedom from supervising controls and acknowledgement from non-professional library workers of acquired status. The history of librarianship in America is a struggle to provide this sort of professional status for graduates of library schools. It is no wonder then that some librarians question the value of marketing which they perceive as perhaps reducing their status to that of a bookstore clerk. For while professionals generally perceive no conflict between their professionalism and promoting library products or encouraging library use, they hesitate to relinquish their role as arbiter in determining what those products will be and how access to them shall be gained. But, unless staff members recognize the importance of *designing the organization* to serve not the needs of the librarians but to serve the needs of chosen markets, the library is not engaging in marketing even though it may be actively promoting library use.

RESPONDING TO THE MARKET

Kotler maintains that organizations fail to be responsive, i.e., make every effort to sense, serve, and satisfy the needs and wants of their clients and publics within the constraints of budgets, for three reasons. The first reason offered by Kotler is that organizations may lack the resources or the power to hire, train, motivate and monitor the performance of employees. The second reason is that customer satisfaction may not be important to the members of the organization and its management. The third reason offered is that the organization may be deliberately acting in such a way as to discourage use by the public.

The conditions underlying Kotler's three reasons for unresponsiveness are found in varying degrees in all libraries. But, it is not possible to change libraries from their current varying states of unresponsiveness to being marketing-oriented, responsive organizations merely by educating management personnel in marketing fundamentals. Implementation of a marketing plan requires a commitment from every member of the library staff. If staff members are continually forced to choose between achieving professional and marketing objectives, they probably will choose the objectives whose accomplishment will lead to the greater personal rewards. Sitting passively at the reference desk waiting for someone to ask a question is very appealing to many librarians. Once a question is asked, they are comfortable only in seeking the appropriate information. But, if the management were to insist that reference librarians move away from the desk and initiate reference transactions with patrons, many staff members would find such behavior uncomfortable. It is not that management lacks the resources to hire, train, motivate and monitor the performance of employees that causes library failure to achieve a true marketing orientation. Rather, it is because library managers themselves are professionals who seek to hire and reward like-minded individuals. If library managers desire to change the behavior of their staff members, they must first change the way they reward staff behavior. If a library manager primarily uses technical competence as criteria for distributing organizational rewards, then staff members will strive to become competent, efficient, consistent and accurate. On the other hand, if managers begin to also recognize and reward those individuals who are willing to develop organizational systems that are accurate and responsive, consistent and compassionate, efficient and sensitive, then librarians might be more inclined to behave in a market-oriented manner toward patrons. At the present time, most library operational systems are designed to meet the library's needs. New systems and individual capacities combining librarians' needs and public needs will have to be created before the library will become truly responsive.

In order to assist library managers in implementing marketing in their libraries, we suggest that directors keep in mind what we call the "ABCs of implementing marketing." These are:

— Achieving a Position
— Balancing Demands with Resources
— Compensating Performance

ACHIEVING A POSITION

The principle underlying positioning is the identification of the major attributes used by the target market to evaluate potential and choose among competitors. It is a process of understanding the needs of various target markets and of communicating to the targets the advantages of library use when compared to the alternatives for satisfying informational or recreational needs. Positioning is not just advertising or promotion, although advertising is often used to communicate a library's position, rather it refers to the per-

ception of the library's placement within the array of competitors for the patron's and funding sources support.

One barrier to achieving any particular position is staff resistance. Someone hired to be a general reference librarian may balk at the prospect of becoming a readers' advisor should the library decide to assume a strong position in the family entertainment market. Someone with a background and expertise in the arts and humanities may resist efforts to reposition the library as a community information and referral center. Someone who has enjoyed cataloging science and technology may not approve of the library's decision to reduce emphasis in science and take a strong position in the business and economics information market. As regional and multitype library networks become more common, it is conceivable that public libraries will be making positioning decisions. The library that tries to be all things to all people will become less common as libraries begin to respond to the needs of their community by developing unique marketing positions tailored to the demographic characteristics and the unmet needs of the community. Achieving a position might make good marketing sense, but to some professionals working in the library, it is an objective that conflicts with what they understand about the library's mission and about their role as librarians.

Unlike businesses, libraries cannot easily terminate those who disagree with management's objectives. A manager who understands the necessity for a marketing orientation needs to be patient and understanding with staff members who remain unconvinced. Disagreements will be frequent and sometimes uncomfortable for all concerned. Achieving a position can be an exciting, satisfying and ego-boosting goal for the entire staff if it is presented as a method of responding to the community.

BALANCING DEMANDS WITH RESOURCES

The goal of any marketing effort is to change the behavior of the target market. In library marketing the change sought is usually increased use by the selected targets. In marketing-oriented libraries, more use is better than less. For the most part, the patron manifests satisfaction with the library by repeat use.

It is possible that successful marketing may increase utilization to the point where staff may become overwhelmed. The library traditionally placed limits or controls on market demand by enforcing silence rules, closing stacks, restricting hours, and fining. In addition to these methods, the library staff controlled demand through a system of subtle, and sometimes not so subtle, behaviors designed to communicate to the market that there were definite limits to how far the staff was willing to go to accommodate the patron. In profit making organizations, price acts as an effective control on demand, but in non-profit organizations, especially non-revenue organizations, demand cannot be controlled by price. Given the inability of libraries to quickly respond to increased demand by adding staff, staff behavior, policies and rules have been the only means available to the library to limit demand.

Library architecture and staff demeanor have changed in recent decades to create a library environment which is less imposing, less restrictive, and more accessible. Libraries have advocated the concept of free and unlimited service. The consequences of these changes include vagrants sleeping in urban public libraries, sexual deviants molesting patrons in the stacks, and teenagers

monopolizing surburban reference rooms weekday evenings. It has been difficult for libraries to have an "open door" policy promising free and easy access and yet place restrictions on use by some segments.

In order to balance demands with available resources, libraries have instituted circulation restrictions, limited the number of reference questions per telephone inquiry and placed limits on "free" on-line searching. Other controls on library use include full-time security patrols and restricting teenage use.

Even with these balancing mechanisms, many librarians find that they are sometimes subjected to unreasonable service requests. Because the public in general is unsure to what level of service it is entitled, it is not uncommon for some members of the community to insist on service above and beyond that which the library feels is adequate. For these patrons, a policy promising free and unlimited services gives them the right to treat librarians as servants. Without the ability to demand money in exchange for service, the librarian must respond to the demand or establish rules (written or unwritten) governing the delivery of service.

Some librarians are fearful that increased marketing activity will have the desired effect of increasing library use, but increased use might also bring with it the potential for abuse. A librarian on the 6 to 10 P.M. shift with a library full of rowdy teenagers has good reason to be apprehensive about making the library more accessible and perhaps more vulnerable to certain market segments. Unless demand can be balanced with resources, the library's staff may become deluged with special requests and demands and be unable and/or unwilling to meet them.

There are several strategies available to libraries which help balance scarce resources with demands. The library will probably wish to avoid instituting rules and policies which will affect all segments and therefore might adversely impact the selected targets. Instead, a multi-branch library might consider branch specialization, i.e., The Children's Library, The Business and Economics Library, The General Literature Library, The Reference Library, etc.

Libraries unable to implement branch specialization may wish to prepare and publish service policies so that both librarian and patron will have a clearer understanding of the library's service limitations. This strategy has the advantage of being inexpensive yet it makes public the range of services patrons are entitled to receive given the library's limited resources. It seems important that there be a uniform service policy within a library. Each staff member ought to know what range of services will be offered and agree with the extent to which those services will be delivered to individual patrons.

COMPENSATING PERFORMANCE

One way to motivate librarians to substitute marketing objectives for technical ones is to reward them when they perform appropriately. Obviously, in some areas technical expertise is vital, but technical competencies ought to become less important to a marketing-oriented organization as an individual moves up in the administrative hierarchy. At some point the technical appropriateness of a serials entry ought to become less important than its ability to provide an access point for the patron.

Libraries have traditionally rewarded their staffs according to various professional criteria. Only rarely do these criteria include marketing-oriented behavior. Most of the time professionals are rated on subjective evaluations or attitudinal or personality traits.[11] If librarians include performance measures as part of their appraisal and compensation systems, they are usually no more than listings of routine tasks whose completion is perceived to be an objective. Most technical service librarians are able to produce a list of professionally satisfying objectives. But librarians should be encouraged to produce a list of objectives indicating a recognition of the importance of the market if a marketing plan is to become more than an academic exercise. Staff members should be rewarded if the objectives are accomplished.

Many library managers believe that bureaucratic rigidities, nonconfidential payroll records, union contracts and civil service protections prevent the implementation of performance-based monetary reward systems. Unable to manipulate the monetary reward system, library managers reward performance by promotion into newly-created job classifications or creating changes in the organizational chart enabling highly performing staff members to enjoy a more favorable working climate.

The pitfall in using these kinds of administrative rewards is that because they lie outside the formal reward structure, the reasons for granting the reward to an individual may never be fully articulated. Unless the person receiving the promotion or title change understands the relationship between his or her performance and administrative outcomes, these kinds of non-monetary rewards may not provide a continuing source of motivation to engage in appropriate behavior. Performance that is seldom rewarded will become increasingly less important to most workers. But, if the link between performance and rewards is made clear to the staff and reinforced by management's actions, then staff performance ought to improve in the areas rewarded. Employees believing that rewards are distributed according to a system unrelated to performance will have a low expectation that their efforts and abilities will result in being rewarded and therefore have diminished interest in improving performance.

Because the traditional role of a professional librarian may be perceived as being in conflict with that of a marketing-oriented librarian, it is crucial to the success of a marketing plan to ensure compliance with marketing objectives. Excellent target market research, excellent audience-oriented program planning, excellent product design will all be costly, fruitless, wasted activities if the library staff cannot be convinced to behave toward the public in a manner consistent with a marketing orientation. Unless library managers inform librarians of behavior requirements they will substitute a variety of role models, many of which are not appropriate to a marketing-oriented library. Of course, managers could select only those who share the belief in the value of marketing. But, because only technical/professional competencies and not marketing ones are taught in most library schools, a library manager needs to recognize that he or she has the responsibility for training staff so that they will be able to engage in the appropriate behaviors. Finally, although selection and training are important determinants of performance, the most powerful performance determinant is the availability of rewards. By compensating those who behave in a marketing-oriented way, the library manager instructs the entire staff in appropriate behavior.

It is a great deal easier to write about marketing than to implement it in libraries. Despite the obvious advantages of a marketing orientation over a professional/product orientation, some librarians, in all likelihood, are apt to experience a role conflict between what they believe is appropriate professional conduct and the behavior requirements of a marketing-oriented organization. Rather than dismiss this role conflict as caused by some perversity in the librarian's personality, we have suggested that library administrators (some may even experience the role conflict themselves) implement library marketing by: achieving a position through a program of assisting the staff in learning about marketing and the need for positioning; balancing demand with available resources by developing service policies; compensating performance by rewarding marketing-oriented behavior.

CASE STUDIES

The following case studies are examples of public libraries which have been able to plan and implement successful marketing programs. These cases are supplied to demonstrate that the implementation of (A)—Achieving a position can be accomplished by vastly different methods in response to (B)—A need to balance demands with resources when demand is growing and resources are shrinking and that the answer need not be to reduce service; and (C)—That faced with probable cutbacks an inspired staff can help to not only avoid cutbacks, but obtain raises as a result of their enthusiasm for a bold move.

Janesville Public Library

Janesville, Wisconsin, is a city that prides itself on government efficiency and at the end of 1981 was dealing with the annual budgets for city services. The city transit system got its budget cut by $150,000, the city landfill cut back by $80,000, and the garbage collection budget took a $30,000 beating. Building inspections were cut back in their hours, saving $18,000, and even street sweeping was carved up.

In this budget slashing environment the Janesville Public Library budget was *increased* by 17.1%. One week later an agreement was reached finalizing a contract that made library director Dan Bradbury a dual administrator. His time would now be split between library functions and the duties of Director of Leisure Services which included recreational programs, golf courses, the senior citizens center, ball fields, the ice arena and swimming pool complex. Also included were the city's other cultural activities and some planning for a potential cultural center.

Discussions leading up to the contract had been going on since early June of 1981 with numerous city officials including the city manager, director of personnel and the city attorney. The agreed upon objective for both the city and Mr. Bradbury was to unify the city's informational, recreational and cultural services under one umbrella.

From a memo from Mr. Bradbury to the Board: "For the City, the new structure would unify the strategic planning and budgeting for facilities and services which currently are dispersed among three different city divisions or departments. For the library, the new structure would firmly identify the library as an integral component in the full range of municipal services while maintaining its autonomy of operation. In the long run the closer relationship with the city should facilitate the achievement of many of our library objectives—increased co-operation and coordination with Recreation Department Programming, improved communication and cooperation with all city departments, development of municipal reference and other services and participation in planning an eventual civic/cultural center complex."

One of the realities in government at almost any level today is that a tough general economic situation has had a severe impact on social services. At the same time that unemployment is rising, revenues are falling, government outflow increases and so-called "free" services have more customers. Each of the social services has its own axe to grind and wants to protect its own vested interests and it is unlikely that a director of a department will volunteer to take a cut. This is particularly true when demand for the services is increasing. In the face of a 15–20% unemployment rate in Janesville, due in large part to its major employer being General Motors, it would be difficult for all public services to survive equally intact. Still the library got a 17.1% increase.

While no formal marketing plan existed at the Janesville Public Library, a case could well be made that some basic marketing strategy was employed. In this declining economic setting the cultural, recreational and leisure activities providers have become competitors for limited resources no different than Coke, Pepsi and R.C. compete in the soft drink market. Just as no grocery store would remove Coke from the shelves in favor of Pepsi because of the public that wants Coke, neither will a city cut out a program with a voting block constituency that wants that service. The problem for the city government is how to measure the various services and the values placed on them by the public. Then funds must be allocated based on that assumption of value.

Janesville Public Library had already indicated its desire to reduce costs among agencies by offering to coordinate acquisitions, cataloging and processing of library materials for five other public libraries in the county and a dozen school media centers, resulting in substantial savings to all agencies. Janesville Public Library also had begun a volunteer program which had contributed over 6500 hours of time to the library and had a 450 member Friends of the J.P.L.

group. The Friends had raised over $17,000 for equipment purchases in about two years. In 1980 a foundation was established for the purpose of soliciting and administering grants, gifts and endowments to benefit library programs in Janesville and it has raised nearly $50,000.

The public library was clearly positioned as the low cost, efficient provider of services to a large portion of leisure activities users. Positioning is a very important component of marketing and economic conditions and city council mood indicated that being an efficient provider of services was highly desirable. By responding to changing conditions in the leisure activities market, a portion of which the library served, Mr. Bradbury could present a solid case for the library becoming a co-ordinator of leisure activities and not just another competitor for funds.

Strategically this new arrangement provided both the city and the library with some satisfaction. The city could toot its horn because it was encouraging more cost efficiency and interdepartmental cooperation, and doing so with high visibility services. The library in turn would gain a larger constituency, broader program base and be a greater power to be contended with at city meetings. The citizens would be exposed to less duplication of services such as film programs or bicycle programs being run simultaneously by two departments. The enlarged role of the library would expose many non-users to library service options.

For 1983 the city budget increased overall only 4% above 1982. The library's budget increased by 12% over the 1982 budget amount and Mr. Bradbury's contract to act in the dual capacity was renewed for 1983.

This may not be an appropriate plan for every occasion but it points out that, if the organization is to survive and continue to offer service, then the needs of the public (funders) must be put above personal wishes. Institutions must be adaptive to changing conditions and improve the linkages between themselves and governing bodies. What the future will bring for J.P.L. is now somewhat predictable and as director Bradbury says about the arrangement, "so far, so good."

Lake Villa Public Library District

Lake Villa is a small country town in a resort area of Northern Illinois. Its public library, like many in the area, had started as a reading club with a dedicated group of volunteers making it work. In the late sixties the library was housed in a rented tavern with the periodical backfile in the bathroom. The floors creaked under the load of the collection and the patrons who crowded their way through the narrow aisles to search for books. Only one small table was available for patrons and there were no public restrooms. Clearly there was a need for a new library facility but no plans had been made and since the library was a township unit it would have required approval of the town board for any plans for a new building program.

The library had been trying to save a little money each year out of its operating budget in hopes of being able to some day build a new headquarters. So far there was $20,000, which was far short of the needed $1 million to build an adequate structure. The situation facing Lake Villa in 1968 wasn't much different than the problems that faced thousands of small libraries. Yet, there was a solution.

In 1968 a new board member was elected who brought with him a strong background in marketing. A year later the beginnings of a plan were in place. It called for abandoning the attempt to save money for a building and spending it instead on services. The underlying philosophy was to identify the services most wanted by the community and then go all out to provide them. By increasing circulation and service levels a by-product would be greater crowding problems and awareness of the problem by more library users.

A fortunate change in Illinois Law took place around this time which said a township library could hold a referendum to convert to a district which would give the library autonomous taxing authority, within limits. The Lake Villa Library held the referendum and the issue passed overwhelmingly.

Following the referendum a survey was taken to find out a little more about the library's patrons. Where did they come from: work or home? Were they combining the library with another stop? How far did they come? Did they find what they wanted? What hours should the library be open? The location of the library was not near any major shopping and only the post office was in the same block. It was important to assess the habits of patrons in order to learn what strings to tug when the bigger question came later.

It was learned that an investor was interested in putting in a shopping center on some land he owned on the major traffic artery in the township. The investor was approached on behalf of a mayor in the library's service area to feel out a land donation for a potential library site. Discussions followed and when the land owner saw the library's survey results showing that the overwhelming majority of library patrons would go to the library no matter where it was he quickly realized it would be a great drawing card for his shopping center if it was located on his land. He offered to give the library five acres on the main highway if the library board would build a new building on the site.

Before the board accepted this gift it called all the elected officials and asked them to appoint people to serve on a site advisory committee to investigate possible new sites for a building. This committee represented all the political and social interests in the community. The library board president charged them with making a site recommendation and then going back to their respective constituencies and supporting a referendum to fund a bond issue for a new library to be built on the selected site. They agreed and voted to recommend the site being donated by the developer.

The status of the library service in Lake Villa was greatly improved by this point with a 100% increase in funds spent on materials (no savings account for a new building), a 50% increase in open hours, a staff that sensed a change and was very enthusiastic and a community with 73% of its residents holding current library cards. On Saturdays people could barely move inside the old rented tavern.

An architect was retained and renderings were submitted. The board wanted a meeting room, lounging areas, high energy efficiency incorporating passive solar heating, a large children's area and a design so minimal staffing could operate the library. A triangular building with insulation on the exterior was proposed that when combined with a sun wall on the south would be very cheap to heat.

The site selection committee supported it to their communities, the staff talked up its energy innovation to patrons, the papers did stories, and the library did a newsletter mailing to the whole township.

The big question was popped and little Lake Villa township's library patrons said YES to a one million dollar building and a 60% increase in the library budget. The vote was two to one for the library. The plan took six years to accomplish and took library service from part-time and inadequate for community needs to a library facility and service level as good as any town its size in the country. This was a marketing plan that: identified the need, determined who could positively influence a solution and how to persuade them to do so, who could lend financial help and how to diffuse possible problems with political enemies.

Several key points are worth covering in this example of marketing in a public library setting.

The size of the project and the apparent resources of the community are not the principle concerns. Cold logic can be overcome by emotion and ground swell and even a little rural town can marshall the resources to provide good library service funding if they are presented with a proper plan. The combination of a small tavern with library staff obviously struggling with deplorable conditions and a willing land donor helped to bring the project to fruition. But careful work with all the political and special interests was very critical to success. Spending money wisely on the materials that were most asked for helped insure support from satisifed users and clarified the issue. The board was asking for a new building and not operating funds.

By having a mayor intercede with the developer on behalf of the library it indicated a wider concern and helped acquire the gift. The village, which then had a vested interest, was able to provide concessions to the builder to make his shopping center more economical.

There are different constituencies in each community and it takes time and planning to win them over to your side. Finding their buttons and learning how to push them is lots more effective than pressure. Pressure is simply not compatible with the image of public libraries, but satisfying patron needs is highly compatible. The basis of marketing in this case might be stated as: Find the need and fill it. Ask for your reward and if you

were correct about the need and you filled it successfully you will be rewarded.

These cases illustrate in real world examples that marketing principles do work, even in very adverse conditions. Both libraries repositioned, one from a provider of information to recreation services, and the other from a part-time reading library to a full service facility offering public areas to many groups previously unserved. Both institutions were using marketing techniques to increase their funding in order to respond to greater service demands from patrons. As a result of these efforts the Janesville staff got raises when other departments in the city got none, and the Lake Villa staff became full-time and had compensation increased accordingly. The active recognition of political bodies as an important constituency of these libraries contributed immeasurably to the success of their efforts.

REFERENCES

[1] O. Gene Norman, "Marketing Libraries and Information Services: An Annotated Guide to the Literature." RSR (Spring 1982), p. 69–80.
[2] Norman, p. 80.
[3] Norman's literature review includes 94 citations.
[4] Barbara Conroy, "Management and Marketing of Public Services." *Journal of Library Administration*, v. 3(1) (Spring 1982), p. 9–12.
[5] John P. Dessauer, "Are Libraries Failing Their Patrons?" *Publishers' Weekly*, 217 (January 18, 1983), p. 67–68.
[6] John Berry, "The Marketization of Libraries," *Library Journal*, 106 (January 1, 1981), p. 5.
[7] Dessauer, p. 68.
[8] John B. Miner and Norman R. Smith, "Can Organizational Decline Make Up for Motivational Decline?" *The Wharton Magazine*, v. 5(4) (Spring 1981), p. 29–35.

[9] Miner and Smith, p. 35.
[10] Philip Kotler, *Marketing for Nonprofit Organizations*, 2nd. ed. Englewood Cliffs, NJ: Prentice-Hall, 1982, p. 23.

[11] Andrea C. Dragon, "The Measurement of Professional Performance: A Critical Review," *Annual Review of Library Administration and Organization*. In press.

RAYANA FAMILY PLANNING PROGRAM

INTRODUCTION

Eduardo Martilla could easily see the five brand new distribution vans of the Rayana Family Planning Program (known locally as RFPP) parked in the lot beside his office. They had arrived the day before as the latest contribution of the All-Nations Family Planning Foundation. All-Nations has been the principal supporter of RFPP since its modest beginnings five years earlier. Three months ago, Sr. Martilla had mentioned to All-Nations his desire to add more delivery capacity to his program and to add at least one new product or product line this year. All-Nations had encouraged Martilla to submit a formal proposal for the vans and for the new introduction. The van proposal was submitted two months earlier. However the second proposal still sat on Martilla's desk awaiting his decision as to whether to propose adding an IUD or a line of noncontraceptive products.

Eduardo Martilla was pleased by the promptness and generosity of All-Nations' support. It indicated once again their confidence in him and in RFPP's accomplishments under his dynamic leadership. Martilla was a man of few doubts about his mission

and about his own abilities to achieve them. He was certain he could meet the challenge he had so glowingly outlined in the draft proposal to All-Nations' executive director Bruce Kirkland.

RAYANA

Rayana is a small South American country with a 200-mile coastline, two major mountain ranges, and dense jungle covering 40 percent of the nation's nonmountainous surface. The mountain ranges and coastline effectively divide the country into three regions and make communications and travel between the regions difficult.

The last census was conducted in 1977. Official projections based on a growth rate of 2.8 percent per year estimate the population in January of 1986 to be 39 million. Population density ranges from 550 per square mile in the foothill areas to over 10,000 in certain sectors of the immense capital city of Bacaville. The population of Bacaville is estimated to be 6 million and is growing at a rate of 4 percent per year due to a significant influx of natives from rural areas. The only other city of major size in Rayana is the coastal city of Aubrey with about 1.8 million

The case was prepared originally for a seminar put together by The Futures Group in Washington.

Prepared by Alan R. Andreasen, Graduate School of Management, UCLA. Used with permission.

in population. The total population is divided about equally among the three regions of the country.

Average age of the population is estimated to be 15.8 and the average family size, 7.2. A recent study estimated that some form of contraception was being used by 11 percent of women of child-bearing age. Sixty percent of the population considers Spanish to be their major language, with a minority in each of the three regions having their own indigenous dialect. Literacy is officially reported to be 34 percent for the entire country. The country is bound together physically by a barely adequate road system supplemented by barges on the two rivers. Communications are by five regional radio stations which cover an estimated 80 percent of the population and a state-owned television system which serves a million private homes and uncounted central meeting places in towns and villages throughout the eastern and southern regions. There are currently five national newspapers, two local papers in Aubrey, and regional indigenous-language papers in each region. Spanish-language magazines and newspapers are imported from nearby countries and foreign TV and radio programs are available to those with the necessary sophisticated receivers.

The country's economic base is the mining of bauxite. There is also a modest fishery industry and jute and banana crops for export markets. Per capita income in 1979, the latest year in which the government had made an estimate, was $920 (U.S.). As in many underdeveloped countries, the skewness of the income distribution is marked. Less than 8 percent of the population, mostly residing in Bacaville and Aubrey, controls 40 percent of the country's income. GNP in 1985 is estimated to be growing at a rate of 3 to 4 percent per annum.

Rayana's government is a democracy—of sorts. The political system is based on the British Parliamentary model wherein the majority party in the elected Assembly appoints the Prime Minister. An election was held in 1984 and won by the Progressive Liberal Party with 83 percent of the popular vote and 29 of 32 seats in the Assembly. The present Prime Minister is Fernando Ortega, the ex-general who engineered the coup that overthrew the autocratic and sometimes brutal dictatorship of Emilio (El Toro) Semilla in 1979. Before the elections of 1984, Ortega ruled as a self-appointed Prime Minister. His brother, Juan, was appointed Minister of Health and Family Planning in the current regime in 1981.

THE RAYANA FAMILY PLANNING PROGRAM

Any account of the Rayana Family Planning Program (RFPP) must begin with its director. Many argue that the success of the program to date is entirely attributable to the energy, creativity, and leadership talents of Eduardo Martilla. At the same time, critics of the program hasten to point out that Eduardo's charisma might not have gotten him quite so far had he not had the foresight to marry El Toro's first cousin in 1972.

Despite his dictatorial ways, El Toro recognized very early in his career the crucial need for family planning in his country. Soon after seizing power in 1968, he realized that the country's high annual population growth rate was likely to put great stress on its agricultural and economic bases. Despite objections from the Roman Catholic clergy (which claimed to represent 78 percent of the populace), Semilla spoke out forcefully for family planning in his country.

Eduardo Martilla became an early advocate of family planning in Rayana. A physician by training, Martilla entered public service not long after his marriage in 1972. He initially obtained a post in the Ministry of Health and shortly rose to the position of Deputy Minister with responsibilities for various aspects of family planning. In that role, he greatly expanded the number of public health clinics and the proportion of these staffed by full-time family planning advisors. He also increased the public health service's capabilities to conduct examinations, insert IUDs, and perform "menstrual regulations."

Martilla was appointed by his cousin-in-law to be Rayana's Ambassador to the United Nations in 1975. While at the U.N., Martilla learned a great deal about government family planning programs in several other countries. He also became familiar with the wide range of financial resources available for such ventures and had the opportunity to visit programs in Thailand and Egypt. Most importantly, Mantilla made the acquaintance of Bruce Kirkland at the All-Nations Foundation.

All of these contacts became very useful to Martilla in the period immediately after the coup in the fall of 1979. After testing the political climate under the new regime, Martilla learned that the new government would not stand in the way of a private sector family planning program such as the one Eduardo Martilla had long thought of developing. With the encouragement and considerable financial assistance of Bruce Kirkland, the Rayana Family Planning Program was begun in the early months of 1980.

THE RFPP PROGRAM

RFPP was formed as a independently chartered nonprofit corporation with the formal approval of the Ministry of Health and Family Planning. Since its inception, the program has not been required to report its plans or progress to the Ministry or to seek its approval except for the registration of any imported medical products. Sr. Martilla, however, does keep his contacts at the Ministry informed of any major developments at RFPP and attempts to make an informal progress report to them once a year.

The RFPP program began in 1980 with two products supplied at no cost by All-Nations. One was a low cost condom already packaged and branded in the U.S. as "Panther." Panther was sold in a number of other countries under contraceptive social marketing projects. The other product was a regular-dose oral contraceptive that RFPP repackaged locally and labelled "Ovadyne." In January 1982, RFPP added a second condom priced at a 50 percent price premium over Panther. The new brand, called "Gold Star," was in fact the Panther product repackaged in a fancier outer wrapping and treated to an extensive "image" campaign on radio and on local billboards and posters. It was available in 3-unit and 12-unit packets. Panther was available in these 3-unit and 12-unit packets and in boxes of 100. A low-dose oral contraceptive branded "Low-Ova" was also added in June 1983.

Sales from 1980 to 1985 for the four products for the three regions and the two principal cities are given in Table 1. Bacaville is located in the Eastern Region and Aubrey is in the South. Sales and other records are maintained by RFPP on an IBM PC-AT installed in the central office in 1985.

RFPP's distribution system is regionalized with offices, warehouses, and regional managers in Bacaville, Aubrey, and Sierra Azul in the Western Region. Government regulations permit sales of orals without prescriptions in pharmacies only. Condoms are sold virtually everywhere. Sixteen distributors and 36 route salespeople cover pharmacies and small food and general merchandise outlets throughout the country. RFPP calculates

TABLE 1: Sales[a] performance 1980–1982

	Panther (Units)	Gold Star (Units)	Ovadyne (Cycles)	Low-Ova (Cycles)
1980				
Bacaville	372,447		34,990	
Other Eastern	95,990		2,910	
Aubrey	187,800		12,800	
Other Southern	47,386		2,770	
Western	59,420		3,336	
	763,043		56,806	
1981				
Bacaville	1340,338		54,998	
Other Eastern	266,880		18,700	
Aubrey	690,654		19,886	
Other Southern	112,290		8,960	
Western	160,887		17,666	
	1571,049		119,510	
1982				
Bacaville	2140,886	23,998	198,998	
Other Eastern	670,880	1,398	46,980	
Aubrey	1280,554	21,124	112,300	
Other Southern	290,342	4,664	33,912	
Western	220,210	10,600	21,887	
	4602,872	61,784	414,077	
1983				
Bacaville	2818,444	187,657	382,930	89,935
Other Eastern	1137,998	12,710	155,887	9,993
Aubrey	2098,762	148,352	258,264	76,830
Other Southern	588,238	56,993	78,993	8,783
Western	347,210	100,879	67,444	8,578
	6690,652	506,591	943,518	194,119
1984				
Bacaville	3098,213	304,119	500,322	243,210
Other Eastern	1321,654	45,876	199,720	47,193
Aubrey	2249,990	248,910	327,251	187,018
Other Southern	682,802	112,238	128,433	23,100
Western	479,444	97,597	86,381	18,050
	7832,103	808,740	1242,117	518,571
1985				
Bacaville	3325,268	329,765	529,887	421,970
Other Eastern	1686,842	56,288	211,987	82,100
Aubrey	2552,443	300,441	376,321	248,128
Other Southern	762,210	154,823	167,308	64,018
Western	520,993	110,491	96,740	97,856
	8847,756	951,808	1382,243	911,072

[a]Sales figures include free goods given out as distribution incentives.

314

that 60 percent of condom revenues come from pharmacies, 30 percent from general merchandise and food outlets, and the rest from miscellaneous sources including clinics. Records produced by the salesforce indicate that there are about 7,000 pharmacies in the country and 50,000 other shops. Market share figures within the various markets are not available. However, Martilla believes that he has about 85 percent of the commercial condom market which, in turn, is about 70 percent of total distribution in the country, the remainder being supplied by the government program. Similarly, Martilla estimates RFPP has 65 percent of the commercial orals market which, in turn, is 55 percent of the country's total.

Support for the distribution system comes from RFPP's own internal advertising department which prepares packaging, posters, and print and radio advertising. Budgets for these expenses along with other marketing costs are reported in Table 2. RFPP's most ambitious advertising program is currently a major TV and billboard campaign begun in 1985. This program is budgeted at $350,000 for three years and is designed to promote the general concept of family planning in rural areas. The campaign does not stress RFPP brands. Kirkland and Martilla agree that the country badly needs such a campaign and All-Nations came up with the long-term funding to ensure it was fully carried through. The TV campaign was prepared and executed by Colona Graphics, the country's largest locally-owned agency. Billboards and other print materials are handled by RFPP's own advertising group.

The Rayana Family Planning Program in January 1986 had a total staff of 167. The overall organizational design is given in Figure 1. (By contrast, the government of Rayana is estimated to have over 6,000 field workers and clinic staff with some type of

TABLE 2: Revenue and marketing expenses, 1985

	$(U.S.)	Percent
Sales		
Panther	$ 265,433	16.2
Gold Star	42,831	2.6
Ovadyne	732,589	44.6
Low-Ova	601,308	36.6
Total	$1,642,161	100.0
Expenses		
Packaging	$ 123,418	7.5
Sales force salaries and commissions	432,496	26.3
Advertising[a]	484,210	29.5
Marketing research	37,290	2.3
Warehousing	213,867	13.0
Transportation	171,113	10.4
Accounting/control	87,211	5.3
Administration	133,499	8.1
Total Expenses	$1,683,104	102.5
Profit or (Loss)	(40,943)	(2.5)

[a]Does not include TV/billboard campaign funded by the All-Nations Foundation.

involvement in family planning throughout the country.)

RFPP strategy aims condoms at all men and orals at younger women. The principal theme of messages directed at both markets is the need for everyone to practice responsible family planning. Secondary themes emphasize the health and economic implications of large families for both parents and children and the benefits to Rayana itself of a slowing in the rate of population growth. Somewhat greater use has been made of point-of-sale materials in recent months. RFPP staff, however, has lately been urging a revision of oral package inserts and new posters to reduce reported misuse of orals, especially among rural and first-time users.

Prices of each product have been un-

FIGURE 1: Rayana family planning program organizational chart

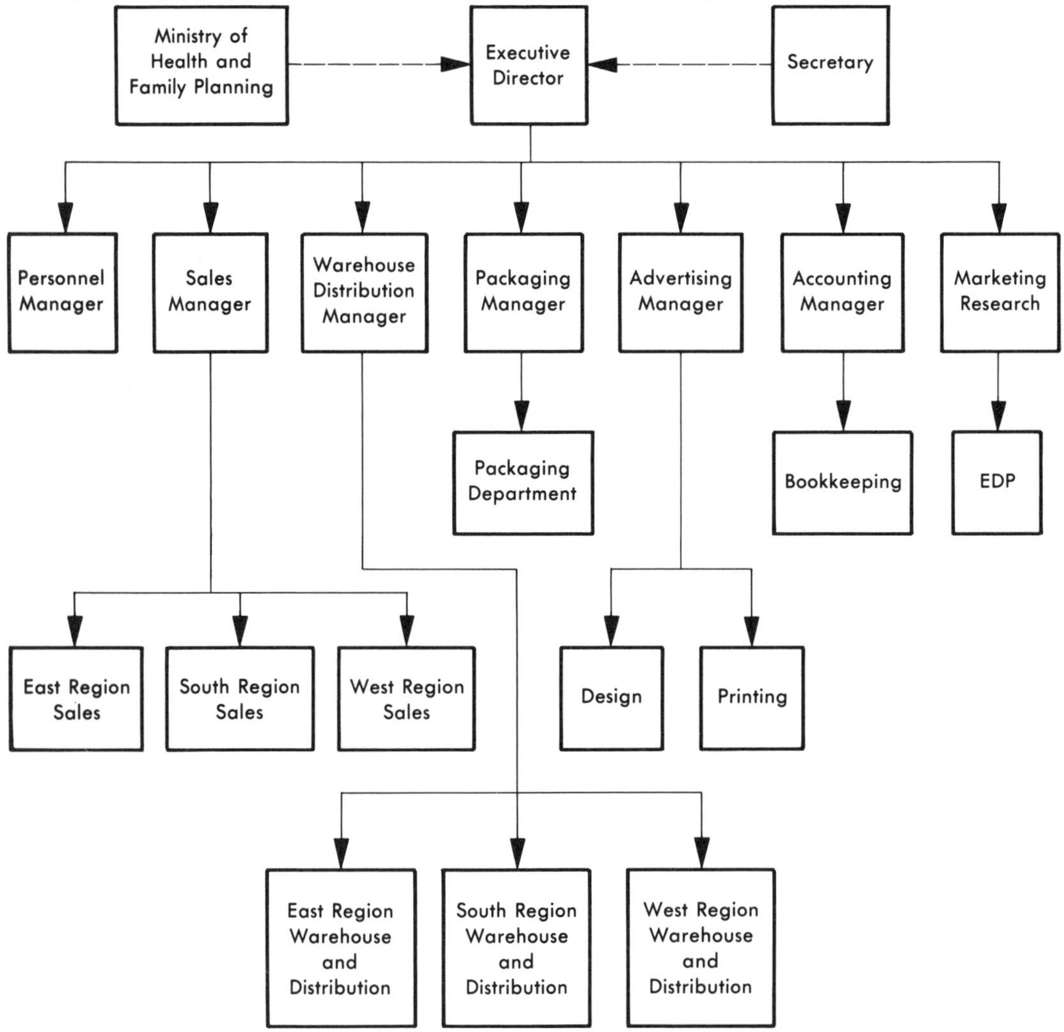

changed since they were introduced. In U.S. dollars they are as follows:

Panther	3¢ per unit
Gold Star	3.4¢ per unit
Ovadyne	53¢ per cycle
Low-Ova	66¢ per cycle

Cost per couple-years-of-protection was $6.13 U.S. in 1985.

THE NEW PRODUCT INTRODUCTION

Eduardo Martilla has spent the last two years consolidating RFPP's organizational structure, increasing coverage of retail outlets (now estimated by him to be 95 percent) and improving the skills of his sales personnel. In recent months, Martilla's considerable energies have been devoted to the All-Nations RV/billboard campaign. He has also become increasingly active in politics within the Progressive Liberal party. (It is rumored that he plans to run for the Assembly in 1988.)

With these efforts under control and with sales of existing products apparently slowing, Martilla is now looking into the possibility of expanding his product offerings.

RFPP is considering two alternative new offerings as part of its line expansion. One possibility is the addition of a line of four noncontraceptive products including aspirin, a first aid kit, an antiseptic, and packets of oral rehydration salts. Martilla feels that his distribution system has both the channels to reach the pharmacies and other outlets that would handle these products and the excess capacity to accommodate them with little negative impact on present contraceptive lines. Three of the four products would be acquired directly from local manufacturers at competitive rates. The fourth, oral rehydration salts, would be provided free by the West German Gesundheit Foundation. The aspirin and antiseptic products would be one

of the three popular brands currently available in Rayana and each would be carried in two sizes. The first aid kit would be assembled from "generic" items and packaged by RFPP in Bacaville. A projected profit and loss statement for the first five years of this undertaking is given in Table 3.

The other offering that RFPP is contemplating is the Copper-T intrauterine device. This product would be made available free of charge by the All-Nations Foundation. The product would be distributed to pharmacies, physicians, and local hospitals and clinics. While RFPP has adequate distribution to pharmacies including some in hospitals, it does not now have regular contacts with physicians. Thus, if the Copper-T product were added, an additional three salespeople would have to be hired for each regional office. To date, RFPP has made some efforts to promote its oral contraceptives to physicians and clinics but is relying primarily on its extensive media campaigns to create the consumer demand that will "pull" these

TABLE 3: Noncontraceptive marketing project

Sales	1986	1987	1988	1989	1990
Antiseptic	$ 46,000	$ 57,600	$ 69,120	$ 82,950	$ 99,500
Aspirin	118,000	188,800	226,560	271,870	326,250
First aid kit	90,000	144,000	172,800	207,500	248,800
ORS	60,000	105,000	137,500	246,250	319,375
Total	$314,000	$495,400	$605,980	$808,570	$993,925
Cost of Goods	175,400	234,000	281,080	337,400	404,730
Gross margin	$138,600	$261,400	$324,900	$471,170	$589,195
Expenses					
Packaging	$ 27,000	$ 40,500	$ 48,600	$ 58,320	$ 70,000
Sales force (commissions only)	29,400	45,540	56,600	70,860	89,390
Advertising	80,000	60,000	40,000	50,000	80,000
Warehousing	29,400	45,540	56,600	70,860	89,390
Transportation	20,580	31,850	39,620	49,600	62,600
Admin./Acctng.	40,000	40,000	40,000	40,000	40,000
Total	$226,380	$263,430	$281,420	$339,640	$301,380
Profit or (Loss)	($ 88,200)	($ 2,030)	$ 43,480	$131,530	$287,815

TABLE 4: IUD project

	1986	1987	1988	1989	1990
Sales	$ 90,000	$112,000	$128,400	$180,000	$208,100
Expenses					
Sales force (salaries only)	$ 56,400	$ 59,200	$ 62,500	$ 65,600	$ 68,900
Advertising	35,000	35,000	35,000	35,000	35,000
Warehousing	2,200	2,640	3,160	3,800	4,560
Transportation	4,400	5,280	6,320	7,600	9,120
Admin./Acctg.	10,000	10,000	10,000	10,000	10,000
	$108,000	$112,120	$116,980	$122,000	$127,580
Profit or (Loss)	($ 18,000)	($ 120)	$ 11,420	$ 58,000	$ 80,520

products through the distribution channels by making it difficult for OB/GYNs, clinics, and pharmacies *not* to carry RFPP brands. Martilla believes that revenues for the IUDs will be quicker coming but slower growing than for the noncontraceptive line. His estimate of revenues and expenses for the first five years of IUD sales are given in Table 4.

AMTRAK

In late 1975, the management of Amtrak faced a number of major decisions concerning their Detroit–Chicago route. They were considering purchasing a number of new Amfleet trains to put on this run. There were also questions about what services to offer on these trains if they were purchased.

HISTORY OF AMTRAK

Amtrak was established through federal legislation on April 30, 1971, as a last-ditch attempt to revitalize intercity rail service in the United States. Railroads, during the previous 10 years, had found it difficult to compete with other modes of transportation—in particular, the private automobile (and the new interstate highway system it used), and the jet aircraft in domestic service. Travel by rail in the United States had declined from 70 percent of all intercity travel in 1947, to less than 5 percent in 1971.

Amtrak, a single nationwide passenger rail system, was designed to lure travelers back to the rails. In an era of increasing awareness of energy limitations, and of ever-growing numbers of people utilizing modes of transport other than the auto, revitalization of American rail service was viewed as a necessity. Amtrak's goal was increased ridership

Reprinted from K. L. Bernhardt and T. C. Kinnear, *Cases in Marketing Management*, copyright © Business Publications, Inc., 1985, by permission of the publisher.

through refurbished equipment, modernization of terminal facilities, speed increases, and greater overall convenience.

At the time of the Amtrak takeover, no intercity passenger rail cars had been built in 10 years, and no passenger technology existed in the country to design and build modern cars. Stations were antiquated and without modern facilities of any kind in many cases. Equipment was in an almost constant state of malfunction, and was seldom cleaned. Connections were often impossible, or highly inconvenient. Rail service held little attraction for anyone except fearful flyers and train buffs. The National Railroad Passenger Corporation (Amtrak's official name) had its hands full.

For the purpose of service development, the various railroad lines and routes were divided into two categories: long-haul services and short- and medium-distance corridors. Long hauls were generally those routes of 700 or more miles, serviced by overnight or two day trains (e.g., The Broadway Limited, 900 miles, 17 hours, overnight between Chicago and New York). Corridors were lines over which several trains a day in each direction were operated. In particular, the corridors of less than 300 miles were thought to be ideally suited for high-quality, high-speed service, which could compete with the airlines. This style service if implemented, it was reasoned, could attract business travelers and others for whom travel time was of great importance. Amtrak had a good reason to believe this would work too: the New York–Washington corridor had offered such service since 1969—the Metroliners—and was very successful.

THE DETROIT–CHICAGO CORRIDOR

In the case of the Detroit–Chicago corridor (279 miles), Amtrak saw an opportunity to duplicate the fine operation between New York and Washington. As late as the early 1960s, the New York Central Railroad (which originally operated Amtrak's Detroit–Chicago line) had offered high-quality rail service on the route. Running times between the two cities were as fast as four and a half hours, and luxurious meal and parlor car service was offered. With the completion of Interstate 94 through to Detroit from Chicago, and the introduction of the 727 jet on ''short-hop'' flights, much of the market for this type of service disappeared. The train was no longer fast enough. As travel volume dwindled, services were cut.

First the parlor cars (first-class service aimed toward business travelers) came off, then the diners with their sitdown meal service. Coaches and snack bars remained. When Penn Central was formed in 1967 (via the merger of the Pennsylvania and New York Central Railroads), high losses were viewed as reason to further cut service quality. Car cleaning was minimized; maintenance became irregular. In 1969, running times were lengthened to five and a half hours. The Penn Central in its annual report served notice it wanted as few passenger trains as possible. Just prior to Amtrak's takeover of the route, Penn Central offered three trains in each direction a day over the route, one without food service at all, the other two with limited snack service. On-time performance was poor. Rats were once reported in the coaches. The service offered was as poor as it could possibly be.

On May 1, 1971, Amtrak took over this corridor. And as with many routes throughout the country, its first major step was to cut the frequency of service. Thereafter, two trains a day in each direction operated between the two cities. It was, according to Amtrak, a temporary economy move to limit the deficit. Further, said Amtrak in newspaper advertising, the remaining trains would be vastly improved.

Improvement was first accomplished by running the trains (the *Wolverine* and the *Saint Clair*) with cars from the C&O Railroad. Its equipment was in far better shape than the Penn Central's, which was immediately withdrawn from service to be rebuilt. The replacement equipment was more comfortable and better maintained, but meal service was still very limited. The schedule remained five and a half hours from endpoint to endpoint. Amtrak also began an advertising program in Detroit, basically just to tell people that the trains were there (many had forgotten or didn't know rail service existed to Chicago). As with other areas of the country, Amtrak promised refurbished cars within a year. The result was a stop in the decline of ridership, and a gradual turnaround by the end of the first year of operation. Unlike the original plans, refurbished cars began to arrive piecemeal—a car here or there, mixed in with older, untouched equipment. But this nonetheless showed good intentions. Schedules were adhered to better as well, and connections at Chicago were improved. This was aided by Amtrak's consolidation of all operations to one Chicago terminal—Union Station—and the elimination of across-town transfers.

But there were many problems with the initial effort as well. Amtrak operated its trains by contractual agreement with the railroads—in this case, Penn Central. Because of this, they had only indirect control over on-board staff, and the dispatching and running of trains. Problems en route were handled by the railroad in the old manner—which often meant not handling them at all. Amtrak couldn't instruct attendants as to the way to deal with passengers, because the attendants still worked for the railroads. Amtrak, because of the situation, could say little about service quality or uniformity.

Equipment was also maintained by the railroad. Often, after individual cars had been rebuilt (at very high cost), they fell into disrepair because of continued poor maintenance. The age of the equipment was also a problem. The average car was 20 years old. While pleasant inside and comfortable to travel in, they were too old to be completely reliable. Air-conditioning failed or heating gave out while trains were en route. Since no passenger railroad cars had been built in the United States for almost 10 years, no technology was immediately available to construct new equipment.

Stations along the route presented many problems. Without exception, they were rundown, dirty, and without modern facilities. The Detroit station, once a busy rail center, was a decaying edifice, vast and frightening. Serving only four trains a day when Amtrak first took over, it was far too large for its task. Located on the west side of Detroit, it was inconvenient for persons from the east and north suburbs to get to it. The Niles, Michigan, station had no heat, and in Battle Creek the main body of the station had been closed for several years. Conditions were so bad, several of Amtrak's advisory board recommended that three of the stations be ripped down rather than trying to fix them up, and new ones be built in their place.

THE ENERGY CRISIS

In 1973, after two years of operation, refurbished equipment ran on the corridor exclusively, stations were painted at last, and on-time operation (on the same slow schedule) became a reality. Then, in the fall of that year, the energy crunch descended on the nation. Gasoline prices and air fares went up substantially, and millions of Americans were forced onto public transportation. Suddenly, Amtrak had its hands full. Trains that were never more than half full were carrying three times their normal load. Overcrowding became commonplace. On the corridor, trains were unreserved (meaning that there was no limit on the number of tickets sold per train). Trains that could comfortably seat 300 people were carrying about 600. Food would run out almost before the trains left their originating stations. Passengers, due to the crowding, sometimes stood for four or five hours, or sat on suitcases in the aisles. Personnel became rude and discourteous. Fistfights broke out on occasion between conductors and irate passengers. The refurbished equipment in many cases couldn't take the abuse and wear it received from carrying this many people. The interiors became damaged and weren't repaired. Heating and air-conditioning were as erratic as ever. Malfunctioning equipment was allowed out on the line for the first time in Amtrak history, so that more cars were available to seat more people.

Amtrak received a ghastly black eye during the energy crunch. It was not able to adequately meet the hordes of people who suddenly came back to the rails. The Detroit–Chicago corridor in particular fared dismally in terms of service, with equipment, food service, and personnel getting more complaints than almost anywhere else in the system. But in two areas, things were positive. On-time performance remained good despite the crowds (which often slowed things down elsewhere) and ridership remained high into the summer of 1974.

THE TURBOLINERS

Based on these final two factors, Amtrak made a firm commitment to upgrade service on the route. In late 1973, the corporation leased two French Turboliner trains for experimental use on the St. Louis–Chicago corridor. Since no modern passenger equip-

ment was yet available in the United States, Amtrak went to Europe where new trains could be acquired almost immediately. The Turbos' better schedules, improved food service, and high on-time reliability resulted in greatly improved ridership to and from St. Louis. Amtrak decided to purchase these two and four more sets of Turbo equipment, and to place some of them in service between Detroit and Chicago. In April of 1975, the Detroit–Chicago corridor became all Turbo. As part of the service improvement program, an additional midday train was added, bringing the number of trains on the route to six daily; that is, in each direction, a morning, noon, and evening train. The new equipment was extremely sleek and modern. Its exterior was reminiscent of the Japanese "Bullet" train, and its interiors were plush, quiet, and featured giant windows and automatic sliding glass doors between each car. Food service was provided cafeteria-style, with an area adjacent to the galley for eating and lounging, and fold-down trays available at each coach seat.

Because of the new technology that the equipment utilized, it was maintained at a special service facility in Chicago constructed specifically for this purpose. Service personnel were specially trained to work on board the new trains and thus the quality level of individual service was vastly improved. The introduction of the new service was accompanied by an innovative and clever advertising campaign on Detroit and Chicago television stations, and on local radio stations along the route. Perhaps because of the new trains themselves, or the extensive advertising, or the added service, or the coordination of the entire promotion, ridership on the corridor increased 72 percent the first month, and over 150 percent within three months. The trains ran regularly at their 300-passenger capacity. They were so successful, in fact, that a whole new set of problems arose.

Foremost among them was a problem related to their new technology. Because the equipment was foreign, it was constructed in a manner quite different from traditional American railway design. Hence, the maintenance people "out on the line" (that is, anywhere but at the service facility) didn't know how to work on the new trains. The troubleshooting manuals on board each train were no help to them either—they were in French. As a result, if air-conditioning failed on a trip, it probably remained broken until the train returned to its Chicago maintenance facility. Sometimes that meant several trips if loads were heavy, and 300 . . ., 600 . . ., 900 uncomfortable passengers. More than once public address announcements were made asking anyone who could read French to come to the cockpit and translate the manual for the English-only maintenance personnel.

The popularity of these trains led to another problem—overcrowding. Unlike conventional American equipment, cars couldn't be added or removed from the Turbos. They had a fixed number (five) and a standard carrying capacity of 300 people. They ran as unreserved trains, however, meaning that Amtrak would sell tickets to as many people as wanted to ride, and often that was over 300. On weekends, some passengers stood for five and a half hours, all the way to Detroit, or Chicago. Even when there were no technical or capacity difficulties, the sleek, new Turbos still serviced stations in Michigan that were at least 50 years old, and which for the most part hadn't been renovated. Ann Arbor was the single exception, but its refurbished station was far too small for the growing number of passengers using the facility. These difficulties marred the generally good impression the turbotrains gave in advertising, and on the many good trips they made. The public failure resulted in a somewhat negative reputation. This was by no means pervasive though, and the trains continued to do well on the route. On subsequent routes where Turbos were assigned, ridership increased as well, seemingly justifying the argument that if modern services were provided, the American public would travel by rail.

The success of this equipment also occurred, it should be pointed out, without great schedule improvement. Due to track conditions, the high-speed capabilities of the new trains could not initially be used, so it was the trains themselves, rather than their speed, that accounted for their popularity. With track improvement, it was reasoned, they would be even more attractive to intercity travelers.

Research data indicated that the average age of Detroit–Chicago train riders was 35 years old, with about 65 percent traveling on vacations, 25 percent on business, and 10 percent for other reasons.

THE DECISIONS TO BE MADE

In late 1975, the management of Amtrak faced a number of decisions with respect to the Detroit–Chicago route.

1. The first decision concerned the possibility of purchasing a number of Amfleet trains for the route. These trains were being built by the Budd Company of Philadelphia for use on a number of Amtrak routes. Amfleet trains combined the modern aspects of the European Turboliners (speed, new interiors, standardized seating and food service) with the flexibility of old-style conventional equipment. On an Amfleet train, cars could be added or removed as load factors

changed. Since they were American built, the difficulty of foreign technology was eliminated. In addition, Amfleet trains offered the possibility of first-class, daytime accommodations featuring reserved seats and at-seat meal service.

In order to run three trains a day in each direction, Amtrak would have to purchase four locomotives and 24 Amfleet cars. The average Amfleet train on this run was thus expected to have one locomotive and six cars. Each locomotive would cost about $540,000. The price of cars varied depending on whether the car was a coach, first-class, parlor, dinette, and so on. On average the cars would cost Amtrak $425,000 each. A car would hold up to 84 passengers, with 60 in some cars. The useful life of this equipment was expected to be 20 years.

2. The second decision related to whether or not first-class accommodations should be available on the Detroit–Chicago Amfleet trains, if these trains were purchased. This service would include reserved seating and meal service at that seat. Reserved seats were spaced two together and a seat by itself, giving three seats across the car. About 10 percent of the seating capacity of an average six-car train could be available for first-class service. The incremental cost of meals and personnel to Amtrak of each first-class seat sold was estimated to be about $5.

3. A related decision here concerned the price of a first-class ticket, if such service were made available. The price of a coach ticket was $17.50 one way. This compared to $19.50 for the five-hour bus ride, and $39 for a coach seat, and $58 for a first-class seat for the one-hour plane ride.

4. At first, the Amfleet trains would continue to take five and a half hours to travel from downtown Detroit to downtown Chicago. They were capable of traveling much faster, but track conditions would not allow this. Amtrak was considering spending $3 million on track and signal improvements in the next year. This money and a great deal more to be put up by Conrail (the regional freight railway of the northeast) could improve the tracks such that travel could be cut to under four hours within a few years. The Amtrak funded improvements were expected to have about a 10 year useful life. The management of Amtrak was wondering whether or not they should spend this money, and aim for shorter run times.

5. There were five major stations on the Detroit–Chicago run. Amtrak was considering upgrading them. The cost to Amtrak would be $150,000 per station. The rest of the cost would be covered by the state of Michigan, and local cities. A 20-year useful life was expected on each improved station.

6. Amtrak's advertising agency was Needham, Harper, and Steers. They had developed an advertising campaign for the Amfleet trains in general, and the Detroit–Chicago corridor more specifically. They planned to use a mix of television, radio, and newspapers. The media costs to Amtrak for the Detroit–Chicago run were proposed to be $300,000 per year.

The management of Amtrak wondered what decisions should be made with respect to the Detroit–Chicago corridor.

TUESDAY EVENING CONCERT SERIES

Because of the rapid increase in artists' fees, the Board of Directors of the Tuesday Evening Concert Series (TECS) was considering, in the fall of 1973, increasing the price of season memberships for the 1974–1975 season. Besides three pricing proposals before the board, there were also three policy decisions under consideration:

1. What caliber of artist should TECS contract?
2. How can the series best be promoted?
3. How often should ticket prices be raised?

BACKGROUND INFORMATION

TECS was a nonprofit organization founded in 1948 and affiliated with the University of Virginia. According to the constitution: "The purpose of the Tuesday Evening Concert Series is to make available to the general public, including students, faculty, and local residents, a nonprofit series of musical events designed to enrich the cultural life of the community." The operating philosophy of the TECS was to provide a variety of chamber music (music for soloists or small ensembles), excellently performed, at relatively inexpensive prices.

The series itself consisted of eight concerts performed on Tuesday evenings in the period from October to April. The university provided the use of Cabell Hall (seating capacity 1,000) for the concerts at no charge. Admission to the concerts was, for the most part, restricted to season ticket holders of the TECS. Season memberships in the 1973–1974 series were priced at $9 for students and $12 for regular members and entitled the holders to a nonreserved seat in Cabell Hall.

The TECS was run by a volunteer board of directors consisting of 10 student members and 16 nonstudent members (mostly faculty and spouses of faculty). Ernest Mead, Chairman of the Music Department, and Vincent Shea, the connoisseur Financial Vice President of the University, were ex-officio members of the Board. According to the bylaws, the president of the series must be a student. Although the board had the final say in the selection of performers, Mrs. John Forbes had handled all the actual booking of the artists for the last 12 years, with the support of the program committee. The programs were presented to the TECS Executive Committee and Messrs. Mead and Shea. Before the final program decision was made, the board of directors' approval was sought.

COST INFORMATION

The major operating expense of the series was the cost of the artists who performed at the eight concerts. Historically, artists' fees accounted for approximately 87% of the series' expenses; programs, advertising, printing, and receptions comprised most of the remainder.

The artists were usually contracted for a year or more in advance through their book-

This case was prepared by Thomas A. Bubier and William P. H. Cary under the supervision of Professor Leslie E. Grayson of the University of Virginia. Copyright 1973 by the Sponsors of the Colgate Darden Graduate School of Business Administration, University of Virginia. Reprinted with permission from the Sponsors of the Colgate Darden Graduate School of Business Administration, University of Virginia.

EXHIBIT 1: Total artists' fees for eight programs

Season	Artists' fees	Percent change over previous season
1966–1967	$ 8,200	+30.2
1967–1968	7,980	−2.7
1968–1969	8,175	+2.4
1969–1970	8,954	+9.5
1970–1971	9,800	+9.4
1971–1972	10,700	+9.2
1972–1973	11,600	+8.4
1973–1974	12,600	+8.6

ing agencies, which handled the transportation and negotiated the performance fees. The great majority of artists gave their agency an "asking price" which was then subject to negotiation with interested parties. The amount of flexibility in the asking price varied from artist to artist. In general, the greater the reputation of the performer, the firmer the asking price was likely to be.

As Exhibit 1 illustrates, artists' fees for the eight concerts increased considerably in recent years. The overall increase from the 1966–1967 season to the 1973–1974 season was 54%. For the last four years, artists' fees increased at slightly less than 10% per year.

In the past seven years, nine artists or

groups of artists appeared more than once. The prices for which they appeared are outlined in Exhibit 2. Since several of these performers continued to appear at considerably reduced fees, Exhibit 2 probably understates the degree to which artists' fees increased in recent years. For comparison purposes, Exhibit 3 provides some additional measures of general price trends in the 1966–1973 period.

A number of factors influenced the final price at which an artist or group of artists appeared for the TECS. The Tuesday restriction on performance dates tended to limit the negotiating position of the TECS vis-à-vis a booking agent who was trying to fit his client into a crowded schedule of concerts. Similarly, the proximity of Charlottesville to the artists' adjoining concerts had a bearing on the price charged. A pianist who was performing in Washington or Richmond on Wednesday would normally come at a lesser fee than if he or she were playing in St. Louis the next day.

Another factor that operated to reduce costs for the TECS was the booking of performers in a "package" from one agency. In past years the series has dealt with two or three major New York agencies for the ma-

EXHIBIT 2: Fees paid to TECS performers who appeared more than one time

	1966	1967	1968	1969	1970	1971	1972	1973
Rampal and Veyron-Lacroix[a]		$700		$700				$1,500
Peter Frankel			$1,500	$1,500				
Janos Starker		$1,100				$2,000		
The Marlboro Trio					$800		$900	
Festival Winds[b]				$1,400				$1,350[b]
The Early Music Quartet			$750			$1,100		
The New Cleveland Quartet[b]						$950		$1,250
The Juilliard String Quartet	$1,000		$1,700		$2,000			
The Hungarian String Quartet[b]					$1,100		$1,300	$1,250[c]

[a]Appeared in the 1972–1973 season.
[b]Booked to appear in the 1973–1974 season.
[c]Part of a four-concert "package" from one agency.

EXHIBIT 3: Selected price trends, 1966–1973

	1966	1967	1968	1969	1970	1971	1972	1973	Percent increase (1966–1973)
Consumer Price Index									
All items	97.2	100.0	104.2	109.8	116.3	121.3	125.3	132.7[a]	36.5
All services	95.8	100.0	105.2	112.5	121.6	128.4	133.3	138.4[a]	44.5
Out-ot-state undergraduate tuition at UVA	$1,037	$1,037	$1,042	$1,057	$1,214	$1,217	$1,374	$1,447	39.5
Regular membership (TECS)	$10	$10	$10	$10	$10	$12	$12	$12	20.0
Student membership (TECS)	$7.50	$7.50	$7.50	$7.50	$7.50	$9	$9	$9	20.0

[a]July.

jority of its concerts. Thus in the 1973–1974 season, for example, a package of four performers was bought for $7,000, a considerable saving over the sum of the artists' individual prices.

The nature of the series itself enabled it to attract performers of outstanding ability within its limited budget. Because of the reputation of the TECS as a discerning and discriminating series, various artists had performed at reduced rates. Furthermore, many outstanding performers were so impressed by the hall's excellent acoustics, the audience, and the university in general that they were willing to appear again at reduced fees.

These good relations between agents, artists, and TECS were largely due to the efforts of Mrs. Forbes as chairman of the program committee, and of the committee itself.

REVENUE INFORMATION

Historically, season memberships accounted for about 83% of total revenue. Exhibit 4 illustrates the change in season memberships from 1966 to 1973, and Exhibit 5 provides total revenue figures over the same period. Although both the regular and student memberships fluctuated, the number of student memberships sold had been par-

EXHIBIT 4: Season memberships[a]

Season	Regular	Percent change over previous season	Student	Percent change over previous season	Total	Percent change over previous season
1966–1967	634	−1.1	328	+2.8	962	+0.2
1967–1968	561	−11.5	230	−29.9	791	−17.8
1968–1969	687	+22.5	349	+51.7	1036	+31.0
1969–1970	725	+5.5	320	−8.3	1045	+0.9
1970–1971	628	−13.4	274	−14.4	902	+13.7
1971–1972	731	+16.4	335	+22.3	1066	+18.2
1972–1973	688	−5.9	349	+4.2	1037	−2.7

[a]The capacity of Cabell Hall is 1,000 persons.

EXHIBIT 5: Total ticket revenue

Season	Total ticket revenue[a]	Percent change over previous season
1966–1967[b]	9,916	+49.2
1967–1968	8,162	−17.7
1968–1969	11,072	+35.7
1969–1970	11,499	+3.9
1970–1971	9,782	−17.6
1971–1972[b]	13,562	+38.6
1972–1973	13,815[c]	+1.9

[a] Total income minus interest on savings deposits.
[b] Ticket prices increased.
[c] First year in which tickets were sold for the second half of the series and individual tickets at the door.

ticularly volatile in recent years. Of the last five seasons, four were sellouts. A particularly successful season was often due—at least in part—to an active membership chairman.

In addition to the revenue derived from the sale of season memberships, the TECS also generated revenue from a number of other sources. In 1972–1973, eighteen sponsor memberships were sold at $36 each. These memberships consisted of two season tickets for the sponsor and a third which went into a pool of tickets available free to local high school students. Sponsor memberships were sold largely to local businesses.

A total of $598 was generated through the sale of memberships to the second half of the 1972–1973 series. Other sources of revenue included ticket sales at the door (only when season tickets were sold out: $94 in 1972–1973), interest on savings deposits, and the McIntire Fund. After each season the McIntire Fund gave the TECS a subsidy according to the following formula: the difference between the regular membership price and student membership price ($3 in 1972–1973), multiplied by the number of student members, up to a maximum of $1,000.

TECS also received an indirect subsidy from Mrs. Forbes. The job of Program Committee Chairman was about half-time, and a person qualified to replace her could have expected anywhere from $5,000 to $7,500. She also spent (without reimbursement) about $100/year on long-distance phone calls and $250 for a once-a-year concert managers' convention in New York City. She had just been elected to another three-year term (1973–1976) as Program Committee Chairman. Assuming that she might be reelected in 1976, she would be unable, for personal reasons, to continue to serve in this capacity beyond 1979.

MARKET

Exhibit 6 gives some indication of the market for TECS members in recent years. Clearly, the potential demands for series tickets within the university community had increased very rapidly since 1966.

In addition to increasing ticket prices, the TECS took several other steps to increase total revenue. For instance, in recent years TECS oversold the concerts by about 100 seats. Because some members only attended a few of the eight concerts, there were al-

EXHIBIT 6: University population

Year	UVA student body	UVA faculty and staff
1966	7,873	766
1967	8,597	867
1968	9,011	1,015
1969	9,735	1,115
1970	10,852	1,200
1971	12,351	1,260
1972	12,907	1,404
1973 estimate	13,500	1,524
Percent change, 1966–1973	+71.5	+96.4

Source: Office of Institutional Analysis.

ways a certain number of empty seats at any given performance. A head count of empty seats conducted in the fall of 1972 revealed that, on the average, about 125 seats were unoccupied during the first four concerts. Consequently, the series now attempted to sell roughly 1,100 memberships and had increased the target to 1,200 for next year.

A second related course of action the TECS adopted in 1972–1973 was the sale of memberships for the second half of the series. After counting the average number of empty seats at the first four concerts, the series then attempted to sell half-season memberships at $8 for regular members and $6 for students. In other words, the series was oversold twice: once at the beginning of the season and once midway through the season. In the event that more than 1,000 people appeared at Cabell Hall, approximately 40 folding chairs could be set up in the aisles to accommodate the overflow.

Finally, the board of directors recently passed a resolution allowing the solicitation of charitable contributions. Although the board did not wish to actively promote contributions, there would be a notice on the 1973–1974 ticket order form to the effect that tax-deductible contributions would be accepted.

POLICY AND PRICING DECISIONS

At recent board meetings a number of policies central to the ticket pricing problem were discussed. There was some disagreement as to which policies TECS should adopt, and it was recognized that, at the next board meeting, these differences would have to be settled before the pricing decision could be made.

First, there was the question of the caliber of artists that TECS should bring to Charlottesville. Although everyone agreed that the quality of the performances was good, some felt that it should be "great" ("it is great only one-fourth to one-half of the time now"). Those who advocated upgrading the quality of the series pointed out that the "masters" drew standing-room-only crowds, while other performers did not fill the hall. In the fall of 1973, the maximum fee for one artist or group was $2,000; one proposal was to raise this to $3,500 for two of the eight concerts. Another proposal was to abandon the fixed maximum fee altogether and adopt a total fixed budget of $20,000, allowing TECS occasionally to present those elite artists who charged upward of $5,000. Both proposals recognized that, since membership could not be increased significantly, a price increase would be necessary. Opponents of the proposals were skeptical that the Charlottesville audience would be willing to pay the price necessary to attract artists of substantially higher caliber than those presently available. They also argued that some members enjoyed the highly experimental nature of some of the programming, the ambience of the concerts, and that it was possible to enjoy an evening of fine music, competently—but not "greatly"—played, in an attractive setting.

Related to the issue of quality was the question of promotion. Some board members felt that low prices arouse suspicion about the quality of the product, whereas high prices increase the perceived value. In fact, when prices were raised in 1966 and again in 1971, season memberships also increased (Exhibit 4). It was further argued that increased prices would enable TECS to book "big names," and that this would be a promotional benefit. Opponents of this strategy pointed out that, with the present level of quality, the series had sold out four of the last five years.

An important consideration in directing promotional efforts efficiently was the ratio of student memberships to regular memberships. With the present price differential of $3, the first 333 student memberships actually brought in the full $12 because of the McIntire Fund subsidy. Each student membership over 333, however, generated $3 less in revenue than a regular membership. Furthermore, if the differential between regular and student prices increased, it would become financially desirable to have fewer student members.

A final recommendation for promoting TECS involved establishing better communications between the board and the members via meetings and/or newsletters. It was argued that increased communication would stimulate interest and involvement.

Many of these policy proposals entailed an increase in ticket prices, and the board members recognized the necessity of raising prices occasionally. However, there was disagreement on how often prices should be raised. Frequent price increases may antagonize the membership, even though inflation of artist fees may justify it. Long periods without increases could be damaging in two ways: revenue is lost while costs are rising, and a momentum is established, making it even more difficult to raise prices later. One proposal offered to the board advocated not increasing the price more frequently than every three years. Other members felt that prices should be raised whenever necessary to effect the board's plans and policies for the coming season.

After the board settled these matters of policy, a decision would have to be made concerning ticket prices for the 1974–1975 season (tickets for 1973–1974 were already

on sale). There were three proposals before the board:

	Student membership	Regular membership
Present prices	$ 9	$12
Proposal I	13	16
Proposal II	9	24
Proposal III	15	20

The first (I) proposal was intended only to keep pace with inflation and would not permit upgrading the series.

The second (II) was suggested specifically to allow for two "special" concerts per year, at which artists presently out of TECS's price range would appear.

The third (III) was advocated as a means of financing a significant increase in the quality of the series.

Prices "comparable" to the TECS tickets are quoted below:

Present prices, regular membership	$1.50
Proposal I prices, regular membership[a]	2.00
Price of movie in Charlottesville	2.00
American Film Theater Series[b]	3.75
Carnegie Hall, cheapest ticket	3.00
Kennedy Center, cheapest ticket	3.00

[a]Same calculation can be made for proposals II and III.
[b]Eight Enchanted Evenings, series cost—$30. Available in Charlottesville.

The three proposals had unequal following among the board members. The board had to make a pricing decision in the early fall of 1973, as the program committee needed to know what the budget would be for the 1974–1975 season; artists were booked a year in advance.

KENT STATE UNIVERSITY: COPING WITH AN IMAGE CRISIS

"Kent State University was perceived by the respondents as having a friendly and attractive campus with an active social life and considerable freedom to 'do your own thing.' . . . It is still viewed as a school which has had campus unrest. Although students generally claimed unrest was unimportant in their college choice decision, it still showed up as the most negative component of attitude."

This was the conclusion of a study done by Kent State University marketing professors Albert Heinlein and Robert Krampf. Krampf and Heinlein obtained 200 responses from a sample of 1,000 college freshmen who sent their ACT scores to Kent State during the 1975–1976 academic year, two years prior to the 1977 Kent State campus protests concerning the construction of a gymnasium near the site of the May 1970 shootings.

Dr. Bruce Allen, special assistant to the president at Kent State, was reviewing the Heinlein-Krampf study and other data in preparation for a special student recruiting campaign. The date was July 1, 1978, and Dr. Allen, in conjunction with KSU's advertising/public relations agency, had been allocated approximately $100,000 to implement a program to avoid a 30 to 40% decline in the 1978 freshmen class. The situation was critical, as shown in Table 1. These figures were especially distressing when considered in the context of a 1,000-person decline in student enrollment the prior year. The university was already in serious financial difficulties and another bad year could result in re-

TABLE 1: Statistics on new undergraduate admissions

Reporting date	Cumulative total new undergraduate student admissions		Change 1977–1978
	For 1977	For 1978	
March	2454	1434	−1021 (−42%)
May	3263	2088	−1145 (−36%)
June	3905	2515	−1390 (−36%)

TABLE 2: Full-time equivalent enrollment (combined fall and summer enrollment eligible for state subsidy)

Year	FTE[a]	Fall headcount
1960	9,984	9,974
1961	10,937	10,510
1962	11,770	11,061
1963	13,294	11,949
1964	15,342	13,425
1965	14,809	14,833
1966	18,217	17,223
1967	19,038	18,528
1968	20,792	19,996
1969	21,930	20,747
1970	22,332	20,950
1971	21,774	20,271
1972	21,079	19,773
1973	19,607	18,534
1974	19,309	18,360
1975	20,109	20,060

[a]Full-time equivalent students.
Source: Ohio Basic Data Series.

Prepared by Dr. Bruce H. Allen, Associate Professor of Marketing, De Paul University.

TABLE 3: Fall headcount enrollments,[a] 1969–1977

Rank	1969	1970	1971	1972	1973	1974	1975	1976	1977
Freshman	7,429	7,488	5,372	5,362	4,958	5,305	6,030	6,147	5,530
Sophomore	3,665	3,613	4,119	3,550	3,196	3,216	3,380	3,470	3,309
Junior	3,289	3,573	3,713	3,679	3,264	3,132	3,250	3,164	3,145
Senior	3,605	3,519	3,777	3,776	3,436	3,155	3,375	3,270	3,106
Special undergrad	144	181	253	251	270	279	363	367	317
Total undergrad	18,132	18,374	17,234	16,618	15,124	15,087	16,398	16,418	15,380
Master's	1,943	2,016	2,048	2,002	2,102	2,142	2,321	2,415	2,444
Doctoral	512	613	703	681	778	768	744	746	804
Special grad	323	354	438	430	472	459	597	795	725
Total grad	2,778	2,983	3,189	3,113	3,352	3,369	3,662	3,956	3,973
No rank	3	13	371	24	83	2	0	0	0
Grand total	20,913	21,370	20,794	19,755	18,559	18,458	20,060	20,374	19,353

[a]Official 15th-day enrollment figures.
Source: Registrar's Report.

trenchment and a severe campus morale problem.

BACKGROUND

In preparation for the emergency student recruiting campaign, Dr. Allen and the ad agency reviewed the history of Kent State's image problems:

- Prior to May 4, 1970, Kent State was a relatively unknown regional university in a rural area located 15 miles from Akron and 60 miles from Cleveland.
- On May 4, 1970, 78 Ohio national guardsmen fired 54 rounds of ammunition into a group of Vietnam war protesters on the KSU campus who were demonstrating against the policies of the Nixon adminis-

TABLE 4: Percentage change headcount enrollment,[a] 1969–1977 (fall quarter)

	1970	1971	1972	1973	1974	1975	1976	1977	Change 1969–1977
Freshman	+0.8	−28.3	−0.2	−7.5	+7.0	+13.7	+1.9	−10.5	−25.9
Sophomore	−1.4	+14.0	−13.8	−10.0	+0.6	+5.1	+2.7	−4.6	−9.7
Junior	+8.6	+3.9	−0.9	−11.3	−4.0	+3.8	−2.7	−0.6	−4.4
Senior	−2.4	+7.3	0	−9.0	−8.2	+7.0	−3.1	−5.0	−13.8
Special undergrad	+25.7	+39.8	−0.8	+7.6	+3.3	+30.1	+1.1	−13.6	+120.1
Total undergrad	+1.3	−6.2	−3.6	−9.0	−0.2	+8.7	+0.1	−6.3	−15.2
Master's	+3.8	+1.6	−2.2	+5.0	+1.9	+8.4	+4.0	+1.2	+25.8
Doctoral	+19.7	+14.7	−3.1	+14.2	−1.3	−3.1	+0.3	+7.8	+57.0
Special grad	+9.6	+23.7	−1.8	+9.8	−2.8	+30.1	+33.2	−8.8	+124.5
Total grad	+7.4	+6.9	−2.4	+7.7	+0.5	+8.7	+8.0	+0.4	+43.0
Grand total	+2.2	−2.7	−5.0	−6.1	−0.5	+8.7	+1.6	−5.0	−7.5

[a]Official 15th-day enrollment figures.
Source: Registrar's Report.

Learning is Something You Live With
...at Kent State

Can you trap learning within the covers of a book? Hem it in by the walls of a classroom? Measure it by a clock?

At Kent State, we believe learning is something you live with . . . We believe an idea becomes an experience and then a commitment.

An idea from a biology class last week can come alive when you walk through Riveredge Park; your experience in the student-run Ambulance Service will help management class ideas make sense. We believe doing can be learning, just as learning is doing.

Kent State is a community for learning, an easy drive from anywhere in northeastern Ohio.

Because it is so convenient, fully 25 per cent of our 20,000 Kent Campus students choose to live at home and commute. The living styles of our students are as varied as the 167 ways to learn a living offered at Kent State.

On campus, students live in traditional residence halls, apartments, and in special living-learning communities where they share their experiences while majoring in architecture, music, foreign languages, peaceful change, and honors studies.

Kent State University Supports Equal Opportunity in Education and Employment

Students living off campus in fraternity and sorority and other private housing are linked to campus by a modern, "no-fare" bus system.

Discover the Kent State you need to know—the 1.2 million volume open stack library, our expanded research facilities, the experimental theatres, Blossom Center, major college sports and nature conservancy centers.

Kent State University is a major Ohio research institution with special interests ranging from America's first novel to liquid crystals, from water pollution control to computer-assisted instruction, from its laboratory school to its Gilbert and Sullivan program.

Kent is all you need from a university and more . . .

Kent State University

a Living /
Learning
Center for
Northeast
Ohio

FOR INFORMATION,
Call 1-216-672-2001

EXHIBIT 2: Television ad campaign

DR. MICHAEL SCHWARTZ
INTERIM PRESIDENT
KENT STATE UNIVERSITY

tration. Four students were killed and nine were wounded. Following the shootings, there were numerous commissions, committees, and court actions reviewing and investigating the courses of the tragedy.

• As a consequence of the unfavorable publicity surrounding the shootings. Kent State's enrollment growth trend was ended in 1971. Total enrollment declined until 1975, when it again approached the level of the early 1970s (see Table 2). The impact of the image difficulties was clearly manifest in the 28% decline in the 1971 freshmen class (see Tables 3 and 4).

• In response to this image problem, Kent State established a strong public affairs and development division, which coordinated 1973, 1974, 1975, and 1976 radio/TV/ print/ advertising/public relations campaigns (see Exhibit 1).

• Kent State University enrollment in the fall of 1975 and 1976 reached levels approaching the peak numbers in 1969 and 1970.

• In 1976, the KSU board of trustees voted to construct a gymnasium annex adjoining the present fieldhouse structure located near the site where national guardsmen pursued student protesters and the shootings occurred. Construction was to begin in 1977.

• In late 1976 and 1977, KSU student leaders, some faculty, and other former antiwar leaders voiced anger and protest over the location of the gym annex. They accused the KSU board of administration of a "cover-up" attempt at "burying" the KSU shootings incident and its symbolism in an effort to camouflage the guilty parties. The media publicized the story.

• In spring 1977, students and other sympathizers set up a "tent city" on the proposed construction site. The university president did not remove them and subsequently resigned. The media publicized the story.

• In summer 1977, students left for vacation and a fence was built around the construction site. Protesting students, clergy, and

Message Analysis

While a 60-second message contains only about 150 words, it is entirely possible to convey many pieces of information both directly and subliminally. This was true in the construction of the message used in this campaign.

A dissection of the message would reveal many elements—not all of which would be consciously perceived by the viewers any more than attitudes formed by the broadcast of news about the protests were consciously perceived. Among those elements were these:

Message: Actual script	Analysis
Visual: a message of importance to all Ohioans	An authority-enhancing device aimed at increasing the credibility of the message (i.e., this is not a routine message or commercial).
If you've been watching the TV news lately, you might think the only thing that goes on at Kent State is demonstrating.	A straightforward admission of fact—with a wry twist—aimed at increasing viewership, comprehension, and credibility. Too often, by failing to state the obvious negative, such messages reduce rather than increase believability.
In fact, the business of Kent State is teaching and learning, looking for the solutions to pressing human problems, helping people to find career opportunities, and serving the citizens of Ohio.	Use of word *business* is intentional to underscore positive connotations of the word fiscally and in terms of management. Subliminally, this challenges assumptions that the management of Kent State encourages anarchy, etc. The listing of goals might have been news to many viewers. The visuals enhanced these concepts with science research, medical training, and others strongly supported and accepted programs.
That's what Kent State is really all about. When fall term begins on September 12, some 19,000 students will come to the Kent campus and another 8,000 to the seven regional campuses.	"What it's really all about" underscores for the viewer to overlay this impression over previous mental images and to accept the new images as more accurate. "When fall term begins" by its very utterance denies any concerns that the university might not or should not reopen. The date of September 12 is a hidden advertisement to potential students and an advisory to existing students since the quarter began two weeks early this year. "Some 19,000 students"—aimed at subliminally impressing the fact the demonstrations involved only a small portion of the student body. "The seven regional campuses"—underscoring another piece of news to many viewers—that Kent is a regional educational system.
And we expect several thousand more for our continuing education programs	Intended to further broaden the image of the university as serving more than young people. . . .
They will have a common purpose—to study in more than 160 career fields.	Underscores the broad curriculum at Kent. "To study" again subliminally the impression of nonstop protest because these people have study as "a common purpose."
We have a job to do at Kent State. . . .	"Job" —not "goal," not "mission," not "objective," but plain, Anglo-Saxon "job." It is clear that we mean business, that we're not scatter-brained or ivory tower fakirs.
For our students and for all of the citizens of Ohio. . . .	Again, broaden the base beyond those we serve di-

| And that is to help people by providing them the best in educational opportunities.

That's our job and we're doing it. | rectly to all of those watching. . . .

"Helping people" and "providing opportunities" are the key terms.

Visual: For information, call, etc.

A bit pugnacious but intentially so. Again, we're hardheaded about what we're supposed to be do- | ing. This is softened somewhat by the visual of beautiful, peaceful campus—another subliminal message.

Intended to pick up any individuals who were inspired to action by the message. |

Source: The Daily Kent Stater.

outside sympathizers climbed the fence, were arrested, and taken to jail. The media heavily publicized the story.

- In summer 1977, the university ran an advertising campaign to counter negative publicity. The interim president served as spokesperson (see Exhibits 2 and 3).
- Fall 1977 brought a 1,000-student enrollment decline (see Exhibit 4) and a massive October antigym demonstration on the Kent State campus. A rally was held on the campus, with a large group of students and former antiwar activists in attendance. Following the rally, groups of protesters began to tear down the fence, the County Sheriff's troops used tear gas and force to restrain them, and a number of persons were arrested. The media were out in force to cover the story.

Following the October arrests, the activism calmed but the image of Kent State had been reimplanted in the minds of the northeastern Ohio citizenry as a troubled, radical, unsafe, and unstable campus. The new president had reorganized his administration, four or six vice-presidents had left, and the public relations director had resigned.

Realizing the severe negative fiscal impact another precipitous decline in enrollment

EXHIBIT 4

Source: The Daily Kent Stater.

EXHIBIT 5: Newspaper ad

Ad agency retained to "market" KSU

Kent State University has hired Dix & Eaton Inc., Cleveland-based advertising and public relations firm, to help direct the university's marketing efforts.

Agency officials met last week with representatives of most of the university's departments—from security guards to graduate schools—to discuss the upcoming marketing effort.

KSU has been trying to overcome the negative image created by the student disturbances on campus and the killing and wounding of students eight years ago. But Henry Eaton, president of the agency, said remaking KSU's image is only a part of the problem.

"This is a very real marketing problem," said Eaton, noting that the university faces a declining "market" of potential students while at the same time facing competition for students from nearby Cleveland State University and state schools in Youngstown and Akron.

"Even if May 4th never happened, the university still would be faced with a critical marketing problem," said John R. Wirtz, a Dix & Eaton account executive and a 1974 graduate of the KSU School of Journalism. Wirtz will be on the agency team that will work with university officials to develop the new program.

The agency will be working with Bruce Allen, assistant professor of marketing at the university. The agency already has met with several students and faculty members to get their reactions and comments about proposed new campaign.

Wirtz said he even had offers of help from a KSU graduate now working for another Cleveland public relations firm.

Although work has just begun on the efforts, the agency said the university is contemplating a short-term media campaign to run in time for the start of fall classes.

Source: The Cleveland Plain Dealer, July 23, 1978.

would have on the campus, in July 1977 the President assigned Bruce Allen, a KSU marketing professor with expertise in college and university marketing to undertake a special assignment. In conjunction with the Dix and Eaton Public Relations/Advertising Agency, the task was to do what was possible by September to increase enrollment for fall 1978 and to begin recruiting students for fall 1979 (see Exhibit 5). Dr. Allen and the agency realized that a program had to be designed and implemented very quickly.

THE SUMMER 1978 INITIATIVES

In planning the action initiatives to be taken over the summer of 1978, the planning group of Dr. Allen, Dr. Robert McCoy (executive assistant to the president), and the ad agency separated their task into two phases. Phase I was to be focused on an intensive campaign to achieve the maximum enrollment for fall registration in early September. Phase II was the carrying forward of phase I

to begin the student recruiting program for the fall quarter of 1979.

The initial step was to initiate a public media communications campaign to reach two basic markets. One market was recent high school graduates who might be undecided about attending college and could be "last-minute" full-time student enrollees at Kent State. The other market consisted of older adult part-time students who typically made college attendance decisions near the time of registration. Through research on reasons why students chose to attend Kent State (see Table 5) and on the current study body's permanent residential locations it was determined that the northeastern Ohio corridor encompassing the metropolitan areas of Cleveland, Akron, Canton, and Youngstown, would be targeted through advertising and public relations. This composite market area comprised a population of almost 3 million people.

The planning group also realized that strong competition existed within northeast-

TABLE 5: Criteria used in the college selection process based on responses from Kent State University[a]

Criteria[b]	Number of responses	Percent of persons responding	Percent of total responses
Location	54	74.0	19.2
Course of study	37	50.7	13.2
Academic reputation	36	49.3	12.8
Cost	32	43.8	11.4
Size	22	30.1	7.8
Social life	17	23.3	6.0
Appealing surroundings	15	20.5	5.3
Friends/relatives attend	15	20.5	5.3
Physical facilities	15	20.5	5.3
Other	14	19.2	5.0
Faculty/student association	6	8.2	2.1
Activities	5	6.8	1.8
Athletics (intercollegiate)	4	5.5	1.4
Financial aid	3	4.1	1.1
Admission requirements	2	2.7	0.7
Athletics (intramural)	1	1.4	0.4
Parents' approval	1	1.4	0.4
Recommendations of high school counselor	1	1.4	0.4
Recruiting effort	1	1.4	0.4
Total	281		100.0

[a]Based on 73 respondents.
[b]Criteria and number of responses were obtained from analysis of open-ended question concerning college selection criteria.
Source: Robert Cook, Kent State University DBA dissertation, 1977.

ern Ohio and the remainder of the state for resident students (Ohio State, Bowling Green, Miami University, and others) as well as for commuter students (University of Akron, Cleveland State, Youngstown State, and Case Western Reserve). Community colleges and other four-year private colleges were also competing for high school graduates and adult students. To make matters more serious, Kent State was ranked behind many of its competitive institutions as a first choice of prospective students taking the ACT exam (see Table 6).

The planning group set a goal of having an intensive advertising campaign reaching northeastern Ohio implemented by early August to run for five weeks until registration in early September. Following an analysis of media coverage and costs in light of budget limitations ($100,000 for the entire year), the ad agency recommended a campaign combining radio and print media. Television was ruled out because of the relatively high cost per message and the necessity of covering numerous media markets while targeting on market segments by age and socioeconomic characteristics.

The next step was to arrive at a campaign

TABLE 6: Within-state institutional preferences listed according to the number of times selected choice 1, 1977–1978

College code	Institution	Location	First choice	Second choice	Third choice
3312	Ohio State University	Columbus	10,038	6,931	5,262
3240	Bowling Green State University	Bowling Green	4,621	4,620	3,698
3294	Miami University	Oxford	4,061	3,779	3,159
3340	University of Cincinnati	Cincinnati	3,798	2,943	2,462
3338	University of Akron	Akron	3,044	1,778	1,401
3368	Youngstown State University	Youngstown	2,115	857	710
3314	Ohio University	Athens	2,019	2,595	2,360
3284	Kent State University	Kent	1,926	2,591	1,988
3344	University of Toledo	Toledo	1,559	1,373	1,181
3270	Cleveland State University	Cleveland	1,510	1,340	1,001
3295	Wright State University	Dayton	1,328	1,088	883
3342	University of Dayton	Dayton	741	1,058	1,064
3265	Cuyahoga Community College—Western	Parma	641	378	279
3244	Case Western Reserve University	Cleveland	632	629	629
3310	Ohio Northern University	Ada	492	585	623
3277	Lakeland Community College	Mentor	491	250	194
3261	Columbus Technical Institute	Columbus	482	492	373
3332	Sinclair Community College	Dayton	452	397	349
3236	Baldwin Wallace College	Berea	363	458	411
3242	Capital University	Columbus	358	602	552
	All other in-state institutions		12,584	12,998	12,138
	Total		53,255	47,742	40,717

Source: The American College Testing Service.

theme or positioning. The ad agency's first suggestion was rejected. They recommended the use of an upbeat rock-and-roll jingle used for 20 to 30 seconds of a radio ad, with the other 30 seconds conveying a direct action-oriented suggestion for the listeners to enroll at Kent State. Given the high degree of publicity that the university had been experiencing, the administration rejected the idea for fear that the public would see this as a "slick Madison Avenue" desperation attempt by a school in crisis to "drag in additional bodies."

An emergency meeting of the planning group was called to address this problem.

Dr. Allen suggested the application of basic marketing principles which state that consumers will purchase a product that is perceived as being different and superior in its ability to meet their needs. The ad agency and the Kent State Communications Department went into a brainstorming session and arrived at the following potential themes for the campaign:

- We are different and we'll show you the difference is better
- Your future is our business
- Plan for tomorrow at KSU
- Have your tomorrow at KSU

Kent State made the difference for Carol Morgan.

Carol Morgan is married, the mother of three children, a full-time junior high school art teacher, and a graduate of Kent State University. She is currently working on a Master of Fine Arts degree at KSU. In her own words, here's how she put the Kent State difference to work for her:

"I think Kent State is a fantastic place. It has one of the top art programs in the entire United States and I really believe it was the best possible place I could have come to school.

"I was out of high school for 10 years before starting college, never had any formal art training, and was scared to death. But the professors I had in my first few courses really helped me. They took a lot of extra time with me, whenever I needed it—and that's something I've never forgotten. It gave me the encouragement I needed to go on.

"I don't think age has anything to do with going to college if you're willing to take the time to learn what you need to know. I'm really pleased with the University and I hope my children will come here. For me, Kent State definitely made the difference."

Put the Kent State difference to work for you. Registration is August 30 to September 18. For more information call us collect at 216/672-2001.

EXHIBIT 6

- KSU road to everywhere
- Find yourself
- A ticket to where you want to go
- Passport to the future
- Progression to passport
- A different direction
- Kent can
- Kent State is growing great
- The time, the place, the people (your future)
- Because we're different, we're better
- Kent State makes a difference . . .
- . . . Makes all the difference
- It can make a difference for you

The "Kent State Makes a Difference" theme was selected unanimously by the planning group and KSU administration. It was then decided to use satisfied customers—present students, alumni, and parents—to convey the "Kent State Difference" to the public of northeastern Ohio. It was also determined that a variety of spokespersons—by age, ethnicity, program major, and perceived

EXHIBIT 7: Script for Carol Morgan ad

KSU Spot 3

Testimonial: Carol Morgan
Ancr. 1: Lee Taylor   *Running time: 60 seconds*
Ancr. 2: Jan Zima   *Mono. 7½ ips*

Music up and under

C.M.: "I'm Carol Morgan, married and the mother of three children. I'm a full-time art teacher in a junior high school, starting my master's work. . . .
"I was, actually, 28 when I started school, and . . . I checked around and it was the best school in the area that I could possibly come to."

L.T.: "Kent State makes a difference."

C.M.: "(And) it did make a difference. I started in a field that was new to me and I was fortunate. . . . I had profs who were willing to take their time to help me and I've never forgotten that. I'm really . . . really pleased with the university. I hope my children will come here."

L.T.: "Kent State makes *all* the difference."

J.Z.: "Put the Kent State difference to work for you. Applications are being accepted now, and registration is August 30 through September 18.
"To get in touch, call us collect at 672-2001. That's 672-2001 . . . and do it today."

L.T.: "Kent State makes all the difference."

C.M.: "It did make the difference for me . . . a great deal."

Music up and out

---

benefits—would be chosen for the campaign. The same spokesperson was to be featured per week, or biweekly, in newspapers and on radio in each major market. Each person would be interviewed concerning his or her Kent State experiences and excerpts of the interviews would be used in the ads. Newspaper ads would be placed in the entertainment section of the Thursday, Friday, or Saturday edition; radio spots would run during morning and evening "drive" time and late-evening time slots. The advertising campaign was planned to run from August until early September to stimulate fall registrations, and from October through December to influence persons taking the ACT and SAT exams to send their scores to Kent State. Overall, the campaign was budgeted at $60,000 of the available $100,000 budget.

Exhibits 6 through 10 provide examples of the advertising.

Other phase I enrollment/image initiatives taken involved:

- Formation of the Institutional Advancement Steering Committee to inform the campus what action was being taken to cope with the image and enrollment problems
- Telephone contact with every current student who had not preregistered and applicants who had not completed their admissions process, to determine their status and assist them in registration
- Publication of a back-to-school summer newspaper describing the exciting events planned for the coming academic year
- An in-depth study of why new freshmen

Kent State made the difference for Paul Warfield

Paul Warfield won't have any trouble making the transition from an All-Pro player in the National Football League to a member of the Hall of Fame in Canton, Ohio. It's only a matter of time.

A greater challenge for Warfield—as well as other former athletes—is making the successful transition from one career to another.

In his own words, here's how Kent State University helped Warfield prepare to move from the playing field to broadcasting.

"While I attended Kent State University during the off-season for three years, I was especially impressed by the quality of instruction in the telecommunications program.

"I feel very proud that I was able to go to Kent State. The University's academic program, whether in telecommunications or whatever, is excellent. Depending on what students want, they can find it at Kent State. There are strong academic programs, social life, fraternities and sororities, intercollegiate athletics. It is all at Kent State University.

"Kent State does make a difference."

When you register for pre-college tests—either ACT or SAT—make sure Kent State gets your test results. We'll do the rest. For more information, call the Admissions Office collect at (216) 672-2001.

Kent State makes a difference

EXHIBIT 8

EXHIBIT 9: Script for Paul Warfield ad

KSU Spot 6

Testimonial: Paul Warfield
Air: 10/22-10/29
Running time: 60 seconds

Music up and under

Ancr. 1: Paul Warfield talks about Kent State University
P.W.: Well, I feel very proud that I was able to go here to school and rightfully so, because here in Northeastern Ohio, in television work, there are a lot of Kent State alumni who are doing quite well. There are many others who are working not only on camera but behind camera in Cleveland. . . .
Ancr. 2: Kent State makes a difference.
P.W.: The academic program here, regardless of whether it is in Telecommuncations or whatever, is excellent. Depending on what a student wants. I think he can find it here at Kent State. You know, he can find certainly social life, interfraternity life, academics, intercollegiate athletics . . . it is all here at Kent State University. . . .
Ancr. 2: Kent State makes all the difference.
Ancr. 1: Put the Kent State difference to work for you. When taking the ACT or SAT, make sure Kent State gets your test results. To get in touch, call us collect at 672-2001 . . . that's 672-2001.
Ancr. 2: Kent State makes all the difference.
P.W.: It does make a difference.

Music up and out

---

visiting the campus for summer orientation chose to attend Kent State
- Other individual public relations activities

PHASE I RESULTS

Following implementation of the first stage of the advertising campaign and other enrollment initiatives, the fall 1978 statistics were compared with those of the previous year (Table 7).

The Kent State administration was very pleased with the progress made between July 1 and October 1978, documented in Table 8.

PHASE II STRATEGY

In late November, the KSU administration wondered whether phase II of the current advertising program should be continued past December 1978. An expenditure of $20,000 per month on advertising was a controversial issue among members of the campus community, especially faculty. Faculty and student groups were questioning whether the image problem had naturally subsided with the passage of time, a tranquil campus situation, and lack of media attention. Some academic deans whose budgets had been cut actually believed that the advertising had little or no impact on the enrollment situation and argued that public approval of the new administration's "no nonsense" approach was the cause for the increase in student interest toward KSU. An additional factor affecting the president's decision was that the October 1978 ACT test scores had been received, reflecting a 78% increase over the same period in 1977 and

EXHIBIT 10: Media buys for Paul Warfield spot 6

Radio station	Gross		Net	
WGAR	12 spots at $54 =	$648.00	$ 550.80	
WWWE	12 spots at 66 =	792.00	673.20	
WABQ	15 spots at 12 =	180.00	153.00	'
WAKR	10 spots at 47 =	470.00	399.50	
WKNT	25 spots at 8 =	192.00	192.00	(net only)
WKBN-AM	12 spots at 22 =	264.00	264.00	(net only)
WDOK	12 spots at 56 =	624.00	530.40	
		$3,170.00	$2,762.90	

Newspaper	Gross	
Plain Dealer (1½)	3 col. × $10 =	$543.90
Beacon Journal (2⅛)	3 col. × 10 =	367.50
Record Courier (1⅜)	4 col. × 10 =	120.40
Canton Repository (1½)	3 col. × 7 =	152.88
Vindicator (1⅝)	3 col. × 7 =	137.55
Reporter (1¾)	3 col. × 7 =	84.00
Call & Post (1⅝)	3 col. × 7 =	73.50
Hub (1⁹/₁₆)	5 col. × 10 =	84.37
Parma Post	3 col. × 7 =	132.30
South Euclid	3 col. × 7 =	107.10
Shaker	3 col. × 7 =	132.30
Garfield	3 col. × 7 =	111.30
Chagrin/Solon	3 col. × 7 =	68.25
Metro Student News (1¾)	3 col. × 7 =	176.40
		$2,291.75

TABLE 7: Comparison of enrollment, 1977–1978

	Headcount: number enrolled		Headcount: decrease/ increase	Percent decrease/ increase
	1977	1978		
Undergraduate students				
Freshmen	5,503	4,499	−1,004	−18.2
Sophomores	3,309	3,090	−219	−6.6
Juniors	3,145	2,979	−166	−5.3
Seniors	3,106	3,067	−39	−1.3
Special	317	379	+62	+19.6
Total	15,380	14,014	−1,366	−8.8
Graduate students	3,973	4,317	+344	+8.7
Overall enrollment	19,353	18,331	−1,022	−5.3

TABLE 8: New undergraduate student admissions

Reporting date	Cumulative for fall 1977	Cumulative for fall 1978	1977–1978 change	
			Number of admissions	Percent
March	2,454	1,434	−1,020	−42
May	3,263	2,088	−1,145	−36
June	3,905	2,515	−1,390	−36
September	5,384	4,008	−1,376	−26
Fall (October) registrations	5,503	4,499	−1,004	−18

TABLE 9: ACT score reports sent to Kent State for the classes of 1977–1979[a]

Testing date	1977	1978	1979	Change 1978–1979	
				Number	Percent
Oct.	1,824	1,166	2,071	+905	+78
Nov./Dec.	3,461	2,573	—	—	—
Feb.	1,923	1,501	—	—	—
Apr.	1,703	1,053	—	—	—
June	1,607	1,406	—	—	—

[a] —, not available at the date of the case.

even a 14% increase over 1976 (prior to the gym controversy) (Table 9).

A decision had to be made by December 15 as to media buys and budgeting for January through September 1979. The administrative officers wondered what statistics might be available, or could be collected, to determine the impact to date of phases I and II. They were also concerned as to the impact on enrollment if the advertising program were inadequately funded over the next eight months of the 1979 recruiting season.

PART IV

CONTROLLING MARKETING STRATEGIES

Controlling the marketing activities of a firm is very important to the strategic planning process for nonprofit organizations. The interrelation between the different marketing elements is crucial for overall marketing success. Control of these elements is necessary to insure a continuity in long-range marketing strategies.

In "The Marketing Audit: A Tool for Health Services Organizations" Eric N. Berkowitz and William A. Flexner highlight the important concerns in the "hands-on" development and implementation of a marketing plan for health care services.

The Marketing Audit: A Tool for Health Service Organizations[1]

ERIC N. BERKOWITZ • WILLIAM A. FLEXNER

Marketing is increasingly recognized as an effective tool in the management of health services. Some potential benefits recently cited in the literature include: improved capacity to respond to the needs and wants of consumers, personnel and the community in general; clarification in the development of long-range strategies and objectives; and more effective allocation of resources within the organization [1–3].

Marketing of health services involves analyzing organizational interactions (transactions) with donors, patients, employees and regulators of the organization [4]. However, before undertaking any marketing program, the factors that affect the organization's internal operations and its relations with the environment must be assessed. As Ireland notes [5]:

> Ideally, a hospital that is developing a marketing program should begin by conducting a series of research studies to gather information that will help define the characteristics, needs, and wants of its market and marketing segments, so that it can develop or revise its services and accommodations accordingly.

Unfortunately, assessments such as Ireland proposes are often done late in the planning process of health organizations. However, an early marketing inquiry—the marketing audit—may be more beneficial.

TWO APPROACHES TO PLANNING

Typically, the planning sequence in health organizations includes the specification of goals, translation of these into operational objectives, development of strategies to achieve the goals and objectives, implementation of the strategies, and finally feedback or evaluation to modify or adjust current strategies and implementation procedures [6]. Figure 1 shows this sequential process.

In this planning approach, understanding the organization's environment and particularly its marketplace usually occurs after the product and service strategies have been defined. While this information may aid in "selling" the product or services being offered, the timing is too late to determine whether the products or services being produced are those that are wanted or needed.

Marketing literature and practice provide another planning sequence. (See Figure 2.) In this model, the consumer of health services (whether viewed as the physician, the patient, the government or some other purchaser) is recognized as the focal point for making the key choices that dictate the organization's success. With a marketing approach, the consumer is considered at the beginning of the planning process [7]. Consumers may be grouped into segments based on behavior or needs. Included in this initial analysis are a consideration of both the in-

[1]From *HCM Review*, Fall 1978, pp. 51–57, by Eric N. Berkowitz and William A. Flexner. Reprinted with permission of Aspen Publishers, Inc., © 1978.

FIGURE 1: A typical health planning model

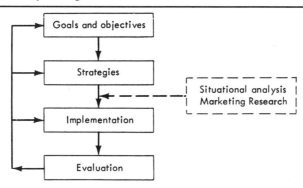

ternal capabilities of the organization, and the preferences and needs of the organization's current and potential consumers. This examination of the organization's internal aspects identifies the range of activities that can be performed, as well as the strong and weak points among these activities.

Once this situational or segmentation analysis is completed, the second step in the process associates various strategies with

FIGURE 2: A marketing planning model

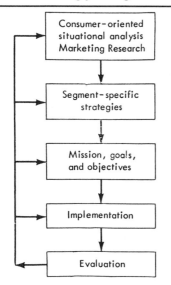

particular segments of consumers. Forecasts of the potential demand from each segment are then often attempted. Only after this step has been completed does the organization consider specific goals and objectives, and the means for implementing the chosen strategies.

As can be seen, the two approaches differ only in terms of the process flow. This difference, however, is critical in terms of structuring consumer-responsive strategies and plans. Traditionally, health service organizations have planned from the inside to the consumer. Yet regulatory, resource and competition trends are requiring the change from a traditional to a marketing planning strategy. A marketing approach starts the process with the consumer, letting the consumer's needs and wants guide the strategy of the organization. Here the consumer is at the beginning of the planning process, around which selective strategies, objectives and goals are constructed. For any organization changing to a marketing orientation, the process should begin with a marketing audit.

THE MARKETING AUDIT

Audits have typically been a procedure used in accounting for internal control. Because marketing can be a critical activity contributing to the efficient and effective operation of any organization, the need for marketing audits in nontraditional businesses is increasing. As many health organizations begin to recognize the marketing function and to formulate marketing objectives, an early marketing audit is essential. This process provides a foundation on which to develop programs and standards for evaluation.

The Meaning of a Marketing Audit. In its most basic sense, an audit is an evaluation of a firm's activities. Bell has suggested that "a marketing audit is a systematic and thorough examination of a company's marketing position" [8]. Shuchman more precisely outlines this practice as [9]:

> a systematic, critical, and impartial review and appraisal of the total marketing operation: of the basic objectives and policies and the assumptions which underlie them as well as the methods, procedures, personnel, and organization employed to implement the policies and achieve the objectives.

A variety of reasons for conducting a marketing audit exists. The dynamic nature of society and the health care industry, in particular, requires up-to-date information for the organization to operate effectively. One must periodically monitor the organization's position and activities to assess its responsiveness to market needs and preferences.

In this dynamic environment, a marketing audit has many purposes [10]:

- It appraises the total marketing operation.
- It centers on the evaluation of objectives and policies and the assumptions that underlie them.
- It aims for prognosis as well as diagnosis.
- It searches for opportunities and means for exploiting them as well as for weaknesses and means for their elimination.

- It practices preventive as well as curative marketing practices.

The Nature of an Audit. Conducting an audit can be an extremely complex task. In essence, it involves examining the entire scope of the organization's activities. Through a broad-based approach, certain cogent issues within each area of marketing operations (product and service design, promotion, price, location) can be identified for analysis in greater depth. Figure 3 shows the scope of the marketing audit procedure.

The audit process is represented as a series of circles expanding outward from the consumer. One begins by looking at the size of the consumer market and the various ways that it can be divided or segmented. To this information must be added information concerning one's own health service organization. Often there are internal constraints that must be determined before devising marketing strategies. Beyond the organization, an assessment needs to be made of the competition, its strengths and weaknesses.

Cutting across each of these circles are the organizing or controllable variables that ultimately come together to define the marketing strategy. These marketing mix variables include the product or service offered, the price at which it is offered, the way in which it is promoted and the channels through which the product or service is distributed [11]. At each stage of the marketing audit, these variables must be considered.

Areas of Inquiry in the Marketing Audit Procedure. For any organization, some factors may appear more relevant than others. The more important and common areas of inquiry for each circle represented in Figure 3 will be listed here in the form of questions to serve as a guide in the marketing audit process. These questions indicate that an audit is an information gathering process.

FIGURE 3: The scope of the marketing audit

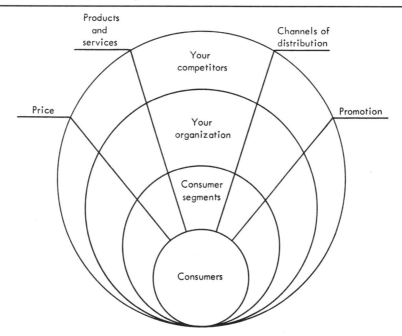

Analysis will then depend on the audit team's foresight and management skill.

The market and market segments

1. How large is the territory covered by your market? How have you determined this?
2. How is your market grouped?
   a. Is it scattered?
   b. How many important segments are there?
   c. How are these segments determined (demographics, service usage, attitudinally)?
3. Is the market entirely urban, or is a fair proportion of it rural?
4. What percentage of your market uses third party payment?
   a. What are the attitudes and operations of third parties?
   b. Are they all equally profitable?

5. What are the effects of the following factors on your market?
   a. Age
   b. Income
   c. Occupation
   d. Increasing population
   e. demographic shifting
   f. Decreasing birthrate
6. What proportion of potential customers are familiar with your organization, services, programs?
   a. What is your image in the marketplace?
   b. What are the important components of your image?

The organization

1. Short history of your organization;
   a. When and how was it organized?

b. What has been the nature of its growth?

c. How fast and far have its markets expanded? Where do your patients come from geographically?

d. What is the basic policy of the organization? Is it on "health care," "profit"?

e. What has been the financial history of the organization?
   (1) How has it been capitalized?
   (2) Have there been any accounts receivable problems?
   (3) What is inventory investment?

f. What has been the organization's success with the various services promoted?

2. How does your organization compare with the industry?

   a. Is the total volume (gross revenue, utilization) increasing, decreasing?

   b. Have there been any fluctuations in revenue? If so, what were they due to?

3. What are the objectives and goals of the organization? How can they be expressed beyond the provision of "good health care"?

4. What are the organization's present strengths and weaknesses in:
   a. Medical facilities
   b. Management capabilities
   c. Medical staff
   d. Technical facilities
   e. Reputation
   f. Financial capabilities
   g. Image

5. What is the labor environment for your organization?
   a. For medical staff (nurses, physicians, etc.)?
   b. For support personnel?

6. How dependent is your organization upon conditions of other industries (third party payers)?

7. Are weaknesses being compensated for and strengths being used? How?

8. How are the following areas of your marketing function organized?
   a. Structure
   b. Manpower
   c. Reporting relationships
   d. Decision-making power

9. What kinds of external controls affect your organization?
   a. Local?
   b. State?
   c. Federal?
   d. Self-regulatory?

10. What are the trends in recent regulatory rulings?

Competitors

1. How many competitors are in your industry?
   a. How do you define your competitors?
   b. Has this number increased or decreased in the last four years?

2. Is competition on a price or nonprice basis?

3. What are the choices afforded patients?
   a. In services?
   b. In payment?

4. What is your position in the market—size and strength—relative to competitors?

Products and services

1. Complete a list of your organization's products and services, both present and proposed.

2. What are the general outstanding characteristics of each product or service?

3. What superiority or distinctiveness of products or services do you have, as compared with competing organizations?

4. What is the total cost per service (in-use)? Is service over/underutilized?

5. What services are most heavily used? Why?

a. What is the profile of patients/physicians who use the services?

b. Are there distinct groups of users?

6. What are your organization's policies regarding:

a. Number and types of services to offer?

b. Assessing needs for service addition/deletion?

7. History of products and services (complete for major products and services):

a. How many did the organization originally have?

b. How many have been added or dropped?

c. What important changes have taken place in services during the last ten years?

d. Has demand for the services increased or decreased?

e. What are the most common complaints against the service?

f. What services could be added to your organization that would make it more attractive to patients, medical staff, nonmedical personnel?

g. What are the strongest points of your services to patients, medical staff, nonmedical personnel?

h. Have you any other features that individualize your service or give you an advantage over competitors?

Price

1. What is the pricing strategy of the organization?

a. Cost-plus

b. Return on investment

c. Stabilization

2. How are prices for services determined?

a. How often are prices reviewed?

b. What factors contribute to price increase/decrease?

3. What have been the price trends for the past five years?

4. How are your pricing policies viewed by:

a. Patients

b. Physicians

c. Third party payers

d. Competitors

e. Regulators

Promotion

1. What is the purpose of the organization's present promotional activities (including advertising)?

a. Protective

b. Educational

c. Search out new markets

d. Develop all markets

e. Establish a new service

2. Has this purpose undergone any change in recent years?

3. To whom has advertising appeal been largely directed?

a. Donors

b. Patients

(1) Former or current

(2) Prospective

c. Physicians

(1) On staff

(2) Potential

4. What media have been used?

5. Are the media still effective in reaching the intended audience?

6. What copy appeals have been notable in terms of response?

7. What methods have been used for measuring advertising effectiveness?

8. What is the role of public relations?

a. Is it a separate function/department?

b. What is the scope of responsibilities?

Channels of distribution

1. What are the trends in distribution in the industry?

a. What services are being performed on an outpatient basis?

b. What services are being provided on an at-home basis?

c. Are satellite facilities being used?

2. What factors are considered in location decisions? When did you last evaluate present location?

3. What distributors do you deal with? (e.g., medical supply houses, etc.)

4. How large an inventory must you carry?

The marketing audit is the starting point. Examining the issues raised in these questions will allow a more viable, effective marketing strategy to be developed. For the health organization beginning its marketing plan, the audit process will establish parameters for the program and goals to be accomplished.

Many of the questions raised within the marketing audit already are being considered in some form by health planners. In this sense, marketing planning may seem no different from methods presently used. Yet the key difference is *when* these questions are examined. A marketing orientation begins with the consumers of the service. The audit process then continues internally after information is gained from the marketplace. This approach follows an external sequence, while traditional health planning methods proceed in the opposite direction.

Because the health care organization operates in a dynamic environment, the audit should become a part of the regular planning sequence. Each question should be reevaluated to highlight changes that may have important strategic implications for the organization in fulfilling its goals.

The marketing audit provides guidance for improving the organization's profitability, competitive position and overall performance. This is accomplished by clarifying the setting in which strategies, goals, and objectives related to future action can be intelligently generated.

NOTE

1. The authors thank Steven R. Orr, Vice President, Corporate Planning, Fairview Community Hospitals, Minneapolis, Minnesota, for his assistance in the preparation of this article.

REFERENCES

[1] Ireland, R. C., "Using Marketing Strategies to Put Hospitals on Target," *Hospitals,* 51 (June 1, 1977), p. 54–58.

[2] O'Halloran, R. D., J. Staples, and P. Chiampa, "Marketing Your Hospital," *Hospital Progress,* 57 (1976), p. 68–71.

[3] Clarke, R. N., "Marketing Health Care: Problems in Implementation," *Health Care Management Review,* 3:1 (Winter 1978), p. 21–27.

[4] Shapiro, B. P., "Marketing for Nonprofit Organizations," *Harvard Business Review* (September–October 1973), p. 123–32.

[5] Ireland, "Using Marketing Strategies," p. 55.

[6] Hyman, H., *Health Planning.* Germantown, MD: Aspen Systems Corporation, 1975, Ch. 3.

[7] Keith, R. J., "The Marketing Revolution," *Journal of Marketing,* (January 1960), p. 35–38.

[8] Bell, M. L., *Marketing: Concepts and Strategies,* 2nd ed, Boston: Houghton Mifflin Co., 1972, p. 428.

[9] Shuchman, A., "The Marketing Audit: Its Nature, Purposes, and Problems," in *Analyzing and Improving Marketing Performance, Report No. 32,* New York: American Management Association, 1959, p. 13.

[10] Shuchman, "The Marketing Audit," p. 15.

[11] McCarthy, E. J., *Basic Marketing: A Managerial Approach,* 5th ed., Homewood, IL: Richard D. Irwin, Inc., 1975.

PART V
COMPREHENSIVE CASES

The purpose of this final section of the book is to provide students an opportunity to work with comprehensive cases that require a variety of integrative, programmatic solutions, so no articles are included.

The first case, "The Milwaukee Blood Center" concerns a major regional blood center serving six counties in Wisconsin. Demand for blood exceeds the available supply. Research data is available to help decision makers design a comprehensive marketing strategy.

The cafeteria and coffee shop of "The Michigan League" is experiencing declining sales while other aspects of the League's operation are thriving. Pat Lawson must determine the main problems and opportunities facing the League and develop a comprehensive marketing strategy to reverse the current trend.

The director of "The Lively Arts at Hanson" faces a number of difficult problems associated with declining attendance at organization-sponsored events. A detailed marketing strategy for the coming season is needed.

THE MILWAUKEE BLOOD CENTER

The Milwaukee Blood Center (MBC) was established in 1946 by the Junior League to meet the emerging needs for blood in the Milwaukee area. The MBC has experienced substantial growth and is now a major regional blood center. The Milwaukee Blood Center is a member of two blood banking trade associations: the American Association of Blood Banks and the Council of Community Blood Centers. MBC is affiliated with the Medical College of Wisconsin. For a discussion of the current state of blood donation in the United States see the Appendix.

In 1976, the Milwaukee Blood Center moved to a new location at the western edge of the downtown area and adjacent to Marquette University. Within several blocks of their location there are five hospitals which MBC serves. The first floor of the building was renovated for use in blood collection. Free parking is provided behind the building for donors. The MBC also makes extensive use of the five mobile units for drawing blood at business and organization sites. Furthermore, three satellite stations are utilized in suburban and neighboring city locations.

CURRENT SITUATION

In fiscal 1979, volunteer donors in southeastern Wisconsin gave 91,500 units of blood to support patients' needs in the 33 hospitals that the Milwaukee Blood Center served. As Exhibit 1 shows, donations have increased steadily during the decade of the 1970s and the 1979 total was 5,500 over the previous year.

However, local demand for blood *exceeded* local donations by 3,100 units, which had to be obtained from other blood centers. The major objective of donor recruitment programs is to make this region self-sufficient.

Eighty percent of the blood collected in the region was given by members of 900 donor clubs sponsored by business, schools, churches, and other civic, labor, and community groups in southeastern Wisconsin. The other 20% was drawn from individuals at MBC's central location in Milwaukee and parttime satellite stations located within the six-county area that the center serves.

These donors made it possible for the Milwaukee Blood Center to keep pace with the increasing demand for blood products in the region. Patients in the 33 hospitals served by the center required 5,400 more units of whole blood and packed red blood cells than were needed in 1978. The MBC also experienced a dramatic increase in the need for blood components.

The increased need for blood and blood components is related in part to the growing number of open heart, hip replacement, and kidney transplant operations being performed. Regular transfusions of blood platelets are demanded by a growing number of patients undergoing chemotherapy for cancer.

This case was prepared by Professor Patrick E. Murphy, University of Notre Dame, and Ron Franzmeier, Zigman-Joseph-Skeen, as a basis for class discussion rather than to illustrate either effective or ineffective handling of an administrative situation. Reprinted with permission from Marquette University, © 1980.

EXHIBIT 1: Number of volunteer blood donations, 1970–1979[a]

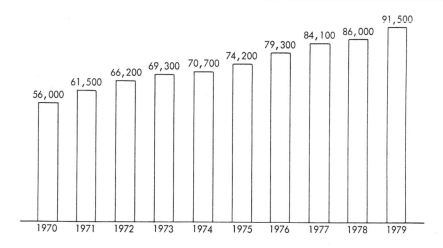

Values by year:
1970: 56,000
1971: 61,500
1972: 66,200
1973: 69,300
1974: 70,700
1975: 74,200
1976: 79,300
1977: 84,100
1978: 86,000
1979: 91,500

[a]During fiscal year 1979, 60,000 donors provided the 91,500 units of blood collected in the region. As demand continues to increase, the Blood Center must recruit more donors to avoid having to ask for more donations each year from the same people.

A MARKETING APPROACH

Administrators at MBC felt that the amount of blood collected from donor clubs was reaching a steady-state position. In fact, a few mobile drives had to be canceled because of layoffs or slowdowns at local industries. Also, the demographic projections for the southeastern Wisconsin area indicate that the area will not grow in population. Therefore, the administration felt that a program aimed at the individual donor was needed. To facilitate this process the Milwaukee Blood Center sought the services of a local marketing consulting firm.

With the assistance of the consultant, the administrators were able to relate the marketing-mix elements to the process of blood donation. The product/service that they are offering is the unique satisfaction which the donor receives from the act of contributing a pint of his/her blood. This satisfaction cannot be derived from writing a check or volunteering time. The price not only represents the real cost of physical discomfort of the donor, inconvenience, and time lost that could be spent in other ways, but also the psychological cost of fear of the total experience. The place or distribution element is directly related to the center's location or availability of mobile units or satellite stations. Finally, promotion entails the personal selling effort engaged in by the donor recruiters and the mass-media efforts. The Milwaukee Blood Center employs four full-time donor recruiters who call on industry and other donor clubs.

The mass-media promotion used by the Milwaukee Blood Center took the form of Public Service Announcements. These announcements are free, but often aired late at night or at times when few people are watching or listening. Also, publicity is utilized by the Blood Center when they are experiencing a large shortage of donations. The problem with this type of promotion is that the Blood Center has no real control over the frequency with which their message reaches the target audience. Therefore, the Blood Center has relied heavily on other means of reaching prospective donors, such as printed brochures, direct-mail materials, and telephone solicitation.

MARKETING RESEARCH

The consultant and administration agreed that before a marketing program could be developed for the MBC, marketing research was necessary. Specifically, they needed to know more about their market area's donation patterns and certain attitudes of thought leaders and donors toward the Blood Center.

One part of the marketing research encompassed a study of the present geographic market area. It includes six counties which comprise the southeastern region of Wisconsin. These counties are: Milwaukee, Waukesha, Ozaukee, Washington, Racine, and Kenosha. Exhibit 2 shows the population and donation profile of this area for fiscal 1979. One important figure in this table is the percentage of population which actually donates. It is only 3% for the Blood Center area, while the national figure is between 5 and 6%. In the county-by-county breakdown, Racine and Kenosha residents are not donating at a percentage equal to their population proportion.

A second phase of the initial marketing research effort entailed a "thought leader" study. Approximately 10 governmental and mass-media leaders in Racine, Kenosha, and Waukesha were interviewed regarding their

EXHIBIT 2

Market—donor statistics

Region's population	1,710,000
Donors	55,000 (3.2%)
Donations needed	102,000 (6%)

Population and donation profile of counties served by Milwaukee Blood Center

County	Population	Percent of MBC region population	Units drawn in county	Percent of total units drawn in MBC region
Milwaukee	982,000	57.4	56,000	61
Waukesha	276,000	16.1	15,800	17
Ozaukee	68,000	4.0	4,200	5
Washington	80,000	4.7	4,000	4
Racine	178,000	10.4	6,600	7
Kenosha	126,000	7.4	4,000	4
Other	—	—	1,400	2
Approximate region total	1,710,000	100	92,000	100

EXHIBIT 3: Reasons why people have not donated blood before

	Was a reason (%)	Was not a reason (%)	No answer; don't know (%)
You thought you had a medical condition which kept you from giving.	16	83	1
You thought giving blood was painful.	29	70	1
You never knew your blood was needed.	30	70	0
You were afraid of giving blood.	30	70	0
You didn't know where to go to give blood.	31	69	0
The location of the MBC was inconvenient.	22	77	1
No one ever asked you to donate before.	62	37	1
You were too busy to give blood.	37	61	2

perception of attitudes that people in their area had toward the Blood Center. Thought leaders in Milwaukee were not surveyed because the Blood Center administrators had frequent contact with them. One consistent finding was that they felt there was some reluctance of people in these cities to donate to the "Milwaukee" Blood Center. Most citizens did not realize that the Blood Center served the entire southeastern Wisconsin region.

Research was also conducted with first-time donors. One hundred first-time donors were surveyed via telephone. They were prompted to donate by the 1979 Winter Blood Telethon which was carried by a local television station. These donors were asked why they had never donated before. Their responses are shown in Exhibit 3. The most frequently mentioned reason was—no one ever asked me to donate. Some of the more obvious reasons, such as "too busy" and "afraid to give," were designated by a much smaller percentage of the donors.

Another survey was conducted at the downtown Milwaukee drawing station. Donors were asked to fill out a short questionnaire while they were being served refresh-

ments after donating; 462 donors responded over a two-week period. One of the major findings of this survey was that nearly one-third of the respondents (32.4%) indicated that they would be likely to donate more often if there was a drawing station located more conveniently to their home.

CONCLUSION

When the consultant presented these research findings to the administration of MBC, they indicated that the consultant should develop a comprehensive marketing strategy (plan) based on these results. The administrators urged the consultants to be innovative and not to be concerned about organizational resistance to change. The only limiting factors that the administration placed on the marketing plan was that they could not afford paid television advertising. Major mass-media resources for the Milwaukee area are shown in Exhibit 4. The Milwaukee Blood Center's Board of Directors is scheduled to meet in three weeks and the administrator wants to present the comprehensive marketing program to them at that time.

EXHIBIT 4: Major mass-media resources in Milwaukee area

| | Newspaper | | | |
	Name	Circulation	Frequency	Cost per column inch
Milwaukee	*Journal*	329,000	Daily	$ 13.58
	Sentinal	165,205	Daily	7.84
	Post	262,000	Weekly (suburban)	3.92
Kenosha	*Kenosha News*	31,620	Daily	4.84
	Kenosha Labor Press	21,500	Weekly	3.92
Racine	*Labor News*	16,000	Weekly	3.05
	Journal Times	40,000	Daily	4.75
Waukesha	*Freeman*	26,000	Daily	3.86

| | Radio | | |
	Name	Format	Average cost (per 30-second spot)
Milwaukee	WTMJ	Mid road	$67.50
	WOKY	AM rock	35.00
	WZUU	FM rock	27.00
	WBCS	Country/western	22.00
Kenosha	WLIP	Mid road	7.75
	WJZQ	FM rock	6.35
Racine	WRJN	Mid road	7.50
	WRKR	AM rock	11.00
	WWEG	Country/western	10.00

APPENDIX:
CURRENT STATUS
OF BLOOD DONATION
IN THE UNITED STATES

The blood collection system in America is going through some major changes, which may not be fully understood by the public.

Credits for Donating. There used to be a national system of credits for blood donors (hence the concept of blood "banking"). If you gave a pint of blood, a credit was given to you, your family, or whomever you designated to be the recipient of that credit. If you or your family needed a blood transfusion, you could draw on those credits and did not have to worry about replacing the blood.

Those who had no credits for previous donations were assessed a penalty charge, called a nonreplacement fee, unless they were able to find someone who would donate to replace the blood used.

This system of credits proved very costly to maintain and involved the transfer of paper credits rather than blood. It also seemed to place an unfair burden on the elderly and others who did not have friends or family members able to replace the blood used. For these reasons, nearly 80% of the blood centers in the country have dropped the system of credits and no longer charge a nonreplacement fee. Blood is simply made available to all who need it and the only charge made is for the costs of the collecting and processing it (and this is covered by most insurance programs).

Paid Donors. It was very common practice at one time for donors to be paid for the blood they gave. Research has determined that the incidence of infectious hepatitis in blood from donors who have been paid is far greater than that in blood which comes from volunteer donors. As a result, most communities no longer pay donors or offer them any reward of monetary value.

Regional Blood Centers. At one time, many small communities had their own blood program—usually organized by the local hospital and industry leaders. Physicians have conducted research into how to use blood efficiently, and about how to separate it into various components. Today, a patient is rarely given whole blood. They receive only those components that are required.

Testing, processing, and separating blood into its components required specialized staff and equipment which would be very costly to duplicate in every community. As a result, the country's blood collection system is being regionalized. Blood is being collected in small communities, but it is transported to regional blood centers, where it is processed.

The blood is stored at these centers, with the quantities and types of blood needed being returned to the small towns so that their supply is always adequate.

As a result of this regulation, many of the small-town blood programs are now a part of regional programs. They are subject to new regulations and have suffered a loss of local identity.

Fewer Restrictions on Donors. Research has greatly improved our understanding of how disease is and is not transmitted through blood transfusions. As a result, many people who once were rejected as blood donors because of some childhood disease can now donate. At one time, the average rejection rate was 12% (i.e., 12% of the people who came in to donate were rejected as donors on the basis of their medical history). Today, only 5% of those who come in are turned away because of past illnesses.

Donors between the age of 17 and 65 who are in good health are eligible to donate. In special circumstances individuals older or younger than those ages may be donors. A person may donate once every 10 weeks (five times per year). However, individuals who donate in the United States usually do so less than once a year.

THE MICHIGAN LEAGUE

Pat Lawson has been manager of the Michigan League for six years. She is in charge of the operation and maintenance of the League building. She acts as purchasing agent and is in charge of the accounting and financial management of the League's activities. As business manager, Pat Lawson is responsible to a Board of Governors and to the vice president for finance. She is expected to report regularly to both.

Recently the staff has noticed a continuing decrease in the number of customers in the cafeteria and coffee shop. However, at the same time the other League functions (conferences, banquets, special events) are operating near capacity. Pat is interested in finding the underlying causes of the decrease in the customer count. She would like to develop courses of action to reverse this trend.

BACKGROUND

The Michigan Leauge is one of three University Activity Centers. The other two centers are the North Campus Commons and the Michigan Union. The Michigan League was built in 1929 with funds raised by University of Michigan women. At the time of the League's construction, women were not permitted to use the Michigan Union. In response to the women's need, the University alumnae built the Michigan League "for the purpose of promoting the social and recreational welfare of the women students in the university." Through the years the emphasis has shifted, and presently for both men and women the primary student building (receiving the major university funding) is the Michigan Union. Currently the Michigan League serves not only the campus community but also the general public.

The League is centrally located one block from the main street of the campus area. It is situated on a highly trafficked street and is very visible. A large sign near the sidewalk advertises the cafeteria and other services. In addition to the cafeteria and coffee shop, the League building has a gift shop, study rooms, conference rooms, a ballroom, several large banquet rooms, student organization offices, and, on the fourth floor, hotel service consisting of 21 rooms. Over the past four years there has been a significant increase in the use of the building by students for study and meeting space.

CAFETERIA

The cafeteria is open Monday–Saturday, 11:30 A.M.–1:15 P.M. and 5:00 P.M.–7:15 P.M. Dinner is served on Sunday from 11:30 A.M. to 2:15 P.M. A full menu is provided for both lunch and dinner. Meal prices range from appoximately $3.00 for lunch to $4.25 for dinner. The cafeteria does not serve alcohol. The League has a limited conference liquor license for scheduled events. A daily special is offered in addition to the other items. The luncheon and dinner entrees are on a three-week cycle and offer a different variety daily. Although there is no table service, the cafeteria maintains a full staff. The cafeteria has

Prepared by Maureen Fanshawe, in James D. Scott, Martin R. Warshaw, and James R. Taylor, *Introduction to Marketing Management*, 5th ed.

Copyright © 1985, by Richard D. Irwin. Reprinted by permission of the publisher.

EXHIBIT 1

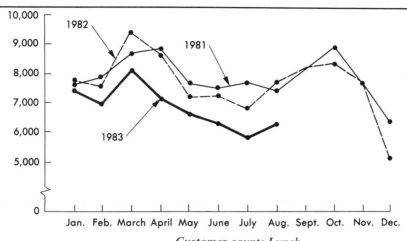

	Customer count: Lunch		
	1981	1982	1983
January	7,641	7,648	7,487
February	7,883	7,586	6,989
March	8,725	9,403	8,067
April	8,816	8,780	7,125
May	7,675	7,267	6,610
June	7,440	7,221	6,290
July	7,659	6,795	5,722
August	7,435	7,724	6,236
September	8,144	8,049	*
October	8,900	8,418	*
November	7,667	7,682	*
December	6,422	5,227	*

*Customer count not yet taken for September–December 1983.

a pleasant atmosphere and emphasis is placed on cleanliness.

NATURE OF THE MARKET

The Michigan League is available to the general public as well as the campus community. Throughout the school year the cafeteria serves approximately 388 lunches and 350 dinners daily. The coffee shop serves 800–1,200 people daily. During the summer months the daily totals are considerably lower. Peak seasons are directly associated with the academic year. From May through August there is a steady decline in business (Exhibit 1 and Exhibit 1A). Special functions scheduled at the League are also affected by the "seasonality" factor. During the months of May–August the League facilities for weddings operate at capacity.

Hill Auditorium and Powers Center are university cultural performance centers, each within one block of the League. Plays, concerts, and ballet are frequently run. On performance nights the League adjusts its regular schedule and menu. There is an in-

EXHIBIT 1A

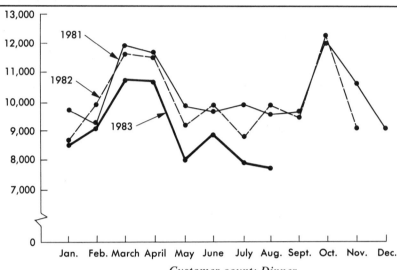

Customer count: Dinner

	1981	1982	1983
January	9,757	8,666	8,635
February	9,265	9,849	9,074
March	11,946	11,636	10,779
April	11,664	11,552	10,718
May	9,894	9,170	8,098
June	9,688	9,838	8,941
July	9,943	8,766	7,925
August	9,628	9,844	7,812
September	9,673	9,572	*
October	12,152	12,164	*
November	10,778	9,168	*
December	9,253	7,555	*

*Customer count not yet taken for September–December 1983.

crease in the cafeteria customer count on these evenings. This increase is not as high as Pat believes it could be. She has attributed this fact to the large number of area restaurants serving alcohol which are available to the Hill Auditorium and Powers Center patrons.

The results of a 1978 survey performed by the League Cafeteria revealed that present customers use the cafeteria on a regular basis and for the following reasons: they enjoy the food, location, no tipping feature, cafeteria-style service, and atmosphere. Also pro-

vided by this survey were positive and negative comments about the cafeteria (Exhibits 2 and 2A).

A third and final part of the survey requested customer suggestions. Many of the suggestions were for bigger salads, a salad bar, to expand the variety of vegetarian dishes and specials, and to include a vegetable or salad with the student special. Presently the League has comment and suggestion cards available in the cafeteria, coffee shop, and hotel rooms. After each special

EXHIBIT 2: Survey results for Michigan League (1978)

	Tuesday noon (170 surveys)	Tuesday night (128)	Thursday night (130)	Sunday (140)
How Often				
First time	2	2	2	4
Infrequent	40	19	25	33
Often	125	107	88	102
Enjoy				
Food	128	117	101	132
Location	154	105	85	98
Cafeteria	126	98	86	122
No tipping	117	100	87	116
Atmosphere	91	91	88	117
Music				
Prefer music	41	54	43	37
Prefer no music	41	27	5	46

Cumulative results (568 surveys)

How Often	
First time	10
Infrequent	117
Often	422
Enjoy	
Food	478
Location	432
No tipping	426
Cafeteria	432
Atmosphere	387
Music	
Prefer music	175
Prefer no music	119

function, a short rating and suggestion card is sent to the person who made the arrangements.

SPECIAL FEATURES AT THE CAFETERIA

The League cafeteria offers daily specials. These specials are available to the students at a reduced price. A luncheon special costs $2.50, and a dinner student special costs $2.75. The cafeteria sells approximately 125 luncheon and 60 dinner specials daily. The student specials are less than the cost of dormitory dinners. Students find it the "best food for the price in town." Over the years, the board has felt "that providing good food to students at the lowest possible cost in an attractive university setting was an important responsibility of the League." The League has a student tax discount but does not have senior citizen discounts.

From October through July, every Thursday evening at the cafeteria is "International and American Heritage Night." Each Thursday night the menu consists of foods from the featured country or state. International night has been successful. On this night the cafeteria serves an average of 475 customers.

EXHIBIT 2A

Frequent comments: Positive	
Enjoy the food	74
Variety	25
Reasonable price	32
International night	17
Service	51
Atmosphere	18
Frequent comments: Negative	
Dull variety	23
Too much gravy	13
Student special	19
Prices too high	28
Cold food	25
Service	
Long, slow lines	38
Discourteous staff	21
Small portions	38
Parking	20

The Michigan League cafeteria "Command Performance dinner" offered the customer a unique dining experience. The customers are encouraged through advertisements to make requests for their favorite foods, to be served at the Command Performance dinner. From these nominations the most requested items are selected to make up the menu for the evening. This special feature has been offered twice and was successful.

Sunday dinner at the cafeteria is served from 11:30 A.M. to 2:15 P.M. White linen cloths and fresh flowers are placed on the tables. The Sunday customer profile at the cafeteria is primarily senior citizens.

COMPETITION

The Michigan League is centrally located on the Michigan campus one block from the campus shopping street and three blocks from downtown Ann Arbor. There are approximately 143 restaurants in the downtown area. Eighty of these restaurants provide full service. The League cafeteria's 1982 share of the Ann Arbor restaurant market was 1.9 percent. In a recent report the Board of Governors recommended that, "The university administration officially recommend that all university departments use the university centers (League, Union, and North Campus Commons) food services, both within these buildings and for catering wherever needed on the university campus."

In direct competition with the League cafeteria is the Michigan Union. The recent revitalization of the union is expected to impact the League. Food revenue may decline as union revenue increases. The Union University Club offers a menu similar to the League's, with prices approximately one dollar higher per meal at lunch and two dollars higher at dinner. The union has table service and serves alcohol. Every Sunday night at the union from 5:30 P.M.–8:00 P.M. is an "all-you-can-eat" Italian Festival for $3.99. The Italian Festival night is successful. A recent addition to the union's lower level, the Michigan Union Grill (MUG), has a variety of food counters and primarily caters to student clientele. The prices are relatively low, to meet the students' budgets, and a student tax discount is offered. Dormitory food service does not operate on Sundays. The other area restaurants have a wide variety of menus but are priced slightly higher than the League. The recent restructuring of dorm food service to include breakfast and flexible hours affected the League's student count adversely.

The recent construction of the Ingalls Street pedestrian mall has drastically decreased parking availability for League patrons. Ingalls Street (which runs adjacent to the League) previously had 45 open-meter parking spaces. More than half of the spaces were destroyed. This loss of parking has been a problem for League patrons. There are two public parking structures, each within one block of the League. It costs two dollars to park in the garage. Across the street from the League is a staff parking lot. Parking is permitted in this lot only after 5:00 P.M. Street parking on North University after 5:00 P.M. has recently been permitted, adding about 12 spaces.

PROMOTION

The League's 1982 advertising budget was $5,500. Of this budget, 91 percent was allocated to the cafeteria. The objective of the cafeteria advertising is to increase awareness in the community. The emphasis of weekly advertisements is usually placed on special-feature nights at the cafeteria. The Command Performance dinner was advertised twice in the *Ann Arbor News*. The League purchased a 2″ × 5″ ad (space is sold by column inch, $7.50 per inch) and ran the ad the week preceding the event. When the League is not advertising for a feature night, a 1½″ × 2″ ad is purchased for $22.50 and run once a week.

For several years the League ran a weekly advertisement for the cafeteria using a limerick theme. Readers would compose an advertising limerick for the cafeteria and mail their suggestions to Julie, Pat Lawson's administrative assistant. She would then select the best limerick entry weekly, to be used in the advertisement. The winning entry received two free dinners at the cafeteria. The League employed this promotional strategy for five years prior to its discontinuance in July 1983. The League staff felt that although they had received a tremendous response, the theme had become overused and repetitive and, as a result, had lost effectiveness.

Presently the League has no measurement of ad effectiveness. In addition, their promotional strategy uses a mass appeal, with minimal attention given to individual market segments. The staff wonders whether the advertising dollars could be more effectively spent by placing emphasis on slow nights rather than on already successful feature nights. To increase the customer count on slow nights, Pat is considering the extension of the feature-night concept to these nights. She also senses a need for an advertising strategy to define her key potential customers and then to target the advertising efforts to this market.

The League also advertises in the *Observer*, a monthly newspaper publication. The cafeteria is listed in the Restaurant Guide section. The price is $25.00/6 months for a four-line listing. The ad is clearly visible but is listed with many other Ann Arbor restaurants. A one-fourth page display advertisement in the *Observer* costs $246.00 (for a one-month edition). However, the *Observer* offers a frequency rate discount. The League has never purchased display ad space in the *Observer*. Presently they purchase only the service ad in the restaurant guide.

The *Michigan Daily* is a student-run newspaper on the Ann Arbor campus of The University of Michigan. The *Daily* has approximately 5,000 subscribers. Advertising space costs $4.75/inch. Presently the League does not advertise in the *Michigan Daily*.

The remaining balance of the advertising budget is used to purchase flyers for the League cafeteria and coffee shop. These flyers are distributed to all new students and staff. Included on this flyer is a coupon for a free beverage, which is heavily used by students. The International and American Heritage Nights schedule is printed on a 2″ × 3″ card and is available throughout the university.

FINANCIAL RESOURCES

The University Activities Centers—North Campus Commons, Michigan Union, and the Michigan League—are owned by the university. The League uses earned revenue to meet its operating expenses. Financial support from the university is made available through allocations. All improvements have been financed from reserves and university loans. Loans are repaid on schedule, and there is only a small balance outstanding. Presently the student fee allocation to the League is $3.50 per student.

The number of customers served at the cafeteria and coffee shop is declining. A statement of the League's revenues and expenses for the year 1982–83 is shown in Exhibit 3. Revenue for the Michigan League for fiscal year 1982–83 was 6 percent greater than for fiscal year 1981–82. This includes: guest room rentals (up 2 percent), meeting room rentals (up 25 percent), banquets and parties (up 16 percent), catering (up 79 percent), and beverages (up 12 percent). However, despite these growth areas cafeteria revenue is down $25,437 (3 percent) and coffee shop revenue is down $6,145 (2 percent). Food costs are in line, but labor costs are 50 percent of total earned income. In a report to the Board of Governors, Pat Lawson states, "A major staff training program is currently underway to increase productivity, but with an already lean, hardworking staff, it is unrealistic to expect much of a reduction in labor costs because of the AFSCME (union) wage rates."

The staff is presently considering several cafeteria improvement projects. The League is unwilling to borrow additional funds until the current loan is repaid. Alternative sources considered are: "A search for major donors (fund-raising committee and fund drive)" and additional financial assistance from the university. The League's fund raising for 1982 collected $69,000. The League is developing a cookbook for sale. The book will be ready for sale in June 1984 and is expected to earn $50,000–$100,000. Pat Lawson believes that although revenue generated by the cafeteria is the most important source of operating funds, it is not a source of funds for projects that might be undertaken in the future.

FURTHER CONSIDERATIONS

In her report to the Board of Governors, Pat Lawson stated a need for financial assistance to meet necessary kitchen modernization costs (new appliances). The projected need totals $500,000. However, Pat is considering a complete remodeling of the cafeteria within the next three years. Total costs for complete remodeling are approximately $750,000. The project would include the necessary kitchen equipment, line restructuring, and a complete redecoration of the cafeteria. The plans for the cafeteria line restructuring are to change it from a straight line to an "open"-style square line (scramble system). This would improve efficiency and provide additional customer convenience by eliminating unnecessary waiting. Customers would be able to proceed directly to the section of items they desired. The development of an "open" line would decrease seating capacity. The cafeteria presently seats 250 persons.

As Pat considers the remodeling plans, she is also hoping to include plans to build a small extension to the cafeteria, which would help to recover the seating lost to the line restructuring. The extension as a "greenhouse"-style design is being considered. She believes that the extension should be built at the same time as the other remodeling is undertaken so that shutdown time is mini-

EXHIBIT 3

Statement of Revenue and Expense
June 1983 and Fiscal 1982–83

	June 1983	June 1982	7/1/82– 6/30/83	7/1/81– 6/30/82
Revenue				
House				
Guest room rentals	$ 14,368	$ 14,335	$ 194,569	$ 189,848
Meeting room rentals	8,273	9,809	120,757	96,540
Front desk merchandise	7,976	8,877	113,718	113,372
Sundry	193	2,920	7,316	10,707
Food				
Cafeteria	59,191	67,692	725,102	750,539
Coffee shop	18,355	22,178	272,373	278,518
Banquets and parties	38,867	47,081	414,803	357,603
Catering	23,315	4,897	105,701	59,095
Beverage	6,401	15,487	83,757	74,582
NCC administrative services	450	450	5,400	5,400
Total operating revenue	$177,389	$193,726	$2,043,496	$1,936,204
Expense				
House				
Salaries and wages	$ 22,004	$ 21,360	$ 184,593	$ 174,272
Front desk merchandise	9,435	6,272	85,585	79,147
Supplies and general	991	1,214	9,893	10,300
Equipment repairs	1,306	92	4,010	4,327
Laundry	602	634	11,476	10,268
Food				
Coffee shop salaries and wages	11,194	11,438	116,170	100,338
Food, salaries, and wages	70,128	68,385	652,021	617,413
Food cost	37,276	41,201	533,873	540,594
Transportation	-0-	-0-	2,531	2,452
Supplies and general	4,260	2,187	37,275	35,429
Equipment repairs	383	704	9,940	9,353
Laundry	2,182	2,644	35,476	29,638
Beverage	(293)	5,163	25,692	27,192
General				
Administrative salaries	11,781	18,599	137,432	131,137
Maintenance wages	2,198	2,182	20,587	23,316
Office	930	613	7,936	6,002
Telephone	(82)	(150)	7,722	8,386
Building maintenance	4,475	4,877	37,901	41,978
Board of Governors	56	415	712	1,443
Publicity	419	281	4,245	5,970
Sales tax	3,485	4,270	51,312	45,618
Insurance	74	148	9,094	10,626
Unemployment insurance	-0-	-0-	2,107	503

EXHIBIT 3 (con't)

Statement of Revenue and Expense
June 1983 and Fiscal 1982–83

	June 1983	June 1982	7/1/82–6/30/83	7/1/81–6/30/82
Revenue				
Bad debts	-0-	-0-	17	60
Miscellaneous	2,408	850	17,479	15,243
Total operating expense	185,842	193,379	2,005,079	1,931,005
Net operating income (loss)	$ (8,453)	$ 347	$ 38,417	$ 5,199
Other income and expense				
U-M allocation	$ 17,781	$ 48,877	$ 319,761	$ 295,919
Interest on investments	33,898	26,430	33,898	26,430
Development fund	6,376	100	62,707	200
Utilities	(12,486)	(15,255)	(214,863)	(204,080)
Student awards	(629)	-0-	(629)	(549)
Debt retirement	-0-	(4,837)	(58,272)	(58,040)
Equipment reserves	(950)	(397)	(11,393)	(4,761)
Building reserves	(1,570)	(466)	(18,854)	(5,589)
Total other income and expense	42,420	54,452	112,355	49,530
Net income (loss)	$ 33,967	$ 54,799	$ 150,772	$ 54,729
Total salaries and wages	$117,305	$121,964	$1,110,803	$1,046,476

mized. The greenhouse room is to extend from the front of the League building, which faces the main street.

Pat believes that the new room would provide several benefits: (1) make the League cafeteria more visible, (2) provide a direct entrance from the street to the cafeteria, (3) increase seating, and (4) improve cafeteria attractiveness. If remodeling plans include construction of the greenhouse room, estimated total costs could be approximately $1 million. Pat is interested in determining the feasibility of the League financing the remodeling project. She believes that the League's opportunities are limited to income provided by loans, fund raising, cookbook sales, and increased business at the cafeteria.

THE LIVELY ARTS AT HANSON

"I'm very frustrated about our attendance figures," noted Barbara Lynn, associate director of the Office of Public Events at Hanson University, a well-known privately funded university in Southern California. "Our programming is high quality, and for the whole season we have only about 30,000 seats to sell, but we have a significant seasonal attendance problem. Our Spring quarter attendance has been running at only 50 percent of capacity over the last few years, down from about 85 percent in the Fall. Winter quarter figures are just marginally better than those of Spring, averaging about 60 percent."

Both she and Tom Bacon, who was finishing his fourth year as director of the Office of Public Events, regarded this seasonal attendance pattern as their most pressing management problem in May 1982 as they contemplated possible remedies for the upcoming 1982–83 season and beyond.

PROGRAM CHANGES

Over the past three seasons, Bacon had implemented a number of changes in the "Arts at Hanson" program. Attendance as a percentage of capacity had increased from 54 percent in the three academic years 1976–79 to 68 percent in the most recent three years. These changes are summarized below:

Programming

The number of performances was reduced from 41 in 1978–79 to 31 for the 1979–80 season. This figure rose again to 36 in 1980–81 and was reduced once more to 25 in 1981–82. Additionally, Bacon had attempted to make the program commercially more viable during the last three seasons than it had been previously. He accomplished this by scheduling relatively more performances by string quartets and guitarists, which usually did very well at Hanson. Attendance data by type of programming for the period from Fall 1979 to Spring 1982 were: guitar—104 percent of capacity, chamber music—79 percent, jazz—75 percent, dance—62 percent, and young concert artists—51 percent. Detailed attendance statistics by quarter for 1981–82 are shown in Exhibit 1.

Personnel

The size of Bacon's staff was increased, permitting more and more effective promotional activities. Even with this increase, however, the total time devoted to the program during the 1981–82 season was not greatly in excess of one person-year, due to the fact that the Office of Public Events was responsible for managing four other University programs in addition to the Arts program during the school year.

The first of these programs was general administration (mainly scheduling) of all public events on the Hanson campus. This function required considerable time and represented a steady workload throughout the academic year. Second, the office was responsible for coordinating all university public ceremonies. Most significant of these was the annual Commencement exercise, con-

Reprinted from *Stanford Business Cases* 1985 with permission of Stanford University Graduate School of Business, copyright © 1985 by the Board of Trustees of the Leland Stanford Junior University.

EXHIBIT 1: 1981–1982 Attendance statistics for lively arts

| | Percent of capacity* | | | | |
	Student	Nonstudent	Total	Capacity	Day
	Fall quarter				
Performance:					
Sour Cream (CM)	49%	55%	104%	720	Tuesday
LA 4 (Jazz)	39	59	98	1,694	Friday
Hartford Ballet 1 (Dance)	38	28	66	1,694	Thursday
Hartford Ballet 2	27	27	54	1,694	Friday
Contemporary Chamber Ensemble	19	19	38	720	Friday
Guarneri Quartet 1 (CM)	49	63	112	720	Tuesday
Guarneri Quartet 2	53	62	115	720	Friday
Guarneri Quartet 3	50	71	121	720	Sunday
Ron Thomas (YCA)	22	37	59	350	Friday
Paco de Lucia (Guitar)	39	69	108	1,085	Friday
Breakdown (average figures):					
Chamber Music (5)	44%	54%	98%	720	
Guitar (1)	39	69	108	1,085	
Jazz (1)	39	59	98	1,694	
Dance (2)	33	28	60	1,694	
Young Concert Artist (1)	22	37	59	350	
Totals (10)	38	48	86	10,117	
	Winter quarter				
Performance:					
AMAN! (Dance)	31%	69%	100%	1,694	Friday
Music by Three (YCA)	14	37	51	350	Friday
Nicanor Zabaleta (Harp)	38	66	104	720	Friday
Pilobolus Dance Theater 1	6	37	43	1,694	Thursday
Pilobolus Dance Theater 2	26	25	51	1,694	Friday
Tel Aviv Quartet (CM)	19	64	83	720	Friday
Fernando Valente (Harpsichord)	26	68	94	720	Friday
Hiroko Yajima (YCA)	7	41	48	350	Friday
Murray Dance Company 1	7	12	19	1,694	Thursday
Murray Dance Company 2	22	21	43	1,694	Friday
Music from Marlboro (CM)	14	52	66	720	Friday
Breakdown (average figures):					
Chamber Music (2)	17%	58%	75%	720	
Dance (5)	18	33	51	1,694	
Young Concert Artist (2)	11	39	50	350	
Other (2)	32	67	99	720	
Totals (11)	19	41	60	12,050	

Performance:	*Spring quarter*				
Mummenschanz (Mime)	17%	26%	43%	1,694	Tuesday
Early Music Consort of London (CM)	35	69	104	720	Friday
Paul Winter Consort (Jazz)	21	24	45	1,694	Friday
Arthur Renner (YCA)	11	51	62	350	Friday
Breakdown (not applicable)					
Totals (4)	21%	34%	55%	4,458	

*Chamber Music events were held in the 720-seat hall, Dance and Jazz in the 1,694-seat hall, and the Young Concert Artist series in the 350-seat hall. For the Guitar Concert, the balcony and back rows of the 1,694-seat hall were not made available for sale, leaving a capacity of 1,085-seats. Other events were scheduled for either the 720- or 1,694-seat hall depending upon the nature of the event. The average production cost per performance was $3,000 in 1981–82.

ducted during June. Although some aspects of Commencement required advance planning and coordination, by far the biggest push came in the two months immediately preceding the event. The third major responsibility of the office was coordination of various university lecture programs, including several endowed lectures. As with general administration, the lecture series imposed a relatively steady workload throughout the year.

In addition, Bacon was responsible for a travel film and lecture series which ran throughout the academic year. Also, during the summer, he scheduled a number of "commercial" attractions (for example, the Preservation Hall Jazz Band) for community enjoyment.

The university administration considered all of these activities to be important in helping fulfill the multiple goals of a major university in the community. Tom Bacon knew that whatever new marketing moves he attempted for "The Arts at Hanson" must be accomplished within strict personnel time constraints.

PROMOTIONAL CHANGES

Name

The name of the program was changed to "The *Lively* Arts at Hanson" for the 1979–80 season, in order, hopefully, to attract more attention to the program and to identify it more positively as a *performing* arts program. This new name was incorporated in a redesigned logo used in all media advertising.

Brochure

The season brochure (now entitled "The Lively Arts at Hanson") was made much more elaborate and eye-catching, starting with the 1979–80 season. Its physical size was doubled (to 8½ by 11 inches) and it was printed in three colors on glossy paper stock. These changes increased the costs substantially. By 1981–82 the total cost of the brochure (45,000 copies printed, of which 30,000 were mailed and 15,000 bulk distributed) had risen to $16,800 (including mailing costs) from approximately $6,500 in 1978–79.

The brochure included listings for not only the Lively Arts program, but also performances by various university departments (e.g., drama and music departments). These nonprofessional performances were clearly separated from the Lively Arts offerings within the brochure. In addition, the sponsoring departments were required to fully absorb their pro rata share—$2,000—of total brochure costs. Bacon planned to maintain this policy into the foreseeable future.

The brochure was sent out to a composite mailing list at the beginning of each season in early September. The mailing list was actually composed of three individual lists. The first list included approximately 15,000 individuals who had previously purchased Lively Arts season tickets, who had purchased individual tickets by check (from which a name and address was obtained), or who had specifically requested to be put on the list (by filling out cards available at all performances).

A second list (about 6,000)—the so-called "Sunset Hills Cultural List"—was obtained from the Council for the Arts in Sunset Hills (a large suburban community adjacent to Hanson). The remainder of the mailed brochures (approximately 9,000 for 1981–82) was sent to local Hanson alumni, priority being determined by proximity of residence to the university campus.

These three lists were not cross-checked against each other for duplication. A spokesperson from University Computing Services, which maintained the lists, said that due to their different coding systems, reprogramming and integrating the lists would be costly and time-consuming. Overall, Bacon had no good feeling for the extent to which duplication existed within the lists. However, he noted that he personally received three mailed copies of the brochure each year.

In addition to program information, the annual brochure included a calendar of all performances (professional and nonprofessional), season ticket information, and ticket order forms for all performances.

Additional Brochures

Supplemental one-page brochures in a postcard format were mailed at the beginning of Winter and Spring quarters to the Lively Arts mailing list, briefly outlining the upcoming quarterly program offerings.

Posters and Flyers

When available from the performers' agents, posters and flyers were distributed around the Hanson campus on centrally located information kiosks, in dormitories, and other places about two weeks prior to each performance. Depending upon availability, additional posters were distributed to other college campuses in the area and to willing local merchants. These posters were of varied quality and Public Events staff had no control over their format. Typically the posters included a blank area at the bottom in which was printed program time and location information. The posters did not include the Lively Arts logo or any other mention of the program itself.

Advertising and Other Promotional Activities

Each performance was advertised for about two weeks prior to the performance itself in the local press and, for some performances, on classical music radio stations. Typical newspaper sources were the *Hanson Daily, Los Angeles Times, Sunset Hills News,* and *Orange County Crier.* Additionally, miscellaneous promotional pieces such as Lively Arts bookmarks were printed in large quantitites and made widely available on campus at the beginning of each season.

EXHIBIT 2: Approximate promotional expenditures—1981–82 season

Annual costs:			
Season brochure*	$16,800		
Program covers	1,200		
Promotional material (bookmarks, surveys, etc.)	1,650		
		$19,650	
Fall quarter costs:			
Advertising			
Newspaper	$ 7,500		
Radio	900		
Other	300	$ 8,700	
Posters & flyers		600	
Other		300	
			$ 9,600
Winter quarter costs:			
Advertising			
Newspaper	$ 7,650		
Radio	1,050		
Other	450	$ 9,150	
Posters & flyers		600	
Winter brochure*		3,150	
Other		450	
			$13,350
Spring quarter costs (estimate):			
Advertising			
Newspaper	$ 3,750		
Radio	750		
Other	150	$ 4,650	
Posters & flyers		300	
Spring brochure*		1,350	
Other		150	
			$ 6,450
Total promotional costs			$49,050

*Includes mailing cost.

Total approximate promotional expenditures for the 1981–82 season are presented in Exhibit 2.

Pricing

Greater flexibility was introduced to the pricing scheme, with price levels varying across different performances according to program cost, expected drawing power of individual performers, and other factors. For example, during Winter quarter 1982, the best nonstudent tickets for the Murray Dance Company sold for $9.00, while the Tel Aviv Quartet seats went for $7.00, and Young Concert Artist series performances sold at $5.00 for nonstudents. Additionally, the overall price level was increased to an average ticket price paid (including student and season discounts) of \$4.97 for 1981–82, compared to \$4.01 for 1979–80.

STUDENT PROMOTIONS

Student Introductory Program (SIP)

Under this program, initiated in 1979–80, each new Hanson undergraduate or graduate student was given a free pass to any one performance during the Fall quarter and also a coupon allowing that student to buy a ticket at 75 cents for any other performance during the year.

Response to the initial free ticket was good, but only a very limited number of students exercised the follow-up 75-cent option. Consequently, the 75-cent coupon was discontinued after only one season. The initial free SIP ticket had been maintained up to the present time, however.

Student Discount Tickets

The price of a ticket to any performance for students was set substantially below the average nonstudent ticket price. During the 1981–82 season the student price was \$4.50 per ticket. Bacon felt this price level was appropriate and equitable and he desired to maintain it as long as possible.

OVERALL ACCOMPLISHMENTS

Tom Bacon was convinced that the program changes represented significant accomplishments for "The Lively Arts at Hanson," notwithstanding the existence of several persistent problems. Overall, he felt there were two major accomplishments:

• Total program attendance had risen steadily from 1976–77 to 1979–80, declining only in the recession year 1980–81. Further

declines in the total attendance for 1981–82 were believed to be due principally to the reduced number of performances.

• Average percentage attendance for Fall quarter had increased markedly from 68 percent in 1976–78 to 85 percent in 1979–81. Bacon attributed this increase to a combination of successful marketing innovations initiated in Fall quarter 1979. These included the expanded brochure, more successful programming and the SIP program.

Together these accomplishments convinced Bacon and Lynn that the Lively Arts was an extremely viable program with a growing base of supporters.

PROGRAM ATTENDANCE

In May 1982 Bacon was undertaking a reappraisal of the entire Lively Arts marketing program employed over the past three seasons to determine what changes, if any, might be warranted. Although he felt strongly that many of his program changes had been successful, he still faced significant problems. Most worrisome of these was a marked pattern of seasonal attendance. While Fall quarter audiences had been very good, averaging nearly 85 percent of capacity, the comparable figures for Winter and Spring quarters were 60 percent and 50 percent, respectively. To compound this difficulty Bacon noted that student attendance had slipped from a high of over 45 percent of the audience during the 1979–80 season to an all-time low of 32 percent for the Winter quarter 1981–82 (Exhibits 1, 3 and 4).

Bacon was concerned about both of these trends:

"The Lively Arts at Hanson" presents first-rate artists in a varied program that should appeal to a broad base of individuals. Look at this season's offerings for example: The

EXHIBIT 3A: Fall quarter audience size (audience size by market segment, 1981–82)

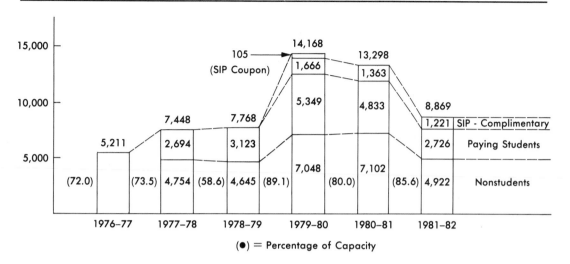

(●) = Percentage of Capacity

Guarneri and Tel Aviv string quartets; Music from Marlboro; AMAN! (a folk dance group); Pilobolus and the Murray Company in dance; the Early Music Consort of London. These artists are representative of the best in their fields.

Our Young Concert Artist series brings some of the most promising young talents in the world to the Hanson audience. These are the artists who will be at the top of their profession in a few years. Already they have received laudatory reviews by major music critics. Moreover, our prices are quite low compared to what one would have to pay to see comparable performers in Los Angeles. The average nonstudent ticket price this year was only about $6.00–9.00. Most city performances cost twice that much.

EXHIBIT 3B: Winter quarter audience size

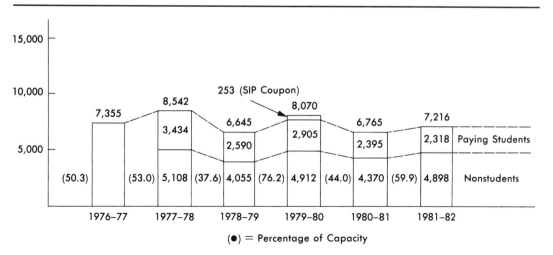

(●) = Percentage of Capacity

EXHIBIT 3C: Spring quarter audience size

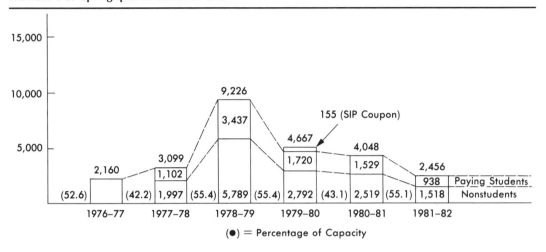

(●) = Percentage of Capacity

EXHIBIT 4: Attendance by quarters, 1976–82

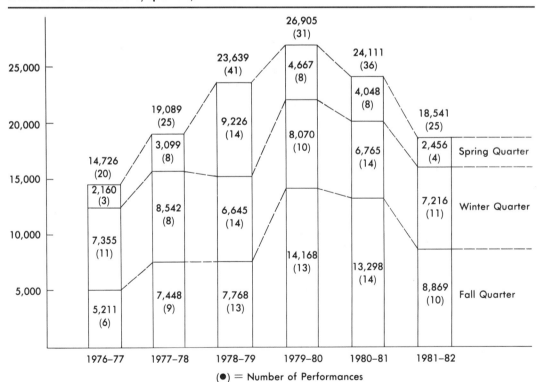

(●) = Number of Performances

Student attendance also bothers me. As a group, Hanson students should be very interested in the Lively Arts program. However, from a number of sources, I have the strong impression that they're really not as aware of our program as I would like. For example, take the Student Introductory Program (SIP). By and large, new students were very willing to take a complimentary ticket, but very few of them exercised the option to purchase a second ticket for 75 cents plus the SIP coupon, as our statistics show.

There are other indications as well. Not concrete to be sure, but present nevertheless. Somehow we have to get through to the students that "The Lively Arts at Hanson" is something very special and very professional, to be distinguished from the whole host of other performance activities with which we must compete for their attention on campus.

"The Lively Arts at Hanson" was not alone in facing a seasonal attendance problem. The performing arts program at State University experienced similar difficulties. Bacon's counterpart at State U. commented that she had had some success in combating this problem by scheduling relatively more "light" and fewer "heavy" performances during Spring quarter, her toughest attendance period. The "light" category encompassed performances which typically sold well at State U., including string quartets, early music, and anything by Bach. "Heavy," on the other hand, included contemporary music and vocalists, which were always difficult to sell. The State U. manager also tended to favor more well-known performers in the Spring.

PROGRAM GOALS

Bacon felt strongly that the program had—and must of necessity have—multiple goals reflecting the multiple dimensions of managing an arts program. For purposes of control and evaluation of the program's progress, Bacon decided after much thoughtful consideration that the following four goals were paramount:

- Establish "The Lively Arts at Hanson" as a major source of first-rate performing arts talent for the extended county community as well as for the immediate Hanson University community.
- Run the series on a close-to-breakeven basis, incurring only a minimal deficit as approved by the university administration.
- Keep prices as low as possible in order to make performances widely accessible.
- Target the total season for overall attendance at 75–80 percent of capacity. Further, maintain the following overall audience proportions: students, 35 percent; nonstudents, 65 percent.

PROGRAMMING DIFFICULTIES

In order to achieve the first of these goals, which he and his staff felt was probably the most important, Bacon knew it would be imperative to continue to present a varied program of artists each season. This was difficult for two reasons. First, the scheduling problems were impressive. Not only did Bacon have to book the artists more than a year in advance in most cases, but also he had to compete with various departmental and student arts productions (e.g., music department concerts, drama department, and theatrical club productions) for a very limited number of available auditoriums on campus and suitable dates.

However, even more troublesome was a second factor. By maintaining a varied program, Bacon was including each season a number of performance types which did not seem to do very well in drawing large audiences, such as the Young Concert Artist series and dance in general. He had broken down his quarterly attendance statistics for the past three seasons and was upset by them. He knew that he would have to try to ameliorate the contrasts in attendance statistics by performance type for the 1982–83 season if possible, but he wasn't sure of the best way to go about it.

SEGMENTATION

Barbara Lynn, who had been working in the Office of Public Events for two years, had some strong feelings about the potential audience:

> I think we have, basically, three groups of people who come out to our performances. First there are the students—mostly from Hanson, but some from neighboring colleges and secondary schools as well. Our sources on campus seem to indicate that Hanson students are not very aware of our program. The students have heard of the Guarneri Quartet—and they know they will be performing—but they don't seem to know that the "Lively Arts" is bringing the Guarneri to campus. I don't know, but maybe our posters and *Hanson Daily* advertising aren't doing the job. They sure cost enough, though!
>
> Second is the group I like to call "Hanson affiliated": University faculty and staff members and their spouses. We haven't made any special attempt to get them interested, but feel they should respond to the advertising both on campus and in the local press.
>
> Finally we've got the community at large—mostly in and around Hanson and Sunset Hills. Many of these people receive our annual brochure and the subsequent quarterly postcard mailings. In addition, they probably read both the *Los Angeles Times* and the *Sunset Hills News*, in which we advertise regularly. They're all great fans in the Fall, but when we have to compete with spring weather their loyalty runs thin. Their allegiance during the Winter is also poor.

> There are other groups, too. For example, local music teachers and their pupils; maybe even some of the companies up in the Hanson Industrial Park. We could probably do a lot here in the way of group discounts. This also might apply to faculty and staff—especially those living nearby on University land. I've got a million ideas I'd like to try out, but not nearly enough time. Especially now, with Commencement to worry about. . . .

IMAGE ADVERTISING

Both Lynn and Bacon were concerned that the perceived image of "The Lively Arts at Hanson" was not as good as it could be. Precise information was not available on this issue, but a number of informal sources supported this belief:

- The manager of the Campus Ticket Office reported that very few buyers ever mentioned the program when purchasing individual performance tickets. Additionally, she said that over the past few years only one of the many students who had worked part-time in the ticket office had heard of the program before beginning work.
- Informal pollings of students in the Hanson Graduate School of Business indicated that only 5–10 percent of them had heard of the program before studying an earlier verison of this case in class.

These and other indicators led Bacon and Lynn to consider the possibliity of an image advertising campaign during the summer in the local press as well as on campus at the beginning of the academic year in September 1982. Lynn also thought that students in Hanson's several graduate professional schools (Business, Law, Medicine, and Education) might be a good target segment. She reasoned that these students were much more dedicated to a particular field than were undergraduates, and therefore probably were less involved in competing general university activities, of which there are many.

Also, professional school students were generally more isolated from the university at large, she thought, and therefore less likely to be aware of the Lively Arts program. Finally, many of the professional school students were married; Lynn felt that the combination of easily accessible, low priced, high quality performing arts entertainment should have tremendous appeal to young professionals on a student budget.

AUDIENCE QUESTIONNAIRE

In order to try to get a handle on some of the characteristics of the audience and formulate an appropriate marketing plan for next year, Lively Art staff had prepared an audience survey. This questionnaire (Exhibit 5) was distributed to most of the audience at ten of the Winter quarter preformances in early 1982. A random sample of about 100 (when less than 100 questionnaires were turned in, the whole group was used) was selected from each performance (in all, over 850 responses were sampled) and the results were analyzed using the computer program available through the university computer center.

By mid-May Bacon had the results of his analysis (Exhibits 6–9). By and large the questionnaire reconfirmed many intuitive feelings he and his staff had had prior to the survey. But they gained several new insights as well. As a result of the questionnaire, Bacon was seriously rethinking some of his marketing strategies for next season.

THE 1982–83 SEASON

Due to the long-range planning horizon implicit in arranging bookings for performing artists, the 1982–83 season was already scheduled (Exhibit 10). Of the 26 performances, 9 were scheduled for the fall quarter, 10 for winter, and 7 for spring. Within this programming context, Bacon sought to use all the market information he had gathered during the season to formulate a well-integrated, *specific* marketing plan.

To operationalize his strategic planning, he thought it would be a good idea to set a specific attendance objective. After much thought he decided upon a season attendance goal of 75 percent, with a 35–65 percent student/nonstudent mix. This was clearly a stretch target, but by setting his overall season goals high, Bacon hoped to really come to grips with his historically most pressing problem: seasonal attendance. He further thought that, at a minimum, his plan should address the following issues:

- *Brochures* Was the "lavish" annual brochure with quarterly postcard follow-ups sufficient, or should *each* quarterly mailing be more like the current annual elaborate brochure?
- *Advertising* How should he allocate his advertising budget? What media should he expand? Contract? Why? What are the possibilities of image advertising over the summer to develop latent demand?
- *Pricing* How might he alter his pricing policy further? What level of prices would be tolerable and consistent with his goals?
- *Season Tickets* Was the "choose-your-own" program[1] viable? Why or why not? What might be employed as an alternative? For example, should the six Guarneri Quartet performances be packaged as a series to be sold at a discount?

---

[1] The "choose-your-own" program allowed season ticket purchasers to structure their own discount season, choosing only those performances they wished to attend, as long as a minimum number of performances was selected.

EXHIBIT 5: Questionnaire distributed at winter 1982 performances (excludes cover letter to recipients)

1. Age:
   - ☐ Under 18
   - ☐ 18–24
   - ☐ 25–34
   - ☐ 35–44
   - ☐ 45–60
   - ☐ Over 60

2. Number of children: _____

3. Education:
   - ☐ Grammar school
   - ☐ 1–3 years high school
   - ☐ 4 years high school
   - ☐ 1–3 years college
   - ☐ 4 years college
   - ☐ Graduate work

4. Annual family income (before taxes):
   - ☐ Under $3,000
   - ☐ 3,000–4,999
   - ☐ 5,000–6,999
   - ☐ 7,000–9,999
   - ☐ 10,000–14,999
   - ☐ 15,000–24,999
   - ☐ 25,000–49,999
   - ☐ Over $50,000

5. Are you a Hanson
   - ☐ student?
   - ☐ faculty member?
   - ☐ staff member?
   - ☐ alumnus?

6. Is any member of your immediate family a Hanson
   - ☐ student?
   - ☐ faculty member?
   - ☐ staff member?
   - ☐ alumnus?

7. In what community do you live?
   - ☐ Hanson
   - ☐ Sunset Hills
   - ☐ Verona
   - ☐ Parkside/Vista Valley
   - ☐ Verdes/Verdes Hills
   - ☐ Ocean View
   - ☐ Other (Please specify) _____

8. How many performing arts programs have you attended at Hanson within the past year?
   - ☐ 1–3
   - ☐ 4–7
   - ☐ 8–10
   - ☐ More than 10

9. How far in advance of this performance did you purchase your tickets?
   - ☐ At the door
   - ☐ Day of performance
   - ☐ 1–3 days before
   - ☐ 4–7 days before
   - ☐ 2–3 weeks before
   - ☐ 1 or more months before

10. Are you presently a subscriber to (check as many as apply)
    - ☐ Lively Arts at Hanson?
    - ☐ Los Angeles Symphony?
    - ☐ Los Angeles Opera?
    - ☐ American Conservatory Theater?
    - ☐ Other art series? (please specify)
    - ☐ _____

11. If you did not buy your ticket on a discount plan, what price did you pay?
    $_____

12. Did you receive a copy of *The Lively Arts at Hanson* in the mail?
    - ☐ Yes   ☐ No

13. How did you hear of this performance? (check as many as apply)
    - ☐ Brochure by mail
    - ☐ Newspaper advertising
    - ☐ Newspaper story
    - ☐ Newspaper photograph
    - ☐ Radio announcement
    - ☐ Television announcement
    - ☐ Poster or flyer
    - ☐ Word-of-mouth
    - ☐ Other (please specify) _____

14. What sources do you usually consult for information about upcoming arts events? (check as many as apply)
    - ☐ *Hanson Daily*
    - ☐ *Campus Report*
    - ☐ *Hanson Observer*
    - ☐ *Los Angeles Times*
    - ☐ *Long Beach News Press*
    - ☐ *Country Recorder*
    - ☐ *Verona Almanac*
    - ☐ *Sunset Hills News*
    - ☐ *Orange County Crier*
    - ☐ KDFC/KIBE
    - ☐ KKHI
    - ☐ KZSU
    - ☐ Other (please specify) _____

15. Do you regularly listen to classical music programs on the radio?
    - ☐ Yes   ☐ No

16. If *Yes* to question 15, which station do you listen to most often?
    - ☐ KKBM
    - ☐ KNFC/KIBC

17. What is your favorite restaurant? _____

18. What is your occupation? _____

19. What kinds of performances do you like to attend? (check as many as apply)
    - ☐ Theater
    - ☐ Contemporary music
    - ☐ Symphony
    - ☐ Modern Dance
    - ☐ Instrumental recitals
    - ☐ Opera
    - ☐ Chamber music
    - ☐ Ballet
    - ☐ Vocal recitals

20. In making a decision to attend a performance, what weight do you give the following factors?
    Name of performers:
    ☐ *Important* ☐ *Unimportant*
    Repertoire to be performed:
    ☐ *Important* ☐ *Unimportant*
    Ticket Price:
    ☐ *Important* ☐ *Unimportant*
    Ease of finding performance hall:
    ☐ *Important* ☐ *Unimportant*

21. What particular artist and/or attraction would you like to see at Hanson?
    _____
    _____
    _____

22. Additional comments you might wish to make concerning the "Lively Arts at Hanson" series of performances:
    _____
    _____
    _____

If you do not return this questionnaire on the night of the performance, please staple or seal it and mail to us. If you mail it, please fill in the date and name of performance below.
Thank you.

_____
Date   Name of Performance

EXHIBIT 6: Audience profile

	Students*	Nonstudents
Median:		
Age group	18–24	35–44
Number of children	0	1
Education level	4 years college	graduate work
Annual family income	—	$25–49 K
Hanson affiliation[†]:		
Students	73%	3%
Faculty	—	10
Staff	1	9
Alumni	3	15
Place of residence:		
Hanson	44%	10%
Sunset	26	35
Verona	1	2
Mateo Park	8	15
Parkside/Vista Valley	1	5
Verdes/Verdes Hills	2	7
Ocean View	5	5
Other	13	21
Performing arts performances attended in Hanson within the past year:		
1–3	64%	49%
4–7	27	27
8–10	4	10
Over 10	5	13
Time of ticket purchase:		
At the door	19%	12%
Day of performance	11	9
1–3 days before	23	12
4–7 days before	16	11
2–3 weeks before	11	12
1 or more months before	20	45
Lively Arts at Hanson:		
Current subscribers	8%	34%
Received brochure in mail	21	56
Information sources for this performance (most frequently mentioned)[‡]:		
Brochure by mail	15%	48%
Newspaper advertising	34	27

EXHIBIT 6 (continued)

	Students*	Nonstudents
Newspaper story	9	14
Poster or flyer	42	14
Word-of-mouth	46	29
Sources usually consulted for upcoming arts events (most frequently mentioned)[‡]:		
Hanson Daily	72%	27%
Campus Report	12	17
Hanson Observer	9	14
Los Angeles Times	32	46
Sunset Hills News	21	54
KNFC/KIBC	18	17
KKBM	13	18
Listen to classical music radio regularly	57%	73%
Station most often listened to:		
KKBM	20%	37%
KNFC/KIBC	39	40
Performance preferences:		
Theater	81%	77%
Contemporary music	41	33
Symphony	63	68
Modern dance	58	51
Instrumental recitals	47	51
Opera	25	32
Chamber music	47	55
Ballet	58	62
Vocal recitals	11	17
Factors important in deciding to attend a performance:		
Name of performers	68%	75%
Repertoire	79	87
Ticket price	68	49
Find hall easily	28	29

*Student/Nonstudent categories were developed according to the response to the occupation question (# 18, Exhibit 5).

[†]Multiple responses were possible for this question. For example, an individual might be a Hanson faculty member and alumnus.

[‡]All other categories mentioned less than 10% of the time by both students and nonstudents.

Source: Audience survey questionnaire.

EXHIBIT 7: Market segments and their characteristics (percent of audience)

	Nonstudent (70.2%)	Hanson students* and spouses (19.3%)	Hanson faculty, staff and spouses (15.9%)
Residence in Hanson-Sunset Hills	45.4%	—	—
Attended at least 4 performances within the last year	50.6	42.7%	49.2%
Purchased ticket at least one month before performance	43.9	12.3	53.0
Lively Arts subscribers**	33.6	4.2	36.8
Information source for this performance:			
Brochure by mail	48.3	10.3	58.8
Newspaper advertising	27.4	36.4	35.3
Poster or flyer	14.3	46.1	20.6
Word-of-mouth	28.9	41.8	30.1
Usual information source:			
Hanson Daily	26.9	87.9	61.8
Campus Report	16.9	13.9	49.3
Hanson Observer	13.8	11.5	14.7
Los Angeles Times	46.2	27.3	44.9
Sunset Hills News	53.5	14.5	61.8

*Student status: undergraduate   42.4%
                graduate student 54.9
**Season ticket purchasers.
Source: Audience survey.

EXHIBIT 8: Attendance and ticket-purchasing behavior of patrons

	Nonstudents*	Hanson students and spouses
Attended 1–3 performances within past year	49.5%	56.1%
Attended at least 4 performances within past year *and* purchased tickets at least one month in advance	34.8	10.2
Attended at least 4 performances within past year and purchased tickets less than one month in advance	15.7	33.7
	100.0%	100.0%

*Within 1–2 percentage points in each category, the figures for Nonstudents also apply to Hanson Faculty, Staff and Spouses, and Hanson Alumni and Spouses, as well.
Source: Audience survey.

EXHIBIT 9: Cross-tabulations of time of ticket purchase by number of performances attended within past year

Time of ticket purchase	Performances attended				Row total
	1–3	*4–7*	*8–10*	*Over 10*	
	Nonstudents				
At door	42	12	2	4	60
Day of performance	35	9	2	2	48
1–3 days before	45	14	3	2	64
4–7 days before	37	12	2	3	54
2–3 weeks before	44	15	2	2	63
1 month or more	68	84	47	59	258
Column total	271	146	58	72	547
	Hanson students and spouses				
At door	14	8	2	4	28
Day of performance	12	6	0	0	18
1–3 days before	23	10	0	1	34
4–7 days before	20	4	5	2	31
2–3 weeks before	10	6	2	0	18
1 month or more	4	12	2	1	19
Column total	83	46	11	8	148

Source: Audience survey.

EXHIBIT 10: 1982–83 season schedule

Fall quarter:
October 22	Chamber Music Society of Lincoln Center
October 28	"Are You Now or Have You Ever Been?" (drama)
October 29	Oba Koso (Nigerian opera)
November 5	Roman de Fauvel (medieval secular music drama)
November 9	Music from Marlboro (chamber music)
November 12	Young Concert Artist
November 14, 16, 19	Guarneri String Quartet—Beethoven Quartet Series (chamber music)

Winter quarter:
January 18	"An Evening of George Orwell" with Jose Ferrer (celebrity)
January 21	Young Concert Artist
February 1, 2, 3	Eliot Feld Ballet Company (dance)
February 11	Young Concert Artist
February 18	Bach Aria Group (chamber music)
February 22, 25, 27	Guarneri String Quartet—Beethoven Quartet Series (chamber music)

Spring quarter:
April 1	Narciso Yepes (guitar)
April 7, 8	Utah Repertory Dance Company
April 15	Young Concert Artist
April 17	American Brass Quintet (chamber music)
April 24, 26	Fine Arts Quartet (with viola)—Mozart Quintet Series (chamber music)